CORPS COMMANDERS IN BLUE

CONFLICTING WORLDS:
NEW DIMENSIONS OF THE AMERICAN CIVIL WAR
T. Michael Parrish, Series Editor

CORPS COMMANDERS IN BLUE

Union Major Generals in the Civil War

EDITED BY
ETHAN S. RAFUSE

Louisiana State University Press   *Baton Rouge*

Published with the assistance of the V. Ray Cardozier Fund

Published by Louisiana State University Press
lsupress.org

Copyright © 2014 by Louisiana State University Press
The essay by Brooks D. Simpson is copyrighted in the name of the author.
All rights reserved. Except in the case of brief quotations used in articles or reviews, no part of this publication may be reproduced or transmitted in any format or by any means without written permission of Louisiana State University Press.

Louisiana Paperback Edition, 2024

DESIGNER: Michelle A. Neustrom
TYPEFACE: Adobe Caslon Pro

Cover photos from Library of Congress; Mansfield photo, National Archives.

LIBRARY OF CONGRESS CATALOGING-IN-PUBLICATION DATA

Corps commanders in blue : Union major generals in the Civil War / edited by Ethan S. Rafuse.
   pages cm. — (Conflicting worlds: new dimensions of the American Civil War)
   Includes index.
   ISBN 978-0-8071-5702-2 (cloth : alk. paper) — ISBN 978-0-8071-5703-9 (pdf) — ISBN 978-0-8071-5704-6 (epub) — ISBN 978-0-8071-8496-7 (paperback) 1. United States—History—Civil War, 1861–1865—Biography. 2. United States—History—Civil War, 1861–1865—Campaigns. 3. Command of troops—History—19th century. 4. Generals—United States—Biography. 5. United States. Army—Biography. I. Rafuse, Ethan Sepp, 1968– editor of compilation, author.
   E467.C79 2015
   973.7'31—dc23
                                                                                            2014011009

For Herman Hattaway

CONTENTS

ACKNOWLEDGMENTS | ix

Introduction | 1

1
Conservatism's Dying Ember
Fitz John Porter and the Union War, 1862
JOHN J. HENNESSY | 14

2
"Too Bad, Poor Fellows"
Joseph K. F. Mansfield and the XII Corps at Antietam
THOMAS G. CLEMENS | 61

3
An "Acting Major General"
Charles Champion Gilbert at Perryville
KENNETH W. NOE | 96

4
"The Longest and Clearest Head of Any General Officer"
George Gordon Meade as Corps Commander, December 1862–June 1863
CHRISTOPHER S. STOWE | 112

Contents

5
Grant's Junior Lieutenant
James B. McPherson and the Vicksburg Campaign, 1863
STEVEN E. WOODWORTH | 156

6
William B. Franklin and the XIX Corps in the Trans-Mississippi, 1863–64
MARK A. SNELL | 181

7
"Always 'Fighting Joe'"
Joseph Hooker and the Campaign in North Georgia, May–July 1864
ETHAN S. RAFUSE | 221

8
Winfield Scott Hancock and the Overland Campaign
BROOKS D. SIMPSON | 261

CONTRIBUTORS | 281

INDEX | 285

ACKNOWLEDGMENTS

First and foremost, I thank John, Tom, Ken, Chris, Steve, Mark, and Brooks for their terrific work, patient cooperation, and the confidently anticipated (but still much appreciated) degree of professionalism they demonstrated throughout the process of putting this volume together. Mark merits special mention in this regard due to his role in the initial stages of the project, when the book's basic themes and approaches were coming together. I am confident I speak for all the contributors to this volume when I thank Kevin Brock for his superb work as copy editor and series editor Michael Parrish for his role in the project. I also thank Rand Dotson, Lee Sioles, Laura Gleason, and MaryKatherine Callaway at LSU Press for their roles in the process of shepherding the book to publication.

This work was conceived as a tribute to Herman Hattaway, whose guidance and example at critical times in the careers of a number of the contributors, above all the editor, is much appreciated. It is unlikely that he will agree with everything that is written in this volume, but it is hoped that he will find more than adequate compensation for that in its existence. Finally, I thank Rachel Lee Rafuse and Corinne Lee Rafuse for all they do to make my work possible and life enjoyable.

CORPS COMMANDERS IN BLUE

Introduction

The question of the American Civil War's place in the evolution of warfare has inspired tremendous debate. Were Civil War armies closer to their Napoleonic predecessors or their twentieth-century successors in terms of organization, doctrine, tactics, and technology? In the area of small arms, for instance, the infantryman's muzzle-loading musket suggests a close tie to the armies of the past. Yet the fact that most of these had rifled barrels and therefore longer range and better accuracy than the smoothbores carried by past soldiers clearly marked a break with the past.[1] The same can be said for field and siege artillery, although the smoothbore twelve-pounder "Napoleon" remained a workhorse of both the Union and Confederate field armies. Among other sources of debate are the degree to which the dramatic expansion of the power of the central governments in the North and South and Federal targeting of civilian resources in the "hard war" of 1864–65 can be said to have marked a transformative break with past practices and anticipated, among other things, the "total war" methods of the world wars of the twentieth century.[2] And of course, the introduction of ironclad warships and submersibles were revolutions in naval warfare, while never before in the history of American arms (and rarely before that anywhere) had governments been forced to mobilize their societies and economies to such a great extent to support their military leviathans.

Yet when it came to organizational structure, the Civil War saw little in the way of innovation. Union and Confederate military leaders closely followed practices from the Wars of the French Revolution and the Napoleonic Wars of the late-eighteenth and early nineteenth centuries. Those conflicts had seen considerable innovation in military organization, with perhaps the most important of these being the corps system, introduced by the French during the nearly thirty years of hostilities that followed the outbreak of their 1789 revolution. Instead of being organized into a single concentrated formation that operated along a single line of march, during the two decades after 1789, French military leaders implemented ideas initially proposed by Pierre de Bourcet, Marshal Victor-Francois de Broglie, and Étienne François, duc de Choiseul during the 1760s. These found their fullest expression in Napoleon's *Grande Armée*, which was divided up into smaller segments known as *corps de armée*. Each corps was in essence a mini-army that contained its own cavalry, infantry, and artillery assets, and their organization both simplified command and control and offered creative commanders greater flexibility operationally and tactically.[3] After the system proved its worth, helping Napoleon win victories at such battles as Marengo, Austerlitz, and Jena-Auerstadt, the other European states emulated his methods and organized their armies into corps.

There were, however, significant differences between the organizational needs of European and American armies that prevented the corps system from being adopted in the United States before the war, although the concept and its value and purpose were recognized. When the Civil War began in 1861, the U.S. Army consisted on paper of a mere 1,105 officers and 15,259 enlisted men organized into ten infantry regiments, four artillery regiments, and five regiments of mounted men. There was no permanent organization larger than a regiment and rarely before 1861 was an entire regiment concentrated in a single place. Instead, units were scattered among nearly ninety garrisons, with seventy-nine of them located west of the Mississippi River. For administrative purposes, the country was divided into regional military departments, each commanded by a senior colonel or brevetted general officer, an officer who had responsibility for whatever units were in his area. This system traced its lineage back to policies implemented during John C. Calhoun's tenure as secretary of war after the War of 1812, as did the staff system that existed to administer the various bureaus responsible for supplying and administering the army. There was, however, no system in place for organizing the various units into a larger force, planning for that eventuality, or for preparing officers for that task.[4]

Arguably, such a permanent system was unnecessary in light of the fact that the European model existed for American officials to follow in the event they needed to assemble a larger body of troops—and the rarity of such events. For the war with Mexico of 1846–48, for instance, the U.S. government raised volunteer regiments, with the states assuming responsibility for them, and in line with European practices, brought them together to form brigades and, when deemed appropriate, combined the brigades into divisions. During the campaign that

Introduction

conquered Mexico City in 1847, Maj. Gen. Winfield Scott's army of about 10–14,000 men was organized into four divisions. If Scott ever considered combining these divisions into corps, there is little evidence of it, but this proved unnecessary in order to achieve decisive battlefield victories over Mexican forces.[5]

In 1861, though, both the North and the South immediately raised armies far greater than any that had previously been seen in North America. In line with previous practice, Union and Confederate authorities left the raising of volunteer regiments to the states. Once states had assembled enough regiments, they would be combined into brigades by Federal or Confederate authorities. Both sides further followed prewar practice by dividing their territory into departments commanded by general officers, who were selected by the Federal or Confederate government and responsible for the organization, administration, and operations of the forces within their particular areas.

For the military campaigns that took place in 1861, though, neither side saw the necessity for organizing units larger than divisions. During the largest major operation of the first year of the war, the First Manassas Campaign, the Union army commanded by Brig. Gen. Irvin McDowell was organized into five divisions virtually on the eve of the campaign, with seemingly little notion that these would or could be permanent organizations. There was no unit organization between the army and brigade levels in the Confederate forces under Joseph E. Johnston and Brig. Gen. Pierre G. T. Beauregard. In the months after First Manassas, the size of Union and Confederate forces swelled to the point where a higher permanent command organization than the brigade was needed if the task of managing forces in the field was not to be totally beyond the ability of a single commander. By the end of 1861, Beauregard had made an abortive attempt, without legal authorization, to inject corps organization into the Confederate forces responsible for defending northern Virginia.[6] It was not until March 1862, however, that the first corps were officially organized, and these by the North. Appropriately enough, given the subsequent military history of the war, this development did not occur without significant controversy.

The Union Army of the Potomac was the first Civil War army to be officially organized into corps. While there was a practical purpose behind the move, in that the dozen or so divisions belonging to the army were clearly too many for one man to control effectively without an intermediate level of command, the organization of corps was also born out of tension between politicians in

Washington and that army's commander, Maj. Gen. George B. McClellan. McClellan, who owed his position in part to the knowledge of European military organizational practices he had gained while a member of a commission the War Department sent to Europe in the 1850s, naturally recognized the desirability of organizing corps and, by the end of 1861, had expressed his views on the matter to his political superiors. Yet during the winter of 1861–62, a significant catch developed that cooled McClellan's enthusiasm for organizing corps at that point. The senior division commanders in his army, the natural candidates for corps command, were older than McClellan and had been senior to him in the antebellum army. Moreover, they did not enjoy as good a relationship with the general as did a number of the more junior division commanders. Further exacerbating the problem was the fact that anti-McClellan elements in Washington had been quick to see potential allies in these senior division commanders and by early 1862 had made a concerted effort to cultivate good relations with them. When the Joint Committee on the Conduct of the War began investigations into the management of the Army of the Potomac in December 1861, the question of corps organization was continually raised, and the existence of a split within the army's high command between McClellan's "pets" and the other division commanders was hard for any observer to miss.[7]

The matter finally came to a head in March 1862, with one of the catalysts being a disagreement between McClellan and President Abraham Lincoln over where the Army of the Potomac should conduct operations. When the general laid out his views on the matter to them, three of his four senior division commanders—McDowell, Edwin Sumner, and Samuel Heintzelman—sided with the president. Fortunately for McClellan, eight division commanders sustained his position, and Lincoln was willing to bow to the views of the majority. The dispute offered unmistakable evidence of the existence of tensions between McClellan and his senior commanders, however, that could have potentially serious consequences for the Union war effort. Soon afterward, Lincoln mandated the organization of the Army of the Potomac into corps and chose their commanders on the basis of seniority.[8] Though Lincoln's decision was eminently justifiable, its timing cast a decidedly unwholesome shadow over the entire question of corps organization by sending the message that the job of the corps commander was in part to act as a check on army commanders. In light of the fact that the system was born under such circumstances, it is not surprising that it would be the rare military campaign of any significance in which there did not emerge conflicts and controversies between army and corps commanders.

Even under more felicitous circumstances, the seeds for trouble were always there. Events would demonstrate time and again that one of the most important things a Civil War army required if it was going to be successful was mutual trust between its commander and his chief subordinates. This was a consequence of the nature of the challenges a nineteenth-century corps or army commander faced. The amount of initiative a brigade or division leader exercised on a major Civil War battlefield was often not especially great, but due to the relatively limited physical space his unit occupied on the field, it was possible for such officers to exercise a considerable degree of direct control over subordinate units. Corps commanders, however, required considerable discretion in how they managed their command, though having direct control over all of their subordinate units was exceedingly difficult, if not impossible. What was true at the corps level was especially so for the army commander, which had significant ramifications for his immediate subordinates. The classic challenge of command is in writing and issuing orders that strike a balance between clearly explaining what the senior officer wants accomplished and how he wants it done and granting subordinate officers sufficient discretion to react appropriately to circumstances. Because there could be no truly objective resolution of this challenge, there was, to say the least, considerable room for disagreement. Not surprisingly, it was the rare Civil War battle from which there did not emerge afterward fierce controversies between army and corps generals. The fact that throughout the war, civil political authorities felt few compunctions about interjecting themselves into such controversies further poisoned the atmosphere in which army and corps commanders had to operate.

Nowhere was the situation worse in the Union army than in the eastern theater. After every one of the major engagements that took place between August 1862 and August 1863, bitter disputes erupted between army commanders and at least one of their corps commanders. Disagreements between Maj. Gen. John Pope and Maj. Gen. Fitz John Porter over the latter's conduct at Second Manassas in August 1862 resulted in a politically charged court-martial whose verdict would ultimately be overturned decades later.[9] Events at Antietam less than a month later all but destroyed a warm personal friendship between McClellan and corps commander Maj. Gen. Ambrose Burnside. After the Union defeat at Fredericksburg in December 1862, Burnside and Maj. Gen. William B.

Franklin became embroiled in controversy over whether the latter acted in good faith in executing orders, while Maj. Gen. Joseph Hooker never forgave Maj. Gen. John Sedgwick for his problematic performance during the Chancellorsville Campaign.[10] And, of course, there was the dispute between army commander Maj. Gen. George G. Meade and Maj. Gen. Daniel E. Sickles's over the latter's management of his corps on the second day of battle at Gettysburg, which became a source of such fierce controversy that it would seemingly generate, in the words of one historian, "a Caspian Sea of Ink."[11]

Moreover, in nearly all of these cases, Republicans in Congress and in the Lincoln administration used their positions to champion officers who sympathized with them. This all but ensured that a dreadful command culture would exist in the Army of the Potomac, which on top of the not inconsiderable challenges the terrain and enemy posed, makes it remarkable that it was able to accomplish anything at all. Indeed, of all the men who exercised corps command in the Army of the Potomac, relatively few were able to last a year in the position; the circumstances surrounding the end of Maj. Gen. Gouverneur K. Warren's tenure were so inextricably wrapped up in personal army and partisan politics that it would be a source of controversy for years to come.

In addition to politics and military disputes, the high turnover in corps leadership was a consequence of the fact that corps command was a natural stepping stone to army command. It was also consequence of the fact that it could be a decidedly dangerous position. Over the course of the war, four corps commanders in the Army of the Potomac—Jesse Reno, Joseph Mansfield, John Reynolds, and John Sedgwick—would be killed or suffer mortal wounds in action.

Despite the hazards, the opportunity to lead a corps was one that officers rarely turned down. Not only did it bring prestige, it offered an opportunity to contribute to the cause of the Union that few could hope to receive. In order for a Civil War army to operate effectively, all understood that it was essential that the men who commanded a corps possess the leadership qualities necessary to handle a large body of troops, for the performance of a single corps commander could mean the difference between decisive victory and decisive defeat in the field. The outcome of such critical battles and campaigns as the Seven Days' Battles in June–July 1862, Vicksburg and Gettysburg in 1863, and the Appomattox Campaign in 1865 often came down less to the skill and character of army commanders than to the great good fortune of having the right corps commander in the right place at the right time—or lack thereof. To have such a profound responsibility entrusted to an officer was in and of itself an honor whose significance and value were beyond calculation.

THIS VOLUME OFFERS eight case studies of corps command in the Union army during the Civil War that are designed to illustrate the critical roles these generals could and did play in shaping the course of the war as well as the variety of internal and external factors that shaped their efforts. In the first essay, John J. Hennessy looks at one of the most controversial of the men who exercised corps command during the conflict's first year. Much was expected of Fitz John Porter when the war began and, thanks to his close friend George McClellan, he quickly established himself as one of the most important general officers in the Army of the Potomac. Porter ably rewarded McClellan's confidence and decision to elevate him to corps command in May 1862 with consistently solid performances in the Peninsula Campaign, particularly the Seven Days' Battles. He was ultimately undone, however, by the climate of suspicion that characterized how influential Republicans in Congress and the Lincoln administration came to view McClellan and his "clique" in the army's high command over the course of 1862, the foremost member of which was Porter. Unwaveringly loyal to his friend and his vision of how the war should be conducted, Porter would pay a steep price in the aftermath of the Union defeat at Second Manassas, when McClellan's enemies in Washington brought an end to Porter's career in a politically charged court-martial whose outcome was as much about the politics of corps command as his actual conduct on the battlefield.

Next, Thomas G. Clemens considers the story of Joseph K. F. Mansfield, who only exercised corps command for two days. Despite this brief tenure, Clemens's description of Mansfield's career prior to September 1862 offers a window into the evolution of the American military system during the previous four decades. Mansfield's military career began at West Point at a time when the military academy was undergoing significant changes that would profoundly affect the army as an institution and how it shaped the experiences of officers who would go on to achieve high command in the Civil War. Unfortunately for Mansfield, a combination of circumstances foiled his not unreasonable expectations that he would be among the men the North would turn to in its search for field commanders during the war's first year. Nonetheless, he was able to make contributions to the Union cause and thus a strong case for the assignment to corps command that came his way in September 1862. Yet on finally achieving that position, he found himself in anything but an ideal situation, commanding a unit containing a high percentage of new troops and being committed to battle in difficult circumstances on one of the worst fields of the entire war. Whether Mansfield could have fully risen to the challenge of corps command will never be known, for he fell mortally wounded shortly after arriving on the field. Nonetheless, as Clemens demonstrates, there is much in this general's career that merits attention from serious students of the Civil War.

Whatever problems Mansfield encountered in September 1862, he could at least take satisfaction in the knowledge that he had attained corps command. The subject of Kenneth W. Noe's essay, Charles C. Gilbert, only received designation as an "acting corps commander," a reflection of the decidedly volatile situation in which his appointment took place. Rebel forces had stolen a march on Federal forces commanded by Maj. Gen. Don Carlos Buell and pushed into Kentucky with hopes of planting the Confederate flag on the banks of the Ohio River and liberating the Bluegrass State from the Yankee yoke. Though neither hope would be realized, the Confederate offensive created a severe crisis for Union authorities, one that was exacerbated by an incident at the Galt House in Louisville that ended with one Union general shot to death by another. When faced with the challenge of finding someone to fill the murdered officer's shoes as a corps commander, and with few friends among those eligible for the position, a beleaguered Buell took an extraordinary action, elevating Gilbert from captain to corps command on the eve of leading his army forward to confront the Confederates. Gilbert's inability to fully rise to the challenges this sudden and rather odd promotion brought would be evident at the confused October 1862 engagement at Perryville, which, while poorly conducted, was followed by the Confederates retreating back to Tennessee.

While Gilbert's name is familiar only to truly hardcore students of the war, the same cannot be said of the subject of Christopher S. Stowe's essay. Before he could become the "victor of Gettysburg" and longest-serving commander of the North's most famous army, George Gordon Meade first had to negotiate the tricky environment of the eastern theater as a corps commander. This entailed not just maneuvering his troops effectively in the field but managing his reputation in the salons of Washington as well, as just about everything the Army of the Potomac did (or did not do) was subjected to intense scrutiny from members of Congress and the Lincoln administration. That this was the case was in part a consequence of the fact that Republicans in Washington had developed a decidedly jaundiced view of the army's officer corps during McClellan's troubled tenure in command. During that time, bitter and fundamental conflicts over operational planning, exacerbated by deep mistrust of the spirit of military professionalization that guided McClellan's efforts and the proximity of the army to Washington, created a hothouse atmosphere for anyone who rose to the level of corps command. These forces, and Meade's ability to negotiate them successfully enough to be the man Washington turned to when the Army of the Potomac marched north to its fateful encounter with the Confederates at Gettysburg, are effectively chronicled by Stowe.

While Meade was struggling to navigate the myriad dangers of corps command in the Army of the Potomac, out west James B. McPherson, the subject of Steven E. Woodworth's essay, was demonstrating what he could do. Much was expected from McPherson, who had graduated first in his class at West Point and contributed significantly to the success of Union operations in the western theater in 1862. In December he ascended to command of the XVII Corps and became a critical member of the sometimes-troubled command team Maj. Gen. Ulysses S. Grant had to work with during the campaign against Vicksburg that began that month. Although the next few months would see more than their share of frustrations for Union forces along the Mississippi River, by July 1863 they were able to claim possession of Vicksburg after conducting one of the great campaigns in all of American military history. McPherson's ability to contribute effectively to the victory, and Grant's ability to set up his young subordinate for success in his debut as a corps commander, illustrate how much personal relationships mattered in Civil War armies and the degree to which a corps commanders' success was contingent on intangible factors, including the command climate in which he had to operate.

Mark A. Snell's essay considers the efforts of one of the most prominent of the men who exercised corps command during the first year and a half of the war, William B. Franklin, after he departed the "main stage" of the eastern theater. Much was expected of Franklin at the outset of the war. He had finished first in his class at West Point and was considered by some the smartest man in the army; however, problematic performances in the Maryland and Fredericksburg Campaigns led to his removal from corps command in early 1863. Franklin's close friendship with McClellan enabled him to rise quickly in the Union army, from brigade commander at First Manassas to division commander in its aftermath, to corps commander during the Peninsula Campaign, and finally to wing commander and "grand division" commander during the Maryland and Fredericksburg Campaigns. Despite his considerable intellect, Franklin failed to rise to the occasion in these operations, with his ineffectual leadership at Fredericksburg, where he commanded more than a third of the army, and the political machinations that followed leading to his removal in early 1863. He received a second chance later that year when he was appointed to command the XIX Corps in Maj. Gen. Nathaniel Banks's Department of the Gulf and, by the end of 1863, was once again in the field, preparing to take an active role in operations west of the Mississippi. Franklin, though, fared no better there—neither his hopes for redemption nor the Lincoln administration's hopes for a great victory in the Trans-Mississippi would be fulfilled. Instead, the Red River Campaign would go down in history as one of the great fiascos of the war, taking down with it what was left of Franklin's reputation as a corps commander. His wounding at Sabine Crossroads in April 1864 as he was rallying his command finally took him out of the war completely.

The fate of another officer who traveled west hoping to rehabilitate a reputation that had taken a bad beating in the East is the subject of the next essay. Remembered best for his tenure in command of the Army of the Potomac, the highlight of which was an ignominious defeat at the hands of a much smaller Army of Northern Virginia in the Chancellorsville Campaign, Joseph Hooker prior to January 1863 had a well-deserved reputation for hard fighting—and self-promotional intrigue. Whether this mixed bag of ability as an officer and deplorable personal traits could achieve success in the western theater was an open question when he was sent there in the aftermath of the Union defeat at Chickamauga. "Fighting Joe's" well-celebrated performance at Chattanooga seemed to confirm Lincoln's high opinion of the general and hopes that whatever problems had arisen during his troubled tenure in command of the Army of the Potomac had been resolved and he would contribute materially to the Union cause in 1864. While Hooker as commander of the XX Corps did in fact make significant contributions to the effort to reach the outskirts of Atlanta, he would not be on hand to participate in its capture for reasons explored in this chapter.

In the final essay, Brooks D. Simpson looks at the performance of one of the most celebrated corps commanders of the Civil War. At Gettysburg, Winfield Scott Hancock made as good a debut after elevation to corps command

Introduction

as one could hope for. In all three days of battle, he played a critical role in the ability of the Union army to fight off the attacks of Gen. Robert E. Lee's Army of Northern Virginia and claim victory when it was over. Despite suffering a serious wound on the last day, hopes were high for "Hancock the Superb" ten months later when he led the II Corps across the Rapidan River in the opening phase of the 1864 Overland Campaign. In the weeks that followed, army commanders consistently placed the general's troops where the action was hottest. Yet from a close study of these operations, Simpson offers a revisionist take on Hancock's performance in 1864, finding reason to question his effectiveness in the management of his corps as it battled its way from the Rapidan River to the gates of Petersburg in one of the truly great—and brutal—campaigns of the war.

IN ADDITION TO PROVIDING insights into the military conduct of the Civil War in general and the commanders and campaigns examined here in particular, the purpose of this volume is to honor one of the great figures in modern Civil War scholarship. In the forty years after finishing his Ph.D. studies at Louisiana State University under T. Harry Williams, Herman Hattaway established himself as one of the towering figures in the field. His contributions to Civil War studies in his roles as a professor and mentor at the University of Missouri–Kansas City; lecturer to Civil War round tables, seminars, and preservation groups; as Distinguished Visiting Professor of History at the U.S. Military Academy; and above all as a scholar of the first order have profoundly influenced a generation of writing and thinking on the war. Professor Hattaway's first book, a prize-winning revised version of his doctoral dissertation, was a study of one man, Stephen D. Lee, whose most distinguished service during the war was in corps command. Since then Hattaway has been one of the great analysts of the organization and conduct of Civil War armies at the operational level. It is thus fitting that a work in his honor has the subject of corps command as its central theme. That such a study focuses on the Union high command is likewise fittingly ironic, for despite his own Southern roots and the fact that his career as a scholar has been distinguished by a number of important works on the Confederate war effort, under his direction two of the contributors to this work produced studies of Yankee officers. It is with profound respect and admiration for Professor Hattaway and the contributions that he has made to scholarship that the editor and contributors have put together this book.

NOTES

1. Grady McWhiney and Perry Jamieson, *Attack and Die: Civil War Military Tactics and the Southern Heritage* (Tuscaloosa: University of Alabama Press, 1982), for years the standard work on Civil War tactics, presented a strong case for the revolutionary influence of rifled weaponry. The notion of a "rifle revolution" has been challenged rather persuasively, though, in recent years. The pioneering work in this regard is Paddy Griffith, *Battle Tactics of the Civil War* (New Haven, Conn.: Yale University Press, 1987). Carrying forward Griffith's arguments are Mark Grimsley, "Surviving Military Revolution: The U.S. Civil War," in *The Dynamics of Military Revolution*, ed. MacGregor Knox and Wiliamson Murray (Cambridge: Cambridge University Press, 2001), 76–77; and Earl J. Hess, *The Rifle Musket in Civil War Combat: Reality and Myth* (Lawrence: University Press of Kansas, 2008).

2. On the powers of the central government in the South and the North, see, for instance, Emory M. Thomas, *The Confederate Nation, 1861–1865* (New York: Harper and Row, 1979); and Richard Bensel, *Yankee Leviathan: The Origins of Central State Authority in America, 1859–1877* (Cambridge: Cambridge University Press, 1991). For skeptical discussions of the notion that the Union's "hard war" marked a significant break with past practices, and thus provided a precedent for the destructiveness of twentieth-century warfare toward civilians, see Mark E. Neely, "Was the Civil War a Total War?" *Civil War History* 37 (Mar. 1991): 5–28; and Mark Grimsley, *The Hard Hand of War: Union Military Policy toward Southern Civilians* (New York: Cambridge University Press, 1995).

3. R. R. Palmer, "Frederick the Great, Guibert, Bulow: From Dynastic to National War," in *Makers of Modern Strategy: From Machiavelli to the Nuclear Age*, ed. Peter Paret (Princeton, N.J.: Princeton University Press, 1986), 105–6; David G. Chandler, *The Campaigns of Napoleon* (New York: Macmillan, 1966), 158–59; Robert M. Epstein, *Napoleon's Last Victory and the Emergence of Modern War* (Lawrence: University Press of Kansas, 1994), 9–32.

4. Herman Hattaway and Archer Jones, *How the North Won: A Military History of the Civil War* (Urbana: University of Illinois Press, 1983), 9–11.

5. The best study of Scott's campaign is Timothy D. Johnson, *A Gallant Little Army: The Mexico City Campaign* (Lawrence: University Press of Kansas, 2007).

6. Though Beauregard's desire to have them designated "corps" was not realized in 1861, the districts in Johnston's Department of Northern Virginia—the Potomac and Shenandoah—provided the nucleus of what became the First and Second Corps in the Army of Northern Virginia when legal authorization for the organization of corps came in November 1862. Robert M. Epstein, "The Creation and Evolution of the Army Corps in the American Civil War," *Journal of Military History* 55 (Jan. 1991): 23–25.

7. In their testimony senior commanders like Samuel Heintzelman complained that they had no idea as to what McClellan's plans were and acknowledged that some division commanders felt "slighted" by McClellan, while junior division commanders William B. Franklin and Fitz John Porter frankly acknowledged to the committee that McClellan had discussed some of his plans with them. Heintzelman testimony, Dec. 24, 1861, in U.S. Congress, *Report of the Joint Committee on the Conduct of the War*, 3 vols. (Washington, D.C.: Government Printing Office, 1863), 1:117, 121,

Introduction

Franklin testimony, Dec. 26, 1861, ibid., 122, 130; McDowell testimony, Dec. 26, 1861, ibid., 131; Porter testimony, Dec. 28, 1861, ibid., 171–72, 178.

8. William B. Franklin, "The First Great Crime of the War," in *The Annals of the Civil War* (1878; repr., New York: Da Capo, 1994), 79–80; "President's General War Order no. 2," Mar. 8, 1862, in *The Collected Works of Abraham Lincoln,* ed. Roy P. Basler, 9 vols. (New Brunswick, N.J.: Rutgers University Press, 1953–55), 5:149–50.

9. Otto Eisenschiml, *The Celebrated Case of Fitz John Porter: An American Dreyfus Affair* (Indianapolis: Bobbs-Merrill, 1950); Henry Gabler, "The Fitz John Porter Case: Politics and Military Justice" (Ph.D. diss., City University of New York, 1979); John J. Hennessy, *Return to Bull Run: The Campaign and Battle of Second Manassas* (New York: Simon and Schuster, 1993).

10. Stephen W. Sears, *Landscape Turned Red: The Battle of Antietam* (New York: Ticknor and Fields, 1983), 258–68, 276–93, 353–57; Ethan S. Rafuse, "'Poor Burn?' The Antietam Conspiracy That Wasn't," *Civil War History* 54 (June 2008): 146–75; Frank O'Reilly, *The Fredericksburg Campaign: Winter War on the Rappahannock* (Baton Rouge: Louisiana State University Press, 2003), 135–38, 460; Hooker to Bates, Apr. 2, 1877, Nov. 29, 1878, Samuel Penniman Bates Collection, 1875–79, vol. 406, Pennsylvania Historical and Museum Commission, Harrisburg.

11. Richard Sauers, *A Caspian Sea of Ink: The Meade-Sickles Controversy* (Baltimore: Butternut and Blue, 1989). Sauers revised and updated his study to produce *Gettysburg: The Meade-Sickles Controversy* (Washington, D.C.: Brassey's, 2003). See also James Hessler, *Sickles at Gettysburg: The Controversial Civil War General Who Committed Murder, Abandoned Little Round Top, and Declared Himself the Hero of Gettysburg* (New York: Savas Beatie, 2010); and Christopher S. Stowe, "Certain Grave Charges," *Columbiad: A Quarterly Review of the War between the States* 3 (1999): 19–46.

Conservatism's Dying Ember
Fitz John Porter and the Union War, 1862

JOHN J. HENNESSY

It is perhaps the highest artistic honor conveyed to American military heroes—the equestrian statue. Of the millions of men who served the Union cause during the Civil War, just thirty have had their service commemorated with such a memorial. Of those, likely none suffered the ignominy of controversy, inaction, and early apathy as did the statue to Union major general Fitz John Porter, located a few yards from his birthplace in Portsmouth, New Hampshire.[1]

A group of local veterans protested any monument at all. The city argued over its proper location. Vandals armed with stone cutters attacked the base of the statue. No pomp attended the groundbreaking in April 1903. Once the statue rose in Haven Park, the city dallied in planning any dedication ceremony, and so the monument sat for years. For a time, an empty meal sack concealed Porter's statuesque face. Later the bag gave way to a U.S. flag. When the city continued to delay a public dedication, someone took it upon himself to unveil the monument without ceremony—in the middle of the night. It would be three years before the city formally recognized the statue of the local boy gone famous.[2]

As much as any figure of the Civil War, Porter's historical life has been framed less by deeds and more by the harsh pens of critics and the loud voices of supporters. (Even the Portsmouth statue was born of a bequest of $30,000 from one of his staunchest public advocates, which is perhaps why the city seemed to be so unenthused by the idea.)[3] Few subordinate commanders on either side caused the spillage of more ink in the decades after the war than did Porter. The verdict of his career is often reduced to the question posed to the 1863 court-martial that led to his dismissal from the army: guilt or innocence? Did he deliberately undermine the efforts of Maj. Gen. John Pope to win a victory at Second Manassas?[4]

Yet Porter's journey through the Civil War is a far more useful lens than the simple question of personal justice or injustice might suggest. As a corps commander in the Army of the Potomac and the closest confidant of that army's commander, Maj. Gen. George B. McClellan, Porter not only stood at the vortex of momentous military events in 1862 but also astride a great and widening gulf between the army and the government it served. He engaged the Confederates on some of Virginia's great battlefields that year. He also engaged—avidly—McClellan's political opponents (some of them in the military) in a struggle over the nature and extent of the Union war effort.

For decades, the dispute between McClellan and the administration has been perceived through the lens of personality—a willful, ego-driven army commander (abetted by like-minded minions) personally offended by and unwilling to work with civilian superiors who irked him. But the quarrel was far more profound than that, for Porter and McClellan represented a conservative philosophy and vision of war shared by a significant percentage of the Northern population—Union-loving people who might best be called "conservative patriots." But unlike the man on the streets of Burlington or Chillicothe, Porter and McClellan were in the army. Their willingness to engage in debate with their civilian masters over war aims was a risky gambit that challenged the American tradition (albeit in 1862 a thin one) of civilian supremacy over the military.

Porter's ultimate fate—dismissal from the army—signaled not just the intellectual defeat of the conservative patriot's vision of war (at least so far as it existed within the army). It also confirmed, in a nation still young, the absolute ascendancy of civil authority over the military, a tradition that has become inviolate. Politicians make policy; the military carries it out. Few in American history paid a higher price in learning that lesson than Fitz John Porter.

In many ways, to look at the Army of the Potomac's relationship with the government it served through Porter's rather than McClellan's eyes is both easier and more telling. Though combative, cautious, and occasionally dismissive, he lacked many of the personality traits that inevitably distract (and even tempt) biographers of McClellan. Porter was energetic but controlled, confident but not self-absorbed, communicative but quiet. He was an accomplished man and competent corps commander whose determined views on the war cannot possibly be ascribed (as McClellan's often are) to an aberrant personality.

His story is thus a vivid window into one of America's most chaotic, important years.

John J. Hennessy

IN 1862 THE CIVIL WAR found its bloody rhythm and transformative purpose. The war that began the year looked little familiar by year's end. The scale of military operations in Virginia trebled. Slaves forced their way to freedom, while the U.S. government moved steadily toward a policy of confiscation and emancipation that would fundamentally alter the nation's longstanding relationship with slavery (and, along the way, significantly diminish the South's ability to sustain a rebellious war effort).

For the Confederates in Virginia, the costs attendant to the South's quest for independence became starkly clear in 1862. The war began its inexorable shift toward destructiveness, ravaging not just armies to an appalling degree but also ever-greater swaths of Virginia's landscape. Early in the year Confederate civilians suffered offense and outrage at the passage or presence of Union armies. By year's end, offense yielded to the hardship of outright destruction as the war increasingly found its way into Southern parlors and living rooms (in Fredericksburg this was literally so). Families and communities North and South suffered the repeated, paralyzing blow of young men lost. A war propelled at year's dawn by enthusiasm was by the year's end fueled by rancor borne forth by determination.

The arc of change in the Union war effort is clear at the distance of more than 150 years. But at the time little was obvious about the war's direction, its changing nature. What comes to us today as bullet points on a scholarly discourse were, at the time, cloaked in chaos, the product of a nation feeling, legislating, calculating, and fighting its way through a conflict that quickly grew beyond anyone's control. Politicians played general. Generals played politics. Congress watched and investigated. The Union army in Virginia coalesced against the threat. Careers blossomed. Others crashed. Some, like Fitz John Porter's, did both.

On the eve of war, many men had resumes like Porter's. Few, however, possessed his military pedigree. His father, John, was a navy captain (though a raging alcoholic), whose temporary posting in Portsmouth accorded his son his birthplace. Fitz John's uncle, David Porter, was a commodore, once commander of the USS *Constitution;* he in turn raised two boys, David Dixon Porter and David G. Farragut (whom he adopted), both destined to Civil War fame on the waters.

Porter's father died in 1831, leaving mother and son to fend for themselves. Largely thanks to his mother, Porter's youth—unstable though it was—yielded a young man smart, wise, and determined enough to gain admission to West Point in 1841. He by then had turned into a solid scholar. He graduated eighth in the nonluminous class of 1845; of his classmates, Porter would become if not the best, at least the most famous.[5]

The following year Porter headed to Mexico as a second lieutenant in the 4th Artillery, part of Maj. Gen. Winfield Scott's army advancing toward Mexico City. George McClellan, an engineer, served with Scott's army too, and the two young officers came to know each other. For his service, Porter received brevet promotions, first to captain and then to major. But this did little to distinguish him from hundreds of other young officers, and after the war he reentered the slow grind of army life. Assignments to teach at West Point, to the Adjutant General's Office in Washington, and to the 1857 expedition against the Mormons offered some variety but little visibility or chance for advancement. And so it would go until war came anew in 1861.[6]

By then the careers of McClellan (a committed and visible Democrat) and Porter were clearly on different trajectories. McClellan soon accepted command of troops in Ohio, with headquarters at Cincinnati. He immediately requested Porter to join his staff as adjutant general—essentially the command's administrative officer. That Washington failed to act on this request might have worked to Porter's ultimate good, for only one of McClellan's early staff officers (William W. Burns) ever found his way to a command position of note. Most, like Seth Williams and Randolph Marcy, were destined to perform staff work and nothing else.[7]

Instead, Porter received assignment to the staff of Brig. Gen. Robert Patterson, who commanded the Union army operating in the Shenandoah Valley during the First Manassas Campaign. Porter's position was important and visible, but the results of Patterson's campaign brought glory to no one associated with that army. Still, Porter emerged with several things essential to his future: a reputation intact, a Regular Army commission as colonel of the 15th Infantry, and a commission as brigadier general of volunteers. His ability and patient diligence in the prewar army had been rewarded. Now all that remained was to find a command that suited his talents and instincts.[8]

That would come courtesy of his friend George McClellan. By the end of July 1861, as the North wallowed in the aftermath of defeat at Bull Run, the Northern press had already painted McClellan as the "Young Napoleon." Success in western Virginia propelled him to the forefront at a time of immense national crisis. Days after the debacle at Bull Run, Abraham Lincoln and Winfield Scott appointed McClellan to command what would become the Army of the Potomac—the largest and most visible army in the land. It was an appointment nearly everyone inside and outside the army approved.[9]

McClellan made sure his friend Porter would figure prominently in the task of building a new army. Within four days of arriving in Washington, he recommended Porter for promotion. Then in late August he placed him in command of William Tecumseh Sherman's former brigade. Porter was among a cadre of fairly young, experienced professional soldiers McClellan put in place—though none of them had any sort of experience that might adequately have prepared them for command in an army that in a few months would exceed 100,000 men. Of them all, Porter would emerge as the commanding general's closest confidant, advisor, and at times proxy. No soldier's career would be more closely tied to McClellan's success or failure than Porter's. No man would be more loyal.[10]

Unconsciously or not, McClellan's highly visible efforts to create a new army melded its identity with his own. He wielded his personality not like a firestick but unpretentiously, as an artist strokes a brush. The army quickly came to see itself as "Little Mac's." Circumstances, inclination, and personal style dictated that Porter would command in his friend's shadow, projecting a very different persona. Porter stood about five feet, ten inches, by every account slender, "erect," and dignified, with dark brown eyes. His wife called him "the handsomest man I ever saw" (as wives are wont to proclaim) but added, "He was entirely unconscious of it." In 1861 a few flecks of gray salted his brown hair; he kept his black beard closely trimmed. Fellow officer William Woods Averell regarded Porter "as the most accomplished gentleman I had ever known." "He was a remarkably handsome man" with an "unaffected dignity of manner," wrote Averell, and an "ease and grace of action." In his youth Porter had been a premier athlete—an excellent swimmer, skater, baseball player, and horseman—and at age forty he apparently still carried himself in the solid way athletes often do. He dressed carefully and possessed a powerful voice, easily heard at a distance. Averell claimed that Porter "could not fail to command attention."

Beyond his assiduous dress, there was little show. Porter was serious, quiet, reserved, even "shy and retiring," said his wife (his daughter later claimed, "in all my life I never once heard my father laugh"). A schoolmate remembered, "He was not eminently sociable, but enjoyed the society of friends." Porter's tendency toward quietude only added weight to the words that did emerge from him—"you would know he meant what he said," recalled a fellow student. A female hospital worker wrote from the Peninsula: "There is a fine spirit in General Porter, ... an expression of devotion about him which inspires great confidence." And Lincoln's secretary John Hay wrote that the general "possessed a solidity of head and intellect that makes success a necessity."

Another classmate called him "high minded and strictly honorable." Indeed, righteousness may well have been Porter's dominant characteristic. He cloaked his political and military thought with a fierce moral certitude, rarely yielding and occasionally attacking in its defense. That moral certitude bound him to McClellan and the conservative vision of the Union war effort they shared. And it ultimately dominated his life, for moral righteousness requires far more energy than moral lassitude. He would pursue redemption for both himself and his conservative philosophies for decades after the war. McClellan treasured his dogged loyalty.[11]

Porter's sense of right and regulation served him well as his unit and the army emerged in late 1861 around Washington. Days after he assumed command, he faced rebellion in two of his regiments, the 2d Maine and 13th New York. Both had fought at Bull Run, and their men thought their obligations to the government had been fulfilled at ninety days. The government disagreed. Porter called them out of camp to the parade ground, summoned their officers, and reminded them of their country's need for them—no doubt with the implied threat that if they continued the ruckus, far worse than a scolding would be coming. He instructed the officers to "go among their subordinates, teach them submission to the rules of service, and maintain discipline." They did. The regiments settled, and both would become mainstays of Porter's command though neither would ever be much for clean camps and quiet reflection.[12]

Beyond such uncommon bouts of suasion, the combination of long service in the military and righteous nature rendered Porter a strict, humorless disciplinarian. His men both feared and admired him. A man of the tumultuous 13th New York called him "cold, heartless, unimpassioned, and a terrible, terrible, terrible disciplinarian ... But such a splendid soldier.[13]

By late fall, Porter's command had expanded to a division—a functional force of about 11,000 men. It included three brigades destined to fight at some of the most famous places on America's battlefields. Of Porter's brigade commanders (Brig. Gens. George Morell, Daniel Butterfield, and John H. Martindale), one, Martindale, would help entangle the general in a web that would eventually contribute to his demise, though no reasonable man would have guessed that in the fall of 1861. Martindale's was one of the peculiar brigades in the army—probably the only one in the Union army with two regiments commanded, at least for a time, by sitting members of Congress. Like his West Point classmate Morell, Martindale had opted out of the military long before the war, becoming a well-known, politically connected, quick-witted criminal attorney in upstate New York (and a Republican antislavery man). In 1861 his West Point credentials qualified him for a commission and command of a brigade that included the troublesome 13th New York and 2d Maine. "A black-haired talkative man, full of great plans to do great things" (wrote Theodore Lyman), Martindale possessed impressive oratorical and even musical skills. In 1862 he and the 18th Massachusetts collaborated on a song, "Touch the Elbow," that became something of a wartime hit. Porter, however, quickly became wary of him: "General Martindale was," he later wrote, "intelligent and active and attentive to his duties when they did not clash with his interests or safety." Porter's medical director called Martindale "a dangerous adversary for an honorable man."[14]

THAT FIRST WINTER of the war did much to lay the foundation for both Porter's rise and eventual fall.

Distance usually afforded officers in the Old Army some insulation from the swirl of politics that governed American life before the Civil War. Not so for the Army of the Potomac. No army in American history would be subject to such close oversight from inquisitive politicians and such relentless coverage from a partisan press as was McClellan's. Nothing did more to shape the culture of the Army of the Potomac than this constant scrutiny, inspiring caution that would endure until the war's end. Officers within it, especially Porter and McClellan, faced an increasingly hostile environment that questioned not only their acts but also their motives. Both quickly grasped that intensifying scrutiny—with its inherent sniping and second guessing (an ageless characteristic of our national capital)—represented something far more than bothersome meddling from politicians. It reflected a growing and deepening division in Washington and within American society over the nature and reach of the war itself.

The hazards of army life in the shadows of Washington came first to Porter in the fall of 1861—the outgrowth of a commonplace event that for the first time brought his political views to public notice. Predictably, the tumult involved John Martindale. In August Col. John Pickell took command of the unhappy and restless 13th New York Infantry of Martindale's brigade. Pickell, "a fat, jolly, solid looking man" sixty years of age, was a graduate of West Point who had lately declared himself a "Union candidate" for Congress from western Maryland. He lost. Porter later proclaimed the colonel an "intense abolitionist" and "like Martindale, [was] annoyed and resentful at being commanded by one who graduated" from West Point years after they had.[15]

After taking command of the 13th New York, Pickell discovered that one of his officers not only owned a slave (a rare but not unique occurrence in the Army of the Potomac) but also kept him in camp. His sensibilities offended, Pickell (as Porter described it) "caused the slave to abandon his master" and took the bondman into his own quarters. The offended slave-owning officer protested directly to Porter. Naively viewing this as an internal matter without political implications, Porter ordered the colonel to return the slave to the aggrieved officer. Porter's thinking reflected a view common at the time: "Slavery existed and we were in a slave state and the owner was entitled to his servant and no officer had the right to use his rank and power to take property from a loyal officer . . . and appropriate it for his own use."[16]

It perhaps did not occur to Porter that others might not see the matter as he did, and so commenced a drama that would help shape political Washington's view of him. In October a new regiment had arrived in Martindale's command, the 22d Massachusetts. The regiment was the work of Sen. Henry Wilson, a powerful and ardent antislavery Republican, who had used the time between congressional sessions to do some recruiting. Not only did the senator recruit the 22d Regiment, he also commanded it (at least for a time). But there was more: Wilson was chairman of the Senate Committee on Military Affairs. A growing and particular interest of his was how the nation's military leaders—charged with prosecuting the war—saw the question of war and freedom.[17]

Senator Wilson was in many ways a pretend soldier (one day he rode thirty miles on an inspection of camps and forts, and the effort propelled him to bed for a week). As such, he instantly engendered mistrust among those in or working with the army. A civilian employee in the War Department described him as many in McClellan's army might have: "He is full of little political stratagems, lacks straightforwardness and sincerity and reliability. He is playing some kind of game with us." Wilson would be in actual command of his regiment for less than two weeks. But his time in Porter's command helped him forge at least one important and enduring connection—with his brigade commander, General Martindale shared Wilson's political views. More importantly, though, Martindale increasingly questioned the commitment and will of his commander. When Porter ordered the slave released from the protection of Colonel Pickell, Martindale quickly reported the incident to Wilson, characterizing it simplistically as a Union general, Porter, returning "a slave to his master."[18]

Months before, soon after Bull Run, Wilson had thundered to his Senate colleagues: "The idea that men who are in arms destroying their country shall be permitted to use [slaves] for that purpose, and . . . that we should disgrace our cause and our country, by returning such men to their traitorous masters, ought not longer be entertained. The time has come for that to cease; and, by the blessing of God, as far as I am concerned, I mean it shall cease."[19] Wilson's views had not yet found their way into policy or law, but clearly in some circles the question of how officers in the army handled escaped slaves had become a litmus. However unconstitutional any other course might have been, Porter had failed that test, and Senator Wilson, abetted by General Martindale, would make sure those in power knew it.[20]

Something else happened during Wilson's short tenure in the field that brought him into indirect confrontation with Porter. Men of the 22d Massachusetts (known ever after as "Henry Wilson's Regiment") stripped a nearby house of weatherboards to make floors for their tents. While such things would be commonplace later in the war (and Wilson would become an important advocate for harsher treatment of Southern civilians), at this point the entire army operated under orders prohibiting such acts. Few things irked both Porter and McClellan more than wanton destruction of civilian property and the enmity it inspired in Southerners, and Porter took prompt steps to correct the Senate committee chairman under his command. Martindale offered to relay the bad news to Colonel Wilson, promising to "do it in such a way as to effect the object and cause no ill feeling." But either through intent or carelessness, Martindale failed. Wrote Porter, "[he] did his part so maliciously and malignantly as to rouse Wilson's bitter and active enmity towards me for many years." Because of that, recalled the general years later, he had run afoul of "influential antislavery senators and representatives . . . and was regarded as a sympathizer to the Confederates."[21]

Porter, of course, was no sympathizer, but the dual confrontations over slavery and private property demonstrated something officers in the army—and

Porter especially—would be slow to learn: as the war dragged along and became more political, the politics of the men waging it mattered more and more. The "sympathizer" label would be the foundation for much trouble to come.

WHILE THE WINTER of 1861–62 brought frenetic activity to the Army of the Potomac, it brought no major movement. That meant little opportunity for anyone to much distinguish himself by success. Porter nonetheless managed to carve out a uniquely visible place in the army, one that would be integral to his eventual rise. And he did it by embracing relatively new technology: balloons. That fall and winter, Porter recruited and used Thaddeus Lowe's fledgling balloon corps, regularly ascending himself. Hours of observation rendered Porter by far more familiar with the landscape west of Washington and Alexandria than anyone in the army. He could, he later recorded, "recognize any changes in the landscape and . . . trace movements of even small bodies of friends or foes." His unique knowledge made him all the more useful to the army's commander. Porter thus assumed a peerless position in McClellan's inner circle.[22]

In November 1861 Lincoln appointed McClellan general in chief of all Union armies. The job required an expansive mind like McClellan's, but it also demanded his full attention and energy. That it did not receive. In addition to tending to the forest of details of managing an armed service spanning two thousand miles of disputed territory in a highly political democracy, McClellan continued in direct command of the Army of the Potomac, preparing it methodically for a campaign whose time (in his eyes) had not yet come. Inspections, reviews, securing the defenses of Washington, and the building of the organizational infrastructure required to sustain in the field an army now more than 100,000 men strong—all of these things required more time than almost everyone outside the army thought wise or necessary. Weeks became months; 1861 became 1862. The very time McClellan so coveted worked against him in other ways, for with each passing day, impatient, disputatious voices grew louder. As British journalist William Howard Russell put it, "McClellan is still reviewing, and the North are still waiting for victories and paying money, and the orators are still wrangling over the best way of cooking the hares which they have not caught yet."[23]

To gain time, to preserve his prerogatives as commander, and to fend off efforts to use the army to accomplish what he saw as unmilitary ends (most notably emancipation), McClellan pushed back hard against his critics. Porter, now his closest confidant, joined him.[24]

At year's end Congress summoned Porter to appear before the brand new Joint Committee on the Conduct of the War. Born of the disasters at Bull Run and Ball's Bluff, the committee existed to inquire into both failures on the battlefield and military policies beyond combat. Its two most prominent members, Republicans Benjamin Wade of Ohio (the chairman) and Zachariah Chandler of Michigan, had both witnessed the disaster at Bull Run. Porter's emerging nemesis Henry Wilson was not on the committee but had done much to shape its purpose when he declared, "We should teach men in civil and in military authority that the people expect that they will not make mistakes, and that we shall not be easy with their errors." As the secret hearings began on Christmas Eve, 1861, committee members, and indeed the public at large, were increasingly viewing McClellan's inaction as a mistake that needed redress. Just a few weeks before, Chandler had privately declared the general "timid and weak."[25]

The joint committee seemed most interested in understanding the dynamics of the army's high command—especially McClellan's tendency to insulate himself with a few like-minded confidants while leaving more-senior officers like Brig. Gen. Irvin McDowell and Brig. Gen. Samuel Heintzelman to wonder. Heintzelman declared that he knew nothing of his commander's plans. "I have not the slightest idea—not the slightest," he complained, then declared that he had "never been consulted upon any military subject" by McClellan. McDowell allowed that he knew a bit more, though little of recent vintage. In contrast, William B. Franklin, a good friend of both Porter and McClellan, testified to his intimate knowledge of the general's plans but refused to share them without his commander's permission.[26]

Porter pulled up his chair in the uncrowded Senate meeting room on December 28. The joint committee did its work behind closed doors, but that did nothing to alleviate Porter's concerns that any information he shared might find its way onto the street, into the press, and into Confederate hands. He admitted to knowing much but parried or evaded nearly every question. When it came clear that the general would not share facts, Senator Chandler asked him for opinions. Should the army go into winter quarters? "That is a question I cannot answer.... I decline to give a military opinion on that point." Why is the army not prepared to move? "You ask a question that I also decline to answer," responded Porter. Can Congress help facilitate the army's movement? "Not that I am aware of. I believe General McClellan is carrying out his plans as rapidly as he possibly can." Had McClellan ever consulted with his officers? "I was present once when a plan was proposed." Nothing more. He revealed no plans and conceded no missteps, no unwarranted delay, and no lack of confidence in the army's future success in McClellan's hands.[27]

Porter never explained his testimony—whether his reticence derived from sincere concerns about secrecy or from growing impatience with what he and McClellan saw as the meddlesome tendencies of politicians. But he left little doubt among observers that he was both an intimate and determined defender of the general in chief. That mattered more and more as that tumultuous, inactive winter of 1861–62 churned along. Porter's appearance before the joint committee came at a moment when fissures in the Union war effort emerged, both within the government and in the public at large. Could, should the war be waged and won solely against Confederate armies? Must slavery perish in order to save the Union? Should Southern civilians be forced to suffer, as one soldier put it, "the awful horrors of a war brought on by their treason"? Three days after Porter's appearance, Chairman Wade warned President Lincoln: "You are murdering your country by inches in consequence of the inactivity of the military and want of a distinct policy in regards to slavery." Porter's residence in the McClellan camp—now well known to Congress—stamped him solidly as a political conservative. He could not know it then, but he had chosen to ride a wave that would ultimately carry him out of the war altogether.[28]

Porter and McClellan were hardly deaf to the critics. Rather, they resolved to defeat them. They engaged opponents within the administration and Congress directly and sometimes openly. Americans have long had a discomfort with military officers who would dispute or debate their civil masters (and especially dislike military men who display insolence in the process, as McClellan sometimes did). But within bounds, the discussion and debate of strategy, policy, and war aims has been a staple of civil-military relations in the United States since its inception. With Lincoln, against Secretary of War Edwin Stanton, and in the halls of Congress, over and over again McClellan argued that the army should not and would not become an agent for social change; it should not be a tool for punishing Southern civilians (they would, he argued, once again and soon be countrymen). The war, he and Porter maintained, should hew to its narrow, original purpose: restoration of the Union as it had been.

It is hard—perhaps unrealistic—to argue that McClellan should not have weighed in on these matters, given the central role his military forces would play in defining the nature of the American Civil War. He and Porter distinguished (and jeopardized) themselves, though, by taking the debates and disputes outside the cloistered halls of government. McClellan mobilized operatives and friends in the Democratic Party and the opposition press, mounting a loose campaign of selective leaks and outright advocacy meant to promote his strategic thinking, defend his operational caution, and to sustain his vision for a limited conflict. "I am fighting to preserve the integrity of the Union & the power of the Govt," he wrote to New York attorney and powerbroker Samuel L. M. Barlow in November 1861. "To gain that end, we cannot afford to raise up the negro question—it must be incidental and subsidiary." The effort amounted to an intellectual declaration of war on those in the administration who disagreed with him. Porter was an ardent participant in what would be a rare public debate by proxy between the civil and the military under the U.S. flag.[29]

When McClellan asked him to cultivate the *New York World,* Porter eagerly complied. Managed and eventually edited by twenty-eight-year-old Manton Marble, the fledgling *World* was a newspaper seeking both a voice and an audience. Marble was ambitious, independent, and personally loyal, determined to carve a niche in New York's chaotic journalistic landscape. Largely by dint of his energy, within a year the *World* would become a loud, sometimes virulent mouthpiece for the Democratic Party. Porter's correspondence with Marble constitutes a vivid record of a "conservative patriot's" view of war and a compelling look at efforts within the army to shape the debate over war aims.[30]

In October 1861 Porter started feeding information to *World* reporter Edmund C. Stedman. As the spring 1862 campaign neared, and as Porter's confidence in Stedman and Marble grew, he became bolder. In early March Stedman reported to Marble that the general "took me to a private room and talked with me an hour, saying he was sure he could rely on your and my discretion. The interview confirmed many things I had believed, shed light on others, and at all events brought me home." In a follow-up letter, Porter directly advocated for McClellan's plan to move the army by water against Richmond. The quicker the troops could get to Richmond the better, Porter wrote Stedman, and "the quickest plan is to take the lower Chesapeake. . . . The object and aim is McClellan's and if sustained he will accomplish it in the shortest time and least loss of life on our side." In turn, Stedman warned Porter about rising opposition to McClellan (the newspaperman advising the military man might be the most remarkable part of this exchange). He warned that that Radical Republicans on Capitol Hill had become a force that "openly hints" at McClellan's possible removal. "You may have the warmest assurances from President and Cabinet, and they may mean what they say," Stedman advised him, "but you cannot depend upon them more than from day to day, because in the end an American Administration always has to bow to the will of the ruling faction." The reporter promised, "we ... shall continue to counteract your detractors as best we can."[31]

Events promptly justified Stedman's warnings. Within a matter of days, Lincoln removed McClellan as general in chief of all Union armies, confining him instead to command of the Army of the Potomac. Lincoln also overruled McClellan's disinclination to appoint corps commanders in the army. The general had wanted to wait, he said, until the division commanders had been tested in battle (though many in Washington presumed—perhaps correctly—that he was simply stalling for the day he could appoint his favorites). Instead, Lincoln appointed corps commanders for him, selecting precisely the men McClellan would have avoided if he could: McDowell, Brig. Gen. Erasmus Keyes, Heintzelman, and Brig. Gen. Edwin Vose Sumner. Conspicuously absent from the list was Porter.

Porter saw these acts as evidence of the growing hostility of Washington (especially Stanton, the Radicals, and abolitionists) not only toward McClellan but also toward the conservative approach he and his commander espoused. And he was right. Antislavery general James Wadsworth would emerge as a key figure in the emerging schism between the army and the government. He saw in McClellan's delays, machinations, and proselytizing a conspiracy. "Is it possible," Wadsworth wondered, "to account for all these errors on the theory of incompetence alone? Is there not in some high quarters a plan for putting down this Rebellion by some other means than by whipping the Rebels?" The theory gaining ground among McClellan's enemies was that the general meant to extend the war long enough for a peace party to rise and negotiate an end to the war with slavery intact. There was, of course, no truth to the assertion, but the cloud of treason would linger with disastrous effect to Porter.[32]

Porter took up the other end of this shadow debate. McClellan will be successful, he told Manton Marble, "if the abolitionists will permit." Victory required the destruction of "rebel leaders" and their armies, not slavery or the Southern populace. In Porter's view an attack on slavery would only compel the Confederates to fight harder (as one soldier put it, the men "view the abolition of slavery . . . as saddling so much additional labor upon them before the present great work is accomplished"). The general claimed the conservatives' view of the war to be omnipresent in the army—"abolitionists in the armies of the U.S. are not looked upon as friends of the Union." Moreover, Porter saw the army as a growing political force to be reckoned with. "The conservative element throughout the army will make itself felt at the next election," he wrote Marble. "If members of Congress could only listen unseen, I believe many would tremble for the probable fall of their political party." In Porter's eyes the emerging Radicals in Washington—especially Stanton—assumed a place analogous to traitorous Confederates. "All [in the army] wish an end to this war," he told Marble, "death to the tyrants and demagogues of the South, and death to the demagogues of the North."[33]

By the time of McClellan's move to the Peninsula in late March 1862, a deep schism between the army and the government it served had emerged. Henceforth, virtually everything each did would be viewed through a lens of suspicion by the other.

LINCOLN QUICKLY GAVE McClellan loyalists fodder for conspiratorial thinking of their own. On April 5, as the Army of the Potomac took position in front of Confederate lines at Yorktown, the president ordered McDowell's corps (the largest in the army) to remain in front of Washington as a safeguard against a Confederate advance that McClellan deemed unlikely if not impossible. It was, perhaps, the most cautious strategic decision of the war, establishing Lincoln as a military thinker whose strategic conservatism far exceeded McClellan's. In the decision to withhold McDowell, Porter saw designs for McClellan to fail, a view he never relinquished. In 1881 he declared to historian John Ropes: "We all knew then—we know now—that there was an influence at work against McC. & you may take it from me for what it is worth, there were two objects to accomplish—McClellan was not to succeed, the war was not to end in a short time. You may put that in your pipe & smoke it silently." Porter claimed that Secretary of the Treasury Salmon Chase, Stanton, and McDowell were all party to the scheme, overawing a president who might have done otherwise without their influence. Even decades later he decried the decision as responsible for "much disaster, loss of life & treasure[,] a cause of misery." It was, Porter told Ropes, "one continued crime," part of a larger, nefarious plan. "You will find if you get behind the scenes that the plan was McClellan should not succeed—that Richmond should not be taken until the south was crushed, & slavery abolished—and that not till it was near or after next Presidential election." The perception (no more accurate than Wadsworth's conspiratorial theories on McClellan) henceforth shaped McClellan's and Porter's view of the government they served.[34]

The evolution of dueling conspiracy theories served as backdrop to Porter's and the army's entrance on the bloody Virginia landscape of 1862. After landing at Fort Monroe, the Army of the Potomac approached the Confederate defenses at Yorktown on April 5. The organization of the army into corps put Porter and his division under General Heintzelman, commander of the III Corps. Porter's subordinate condition displeased McClellan, but his friend's close association with Lowe's balloon corps quickly accorded him a special place in the army's hierarchy. Porter's ascents became regular affairs, and in short order he no doubt had a greater understanding of the Confederate lines at Yorktown than anyone in the Union army.[35]

Later that month McClellan carved out for Porter a special position, "Director of the Siege." McClellan explained that he had discovered many "blunders" in the layout of trenches and needed someone more aware than his own chief of staff, Randolph Marcy, to fix matters. "This new arrangement will save me much trouble," the general explained. "I was very thankful to put Porter on duty at once." The position seems to have been improvised, and it is easy to argue that the extensive knowledge Porter acquired of both Union and Confederate lines from his balloon ascensions justified the assignment. The orders, issued on April 27, gave Porter broad authority over both the evolution and protection of the Union line at Yorktown—the geometrics of the siege. More importantly, they required every corps commander in the army to report not to headquarters, but to Porter, rendering him the equivalent of an executive officer. It was clearly McClellan's way of righting the slight imposed on his friend by Lincoln's imposition of corps commanders in March.[36]

The appointment had little real effect, for the siege ended victoriously for the Union just a week after Porter assumed command. But if any doubts remained among Porter's army brethren that he stood highest in McClellan's esteem and affection, the special appointment at Yorktown removed them. That fact engendered resentment toward both Porter and McClellan. Keyes later declared that McClellan gave "himself up to favorites to an extent unheard of before." Both of Porter's fellow division commanders in the III Corps weighed in with vitriol, especially after McClellan issued an order after the Battle of Williamsburg that seemed to slight them. Brig. Gen. Philip Kearny thought McClellan prone to surrounding himself with "weak favorites." Brig. Gen. Joseph Hooker railed at the commander's penchant for awarding "merit only to favorites and kindred" (referring to McClellan's chief of staff Marcy, his father-in-law). Porter's corps commander, Heintzelman, recorded his dissatisfaction in his diary on April 29: "The conduct of Gen. McClellan is giving great dissatisfaction in this Army, particularly about Gen. Porter." Heintzelman asserted that three generals had complained to him, and "one of them this morning was afraid his name would have to be changed to Porter before he would be able to do anything."[37]

With the siege over and the Confederates in retreat up the Peninsula toward Richmond, Porter reverted to command of his division. It would, however, be a short-lived condition. On May 18 McClellan decided to create two new corps—one for Porter, the V, and one for Brig. Gen. William B. Franklin, the VI, McClellan's two great loyalists. Lincoln had warned McClellan against doing this: "It is looked upon as merely an effort to pamper one or two pets, and to persecute and denigrate their supposed rivals." McClellan likely would not have disagreed; it was probably *for* these reasons, not despite them, that he pushed the new corps through. Porter now commanded his old division, led by General Morell, and a new division (with regular troops at its core) commanded by Brig. Gen. George Sykes.[38]

As the Army of the Potomac crawled up the Peninsula and approached the defenses of Richmond, Porter updated ally Manton Marble at the *New York World*. The progress of the campaign clearly suited him. "The course of this army is a safe one," he wrote, "we do not move but surely, and Richmond falls to us, *perhaps without a battle*." (The rest of the nation shared Porter's hope but not generally his cheery view of McClellan's deliberate methods.) The successful, perhaps bloodless campaign would clear the way for a continued march into the South—a prospect that demanded, in Porter's view, a rejection of all calls for a harsher war. The army "will reconquer the country in a manner which will develop Union feeling and cause Virginia to rejoin [us]," he declared. "This army goes as a disciplined body, not an armed mob, compelled to respect private rights and to win the respect of the people we will be with." The abolitionists were, wrote Porter, "trying to prolong this unnatural war." He predicted that once done with the Rebels, the men in the army might turn their attention to the "abolitionist traitors" at home. "How they are detested here," he declared. He went on to chastise Secretary Stanton for continuing to withhold McDowell's men at Fredericksburg. "Poor fool," he called the secretary of war. This was no intimate musing to a wife or trusted confidant; it was a professional soldier's opinion of his boss expressed to one of the most powerful editors in the North. Not only was all this a vivid example of how one of America's millions of conservative patriots envisioned the war, but it also demonstrated clearly their growing alienation from those who thought otherwise.[39]

Once in front of Richmond, three things shaped McClellan's prospects and plans: the strength of the Confederate defenses, the desire to capture Richmond in a single blow with as little loss of life as possible, and the need to accommodate the impending arrival of McDowell's column, descending directly south from Fredericksburg. Even McClellan's ardent critics in the army—Heintzelman, Keyes, and McDowell himself—thought the junction of these 41,000 men with the Army of the Potomac essential to success at Richmond. Achieving that objective would shape Porter's experience on the Peninsula. His corps would spend more than a month acting as the army's dangling hook, reaching northward in anticipation of McDowell's arrival. The requirement rendered Porter the central subordinate commander in the drama that played out before Richmond in May, June, and July 1862.[40]

McDowell never came. The advance of Maj. Gen. Thomas J. "Stonewall" Jackson through the Shenandoah Valley in late May scuttled Lincoln's plan and inspired him to send part of McDowell's force to chase Jackson. By then, Porter had already moved his corps north of the Chickahominy River to make a connection. Though his major purpose seemed foiled, McClellan spotted a chance to flail a formidable Confederate force near Hanover Court House. To Porter went orders to clear the area, and on May 27, 1862, the general led his corps into battle for the first time.[41]

The Battle at Hanover Court House was a sprawling, disjointed affair, with regiments colliding at odd angles in unexpected places. Porter micromanaged, placing regiments and batteries and rendering division commander Morell largely useless. He also erred at times—though not disastrously—and was called to public account for it by none other than John Martindale. But victory soothed all. Porter succeeded in driving the Confederates away from Hanover Junction. In McClellan's report to Stanton that night, he extolled Porter's performance: "Too much credit cannot be given to his magnificent Division and its accomplished leader." To his wife McClellan gushed: "The old rascal has done all that I could ask.... It is a fair presage of the great victory which awaits us at Richmond."⁴²

Still, Jackson's dash in the Shenandoah Valley preyed on Lincoln's profound worries for Washington, and so McDowell sat at Fredericksburg. In Porter's eyes an immobile McDowell symbolized the perfidy of the nation's leaders. He urged his editor-friend Marble to challenge Lincoln publicly: "Does the President (controlled by our incompetent Secy) design to cause defeat here for the purpose of prolonging the war[?]" For his part, Lincoln was governed not by the military principles of Antoine-Henri Jomini but by the fears of a politician largely uncounseled. The president came to recognize his errors in responding to Jackson's Valley Campaign, though too late to do any good. "I think Jackson's game—his assigned work—now is to magnify the accounts of his numbers and reports of his movements," he explained in mid-June, "and thus by constant alarms keep three or four times as many of our troops away from Richmond as his own force amounts to. Thus he helps his friends at Richmond three or four times as much as if he were there. Our game," Lincoln concluded, "is not to allow this." Had he penned these words a month earlier and acted on them, the president would have marked himself a prescient military thinker. Coming as they did after Jackson had roiled Union designs, they served only as a sorry epitaph to a failed Union campaign in the Shenandoah Valley.⁴³

The fact remained, though, that McClellan had men, materiel, and opportunity enough to achieve success at Richmond even without 41,000 additional troops. Still, the prospect of McDowell's descent from Fredericksburg continued to shape McClellan's position before Richmond. Porter continued to hold ground north of the Chickahominy River, an indefinite, swampy expanse impassable to human or horse. On June 25 the V Corps, newly supplemented by a division of Pennsylvania troops commanded by Brig. Gen. George McCall, stood alone there, connected to the rest of the army only by a handful of floating bridges built by Union engineers. Gen. Robert E. Lee, newly appointed commander of Richmond's defenders, did not fail to note this vulnerable circumstance. In late June Porter and his corps stood at the vortex of the campaign's climax.

On June 26 Lee launched his attack, trying to destroy Porter's command and rupture McClellan's supply line. But the Confederates' plans went awry, and Porter's men parried Lee's attacks along Beaver Dam Creek near Mechanicsville. That night McClellan visited his friend. There would be no chance to withdraw the corps to safety across the Chickahominy; it would have to stand and fight. "Now, Fitz," McClellan said, "you understand my views and the absolute necessity of holding the ground, until arrangements over the river can be completed." In a narrow sense Porter did. But he presumed his defensive efforts north of the Chickahominy would be matched by an offensive, organized by McClellan, south of it. As the commanding general departed that evening, Porter did not know that the he had decided not to advance south of the river but instead to move the army across the Peninsula to a new base, covered by gunboats on the James River. McClellan called the movement a "change of base." Detractors called it a retreat. Indeed, it was both.[44]

None of this changed Porter's momentous task for June 27. That afternoon his corps endured the single largest attack ever launched by an army under Lee's command. The Confederates pummeled the Union position near Gaines's Mill. Porter called for reinforcements, arranged his artillery, plugged gaps, and urged his men—all in a quest to buy time for McClellan to organize the larger movement of the army. Regiments repeatedly sacrificed themselves to seize a ripple of ground or to buy a few more moments. In the end Porter had too few reserves to rush into multiplying holes punched in his lines by Lee's swarming men. It was perhaps the most intense fighting the army had ever done. Porter's lines finally collapsed, leaving behind nearly 7,000 casualties. The result could hardly have been otherwise. Lee had more than 55,000 men on hand, Porter just 34,000. That night, stunned and bedraggled, Porter's men took to the crossings of the Chickahominy and joined the Army of the Potomac's march to the James River.[45]

The swirl of events left little time for contemplation or laurels. Indeed, had Gaines's Mill been like most other battles—bracketed by anticipation on the one side and quiet reflection on the other—Porter's performance, though futile, might well have been widely noted and lauded. He and his men gained McClellan a critical day. But events sped onward, and Gaines's Mill became simply one of the "Seven Days."

As the Army of the Potomac snaked southward across the Peninsula toward the James, Lee tried again and again to slice into McClellan's column, to hack it into pieces that could be destroyed in turn. Savage Station, White Oak Swamp, Glendale—these places became bloody waystations along the path of McClellan's march. Porter and his battered corps suffered no more until their involvement in the campaign's ultimate battle, Malvern Hill.

After the war, Porter declined to celebrate his birthday on August 31—a date associated with travails at Second Manassas—and instead celebrated July 1 each year, the anniversary of the most successful day of his military life at Malvern Hill. As savage fighting raged near the crossroads of Glendale on June 30, the general hauled his V Corps onto the open plateau farther southeast at Malvern Hill. Throughout the night, the rest of the army marched south to find refuge behind Porter's powerful line of interwoven infantry and artillery. With broad, unobstructed fields of fire a mile in front, it was precisely the unshakable sort of position the shaken army needed. Though he never said so, Porter could not have failed to be disappointed in his commander these climactic, critical days. McClellan, seemingly as demoralized as any man in his army, spent most of two days tending to matters far away from combat, on gunboats and looking at potential bases for the army on the James. The army commander despaired the results, pondering potential disaster. "If none of us escape, at least we have done honor to the country," he wrote Stanton. "I shall do my best to save the Army."[46]

In fact, Porter would do far more than McClellan to preserve the army in those dark hours. On July 1 he directed as one-sided a victory as the Army of the Potomac ever won. Lee wasted his troops in futile attacks against Porter's position.

The victory at Malvern Hill convinced many in Porter's command—including Porter himself—that the army should stand and fight anew, perhaps even advance. But that night orders came from McClellan to march the army to its new base at Harrison's Landing. William Biddle, one of McClellan's staff officers, remembered, "The idea of stealing away in the night from such a position, after such a victory, was simply galling." Porter protested to McClellan (likely the only recorded instance of his confronting his friend), though to no avail. Brigade commander Daniel Butterfield called the decision to retreat "heartbreaking." Just after midnight, the army started its march.[47]

Perhaps the only man more demoralized than McClellan that night was Brigadier General Martindale. Martindale's brigade had done a good deal of fighting that day, and the experience left the general depressed almost to insensibility. As the V Corps prepared to move away from Malvern Hill, Martindale called Butterfield, Morell, and Col. Charles Roberts of the 2d Maine together. The descriptions of what he said next vary in details, though not in intent. Martindale pointed to the troops and artillery passing on a nearby road. "See here," Morell remembered him saying, "we all understand what this means. Before the battle we might have made terms. Now, see where we are. I propose we stay here and give ourselves up." The idea met a chorus of dissent. "No!" barked Morell. "We go on."

The weak utterings of a broken-down, middling brigade commander would be largely irrelevant to history except for this: Porter later heard of Martindale's proposal to surrender and decided to act against the abolitionist friend of Henry Wilson. On August 4 he relieved Martindale of command and preferred charges against him: "Misbehavior in the presence of the enemy." In October (notably when the tumult about McClellan, Porter, and the Emancipation Proclamation was at its height), Porter, Morell, Butterfield, and Colonel Roberts testified against Martindale. The rattled brigadier conceded that he talked of surrender that night and offered only a tepid self-defense. The court ruled Martindale's behavior "reprehensible" but offered (as such courts often did) that "the interests of the service" would not be served by further action. Martindale would resume command elsewhere—and indeed would return to duty in Virginia later in the war—but his time with Porter was done. While he had managed to get Martindale out of the V Corps (it would seem rightly so), confronting Martindale meant confronting something much larger that could do lasting damage. As Porter later put it, "[Martindale] was subsequently used by Secretary Stanton and members of the Committee on the Conduct of the War to injure me and to aid my downfall."[48]

By campaign's end, Porter had established himself solidly as McClellan's most reliable corps commander (though none of the others had set the bar high). He later revealed reservations about McClellan's passivity and "slows," but his personal loyalty to his commander never wavered. Nor did their shared commitment to a war waged on conservative principles.

What neither understood completely, however, was that the war around them was changing dramatically. Their commitment to conciliation and their unwillingness to disrupt slavery had been, in late 1861, embraced by most and rejected by few. By mid-1862, as the war evolved, those views had become objectionable in Washington and in the North at large. Soon, some would associate the two generals with treason. Just how intent those in government were to see the war transformed—to supplant McClellan and Porter's conservative approach—became clear that summer when President Lincoln appointed hard-war practitioner and willing emancipator Maj. Gen. John Pope to command of a new force, the Army of Virginia.[49]

John J. Hennessy

★ ★ ★

JOHN POPE WAS THE military embodiment of Radical politicians' vision of war. He advocated using "every instrument which could be brought to bear" against the Confederates. He despised slavery and thought the war a fine means by which to end it. And from the day of his arrival in Washington, he expressed publicly his disdain for McClellan and his conservatism, both military and political.

But Pope was no political general. He was West Point educated, "dark, martial, and handsome ... inclined to obesity ... possessing a fiery black eye, with luxuriant beard and hair," as newspaperman George Townsend remembered. "He smoked incessantly, and talked imprudently." Lincoln probably appreciated Pope's truculence, for change would not come without upset. If so, the president would not be disappointed. Within days of the general's arrival in Washington, he commenced a barrage of criticism—some of it direct, some of it veiled—that clearly signaled his dual purpose: to aggressively win battles (as McClellan had not) and to change the nature of war in Virginia (as McClellan had been unwilling). Pope did not mention it, but he, Lincoln, and Stanton also likely knew that success would, by public demand, result in his superseding McClellan as the dominant Union military leader in Virginia.[50]

McClellan and Porter could not and did not mistake the threat. Because McClellan had controlled the Army of the Potomac, he also had largely controlled how policy with respect to civilians and slavery manifested itself in the Virginia theater. To some eyes, he had not been aggressive enough with respect to slavery and too kind to Southern civilians, but he had in fact hewed closely to standing policy. He worked hard to avoid undue hardships for Southern civilians (as had McDowell at Fredericksburg). And while he did not actively advocate emancipation, he accepted slaves who freed themselves into Union lines and put them promptly to work—for pay. In the wake of the Seven Days, McClellan argued strongly for a continuation of these policies.[51]

Pope, however, portended change. With the administration's blessing, he issued a series of orders that laid waste to McClellan's conciliatory vision of war. Pope directed that his army should live more generously off the land, required male Virginians within Union lines to sign oaths of allegiance, and held local civilians responsible for damage done by Confederate raiders. Beyond that, he issued an obnoxious order to his troops that struck squarely at McClellan's way of cautious war: "I hear constantly of 'taking strong positions and holding them,' of 'lines of retreat,' and 'bases of supply,'" he wrote. "Let us discard such ideas." On July 22 Lincoln announced to his cabinet his intent to issue a proclamation of emancipation. McClellan's pillars of a conservative, conciliatory war stood in dire peril.[52]

Porter's performance on the Peninsula won him promotion to major general of volunteers and perhaps emboldened him to both a more dogged defense of McClellan and strident assault on Pope. On July 17, 1862, he wrote a response to a "friendly inquiry" he would come to regret more than any letter of his life. The inquiry (which apparently does not survive) had come from Joseph C. G. Kennedy, superintendent of the Census Bureau, whose son was serving under Pope in the 9th New York Cavalry. Kennedy was a former Whig and well entwined in Republican circles in Washington, counting both the president and Secretary of State William Seward as friends. As director of the most recent census, he had been called upon to provide estimates of the enlistment-eligible men available and the likely cost of war, and so he had gained some notice in military circles. But there is no evidence that Porter and Kennedy had any prior relationship—he clearly did not know of Kennedy's connections in Washington. This fact renders Porter's unguarded response to him all the more astonishing.[53]

"I regret to see," Porter wrote to this relative stranger in Washington, "that Genl. Pope has not improved since his youth and has now written himself down what the military world has long known, as ass. His address to his troops will make him ridiculous in the eyes of military men abroad as well as at home, and will reflect no credit on Mr. Lincoln, who has just promoted him. If the theory he proclaims is practiced you may look for disaster." Porter went on to explain that the army "put no faith in" Lincoln and would not "till they see evidences as strong as holy writ." The president may indeed be honest, Porter wrote, "but with honesty is expected firmness and decisions, and professions alone will not avail." He regretted Maj. Gen. Henry W. Halleck's recent appointment as general in chief of all Union armies and argued against supplanting McClellan as head of the Potomac army. "There is no more able commander than McClellan, and no one in whom the army has more confidence. Every army has its idol, and McClellan is the idol of this, and I should amply regret for the sake of our country anything being done to supercede him." McClellan, he explained, "is no politician, but moves along with the spirit of a true soldier, to use to best advantage the means placed at his disposal to break down this rebellion." Porter concluded with his continued wish for a policy of conciliation: "All I hope pray and work for is a speedy termination of the war by a restoration of Union feeling."[54]

This was the sort of unrestrained expression more commonly found in private letters to family (McClellan's letters are full of such passages to his wife). Why Porter shared these thoughts with someone he barely knew is either a mystery or a vivid illustration of horrendous judgment. Historians, of course, love such quotable musings, but usually their value extends little beyond illustrating their author's mindset. Not so in Porter's case, for these words had profound consequences. After receiving this letter, Kennedy passed it along to his friend William Seward. In a matter of days or weeks, it would be in Lincoln's hands—and eventually in Pope's too. Porter would scribble some ill-advised passages in the coming weeks, but none would have the effect on his career that this one did. This letter, he later wrote, "furnished the means" by which his career would be demolished at Pope's hands.[55]

IT IS A DARK IRONY that Porter would soon be charged with helping avert the very disaster he so haughtily predicted for Pope. In early August Halleck ordered McClellan to evacuate the Peninsula and move his army to Northern Virginia. As this began, Lee pressed northward against Pope. The urgency, if not the speed, of McClellan's movement increased daily. Porter's corps disembarked at Aquia Landing and marched northwestward from Fredericksburg, reaching the Army of Virginia on August 23—the first of McClellan's men to do so. Porter did not meet Pope personally until August 27 (by then Jackson had already marched to Pope's rear, and things were starting to unravel for the Union general). He received a chilly reception. "I was struck by his irritating manner," Porter remembered, "and his continued bearing towards me, but I could not account for his course." In fact, Pope had already seen the letter to Kennedy, with all its diatribe and dire predictions.[56]

During those desperate last days of August, communication between Pope and Washington lay tattered at Stonewall Jackson's hands. As Pope groped across Northern Virginia in search of Lee and Jackson, the only information escaping his army to Washington came from Porter, who wrote several times to Maj. Gen. Ambrose Burnside at Fredericksburg. His messages included useful information, but Porter could not resist interspersed chortling at Pope's (and the nation's) bad news. "Our line of communication has taken care of itself," he told Burnside on the twenty-seventh, mocking Pope's earlier proclamations. "All that talk of bagging Jackson, &c. was bosh," he wrote two days later. And finally, his most damning passage of all: "I hope Mac is at work, and we will soon get ordered out of this.... It would seem ... that [Jackson] was wandering around loose; but I expect [the Rebels] know what they are doing, which is more than any one here or anywhere knows."

Burnside and Porter were warm friends, but to Burnside the preferences of friendship receded in the face of emergency. Washington begged him for news, so Burnside sent along the best he had, the dispatches from Porter—unedited. Porter likely foresaw this. He concluded one of the notes: "Most of this is private, but if you can get me away please do so. Make what use of this you choose, so it does good." Whether he expected Burnside to redact childish fumings or whether he simply could not see the offense in what he had written is not clear. (He later conceded, "In the haste of dispatch they were carelessly expressed.") But in the end, Porter did not blame Burnside for sending the dispatches to Washington, though the messages did nothing but fuel political perceptions that Porter's commitment to Union victory in Virginia depended on the general in charge.[57]

Pope might have achieved the primary purpose of his campaign by simply withdrawing behind Bull Run and nearer the defenses of Washington, where his and McClellan's armies could have been fully combined (very likely under Pope's rather than McClellan's command). This he opted not to do. Instead, he turned and lashed at Jackson north of the old Bull Run battlefield. On August 29 Porter operated on the left flank of Pope's army, at first with McDowell, then alone, and eventually confronted by Longstreet's wing of Lee's army. Unaware of Longstreet's presence, Pope imagined that Porter might move against Jackson's right flank. But he issued orders both maddeningly unclear and fatally delayed, and so Porter did little that day. His waffling stillness enraged Pope.

One thing shaped Pope's perceptions of Porter—his complaining, pessimistic letter to Joseph Kennedy predicting failure. When, near sunset, he learned that Porter had not moved, the army commander raged, "I'll arrest him!" McDowell defended Porter in a backhanded way, arguing that he was not disloyal, just "incompetent." Pope relented for the moment and brusquely ordered Porter to the main battlefield (along the way, the general lost track of one of his brigades—an additional miscue Pope would note). The events of that day would form the basis for charges of disobedience that would govern Porter's legacy to and beyond his life's end.[58]

The next day, August 30, Porter led the largest assault he would ever command, sending 5,000 of his 10,000 men against Jackson's line at midafternoon. Porter's attack constituted Pope's ultimate effort to damage Jackson. It failed, with nearly one-third losses. This attack and the subsequent retreat set in motion the final, dramatic chapter of Pope's career in Virginia. Half of Lee's army surged forward against the Union left, coming within yards and minutes of destroying the Army of Virginia. Though Pope escaped the battlefield with his command intact, Second Manassas constituted perhaps Lee's greatest victory and likely the most decisive defeat suffered by a Union army in Virginia.

By September 2, as the army streamed back toward Washington, Pope had fixed Porter as responsible for the Union defeat. He largely misunderstood the corps commander's actions on August 29 and failed to realize that key orders to Porter had either been badly jumbled or delayed in their delivery. Instead, Pope saw only two things: Porter's immobility in the face of orders to the contrary, and the vile attitude he had expressed in his July letter to Kennedy. These were enough for him to conclude that Porter had acted maliciously to see the Army of Virginia defeated, to see to it that his summertime prediction of Pope's demise came to pass. That day Pope confronted him with the contents of the Kennedy letter. Perhaps sensing the trouble brewing, Porter sent a "show" note to McClellan, taking a tone of cooperative good will toward Pope he had heretofore eschewed. "You may rest assured that all your friends," he wrote, "as well as every lover of his country, will ever give, as they have given, to General Pope their cordial co-operation and constant support in the execution of all orders and plans." Porter claimed the killed, wounded, and exhausted men in his command "attest to our devoted duty."[59]

The next day Pope sent his report to Washington, accusing Porter of disobeying orders on August 29 and various other delays and failures, all of them, Pope would come to believe, calculated to bring about his downfall. These allegations met a willing audience in the nation's capital. Not only had Lincoln and Stanton seen Porter's letter to Kennedy, they had also seen his dispatches to Burnside, full as they were of disparaging comments. More than that, McClellan had done his friend no favors by adopting a similar tone in one of his own dispatches to Lincoln, wondering out loud if he might "let Pope get out of his scrape." For those in Washington who already believed the army's conservatives were conspiring to conduct war on their own terms, the acts of Porter and the writings of both he and McClellan seemed to offer proof of perfidy afoot. Porter's Republican nemesis, Senator Wilson, saw it so, claiming a "conspiracy among certain generals for a revolution and the establishment of a provisional national government." Even Lincoln came to believe in McClellan's treachery: "He has acted badly toward Pope. He wanted him to fail." The suspicion cast a dangerous glow on Porter too.[60]

Washington doubters knew too that Pope's failure on the battlefield carried immense implications for Lincoln and the Union war effort. The general's attempts to impose harder war could only be institutionalized if he cloaked them in victory on the battlefield. He had not. Lincoln, anxious to issue the Emancipation Proclamation, knew it too must emerge in the glow of victory, not the shadow of defeat. The setback of Second Manassas foiled, for the moment, both hard-war advocates and emancipationists. Even worse in their eyes, Pope's failure turned the war in Virginia back over to General McClellan.

McClellan's reemergence (he had never actually been relieved of his command but rather relieved of most of his army) was an outcome for which both he and Porter had ardently and loudly wished. Events quickly overawed any inclination Porter might have had to rejoice in this triumph born of disaster. On September 5 General in Chief Halleck relieved him of command. Lincoln directed a court of inquiry be convened to investigate Pope's accusations.[61]

The two orders set a future course for Fitz John Porter, but speeding events and George McClellan dictated that his demise would be delayed. Lee's move into Maryland both stunned the nation and refocused the army's attention like a cold splash in the face (indeed, Lee by this act probably did as much to rehabilitate the Union army as did McClellan's restoration to command). Citing the emergency, McClellan won approval to keep Porter in the field, putting him back in command of the V Corps. On September 17 Porter and his corps stood as the Army of the Potomac's reserve on the banks of Antietam Creek.

To the annoyance and suspicion of some, Porter played no active role in that battle beyond sending units to various parts of the field and urging caution at the fighting's late-afternoon climax. As McClellan pondered the wisdom of committing the corps to a final push against the Confederate right in front of Sharpsburg, Porter shook his head. His men, he said, were "the only reserves of the army." Daring normally suited Porter more readily than it did his friend and commander, but on this day he marched in lockstep with McClellan's cautious tread. Porter's men remained where they were.[62]

The Battle of Antietam did nothing to alter the trajectory of Porter's career set at Second Manassas. He remained in command of the V Corps for just eight weeks after Antietam. In the interim he suffered with rage the recriminations against McClellan for his failure to pursue Lee and bore witness to Lincoln's Preliminary Emancipation Proclamation on September 22 and the government's suspension of the writ of habeas corpus on September 24.

A week later, on September 30, Porter went on the rhetorical offensive against a war that clearly had spun beyond what he and other conservatives (in the army and beyond) envisioned it should be. His letter to Marble, ally and editor of the *New York World,* embodied all the classic themes espoused by the war's conservative patriots, with a measure of personal invective woven in. It is perhaps the greatest of all wartime writings from the army's conservative core.

Porter declared that the Emancipation Proclamation "was ridiculed in the army—caused disgust, discontent, and expressions of disloyalty to the views of the administration." Echoing the sentiments of even a few abolitionists in the ranks (including Robert Gould Shaw), Porter asserted that the proclamation would "tend only to prolong the war by rousing the bitter feelings of the south, and causing unity of action among them, while the reverse for us." It was not enough to merely suppress the rebellion, he stated, rather, the Union must be restored, and for that to happen, the good will of the Southern people must be respected and nurtured.

The general argued that what he saw as the wrongheaded management of the war by the administration had taken a toll on the army itself. "Those who have to fight the battles of the country are tired of the war and wish to see it ended and honorably," he fumed. The men's toils, the loss of life, the soldier's constant danger endured must not be rendered "useless" by "politicians working to prolong [the conflict]."

Then Porter for the first time (at least in his known writings) turned on Lincoln. Just a fortnight before, newspapers had carried the president's response to a petition from Chicago churches calling for emancipation. Lincoln demurred with some force: "What good would a proclamation of emancipation from me do, especially as we are now situated?" "How can we feed and care for such a multitude?" "What possible result of good would follow the issuing of such a proclamation?" Now, in the wake of just such a proclamation, Porter railed against a president he saw as weak and subject to political winds. The labor of soldiers, he informed Marble, has been "upset by the absurd proclamation of a political coward, who has not the manliness to sustain opinions expressed but a few days before.... What a ruler for us to admire." And then he leveled the most damning charge a military man can bring against a civilian leader: Lincoln "holds in his hands the lives [of soldiers] ... and trifles with them." Porter foresaw for Lincoln, Radicals in Congress, and the administration divine retribution: "I believe God in his own particular way will punish these wicked rulers and abettors and bring peace to our country in due time."[63]

Like much of the high command of the army, McClellan shared Porter's dim view of the Emancipation Proclamation—not because he did not oppose slavery (he did), but because he opposed the admixture of war and emancipation. McClellan, along with many conservative officers like Brig. Gen. John Gibbon and Hooker, declared that he could not fight for "the accursed doctrine" of "servile insurrection." "It is too infamous," he wrote. But as army commander, McClellan knew that his views meant far more than those of his colonels and brigadiers. He also knew the question was far greater than one of military or social policy, momentous though that might have been. Rather, his response would speak to the function of American democracy. If he declared against the proclamation, tumult would surely follow.

Supporters in the army and advisors beyond it urged restraint on McClellan. Finally, after nearly two weeks, he concurred and chose to submit. On October 7 he issued an order to his troops not about the virtues of freedom or the evils of slavery, but reminding them at length of the American imperative of subordinating the military to civil authority. "The remedy for political error," he wrote, "is to be found only in the action of the people at the polls"—a statement the president surely found foreboding, with midterm elections only weeks away. In rambling, ungrammatical sentences focused entirely on civics rather than policy, McClellan clearly communicated his ambivalence. Nowhere did he cheer the humanity of ending bondage or mention the words "emancipation" or "freedom." He promised only that the army's conduct in implementing the proclamation (once finally issued on January 1, 1863) would be "guided by the same rules of mercy and Christianity that have ever controlled its conduct toward the defenseless"—this last likely a reference not to slaves, but to slaveholding civilians.

An army McClellan had built to restore the Union had, over his objections, now officially become also an instrument of emancipation. It is one of the great ironies of American history that McClellan's victory at Antietam ushered in the very policy he and Porter had labored so hard to keep out of the war.[64]

McClellan's cover note to Lincoln transmitting a copy of his October 7 order made reference to "your proclamation." The wording was no accident, for by the fall of 1862, the chasm between the government that set war policy and the high command of the army that waged the war seemed total. Porter's and McClellan's views on the principles that should guide the war effort had changed little since 1861. But around them, the conflict had changed dramatically, growing in scope and morphing in both method and purpose. Both generals had resisted the transformation to a harder war of emancipation, engaging directly and by proxy in the public debate over the nature of the nation's civil war. Their efforts had strained both the limits of propriety and the administration's patience.

But for Lincoln, a harder dilemma persisted: while he, Stanton, and Congress sought a harsher war that would end slavery, the practical questions of conciliation (or not) and emancipation lay largely in the hands of the military. In 1861 the views of army commanders on war policy mattered little. Now, a year later, they mattered a great deal. One thing was clear to Lincoln, Stanton, and congressional leaders: George Brinton McClellan was no longer the man to carry forth the war they envisioned.

A HEAVY AURA of faithlessness hung over Porter and the Army of the Potomac in the weeks following Antietam. Pope's charges loomed. In early October Porter traveled to Washington to testify against John Martindale, on trial for his behavior at Malvern Hill. He predicted that this alone would antagonize Republican enemies enough for them to want to see "my head chopped." Beyond that, rumors spread that Burnside had also filed charges against Porter, claiming that he had failed to send reinforcements at Antietam. Burnside took to the newspapers to quell this falsehood. Foul (though idle) talk of rebellion wafted from the army's camps in the wake of the Preliminary Emancipation Proclamation. And men in high places in Washington believed that McClellan's inaction after Antietam had something to do with his tepid support for Lincoln's war policies, that the general's "game" was to fight a war or pursue peace on his own terms. The brother of one of McClellan's staff officers even said just such a thing out loud. Lincoln heard of it, gave the man a military hearing, and dismissed him from the service. The cloud over the army darkened.[65]

Porter rose with McClellan. In November 1862 he fell with him too. On November 7, orders arrived in the army relieving both officers, which Porter received three days later. For him, this was no surprise. He had expected to be relieved because, as he put it in a letter to Marble, he had placed "before the country the dastardly acts of Genl Martindale." But much more than that portended Porter's demise.

Porter took leave of the V Corps on November 12. He had never bound himself up with his men as McClellan had, and he eschewed the sort of public display that his friend would famously permit. Instead, Porter called his officers to his tent to bid a private goodbye. He stood in the center, his eyes filled with tears, "sobs choking his utterance," as one witness wrote. Around him men cried.[66] Porter issued the obligatory farewell order to his troops, praising them and confirming the privilege he had enjoyed by commanding them. He concluded with an admonition that spoke clearly to the aura of suspicion that surrounded him: "Among the most gratifying of my thoughts of you will be the assurance that your subordination and loyalty will remain in the future, as in the past, firm and steadfast to our country and its authorities."[67] McClellan shuffled off to New Jersey to await orders that never came. Porter traveled to Washington, with barely three weeks to prepare his defense against the charges leveled by Pope.[68]

Porter's trial, which started in earnest on December 4, was the highest profile court-martial of the war. Its import extended well beyond the mere question of guilt at Manassas. The great issue was had Porter consciously worked to bring about the demise of his and McClellan's great philosophical enemy in Virginia, John Pope, the agent of change in the Union war effort?

It is tempting, even after 150 years, to link Porter's bad attitude with Pope's unfortunate fate at Manassas. While neither Porter nor McClellan performed artfully during Pope's tenure in Virginia, neither is there substantial evidence that they consciously abetted his failure (Pope proved well capable of that on his own). Was Porter guilty of the charges of disobedience and dereliction eventually leveled against him? As nearly two decades' accumulation of evidence by Porter would show (as well as the work of virtually all subsequent historians), clearly not.

But Pope's interest in self-preservation and desire to see Porter punished dovetailed nicely with the government's need to mute discordant voices within the army. It is easy to understand how the negative perception of Porter's acts found traction in the tumultuous months following Second Manassas. Porter stood in opposition to the government's emerging war policies. He had predicted and seemed to root for the failure of the army commander charged with institutionalizing those policies. He had unabashedly advocated for McClellan's reemergence as the dominant Union leader in the eastern theater. And he had been a central figure in the battle that brought about Pope's demise.

The same, of course, might have been said of many others who served in Virginia in the late summer of 1862. But two things distinguished Porter from them: his inseparable, public identification with McClellan and, just as important, his uncharitable statements about Pope and Union war policy that found their way into Lincoln's hands. His written musings and predictions rendered impossible any favorable interpretation of his performance at Manassas, especially in the wake of Pope's accusations. (Even his staunchest allies conceded the case looked dubious for Porter.) To his and McClellan's foes, it appeared that Porter had deliberately acted to abet Pope's defeat at the expense of the nation. Given the atmosphere of suspicion, doubt, and defeat then in the air, and the specter of civil-military relations that threatened to spin out of control, it is difficult to imagine any administration acting in anything but the way it did.[69]

After forty-five days of testimony and deliberation, the court handed down its verdict: guilty. As events would show, the testimony was incomplete and sometimes simply wrong. But the new judge advocate general of the army, Joseph Holt, was managing his first high-profile case, and he and the administration used the verdict to send a message. The court directed that Porter be "cashiered and dismissed from the service ... and forever disqualified from holding any office of trust or profit under the Government of the United States." President Lincoln signed the order on January 21, 1863. The press raged on both sides of the verdict. The *Columbian Register*, a Democratic paper in New Haven, Connecticut, warned that the verdict reflected "the full sense of the revolutionary spirit that now reigns in Washington" and symbolized the "deliberate conspiracy ... against all that remains to us of conservatism and Constitutional principle in the army." A more liberal sheet in Vermont reflected a sentiment that Lincoln surely embraced: "Dismiss such officers from the service, and put others in their places who will heartily cooperate with the commander-in-chief." The *New York Times* called for Porter to be shot rather than merely dismissed.[70]

McClellan's removal might be seen in many ways: as Lincoln's reaction to his operational caution, as a proper recompense for a subordinate who simply could not get along with his bosses, or as an unavoidable outcome for an army commander at philosophical odds with those who directed him. But Porter's relief and dismissal allowed for no such ambiguity, and other officers in the army knew it. The message was clear: the careers of men who mixed their political views and official duties too freely would not thrive. Those who remained in the army—men like John Reynolds, John Sedgwick, Gouverneur Warren, and John Gibbon—generally did not change their conservative stripes; instead, they managed their politics more wisely, embracing quietude rather than advocacy. The cocktail of political machination and indiscreet expression so fatal to Porter's career would not be reprised by others.

After the trial, Porter traveled to New York City a civilian. In the coming decades he built a successful career in business and government, eschewing official controversy in all things except his own case. Porter's reservoir of righteousness fueled an intense campaign for redemption. His papers (today at the Library of Congress) include thousands of letters to and from old army comrades, potential witnesses, and former enemies seeking and offering testimony on the events of August 1862. Hundreds more letters sought to move the levers of Washington politics to have his case reopened. Horace Greeley of the left-leaning *New York Tribune* and even wartime nemesis Henry Wilson eventually came out on Porter's behalf. Former Confederate general James Longstreet provided testimony unavailable during the war. In 1878 Pres. Rutherford B. Hayes ordered the case reopened. New evidence clarified much of what faced Porter on August 29, 1862. Old evidence collapsed in the face of renewed scrutiny. In March 1879 a board of inquiry exonerated Fitz John Porter. Six years later Congress reinstated him to proper rank, though it did so without granting him back pay for twenty-three years of service denied.[71]

PORTER'S CASE PRODUCED a trove of information that clarified or revised conventional wisdom about Second Manassas and John Pope. But that same information did little to revise Porter's own views of the war and his role in it. He never relented in his belief that the government conspired to see McClellan fail. His perception of the Union war effort in 1862 hardly evolved, trapped by a recollection made immutable by the intensity of the experience. "Many things of war times are blanks in my mind," he admitted to historian John C. Ropers in 1894. "Those I do remember are fixed.... I have many points, but I have not the proof, though I know they are true, & references are dead, and doubts by others don't surprise or disturb me." He tolerated criticism of McClellan but never engaged in it himself. The two men remained friends until McClellan's death in 1885 at the age of fifty-eight.[72]

The nation would not forgive Porter easily, for his case reflected deep divisions that were slow to heal. Though he enjoyed wide-scale support within the army in 1862, his dismissal from the service changed minds. When after Porter's death in 1901 the idea for the equestrian statue funded by an admirer became known, some old soldiers rose in protest. They claimed it "a great mistake and greater wrong" to "erect a public monument to a man ... who is believed to have subjected an army to overwhelming defeat, through jealousy and pique, if not cowardice."[73]

Still, Porter got his hometown statue, dedicated on July 1, 1906, the forty-fourth anniversary of his victory at Malvern Hill. Today his likeness sits astride a powerful horse, his arm stretched across his chest in salute. The commonness of the pose belies the tumult that characterized Porter's journey from hero to outcast to something in between (where his reputation still resides).

Lincoln's secretary John Hay wrote that Porter was "ruined by his devotion to McClellan." That is an easy characterization but in the end too superficial. To be sure, no one was more loyal to McClellan. But it was not just loyalty to a man that doomed Porter's career. Rather, his unchanging, righteous commitment to a war that rejected emancipation and harsher treatment of civilians as tools for victory put him at odds with a government increasingly willing to embrace such measures. Just as important, Porter made his disdain for policies, leaders, and colleagues known beyond the appropriate channels of discussion and dissent. He actively worked to reverse the strategy and policies of his civilian lords, and with unwise expression he seemed to cheer the downfall of those who stood in opposition. As a legal matter, Porter was guilty of nothing—he was an innocent man convicted, the first of several "conservative patriots" to fall. But as a practical matter, he rendered himself intolerable. Porter stood as a formidable obstacle in the path of a war transforming, and his demise sent a powerful message to military men tempted to engage in a public attempt to shape American war aims then and later.[74]

Fitz John Porter and the Union War, 1862

NOTES

1. For an overview of the history of the Porter statue, see Ray Brighton, "Controversy Dogged Porter Statue," *Portsmouth [N.H.] Herald*, June 30, 1991; and "Controversial Statue Still Stands," ibid., July 7, 1991.

2. The veterans' protest appears as a letter from "War Veterans" in the *Portsmouth [N.H.] Journal*, June 14, 1902. The various deeds and delays are recorded in newspapers of the period. For vandalism, see *Boston Journal*, Feb. 4, 1903. For reference to the meal sack, see *Boston Journal*, Aug. 13, 1904. For nighttime unveiling, see *Portsmouth [N.H.] Times*, Sept. 8, 1904; and *Boston Herald*, Sept. 9, 1904. The monument was finally dedicated on the anniversary of the Battle of Malvern Hill in 1906. *New York Times*, July 2, 1906. I am indebted to Brent Vosburg of Elizabethtown, New York, for providing clippings from the Portsmouth newspapers cited here. Porter's name often appears with a hyphen between "Fitz" and "John," but in fact Porter's name was not hyphenated.

3. *Wilkes Barre [Pa.] Times*, May 25, 1901; *Portsmouth [N.H.] Journal*, Dec. 1, 1900.

4. The question of Porter's guilt or innocence is most thoughtfully assessed in Henry Gabler, "The Fitz John Porter Case: Politics and Military Justice" (Ph.D. diss., City University of New York, 1979). More recent studies come to similar conclusions about Porter's innocence. See Donald R. Jermann, *Fitz-John Porter, Scapegoat of Second Manassas: The Rise, Fall and Rise of the General Accused of Disobedience* (Jefferson, N.C.: McFarland, 2009); and Curt Anders, *Injustice on Trial: Second Bull Run, General Fitz John Porter's Court-Martial, and the Schofield Board Investigation That Restored His Good Name* (Zionsville, Ind.: Clerisy, 2002). This essay will not revisit the details of Porter's court-martial or the question of guilt or innocence. For my views on the case, see John J. Hennessy, *Return to Bull Run: The Campaign and Battle of Second Manassas* (New York: Simon and Schuster, 1993), 465–66. This discussion will confine itself to the significance of Porter's career as a corps commander in the context of the relationship between Congress, the Lincoln administration, and the Army of the Potomac.

5. For details of Porter's early life, see Wayne Soini, *Porter's Secret: Fitz John Porter's Monument Decoded* (Portsmouth, N.H.: Peter Randall, 2011), 15–19; and Otto Eisenschiml, *The Celebrated Case of Fitz John Porter: An American Dreyfuss Affair* (Indianapolis: Bobbs-Merrill, 1950), 18–25. Neither of these books document their source material, but Eisenschiml's work is notable because he had direct access to Porter's family and includes details of the general's life not found elsewhere. A brief interview with Porter's daughter is in William B. Styple, *Generals in Bronze: Interviewing the Commanders of the Civil War* (Kearny, N.J.: Belle Grove, 2005), 204. See also George Washington Cullum, *Biographical Register of the Officers and Graduates of the U.S. Military Academy from 1802 to 1867*, rev. ed., 3 vols. (New York: Houghton Mifflin, 1891), 218.

6. George B. McClellan, *The Mexican War Diary and Correspondence of George B. McClellan*, ed. Thomas W. Cutrer (Baton Rouge: Louisiana State University Press, 2009), 63, 68. See also Stephen W. Sears, *George McClellan: The Young Napoleon* (New York: Ticknor and Fields, 1988), 15–17; Cullum, *Biographical Register*, 2:218; and Theodore A. Lord, unpublished biography of Porter, Fitz John Porter Papers, container 66/reel 30, Manuscript Division, Library of Congress, Washington, D.C. (hereafter cited as LC).

John J. Hennessy

7. Sears, *George McClellan*, 51–58, 68, 70, 73; McClellan to Scott, Apr. 23, May 9, 1861, in *The Civil War Papers of George B. McClellan: Selected Correspondence, 1860–1865*, ed. Stephen W. Sears (New York: Ticknor and Fields, 1989), 5, 8, 14, 18.

8. Cullum, *Biographical Register*, 2:219. The most interesting modern discussion of Patterson's campaign can be found in David Detzer, *Donnybrook: The Battle of Bull Run, 1861* (New York: Houghton Mifflin, 2004), 98–104.

9. U.S. War Department, *The War of the Rebellion: A Compilation of the Official Records of the Union and Confederate Armies*, 70 vols. in 128 parts (Washington, D.C.: Government Printing Office, 1880–1901), ser. 1, 2:49 (hereafter cited as *OR;* all references are to series 1 unless otherwise noted); William T. Sherman, *Memoirs of General William T. Sherman*, 2 vols. (New York: D. Appleton, 1904), 1:220. See also Sears, *George McClellan*, 93.

10. Russel H. Beatie, *Army of the Potomac: Birth of Command* (New York: Da Capo, 2002), 427. Eisenschiml includes a useful interview with Porter's daughter, who pointedly argued that Porter was not "devoted" to McClellan but rather "loyal" to him. *Celebrated Case of Fitz John Porter*, 310. Beatie's work includes reference to a memorandum from McClellan to Lincoln recommending promotion for Porter and more than two dozen other officers. As the creator of an essentially new army, McClellan wielded considerable power in advancing (or halting) careers. Though this was not patronage in the political sense, his efforts did help imbue loyalty among the officers whose ranks and careers advanced under his command. For examples of this, see Meade to his wife, May 5, 1862, in *The Life and Letters of George Gordon Meade, Major-General United States Army*, ed. George Gordon Meade, 2 vols. (New York: Charles Scribner's Sons, 1913), 1:263; and Sedgwick to his sister, Apr. 14, 1862, in *Correspondence of John Sedgwick, Major General* (1903; repr., Baltimore: Butternut and Blue, 1999), 43–44. "I mean to stand or fall with McClellan," Sedgwick declared. " He has been very kind to me, giving me a large command without my asking for it." In 1863 Sedgwick admitted that he had never so much as visited McClellan socially. Sedgwick to French, Sept. 1, 1863, ibid., 155.

11. The description of Porter is assembled from several sources. See Styple, *Generals in Bronze*, 199; Eisenschiml, *Celebrated Case of Fitz John Porter*, 309, 313, 314, 315; John Hay, *Lincoln's Journalist: John Hay's Anonymous Writings for the Press, 1860–1864*, ed. Michael Burlingame (Carbondale: Southern Illinois University Press, 1998), 298; William Woods Averell, *Ten Years in the Saddle: The Memoir of William Woods Averell, 1851–1862*, ed. Edward W. Eckert and Nicholas J. Amato (San Rafael, Calif.: Presidio, 1978), 338; Katherine Prescott Wormley, *The Other Side of War: With the Army of the Potomac, Letters from the Headquarters of the U.S. Sanitary Commission during the Peninsular Campaign* (Boston: Ticknor, 1888), 52–53; and letters of Nathaniel Gordon, Aug. 20, 1901; Nathan Soule. Aug. 22, 1901; and William G. Perry, all in Porter Papers, container 49. The author is indebted to the late Hugh Engelman of Crystal Lake, Illinois, for providing (in 1994) excerpts of the last letters cited here, which were solicited from Porter's Phillips Exeter classmates after his death in 1901. For a useful sketch of Porter, see Beatie, *Army of the Potomac: Birth of Command*, 106–9.

12. Porter, unsigned memoir, n.d., Porter Papers, container 53/reel 25. By far the best description of morale and viewpoints in the 13th New York appears in Samuel S. Partridge to "My dear Mac," Aug. 14, 1861, "Civil War Letters of Samuel S. Partridge of the 'Rochester Regiment,'" *The Rochester Historical Society Publications, XXII: Rochester in the Civil War* (Rochester, 1944), 82–84. See also "Letter from a Volunteer" (13th New York), *Rochester Democrat and American*, Sept. 2, 1861. This cor-

respondent indicated that the 13th was "still in a 'bad way'" a week after Porter's intervention, and indeed the regiment's officers still struggled with would-be mutineers in December. See "From the 13th" ("A.O.C."), *Rochester Democrat and American*, Dec. 18, 1861; and [Washington, D.C.] *Evening Star*, Dec. 19, 1861.

13. Letter of Samuel S. Partridge, Dec. 27, 1861, Partridge Letters, Fredericksburg and Spotsylvania National Military Park Library, bound vol. 146.

14. U.S. Congress, *Report of the Joint Committee on the Conduct of the War*, 3 vols. (Washington, D.C.: Government Printing Office, 1863), 1:173 (hereafter cited as *JCCW*); Martindale obituaries, *New York Times* and *New York Herald*, Dec. 14, 1881; Thomas H. Mann, *Fighting with the Eighteenth Massachusetts: The Civil War Memoir of Thomas H. Mann*, ed. John J. Hennesssy (Baton Rouge: Louisiana State University Press, 2000), 21, 32–34, 36; Letter of "A.G.C." (13th New York), *Rochester Democrat and American*, Nov. 27, 1861; Fitz John Porter, memorandum, n.d., Porter Papers, container 7/reel 3; George Lyman to Porter, Dec. 10, 1862, ibid., container 6/reel 2; Theodore Lyman, journal, June 8, 1864, Ms. 05560, volume 17/reel 15, Massachusetts Historical Society, Boston. Porter gave the strength of his division in December 1861 as between 10,000 and 11,000 men. McClellan labeled Martindale an "intriguing unscrupulous man, a good show-soldier." McClellan's comments on various officers, George B. McClellan Papers, vol. D-9/reel 71, Manuscript Division, LC. After the war Martindale ran successfully as a Republican for attorney general of New York. For coverage of the court-martial of Colonel Kerrigan of the 25th New York, who also sat in Congress, see the *New York Tribune*, Dec. 12, 14, 1861, Mar. 7, 1862; and *New York Times*, Jan. 10, 1862.

15. Cullum, *Biographical Register*, 1:285; *Alexandria Gazette*, May 14, 1861 (proclaiming Pickell's candidacy); "An Excellent Appointment," *New York Tribune*, Aug. 24, 1861. The description of Pickell appears in "From a Volunteer," *Rochester Democrat and American*, Sept. 2, 1862. Pickell lost the June congressional election to former governor Francis Thomas. *Easton Gazette*, June 15, 1861. Porter, memorandum, n.d., Porter Papers, container 7/reel 3. Pickell's Seminole War diaries are at the Library of Congress. Exactly how this man from western Maryland came to command a regiment from Rochester, New York, is not entirely clear.

16. Fitz John Porter, "Reminiscences of a Life in Peace and in War—of Peace in War and War in Peace: The Autobiography of Fitz John Porter, Late Colonel of the U.S. Army and Major General of Volunteers and for more than twenty years suffering under an Unjust Stigma Inflicted and Maintained by his Government," Porter Papers, container 54/reel 25, 4–5. The slave-owning officer was Lt. Col. Samuel W. Owen of the 3d Pennsylvania Cavalry. Owen was a resident of Washington, D.C. His name does not appear in the census of 1860, and his status as a slave owner could not be confirmed by sources other than Porter. Owen is most famous as the subject of a photograph by Alexander Gardner, *Lt. Col. Samuel W. Owen, 3d Pennsylvania Cavalry, Caught Napping*. By far the best treatment of evolving policy with respect to the Army of the Potomac, slavery, and freedom is found in Glenn David Brasher, *The Peninsula Campaign and the Necessity of Emancipation* (Chapel Hill: University of North Carolina Press, 2012). For a discussion of McClellan and emancipation early in the war, see ibid., 59, 68–69.

17. Ernest McKay, *Henry Wilson, Practical Radical: A Portrait of a Politician* (Port Washington, N.Y.: Kennikat, 1971), 147–50; John L. Myers, *Senator Henry Wilson and the Civil War* (New York: University Press of America 2007), 28–29.

18. Porter, unsigned account, n.d., Porter Papers, container 53/reel 25; McKay, *Henry Wilson*, 150; Benjamin Perley Poore, *Perley's Reminiscences of Sixty Years in the National Metropolis*, 2 vols. (Philadelphia: Hubbard Brothers, 1886), 2:99.

19. *Congressional Globe*, 37th Cong., 1st sess., July 22, 1861, 219. For Wilson's views on the protection of Southern private property, see ibid., 2d sess., May 1, 1862, 1896.

20. Porter asserts the connection between this event and his later poor relationship with Wilson and other radicals in "Reminiscences," 5. It is worth noting that this incident was not reported in the press. Its effect was confined solely to the halls of Congress and within Lincoln's cabinet.

21. Porter, "Reminiscences," 5.

22. Fitz John Porter, "Signal and Balloon Services," Porter Papers, container 52/reel 25, 2. For by far the best description of Lowe's early connection with the army and his eventual alliance with Porter, see Frederick S. Haydon, *Aeronautics in the Union and Confederate Armies*, 2 vols. (Baltimore: Johns Hopkins University Press, 1941), 1:199–203, 220–21, 225, 369. Porter's unique position in the army was noted by many and would be most apparent when McClellan appointed him "Director of the Siege" at Yorktown in April 1862. Thaddeus S. Lowe, *Memoirs of Thaddeus S. C. Lowe, Chief of the Aeronautic Corps of the Army of the United States during the Civil War: My Balloons in Peace and War*, ed. Michael Jaeger and Carol Lauritzen (Lewiston, N.Y.: Edwin Mellen, 2004), 87, 89–92. Lowe's memoir reproduces much of the material in his official report (*OR*, ser. 3, 3:252–318), though with additional personal observations, and so the memoir is cited here. McClellan, among others, pointed out the value of balloon observations "made by intelligent officers." George B. McClellan, *McClellan's Own Story: The War for the Union, the Soldiers Who Fought It, the Civilians Who Directed It, and His Relations to It and to Them*, ed. William C. Prime (New York: Charles L. Webster, 1887), 135.

23. William Howard Russell, *My Diary North and South*, ed. Fletcher Pratt (New York: Harper and Brothers, 1954), 257. A typical example of McClellan's desire for time appears in a letter to the governor of Rhode Island: "I ask only for the delay necessary to make a real army of them—that public opinion shall not urge us to premature action." McClellan to William Sprague, Sept. 27, 1861, in *Civil War Papers of George B. McClellan*, 103. By far the best treatment of the evolving Union war policy toward slavery and civilians is Mark Grimsley, *The Hard Hand of War: Union Military Policy Toward Southern Civilians, 1861–1865* (New York: Cambridge University Press, 1995). For McClellan's role, see ibid., 23, 31–34.

24. McClellan's battle against his critics is beyond the scope of this work but is well covered in Ethan S. Rafuse, *McClellan's War: The Failure of Moderation in the Struggle for the Union* (Bloomington: Indiana University Press, 2005), 134–37, 139–41. Sears's *George McClellan* and Russel Beatie's volumes on the Army of the Potomac also treat the topic extensively. This study will confine its inquiry to Porter's role.

25. Porter's testimony appears in *JCCW*, 1:170–76. For Wilson's comment, which came in the debate over the wording for the resolution that would guide the joint committee, see *Congressional Globe*, 37th Cong., 2d sess., Dec. 9, 1861, 32. Despite the tone of his remarks, it is worth noting that Wilson expressed a good understanding of the immense task of the army's officer corps and its relative inexperience. In that same debate the senator said: "As to the failures in the field, it is very easy, sir, to criticize them; but we should all remember that we have no men in America of military experience on anything like the scale on which they were now required to act. We have had a little

army of fourteen or fifteen thousand men. No man in this country ever led into action before this war twelve thousand men. We have an army now in the field of half a million of men. We have generals who have been trained in the military service of the country, but on a small scale. We are calling the military talent of the country into the field. It takes more than twenty thousand officers to officer the military force now in the field in this country, and we have but very few men that can claim any military experience. Those who have any military experience, have it on a very small scale indeed." See also Bruce Tap, *Over Lincoln's Shoulder: The Committee on the Conduct of the War* (Lawrence: University Press of Kansas, 1998), 19, 21–24.

26. *JCCW*, 1:117, 122, 131.

27. Ibid., 171, 172, 178.

28. Tap, *Over Lincoln's Shoulder*, 104–5.

29. McClellan to Barlow, Nov. 8, 1861, in *Civil War Papers of George B. McClellan*, 128. McClellan's correspondence is replete with examples of his efforts to engage Lincoln and the administration on matters of policy. The most famous was the Harrison's Landing letter: McClellan to Lincoln, July 7, 1862, ibid., 344–45. Ethan Rafuse explores McClellan and his relations with civil authorities in "General McClellan and the Politicians Revisited," *Parameters* 42 (Summer 2012): 71–85. Summations of McClellan's efforts to counter criticisms are legion. See, for example, Sears, *George McClellan*, 132–44; T. Harry Williams, *Lincoln and the Radicals* (Madison: University of Wisconsin Press, 1941); and Tap, *Over Lincoln's Shoulder*, 101–13. For extensive coverage of McClellan's enemies and his defense, see Russel Beatie, *Army of the Potomac: McClellan Takes Command* (New York: Da Capo, 2004), esp. 316–45.

30. Sears, *George McClellan*, 142–44. For the first contact between Porter and Marble, see George T. McJimsey, *Genteel Partisan: Manton Marble, 1834–1917* (Ames: Iowa State University Press, 1971), 35.

31. Clarence Edmund Stedman, *Notes from the Life and Letters of Edmund Clarence Stedman*, 2 vols. (New York: Moffat, Yard, 1910), 1:267–72. The final quote here appears in Stedman to McClellan, Mar. 17, 1862, in McClellan, *Civil War Papers*, 214.

32. James S. Wadsworth to William Cullen Bryant, Feb. 3, 1862, quoted in Allan Nevins, *The War for the Union: War Becomes Revolution, 1862–1863* (New York: Charles Scribner's Sons, 1960), 45n. Philip Kearny was one of the few officers in the army to express himself in support of the idea that McClellan was conspiring to extend the war so that it might end "with little bloodshed." Kearny, *Letters from the Peninsula: The Civil War Letters of General Philip Kearny*, ed. William B. Styple (Kearny, N.J.: Belle Grove, 1988), 108–9.

33. Porter to Marble, Apr. 26, 1862, Manton Marble Papers, LC; Emil and Ruth Rosenblatt, *Hard Marching Every Day: The Civil War Letters of Private Wilbur Fiske, 1861–1865* (Lawrence: University Press of Kansas, 1993), 29. Union general John Gibbon echoed these sentiments when he declared that embracing abolition "is better calculated to prolong the war" than anything else the government could do. Gibbon to his wife, May 19, 1862, John Gibbon Papers, Box 1, Historical Society of Pennsylvania, Philadelphia. At this point in the war, Porter's assertion that there were few men espousing antislavery thought in the army is likely correct. Charles Brewster, an antislavery soldier in the 10th Massachusetts, noted that winter that the conflict "seems to be a war for the preservation of slavery more than anything else." Charles Harvey Brewster, *When This Cruel War Is*

Over: The Civil War Letters of Charles Harvey Brewster, ed. David W. Blight (Amherst: University of Massachusetts Press, 1992), 72.

34. Porter to John C. Ropes, Aug. 8, 1881, Nov. 30, 1893, Ropes Papers, Military Historical Society of Massachusetts Collection, Boston University. See also Sears, *George McClellan,* 175–78. The most extensive treatment of Lincoln's decision to withhold McDowell appears in Russel Beatie, *Army of the Potomac: McClellan's First Campaign, March–May 1862* (New York: Savas Beatie, 2007), 298–319. Years later Porter conceded that he remained dogged in his view of events, suffering no correction even in the face of new information. Porter to Ropes, Mar. 25, 1894, Ropes Papers.

35. *OR*, 11(3):281; Lowe, *Memoirs,* 113–15. A good overview of the balloon operations at Yorktown is in Tom D. Crouch, *The Eagle Aloft: Two Centuries of Balloons in America* (Washington, D.C.: Smithsonian Institution Press, 1983), 373–85. Porter's exploits with the balloon corps also made him, for the first time, famous, when on April 11 his balloon broke away from its tethers and floated for a time over Confederate lines. The adventure was widely reported in the press and minutely recorded by Porter in a memoir. His unpublished account of the ascent appears in his "Signal and Balloon Services." A briefer account with additional details appears in Porter, "Advance on Yorktown," Porter Papers, container 26/reel 111. See also George Alfred Townsend, *Rustics in Rebellion: A Yankee Reporter on the Road to Richmond* (Chapel Hill: University of North Carolina Press, 1950), 95; McClellan, *Civil War Papers,* 235; statement of E. Locke Mason, n.d., Porter Papers, container 51/reel 23; E. Mason to Porter, June 13, 1870, July 22, 1883, ibid., container 51/reel 23; James Allen to Porter, July 16, 1883, ibid., container 51/reel 23; statement of Thomas P. Smith, n.d., ibid., container 51/reel 23; and unsigned statement, likely by Col. Henry Lansing of the 17th New York, n.d., ibid., container 51/reel 23. Press coverage of the event was extensive, if repetitive. See, for example, *Philadelphia Inquirer,* Apr. 16, 1862.

36. *OR*, 11(3):125; Porter, "Advance on Yorktown." McClellan explained the appointment in a letter to his wife. McClellan to his wife, Apr. 27, 1862, in *Civil War Papers of George B. McClellan,* 249. A good discussion of Porter's appointment appears in Beatie, *Army of the Potomac: McClellan's First Campaign,* 455–56. The publicity attending the appointment was slight. See, for example, *Albany Evening Journal,* Apr. 30, 1862. Porter's aide Stephen M. Weld testified that most of the general's journeys away from camp were with McClellan. See Weld to his father, Apr. 21, 1862, in *War Diary and Letters of Stephen Minot Weld* (Cambridge, Mass.: Riverside, 1912), 99.

37. Keyes to Montgomery Meigs, Aug. 21, 1862, Montgomery C. Meigs Papers, Manuscript Division, LC (I am indebted to Dr. Carmen Grayson, formerly of Hampton University, for her assistance with the almost indecipherable Meigs letters); Kearny, *Letters from the Peninsula,* 101; Hooker to John Conover Ten Eyck, May 16, 1862, Schoff Civil War Collection, William L. Clements Library, University of Michigan, Ann Arbor; Samuel P. Heintzelman, diary, Apr. 29, 1862, Samuel P. Heintzelman Papers, Manuscript Division, LC. Beatie identifies one of the complainers as Martindale. *Army of the Potomac: McClellan's First Campaign,* 456. It is worth noting that most officers and soldiers stood solidly behind McClellan. Of course, friction and not contentment breed change, and so my focus is on the points of friction that eventually led to difficulty for Porter. For an excellent example of support for McClellan within the officer corps, see William T. H. Brooks to his father, June 4, 1862, Brooks Papers, U.S. Army Military History Institute, Carlisle, Pa.

38. *OR*, 11(3):181; Lincoln to McClellan, May 9, 1862, in *The Collected Works of Abraham Lincoln*, ed. Roy P. Basler, 9 vols. (New Brunswick, N.J.: Rutgers University Press, 1953–55), 5:208. See also Mark A. Snell, *From First to Last: The Life of Major General William B. Franklin* (New York: Fordham University Press, 2002), 109.

39. Porter to Marble, May 21, 1862, Marble Papers. Some of Porter's vehemence came in response to a then-ongoing public controversy swirling about accusations of the lack of support for the army from Senator Wilson, Porter's perceived nemesis in Congress. For Wilson's defense of himself and a rebuttal, see *Boston Advertiser*, May 15, 19, 1862. See also Myers, *Wilson and the Civil War*, 60.

40. Keyes expressed his dismay over the effect of Washington's meddling on operations on the Peninsula in an April 7 letter to Sen. Ira Harris, which is published in Erasmus D. Keyes, *Fifty Years' Observation of Men and Events, Civil and Military* (New York: Charles Scribner's Sons, 1884), 442–45. Heintzelman did the same in a letter to Senator Wilson on May 21. Myers, *Wilson and the Civil War*, 61. McDowell expressed his dismay in a letter to C. A. Heckscher, June 17, 1862, quoted in Nevins, *War for the Union*, 128. For McDowell's stated reaction to being withheld, see Franklin to Porter, Apr. 7, 1862, Porter Papers, container 3/reel 1.

41. Detailed descriptions of all the battles referenced in this essay are readily available, and so specifics need not be included here. Two excellent accounts of the Battle of Hanover Court House exist: Robert E. L. Krick, "The Battle of Slash Church (Hanover Court House), May 27, 1862," in *The Peninsula Campaign of 1862: Yorktown to the Seven Days, Volume 2*, ed. William J. Miller (Campbell, Calif.: Savas Woodbury, 1995), 1–38; and Michael C. Hardy, *The Battle of Hanover Court House* (Jefferson, N.C.: McFarland, 2006).

42. Ibid., 134; *OR*, 11(1):703–5. Elisha G. Marshall describes Martindale's erratic behavior at Hanover Court House in a letter to Porter, n.d., Porter Papers, container 5/reel 2. Porter later declared that he was "again greatly disappointed in Martindale. He behaved badly at Hanover Court House." Porter, memorandum, n.d., Porter Papers, container 53/reel 25. See also "The Army before Richmond," *New York Times*, June 7, 1862; McClellan to Stanton, May 28, 1862, in *Civil War Papers of George B. McClellan*, 279; and McClellan to his wife, May 28, 1862, ibid., 280.

43. Porter to Marble, June 20, 1862, Marble Papers; Lincoln to Frémont, June 15, 1862, in *Collected Works of Abraham Lincoln*, 5:271. In Porter's letter to Marble, he praised the editor's efforts to "stir up the Secretary of War," which, Porter wrote, "have been watched with strong interest."

44. McClellan's words to Porter are quoted in Sears, *To the Gates of Richmond*, 210. Perhaps the best discussion of McClellan's decision to move his army across the Peninsula appears in Rafuse, *McClellan's War*, 223–25.

45. Beyond Sears and Rafuse, the most detailed modern treatment of Gaines's Mill appears in Brian K. Burton, *Extraordinary Circumstances: The Seven Days Battles* (Bloomington: Indiana University Press, 2001), 100–37. Porter's report appears in *OR*, 11(1):223–27.

46. Porter's daughter indicated that he shunned his actual birthday for another date. Eisenschiml, *Celebrated Case of Fitz John Porter*, 315. For Porter and McClellan at Malvern Hill, see Rafuse, *McClellan's War*, 237–38; and Sears, *George McClellan*, 208–10.

47. William F. Biddle to John C. Ropes, n.d., copy in Porter Papers, container 45/reel 19; Butterfield's testimony, Court of Inquiry for John H. Martindale, Records of the Office of the Judge

John J. Hennessy

Advocate General (Army), Court-Martial Case File KK298, RG 153, National Archives and Records Administration, Washington, D.C.; Burton, *Extraordinary Circumstances*, 366–67.

48. OR. 11(3):352; testimony of Porter, Butterfield, Morell, and Roberts, Court of Inquiry for John H. Martindale; Affidavit of John H. Martindale, ibid.; Porter, "Reminiscences of a Life in Peace and in War," 5–6. This unfinished and unpublished autobiography includes details not found in Porter's correspondence or published works. Exactly what actions Martindale subsequently took to "injure" Porter are not entirely clear. He did testify unfavorably about his commander's performance at Hanover Court House to the Joint Committee on the Conduct of the War, but Porter's antipathy toward him must have been born of more than that. *JCCW*, 1:634–38. For examples of press coverage of the Martindale trial in October 1862, see *Rochester Daily Union and Advertiser*, Oct. 20, 30, 1862. Porter also charged Martindale with abandoning his command the night of July 1–2, 1862, but the court found insufficient evidence to support the charge.

49. McClellan wrote to Stanton that Porter's performance in the Seven Days deserved "the marked notice of the Executive and the nation." *OR*, 12(2, supplement):1111. Porter's daughter recorded that her father had reservations about McClellan's passivity and slowness. Eisenschiml, *Celebrated Case of Fitz John Porter*, 311. His exchange with McClellan the evening of July 1, 1862, suggests similarly.

50. Townsend, *Rustics in Rebellion*, 191–92. The details of Pope's very public campaign to impart a new vision for war in Virginia need not be recounted here. For the most complete treatments, see Peter Cozzens, *General John Pope: A Life for the Nation* (Urbana: University of Illinois Press, 2000), 76–82; and Hennessy, *Return to Bull Run*, 3–5, 11–14. For McClellan's belief that the intent was to have Pope supersede him, see McClellan to his wife, July 18, 1862, in *Civil War Papers of George B. McClellan*, 364, 365.

51. McClellan's most famous articulation of conservative policies is embodied in his "Harrison's Landing Letter." See McClellan to Lincoln, July 7, 1862, in *Civil War Papers of George B. McClellan*, 344–45; and Sears, *George McClellan*, 227–28. Brasher points out that McClellan encouraged slaves to leave their owners and become Union laborers. *Peninsula Campaign and the Necessity of Emancipation*, 215–17. Still, amid it all, McClellan never retreated from his intellectual commitment to conservative principles. On July 12, 1862, he wrote a fascinating letter to Hill Carter, the beset owner of Shirley Plantation on the James River, in which he apologized for "the losses you have suffered, & the inconveniences you have endured." McClellan assured him: "I have done my best to secure protection of private property, but I confess that circumstances beyond my control have often defeated my purposes. . . . I and the Army I command are fighting to secure the Union & to maintain its Constitution & laws—for no other purpose." McClellan to Carter, July 12, 1862, in *Civil War Papers of George B. McClellan*, 352.

52. Hennessy, *Return to Bull Run*, 13–16.

53. For the genesis of Porter's July 17 letter, see Porter, memorandum, n.d., Porter Papers, container 7/reel 3. For Kennedy's connections in Washington, see Richard Lathers, *Reminiscences of Richard Lathers: Sixty Years of a Busy Life in South Carolina, Massachusetts, and New York*, ed. Alvan F. Sanborn (New York: Grafton, 1907), 189–90. For Kennedy's early war writings, see *Daily National Intelligencer* (Washington, D.C.), Oct. 14, Nov. 21, 1861. For reference to the service of his son (Jo-

seph M. Kennedy) in the 9th New York Cavalry (confirmed by the regiment's roster), see *New York Tribune*, May 22, 1869.

54. Porter to J. C. G. Kennedy, July 17, 1862, Porter Papers, container 3/reel 1. Porter shared similar sentiments in a private letter to Manton Marble, predicting that "Pope will be whipped.... God spare us from our friends." But proving he possessed discretion, the general wrote much more guardedly in a response to a man seeking a position on his staff. "'Principles and not men' should be our motto and who leads us to victory is the one we want," he wrote. Porter to Marble, Aug. 10, 1862, Marble Papers; Porter to J. Howard Foote, Aug. 12, 1862, Porter Papers, container 4/reel 2.

55. Porter recorded his views on the letter in an undated memorandum, Porter Papers, container 7/reel 3. He was hardly alone in his harsh musings about the direction of the Union war effort and disdain for Pope. See John Gibbon to his wife, May 11, 1862, Gibbon Papers; Gouverneur K. Warren to his brother, July 20, 1862, Warren Papers, New York State Library, Albany; Alexander Webb to his father, Aug. 14, 1862, Webb Papers, MS 684, Yale University, New Haven, Conn.; William Thomas Harbaugh Brooks to his father, June 4, 22, 1862, Brooks Papers; William W. Averell to his brother, June 15, 1862, Averell Papers, New York State Library, Albany; and W. W. Burns to Alexander Webb, June 13, 1881, Porter Papers. Ambrose E. Burnside spoke directly to the almost universal distrust of Pope's abilities in his testimony before the Porter court-martial. *OR*, 12(2, supplement):1002–3. These and many other letters reflect a mash of resentment rooted both in regret over Washington meddling with the army (an almost universal sentiment), disdain for Pope, and discomfort with the changing nature of the Union war effort.

56. Hennessy, *Return to Bull Run*, 81–82; memorandum, n.d., Porter Papers, container 7/reel 3.

57. Porter's characterization of the dispatches and Burnside's handling of them appears in Fitz John Porter, "Notes on Second Manassas," n.d., Accession 42, University of Virginia Library, Charlottesville. When he wrote this memorandum, probably in the 1880s, Porter seemed to harbor no resentment toward Burnside, instead placing the blame on his own misjudgment of making the intemperate remarks rather than on his friend for sending them to Washington. Ethan S. Rafuse suggests that the later antipathy between Burnside and McClellan—often ascribed to the former's handling of Porter's dispatches—was rooted in other events more closely associated with the Battle of Antietam. "'Poor Burn?' The Antietam Conspiracy that Wasn't," *Civil War History* 54 (June 2008): 146–75. Porter's memorandum seems to support this. Franklin, however, saw perfidy in Burnside's actions. Franklin to Capt. F. C. Adams, Oct. 11, 1879, Frederick M. Dearborn Collection, Folder 225, Harvard University, Cambridge, Mass. See also William Marvel, *Burnside* (Chapel Hill: University of North Carolina Press, 1991), 106–7; and Burnside's testimony in the Porter court-martial, *OR*, 12(2, supplement):1002–5.

58. In later testimony Pope offered what appears to have been a careless reference to the dispatches to Burnside, suggesting they had shaped his perceptions of Porter, and then went on to describe a "letter" written by Porter even before "he knew the orders under which I was acting"—an apparent reference to the letter to Kennedy. It seems unlikely that copies of Porter's dispatches to Burnside would have reached Pope while he was still in the field. For Burnside's testimony, see *OR*, 12(2, supplement):840. See also T. C. H. Smith, "Memoirs," Smith Papers, Ohio Historical Society, Columbus, 166–67; George Ruggles [Pope's chief of staff] to Fitz John Porter, Oct. 14, 1877, Por-

ter Papers; Pope to Porter, unfinished dispatch, Aug. 29, 1862, Ropes Papers. It is well beyond the scope of this work to explore Porter's performance at Second Manassas in any detail. For a complete discussion, see Hennessy, *Return to Bull Run,* 231–35, 268–69, 306. An outstanding recounting of Porter's case and the implications of his actions on August 29 can be found in Gabler, "Fitz John Porter Case."

59. Fitz John Porter, memorandum, n.d., Porter Papers, container 7/reel 3; *OR,* 12(3):798.

60. Rafuse, *McClellan's War,* 270; Hennessy, *Return to Bull Run,* 241–42; Gideon Welles, *Diary of Gideon Welles: Secretary of the Navy under Lincoln and Johnson,* ed. Howard K. Beale, 3 vols. (New York: W. W. Norton, 1960), 1:119.

61. *OR,* 12(3):811, 19(2):188. The orders also relieved Franklin and Porter's wandering general, Charles Griffin, but neither of them would ultimately be subjected to formal charges.

62. Reporter George Smalley quoted in Sears, *George McClellan,* 316. Thomas M. Anderson (commander of the 2d Battalion, 12th U.S. Infantry at Antietam) claimed after the war that George Sykes quoted Porter as proclaiming dramatically: "Remember, General! I command the last reserve of the Army of the Republic." *Battles and Leaders of the Civil War,* ed. Robert U. Johnson and Clarence C. Buel, 4 vols. (New York: Century, 1887–88), 2:656. In a letter to T. T. Gantt, Porter obliquely denied making this statement. *St. Louis Republican,* Oct. 12, 1886. That Smalley recorded a similar conversation certainly suggests that the intent, if not the substance, of Porter's words was conveyed correctly by Anderson.

63. Porter to Marble, Sept. 30, 1862, Marble Papers; Abraham Lincoln, "Reply to Emancipation Memorial Presented by Chicago Christians of All Denominations," Sept. 13, 1862, in *Collected Works of Abraham Lincoln,* 5:420–21. Lincoln's response to the petition for emancipation was written on September 13 and appeared in Washington's Daily *National Intelligencer* on September 26, four days after the Emancipation Proclamation was issued and four days before Porter wrote his letter to Marble.

64. It is clear from McClellan's own writings and other witnesses that he considered carefully how to respond to the Emancipation Proclamation, and it is equally clear that one option he considered was repudiation. Porter's views on this question are unknown. He is not mentioned in the several accounts that record the counsel McClellan received from his subordinate commanders. See Jacob D. Cox, *Military Reminiscences of the Civil War,* 2 vols. (New York: Charles Scribner's Sons, 1900), 1:359–61; William F. Smith, *Autobiography of Maj. Gen. William F. Smith, 1861–1865,* ed. Herbert M. Schiller (1883; repr., Dayton, Ohio: Morningside, 1990), 57; Sears, *George McClellan,* 326–27; Rafuse, *McClellan's War,* 338–42; McClellan to his wife, Sept. 25, 1862, in *Civil War Papers of George B. McClellan,* 481; McClellan to Aspinwall, Sept. 26, 1862, ibid., 482; and McClellan to Lincoln, Oct. 7, 1862, ibid., 493–94. For Gibbon's views on emancipation, see Gibbon to his wife, Nov. 21, 1862, Gibbon Papers. For Hooker's declaration that he would be no "man stealer," see Hooker to Sen. James Nesmith, May 4, 1862, Nesmith Papers, Oregon Historical Society, Portland.

65. Porter wrote to Marble on November 9, "You may soon expect to hear my head chopped ... for ... [bringing charges against] Genl Martindale—his efforts to cause ruin to Genl McC for which he was willing to risk the safety of the army." Porter to Marble, Nov. 9, 1862, Marble Papers. For Burnside's denial of charges against Porter, see *Daily National Intelligencer* (Washington, D.C.), Nov. 17, 1862. For an overview of the case of the disloyal officer, John J. Key, and the general

condition in the Army of the Potomac following Antietam, see Brooks D. Simpson, "General McClellan's Bodyguard: The Army of the Potomac after Antietam," in *The Antietam Campaign*, ed. Gary W. Gallagher (Chapel Hill: University of North Carolina Press, 1999), 44–73. For the complete record of the Key case, see Abraham Lincoln, "Record of Dismissal of John J. Key," Sept. 27, 1862, in *Collected Works of Abraham Lincoln*, 5:442–43.

66. Letter of Signal Officer Louis Fortesque, Nov. 13, 1862, Dreer Collection, U.S. Army Military History Institute, Carlisle, Pa. Porter's departure elicited slight response from the ranks. See Evan M. Woodward, *Our Campaigns . . . together with a Sketch of the Army of the Potomac, under Generals McClellan, Burnside, Hooker, Meade, and Grant* (Philadelphia: John E. Potter, 1865), 225. In noting his departure, a reporter for the *New York Tribune* declared: "By a large part of the army he has long been looked upon as a 'semi-traitor.'" *New York Tribune*, Nov. 19, 1862.

67. *OR*, 19(2):572–73. Many Northern newspapers published Porter's farewell order. See, for example, *Albany (N.Y.) Evening Journal*, Nov. 14, 1862; and *Baltimore Sun*, Nov. 14, 1862. For reaction to Porter's relief, see "Louis," 18th Massachusetts, to "Dear John," Nov. 14, 1862, Porter Papers, container 6/reel 3.

68. The formal charges against Porter were filed not by Pope but by his inspector general, Benjamin S. Roberts. Roberts was clearly acting as the general's proxy in the matter. *OR*, 12(2, supplement):828–29.

69. For commentary on Porter's trial and the strength of the case against him, see the letters of staff officer Stephen M. Weld in *War Diary and Letters*, 152–53, 157.

70. Elizabeth D. Leonard, *Lincoln's Forgotten Ally: Judge Advocate General Joseph Holt of Kentucky* (Chapel Hill: University of North Carolina Press, 2011), 166–71; Abraham Lincoln, "Order Approving Sentence of Fitz-John Porter," Jan. 21, 1863, in *Collected Works of Abraham Lincoln*, 6:67; Anders, *Injustice on Trial*, 258. For editorial commentary of the Porter verdict quoted here, see *New Haven (Conn.) Columbian Register*, Jan. 31, 1863; and *St. Albans (Vt.) Daily Messenger*, Feb. 5, 1863. Virtually all major newspapers offered opinions on the trial. For example, see *Boston Post*, Feb. 2, 1863; *Boston Liberator*, Feb. 6, 1863; and letter of "Scorer," *Rochester (N.Y.) Union and Advertiser*, Feb. 6, 1863. It is worth noting that just four days after Porter's verdict, Lincoln also ordered General Franklin relieved from command. Other than Porter, no officer had been so closely identified with McClellan, despite Franklin's efforts to distance himself from the army commander. He explained: "At that time I knew that a jealous feeling had grown up about Gen M'c friendship for Gen P & me, and I purposely kept away from HdQrs for days together in order to silences slanderous tongues, and when I had business at Hdqrs generally transacted it with staff officers without asking to see the General—merely to break down the feeling if possible." Franklin to the Comte de Paris, Sept. 12, 1876, Porter Papers, container 13/reel 5. See also the discussion of Franklin's fate in Snell, *From First to Last*, 250.

71. Anders, *Injustice on Trial*, 267. See the interview with Porter's daughter, which helps characterize his wartime life and career, in Eisenschiml, *Celebrated Case of Fitz John Porter*, 308–17.

72. Porter to Ropes, Mar. 25, 1894, Ropes Papers. For evidence of Porter's dogged belief in conspiracy, see Porter to Ropes, Aug. 8, 1881, ibid. See also Eisenschiml, *Celebrated Case of Fitz John Porter*, 311. Porter's papers include many examples of criticisms of McClellan offered by others—and no indication that Porter ever responded or refuted them. See, for example, George Hoadly to

Porter, Jan. 30, 1892, Porter Papers, container 44/reel 19; and C. D. Holmes to Porter, Jan. 16, 1893, ibid., container 45/reel 19.

73. Letter of "War Veterans," *Portsmouth (N.H.) Journal*, June 14, 1902.

74. Hennessy, *Return to Bull Run*, 465.

"Too Bad, Poor Fellows"
Joseph K. F. Mansfield and the XII Corps at Antietam

THOMAS G. CLEMENS

"Cease firing, they are our own men!" Lt. John M. Gould, acting adjutant, 10th Maine Infantry, remembered Brig. Gen. Joseph K. F. Mansfield shouting these words as he rode in front of his regiment on September 17, 1862, at the Battle of Antietam. Gould's regiment was committed to battle in the East Woods that morning, with the rest of Mansfield's XII Corps, as part of Maj. Gen. George B. McClellan's plan to drive Gen. Robert E. Lee's Army of Northern Virginia out of Maryland. Several members of 10th Maine attempted to correct Mansfield, advising him that the fire in their front in fact came from Rebels hiding behind trees in the East Woods. Soon thereafter, Mansfield was struck in the chest by a rifle bullet and carried to nearby farmhouse, where he died twenty-four hours later.[1]

Joseph King Fenno Mansfield is a man more remembered for his death than his life. Most studies of Antietam, the only engagement in which he actually exercised field command, do little more than highlight his brief appearance on the field before his mortal wounding and his inexperience in command, noting that he had taken command of the XII Corps only two days before the battle. Consequently, the impression one gains of Mansfield is of as a desk soldier whose best days were behind him, who was out of his depth at Antietam, and at whose feet problems with the XII Corps's performance must be laid. Many authors attribute the command's failure to achieve immediate success at Antietam to Mansfield's mishandling of troops and his untimely demise. Because he fell so early in the battle—and the war—his service has been relegated to a small footnote in Civil War history. Historian Stephen Sears, for instance, refers to Mansfield as merely "an earnest old regular who pulled strings to get a field assignment," while James M. McPherson, in his study of Antietam, only mentions Mansfield's death in passing.[2]

Though understandable in the context of the hugely complex and bloody battle of Antietam, this cursory treatment of Mansfield unnecessarily slights his nearly forty-five years of military service, during which he gained considerable field experience prior to the war, and the leadership skills he demonstrated during his decades of service. Moreover, in many ways Mansfield and his experience at Antietam was emblematic of the profound difficulties the XII Corps, and the Army of the Potomac as a whole, faced during the Maryland Campaign. Thus, it is fitting and worthwhile to revisit Mansfield's career prior to his assuming corps command, the qualities and qualifications as a soldier he demonstrated during that time, the XII Corps as a combat unit, and how both affected the Battle of Antietam.

JOSEPH K. F. MANSFIELD was born December 22, 1803, the son of Henry and Mary (Fenno) Mansfield of New Haven, Connecticut. He was the youngest of their three sons and three daughters, with only two of his sisters outliving him. Descendants of an old New England family, the Mansfields had a history of public service. His father was a sea captain who worked in the West Indies trade. Lamentably, not long after Joseph's birth, his mother divorced his father for carrying on an adulterous relationship with a woman in Saint Croix, Virgin Islands. The family subsequently relocated to Middletown, Connecticut, with Joseph's older brother John becoming guardian of him and the younger children. Despite his family obligations, John volunteered his services when war broke out in 1812. He was subsequently captured in a failed invasion of Lower Canada and died from disease contracted in prison. Shortly before his fourteenth birthday, Joseph Mansfield began his career as a soldier when he entered the U.S. Military Academy at West Point, New York, on October 1, 1817. His uncle, Lt. Col. Jared Mansfield, was at the time serving as the academy's first professor of natural and experimental philosophy and wrote letters in support of his nephew's application for admission. These letters reminded Pres. James Monroe and Secretary of War John C. Calhoun of John Mansfield's sacrifice and testified to Joseph's education and intelligence. His admission may have been facilitated too by efforts on his behalf by a cousin, Joseph Totten, who later served as chief of the Corps of Engineers from 1838 to 1864. Schoolwork and the military program at West Point clearly agreed with Mansfield as he performed well enough to graduate second in the class of 1822. (The class leader,

George Dutton, was also from Connecticut and a cousin of Mansfield.) Like many top graduates, Mansfield was assigned to the prestigious Corps of Engineers. Somewhat unusually, however, as graduates of the academy usually spent a number of months after completing the program holding the rank by brevet, he was immediately promoted to second lieutenant on July 1, 1822. It was a propitious beginning to what would be a highly successful career.[3]

Mansfield entered the U.S. Military Academy at a crucial time in its history. During his first year there, Superintendent Alden Partridge was dismissed, and Sylvanus Thayer took his place. Thayer arrived determined to completely revamp the school and quickly went to work. Jared Mansfield was one of the instructors who enthusiastically welcomed Thayer's arrival, for he had resented Partridge's favoritism, bullying of the faculty, and frequent interruption of classes for close-order drill, which no doubt helped foster a positive image of the new superintendent and his work in the eyes of the professor's nephew. Thayer's reforms, which earned him enduring fame as the "Father of the Military Academy," included emphasis on rigorous academic programs focused on engineering, a strict honor system, and the adoption of systems for officer training he had observed during travels to France. Young Mansfield belonged to the first class of graduates to experience Thayer's efforts to create an institution that would serve as the foundation for the emergence of professionalism in the U.S. Army during the first half of the nineteenth century.[4] Thayer's positive influence reaped huge dividends in the performance of academy graduates in subsequent conflicts and in engineering work that would be critical to the nation's development.

Because his years as a cadet coincided with Thayer's first years at the academy, during which the curriculum was standardized and reformed as was the entire culture of the academy, it can be accurately said that Mansfield was literally present at the creation of West Point as a bastion of military professionalism with engineering at its core. Moreover, his experience undoubtedly confirmed a strong personal tie to the U.S. Army and its development as an institution already encouraged by his family connections. That he performed so well at the academy and was able to receive a commission in the engineers, which in nineteenth-century military circles enjoyed an unequalled level of prestige due to its status as the acme of military professionalism, further reinforced this tie. For better or worse, Mansfield's life and career would be inextricably linked to this dynamic.[5]

Mansfield's first assignment after graduation was as assistant to the Board of Engineers at New York from 1822 to 1825, followed by work assisting in the construction of Fort Hamilton on the east side of the Verrazano Narrows entrance to New York Harbor. From 1825 through 1828 he worked on the defenses of Hampton Roads, Virginia, and from 1828 to 1830 was detached to survey Pasquotank River, North Carolina, taking temporary charge of the works at Charleston Harbor, South Carolina. He was then assigned as superintending engineer of the construction of Fort Pulaski for the defense of the Savannah River in Georgia, where he served from 1830 until shortly before the outbreak of hostilities with Mexico in 1846. While serving at Fort Pulaski, he was promoted on March 5, 1832, to first lieutenant in the Corps of Engineers. When Mansfield arrived at Cockspur Island, site of the proposed fort, in January 1831, another young engineer officer whose performance at West Point had marked him as a man of promise, 2d Lt. Robert E. Lee, was overseeing the construction of defenses designed by Maj. Samuel Babcock. Mansfield, however, disliked the design, and his efforts contributed to Washington's decision to have another engineer, Capt. Richard Delafield, consult with Mansfield on the plans. Lee, rendered a supernumerary by Delafield's arrival, was soon transferred to Virginia to work on Fort Monroe. Significantly, both Lee and Delafield would later serve as superintendents at West Point.[6]

While posted at Fort Pulaski, Mansfield also received a number of temporary assignments that, along with his promotion to captain in July 1838, offered evidence of the high regard in which he was held by the army. These included overseeing repairs on the National Road at Cumberland, Maryland; work on projects to improve the Savannah River and inland navigation between the Saint Marys and Saint Johns Rivers in Florida; construction of the Sullivan's Island breakwater in South Carolina; and overseeing repairs of the Saint Augustine seawall in Florida. Mansfield also served on the Board of Engineers for Atlantic Coast defenses from May 8, 1842, to September 8, 1845. While important to the Corps of Engineers, these assignments ensured that Mansfield would have no opportunity to actually lead troops and prevented him from seeing duty in a combat area during the Second Seminole War of 1835–42. During these years, he also started a family, in 1838 marrying Louisa M. Mather of Middletown, Connecticut, with whom he would have three sons and two daughters. (His oldest son, Samuel Mather Mansfield, would follow in his father's footsteps to attend the U.S. Military Academy, graduating sixth in the class of 1862. Another son, Joseph Totten Mansfield, was named for his cousin but never served in the military.)[7]

When disputes over the boundary between Texas and Mexico brought the United States to the verge of war in the 1840s, the War Department organized the Army of Observation under the command of Brig. Gen. Zachary Taylor and sent it to the Texas border. Mansfield was assigned to Taylor's command as chief engineer and in this capacity laid out a defensive work on the north side of the Rio Grande, Fort Texas (later renamed Fort Brown), which was unsuccessfully attacked by a superior Mexican force in May 1846. In the course of these operations, Mansfield won praise from superiors as the "engineer officer, under whose direction the fort was built, and by whose skillful conduct the defenses were increased and strengthened during the siege." This led to a brevet promotion to major for "gallant and distinguished services in the defense of Fort Brown." When Taylor's army subsequently invaded Mexico, Mansfield accompanied it. He then led the first reconnaissance of the city of Monterrey, which was praised as "important and ably executed." He later received another brevet promotion, this one to the rank of lieutenant colonel, "for Gallant and Meritorious Conduct in the Several Conflicts at Monterey, Mex. while directing the Storming of the Tannery Redoubt, in fortifying Monterey and Saltillo, and reconnoitering the mountain passes, 1846–47." In these operations he received the critical task of scouting the route for Brig. Gen. William Worth's command to follow in order to play its part in Taylor's plan to attack Monterrey from two sides. During this mission, Mansfield narrowly escaped a group of Mexican lancers, which enabled him to also conduct reconnaissances for Brig. Gen. John Garland, who was leading the other portion of the American army.

September 21, 1846, however, was not a stellar day for Taylor. His orders to Garland were unclear as to whether he was to lead a feint against a strongpoint in the Mexican line called the Tannery. Garland thus consulted with Mansfield, and they agreed that Taylor would be disappointed in a withdrawal without major fighting, which led Garland to send his troops forward. Mansfield accompanied the attack, which resulted in the loss of nearly one-third of the troops engaged. He then advised the general to order a retreat, which was done, much to Taylor's disappointment. Mansfield, however, who was severely wounded in the leg during the attack, once again was praised for his efforts, which along with those of Capt. Electus Backus were described as "the brilliant point in this operation." The engineer recovered from his injuries in time to accompany Taylor's army when it marched to confront Mexican general Santa Anna at Buena Vista. In this operation Mansfield once again carried out successful reconnaissances and received compliments from Taylor in his report of the resulting battle. He also received yet another brevet promotion, this one to colonel, for "gallant and meritorious conduct."[8]

When the war ended, Mansfield was still a captain but could claim three brevet promotions. This marked him as a man clearly on the rise and one of several staff officers recognized for their professionalism and extraordinary efforts in this war. Among these was Robert E. Lee, who performed much the same duties for Maj. Gen. Winfield Scott that Mansfield did for Taylor, and like his counterpart, earning three brevet promotions. Other engineer officers who performed well during this conflict would gain fame during the Civil War, including P. G. T. Beauregard, George McClellan, and George G. Meade. To General Scott and other likeminded officers, the war was a vindication of the military academy and their efforts to professionalize the army, to which they had dedicated so much energy since the end of the War of 1812. Mansfield in particular had won notice for engaging in high-risk duties that exposed him to enemy fire and serving as an effective advisor to commanders and subordinates. Evidence of his enhanced status among fellow officers came when engineer officer and recent West Point graduate Lt. George McClellan identified Mansfield as being one of the army's "heroes and other big bugs" in a February 1847 letter to his mother.[9]

Less salutary in the eyes of McClellan and other regular officers was the conduct of the American volunteer soldiers. Many of these men were outraged at the nonbattlefield behavior of Taylor's and Scott's volunteers, whose poor officers and their inability to impose discipline was evident in their unsanitary camps and their unsavory treatment of civilians encountered in their path of march. This, along with their own consistently superb performances, reinforced a poorly concealed sense of superiority and commitment to professionalism among West Point–educated officers, factors that would influence their conduct when compelled to deal with volunteer soldiers on a much larger scale during the Civil War.[10]

AFTER THE WAR Mansfield returned to his engineering duties, with assignment to the Board of Engineers for Atlantic Coast Defenses from March 13,

1848, to April 11, 1853. During this time, he also served briefly on a board tasked with overseeing Pacific Coast defenses and as superintending engineer for the construction of Fort Winthrop at Boston Harbor, Massachusetts. As if this were not enough, he also spent part of these years working on transportation improvements on the James and Appomattox Rivers and on a mission to survey the Rappahannock River in Virginia.[11]

That his performance in these duties had done little to diminish his stature within the army was evident when on May 28, 1853, Mansfield accepted appointment from Secretary of War Jefferson Davis as junior inspector general of the army. This assignment entailed conducting inspections and submitting reports on all army posts and garrisons west of the Mississippi River. It also brought with it a significant jump in rank from captain to colonel. These developments were influenced by factors beyond simple faith in Mansfield's competence as an engineer. First, Davis too was a veteran of Taylor's army and enjoyed status as one of the heroes of Buena Vista; his experiences undoubtedly gave him a favorable impression of Mansfield's abilities. In addition, Mansfield's cousin, Colonel Totten, was then serving as chief engineer of the Corps of Engineers, which probably influenced the selection as well. Finally, in contrast with many who held the position before the Civil War, during his tenure as secretary of war, Davis was an active champion of military reform and professionalization and may have correctly seen in Mansfield someone with the background and experience to bring a similar spirit to the job of inspector general.[12] The jump in rank that came with the appointment is especially noteworthy in light of how seniority almost invariably dictated promotion in the antebellum army. That external factors came in to break with practice in this case is ironic given perceptions that Mansfield himself was—ironically—resentful of those who jumped rank over him during the Civil War. What at this time he may have accepted as recognition of his professionalism would appear quite different to other observers.

During this period, there existed a nearly constant feud between Secretary of War Davis and Winfield Scott, now a brevet lieutenant general and commander of the U.S. Army, over control of the Inspector General's Office. Evidently, Mansfield was able to steer a neutral course and avoid being drawn into the political and personal conflict between these two notoriously prickly personalities. That Scott became a strong supporter of Mansfield during the early days of the Civil War is certainly suggestive of his success in this.[13]

Almost immediately upon assuming his duties as junior inspector general, Mansfield was sent on an inspection trip to the frontier posts and forts located in the territories acquired from Mexico through the Treaty of Guadalupe Hidalgo. (Absence from Washington no doubt also helped him successfully negotiate the Davis-Scott feud.) Designated the Department of New Mexico, the region included much of what is now New Mexico and Arizona as well as sections of present-day Colorado and Utah. The hardships and dangers of travel, even on mundane inspection trips, were considerable in that part of the country, with hostile Indians, bandits, and Mexicans still disputing the boundaries roaming the region. Though traveling by wagon to haul forage and food in hostile environments was enough to challenge anyone's stamina and health, belying his traditional image as a desk general, Mansfield seemed to thrive and produced a report that offered insightful commentary on the region and its inhabitants.

The report fully demonstrated Mansfield's keen eye for detail. He compellingly described the terrain, transportation features, and potential for running railroads through the area. The concerns he expressed for protecting the inhabitants from Indian depredations also spoke to his sense of duty. Mansfield, now a seasoned veteran, also took great interest in the uniforms, weapons, and equipment used by U.S. soldiers. His recommendations for improvements in weapons, tents, and other items reflected a degree of experience and knowledge that made him well suited for the job.

One example of this keen eye for improvement was his recommendation that dragoon units abandon the use of muzzle-loading, smoothbore musketoons, which Mansfield accurately pointed out were difficult to use and slow to load; making matters worse, when slung, the ball dropped out of the barrel. Mansfield suggested replacing them with Sharps carbines, the newest and most highly regarded breech-loading weapon of the time. Other suggestions he offered included improving the pay for the troops and a better mail system. The colonel also expressed disapproval of the practice of soldiers working as farmers.[14] In short, Mansfield took an interest in the needs of the common soldiers and the need for army administration to provide them.

Further inspection trips followed. He visited the Department of California in 1854, traveling from Fort Yuma in Arizona all the way north to Fort Steilacoom on Puget Sound. Once again his skills at observation and analysis were reflected in his reports. He recommended resolving outstanding territorial disputes with Mexico and strongly endorsed the idea of a transcontinental railroad for both military and commercial use. He also sketched maps of the various posts he visited, demonstrating skill as an artist. In addition to developing his competency with a pen and demonstrating an ability to endure the hardships of travel, another benefit of Mansfield's journeys was the opportunity he gained to acquaint himself with many fellow officers. His assessments were usually positive, and many of the men he mentioned on these two trips became prominent commanders during the Civil War. (Ironically, two of them, Israel B. Richardson and George B. Anderson, also would die of wounds received at Antietam.) Yet there is no evidence of any of these officers becoming advocates for him during his effort to a secure a major field command in 1861–62, possibly because the nature of his duties fostered or reinforced preexisting impressions that he was preeminently fit for staff duties rather than having any potential to actually command troops.[15]

In the following years Mansfield made additional inspection trips. He visited the Department of Texas in 1856 and conducted an inspection of the Utah army in 1857. He followed this up with tours of the newly separated Departments of Oregon and California in 1858–59 and lastly of the Departments of Texas and New Mexico again in 1860–61. This last inspection trip, made just before the beginning of the Civil War, produced the usual thorough report on each post, laying out the complement of men garrisoning it, their uniforms, and their equipment. Mansfield conducted this tour traveling by a mule-drawn wagon with a small escort over rutted dirt roads to various far-flung posts. He left Galveston on September 26, 1860, and inspected forts between there and Fort Brown. He then proceeded to Fort Quitman near El Paso and finished his journey on January 23, 1861, by presenting a report to department headquarters at San Antonio.

Curiously, although Texas was seriously considering secession at this time, no mention of the political climate appeared in the reports. But a convention assembled in Austin on February 1, just days after Mansfield left, and approved submitting a secession ordinance to the people of the state.[16] Seventy-one years old and in poor health, Maj. Gen. David Twiggs, the commander of the Department of Texas, was the second-highest-ranking officer in the U.S. Army. A few weeks after Mansfield departed San Antonio, Texas forces surrounded Twiggs's headquarters and convinced him to surrender all U.S. troops and property in the state. Mansfield made no reference to this roiling state of affairs in his official report, yet it could hardly have escaped his notice.[17]

When war broke out in April 1861, Mansfield was immediately assigned the task, along with other regular officers, of assisting the effort to raise and muster into service volunteer regiments being organized by the states in response to Pres. Abraham Lincoln's call for volunteers on April 15. From the nineteenth through the twenty-seventh, he mustered volunteers into service at Columbus, Ohio (where he almost certainly crossed paths with McClellan, who on April 23 assumed command of Ohio troops). He then traveled to Washington, where he would serve until July 25. Mansfield's transfer came at the request of General Scott. The capital region was now the Military Department of Washington, which the orders establishing it explained "will include the District of Columbia, according to its original boundary, Fort Washington and the country adjacent, and the State of Maryland as far as Bladensburg, inclusive. Col. J. K. F. Mansfield, inspector-general, is assigned to the command, headquarters Washington City."[18]

OF IMMEDIATE CONCERN to Mansfield upon arriving in the capital was the threat to Washington posed by Virginia troops occupying the high ground across the Potomac River and establishing batteries there. Thus, he became an eager proponent of seizing the commanding ground in Virginia in order to safeguard the city and the bridges leading to it. "The President's House and Department buildings in its vicinity," Mansfield observed in a report he submitted to Scott on May 3,

> are but two and a half miles across the river from Arlington high ground, where a battery of bombs and heavy guns, if established, could destroy the city with comparatively a small force after destroying the bridges. The Capitol is only three and a half miles from the same height at Arlington, and at the Aqueduct the summits of the heights on the opposite shore are not over one mile from Georgetown.
>
> With this view of the condition of our position, it is clear to my mind that the city is liable to be bombarded at the will of an enemy, unless we occupy the ground which he certainly would occupy if he had any such intention. I therefore recommend that the heights above mentioned be seized and secured by at least two strong redoubts, one commanding the Long Bridge

and the other the Aqueduct, and that a body of men be there encamped to sustain the redoubts and give battle to the enemy if necessary.[19]

To establish a commensurate rank for his assignment, Mansfield was promoted to brevet brigadier general in the U.S. Army on May 6 and, by order of General Scott, took command of Washington, D.C., that day. He was subsequently advanced to the full rank in the Regular Army on May 14, making him fourth in seniority on the list of brigadier generals. Mansfield would exercise the duties laid out in the orders establishing the Department of Washington even after Major General McClellan's arrival in late July.[20]

The task of alleviating Mansfield's anxiety over Confederate occupation of Arlington Heights was carried out on May 23 and 24. Those days saw Union troops carry out a plan the general had conceived for what would be the first invasion of Confederate territory, the implementation of which was delayed until after a referendum ratified Virginia's ordinance of secession. Union forces smoothly executed the operation, its design and implementation indicating that Mansfield possessed some skill at operational planning, though it did produce the first death of a Union officer when Col. Elmer Ellsworth was killed during the capture of Alexandria.[21]

Under Mansfield's direction, work then began on forts and interconnected earthworks in Northern Virginia to protect Washington. His chief engineer, Maj. John G. Barnard, laid out this system of defenses, which proved to be one of Mansfield's enduring contributions to the war effort. The general was also responsible for arresting anyone thought to be aiding the Confederates, and in Washington and Suffolk, Virginia, a number of disloyal citizens were detained on his orders.

Like many of his Regular Army comrades, Mansfield's long years of service had instilled in him a mistrust of volunteer regiments and a belief in the need to give them thorough training before sending them into action. His concerns seemed confirmed when, in the aftermath of Lincoln's call for ninety-day troops, the capital became crowded with poorly trained and underequipped militia and volunteer soldiers.

Another problem Mansfield had to deal with was the fact that, with this gathering of large numbers of men, there ensued an inevitable jockeying for command positions among Regular Army officers. Scott was clearly too infirm to take the field, and the question of who should exercise operational command was one guaranteed to fuel political intrigue as well as professional competition. Mansfield seemed well positioned, given his long experience and the fact that he enjoyed favor with Scott; however, his manifest inclination toward prudence, caution, and undoubted coolness toward the "On to Richmond" fervor that swept through the North in the summer of 1861 (an impression fostered by his closeness to Scott, who opposed attempting a major offensive until at least the fall) left him out of step with public opinion. This was undoubtedly a factor in the promotion of Maj. Irvin McDowell to brigadier general of volunteers and appointment to command the newly organized Department of Northeastern Virginia in late May 1861. Mansfield and Scott were incensed by the move, but McDowell enjoyed the patronage of the influential secretary of the Treasury, Salmon Chase, who pushed for the appointment of fellow Ohioans like McDowell to important commands. Mansfield clearly took it as an insult to see the elevation of McDowell, a man several years his junior and whom he had clearly outranked before they were appointed brigadier general on May 14, 1862, though Mansfield was listed as senior to McDowell.[22] Nevertheless, the message the appointment carried in terms of what it said about Mansfield's standing in the capital was unmistakable, for the new department was organized in such a way that it would be its commander who would conduct active field operations.

That this would anger Mansfield was certainly understandable. After all, he had been in the army longer than only a handful of officers and, during his forty-four years of service, had performed well at every assignment he was given as evidenced by his rise from second lieutenant to captain in sixteen years, earning of three brevet promotions in the Mexican War, wounding in combat, and elevation to colonel thirty years after graduating from West Point. Although he never held an actual field command, as an engineer he had demonstrated a talent for developing plans and some ability to direct others in their implementation. Furthermore, in the course of his trips to frontier posts, he had demonstrated that he possessed both physical vigor and stamina and had produced reports characterized by a thorough understanding of discipline, drill, weapons, and equipment.

Yet there was the matter of his relatively advanced age in comparison with the likes of McDowell and McClellan (neither of whom could claim extensive line-command experience in the field). Moreover, doubts about Mansfield's vigor may have been reinforced by his joining Scott in opposing active operations. Then there was the fact that the one operation he had planned, the capture of Arlington and Alexandria, had resulted in the death of Ellsworth, who was both a friend of the president's and a popular hero in the North.

But the appointment of officers of Mansfield's age to important commands was not at all unusual in 1861. There is little evidence age influenced thinking in this regard in the Confederacy. Joseph E. Johnston, who inspected the Department of New Mexico shortly before Mansfield's travel through Texas, entered the army only a few years after Mansfield, earned similar brevets in Mexico and Florida, and held combat-arms postings to the rank of lieutenant colonel until June 28, 1860, when he was appointed to the staff position of quartermaster general, with promotion to brigadier general. Similarly, Albert S. Johnston graduated from the U.S. Military Academy only four years after Mansfield, was promoted to colonel two years after him, and also spent time in a staff billet. Yet few then or since questioned their fitness for command. P. G. T. Beauregard and Robert E. Lee also entered the army later and made rank slower than Mansfield despite working on similar engineering projects, but both were almost immediately given important commands.

Comparing Mansfield to officers who received high ranks in the Union army during the first year of the war, men like Robert Patterson, Nathanial Lyon, John C. Frémont, Nathanial P. Banks, Henry W. Halleck, McClellan, Ulysses S. Grant, and of course McDowell, reveals other dynamics at work. Patterson had seen little peacetime service and was even older than Mansfield, but he also enjoyed Scott's patronage and had on his record the actual exercise of field command in Mexico. Banks, though, was a politician with no military experience whatsoever. All the others, while they had experience in the prewar army, had entered the service later than Mansfield, were promoted more slowly, earned fewer brevets, and held less responsible prewar billets, yet they quickly moved to top commands in 1861. Certainly, having a political connection or sponsor was a factor in several cases, including those of Lyon, Frémont, Grant, and McDowell. Halleck and McClellan, though neither had ever exercised field command, had in the course of their careers established reputations as military intellectuals, which Mansfield did not possess. John Dix and John Wool also could assert claims to important commands due to their seniority, but it is certainly suggestive that both received what were decidedly administrative posts rather than active field commands.

Many who left a record of their interaction with Mansfield during this time were favorably impressed. Yet the general may well have been viewed, rightly or wrongly, as too much a creature of the peacetime army, dependable and fit for routine duty but lacking the physical dynamism, youth, and charisma needed for field command. He evidently, though, was still capable of nursing resentments, a perception reinforced by his closeness to Scott, a world-class holder of grudges, and complaints by McDowell that he (and Scott) had not been as fully supportive of his efforts to prepare his command for operations as they could have been.[23]

When the disastrous Union defeat at Manassas on July 21 seemed to have vindicated the older men's skepticism about conducting major operations, Mansfield could have been forgiven for thinking his time had come and that his work helping to stem the tide of stragglers after the battle and rally the retreating troops when they reached the capital had further strengthened his standing. Yet authorities decided to summon McClellan to Washington and gave him command of the troops around the capital. Mansfield's subsequent work handling the physical defenses around the city seem to have earned the professional respect of McClellan, who retained the old soldier in command of the city as he built what eventually became the Army of the Potomac. Not surprisingly, though, Mansfield regarded "Little Mac" with some resentment, which McClellan immediately sensed, writing to his wife shortly after arriving in the capital: "I have been assigned to a division composed of the departments of Northeastern Virginia (that under McDowell) and of Washington (now under Mansfield). Neither of them like it much, especially Mansfield, but I think ere long they must become accustomed to it, as there is no help for it." Indeed, after several months working under McClellan's direction, Mansfield complained in a letter to his wife that the younger man had not "exhibited one sign [of] a generous feeling toward me." He also wrote to various politicians, including Treasury Secretary Chase, asking them to help him secure a field command.[24]

IN AUGUST 1861 Federal forces captured the Cape Hatteras inlet on the North Carolina coast and several hundred Confederate defenders. Union troops occupying the area were threatened by Southern efforts to retake the inlet, and on October 1 the USS *Fanny,* a shallow-draft steam tug, was captured by Confederate forces with only slight resistance by the crew. To find out what exactly had happened, Washington sent Mansfield to Cape Hatteras, and four days later he reported the facts of the case to Scott. He also offered several useful suggestions relating to garrisoning the area and the logistical support required. General Wool, commander of the Department of Virginia headquartered at Fort Monroe, appeared far more welcoming toward the general than McClellan had been and found in him a useful "troubleshooter" in the matter. Mansfield was then ordered to Camp Hamilton, near Fort Monroe, where he arrived on October 15. By November 24 he had assumed command of Camp Butler, also near Fort Monroe, from Brig. Gen. John W. Phelps.[25]

A clear indication of Mansfield's aggressiveness and competence is provided in his report on the famous engagement between the USS *Monitor* and CSS *Virginia* on March 8, 1862. The general, then officially the commander of the First Brigade, First Division, Department of Virginia, was not content to simply observe the action but ordered guns under his command to join the engagement by opening fire on the *Virginia*. After the USS *Congress* ran aground and other Confederate vessels tried to send boarders to burn the ship, Mansfield then ordered field guns and infantry of his command to drive the unarmored enemy vessels away. His efforts were not completely successful, for the *Virginia* was able to fire hotshot into the *Congress* and set it afire. Nevertheless, they reflected well on his military character. Aggressive, resourceful, and determined, no one could say that he did not do his best to help resist the Confederate onslaught using all the weapons at his disposal.[26]

As he prepared to move his Army of the Potomac to Fort Monroe that month as the first step in what became known as the Peninsula Campaign, McClellan hoped to incorporate troops from Wool's command into his force in a way that held out the prospect of the active field command that Mansfield so clearly craved. "I desire to form another division, under Mansfield," McClellan wrote in a telegraph message to Secretary of War Edwin Stanton on March 14, "and to annex that division to the First Army Corps as soon as McDowell is confirmed as major-general."[27]

This proposal to elevate Mansfield to division command was perhaps a reflection of the army commander being impressed with Mansfield's prewar record or the positive reports he received of the general's performance in Washington and in the naval action at Hampton Roads. It may also have been designed to get Washington to assign troops at Fort Monroe to his own force. Moreover, at that same time McClellan was feuding with the administration over the formation of corps and the appointment of their commanders. McClellan had months earlier asked permission to create corps even though such organizations were not part of the U.S. military system at the time. When the president finally agreed to this in early March, though, the well-ingrained seniority system interfered with McClellan's hopes. He wanted first to have the opportunity to observe his division commanders and then appoint corps leaders based on merit, which he no doubt hoped would lead to the elevation of younger men like Fitz John Porter and William B. Franklin, who shared his views on operations. Lincoln, however, mandated that the four senior generals, McDowell, Edwin Sumner, Samuel Heintzelman, and Erasmus Keyes—all of whom had expressed either outright opposition to or had serious reservations with McClellan's plans—be given these positions.[28] Mansfield was senior to every one of these officers except for Sumner. Indeed, Heintzelman had served under Mansfield in Washington in April and May 1861. Thus, it is possible that McClellan, in requesting Mansfield for division command, was less motivated by his qualifications than by a hope that his appointment would cast doubts about the seniority system.

McClellan's plans and Mansfield's hopes would be thwarted not only by Washington but also by Wool, who ranked both Mansfield and McClellan. As an old regular whose service began in 1812, Wool shared the resentments of Mansfield and other older officers of McClellan's meteoric rise to command and was determined not to subordinate himself to a man he considered a young upstart. Moreover, because McClellan was relieved from his position as general in chief of all the Union forces and his authority limited to his own army on March 11, Wool could raise a legitimate complaint about meddling by an equivalent officer in areas that were outside his authority. In the end, Mansfield stayed under the old general's command, while McClellan was compelled to operate against Richmond with a smaller force than he wanted and what he deemed to be a badly flawed command team. Once again, Mansfield had missed an opportunity for field command.[29]

While commanding a brigade under Wool, though, Mansfield did have the opportunity to participate in the bloodless capture of Norfolk in early May 1862. Yet even securing a role in this relatively minor action was a struggle. Anxious for a combat assignment, Mansfield advised his commander in late April that he was "ready to march with any force, from a company to ten thousand men." According to one source, though, when the move on Norfolk began, Mansfield was ordered to remain at Fort Monroe, and it was only on direct orders from President Lincoln himself that he was sent to the front. Once again, although no combat was involved, Mansfield's men were fully prepared for resistance, and their commander was active in the operation. While not the field command the general really wanted, he was commanding troops and even managed to earn favorable mention in Wool's after-action report.[30]

On July 22, a few weeks after McClellan's army was driven back from the gates of Richmond in the Seven Days' Battles, the Department of Virginia, command of which had by then passed from Wool to Maj. Gen. John A. Dix, was organized into the VII Corps. Mansfield was designated commander of the division at Suffolk, but with few troops under his authority, it was an almost purely administrative post. Although most sources refer to Mansfield as never holding field command before September 1862, in fact by then he had several months' experience commanding a brigade and a division.[31]

Nonetheless, the general clearly chafed for more active service. On September 5, shortly after the last of McClellan's command departed from the Peninsula, Mansfield decided to write a private letter to Major General Halleck, who had recently been appointed commander of all Union field armies. He assured Halleck that Suffolk was strong enough that it could be held by "three green regiments" and proposed that he take the three veteran—though yet unbloodied—regiments there "up the Potomac to the Army of Virginia," which under the command of Maj. Gen. John Pope had just seen heavy fighting in the Second Manassas Campaign. "I am ready at all times myself," he declared, "to take any command you will think it to the interests of the country to give me, and believe I can do more than I can here." This contradicted reports from Dix that he could not afford to see troops leave his area on account of the danger of Confederate attacks against Suffolk, Yorktown, and other outposts. Evidently, though—no doubt due to the crisis at the capital brought about by Pope's defeat on August 30—Mansfield's offer proved more compelling than Dix's concerns. Shortly thereafter, Mansfield was called north, even though the field command he desired was not yet available.[32]

In the wake of the disaster at Second Manassas, Pope made unfavorable references to the conduct of Generals Franklin and Porter, two of McClellan's strongest supporters and the only two corps commanders in the Army of the Potomac he had actually chosen. Mansfield, as an officer senior to all the accused, soon found himself appointed to a court of inquiry to investigate charges against the two officers. The court first met on September 6 and then again on September 8 but came to no conclusions during those sessions. It was soon thereafter dissolved as a consequence of McClellan's request that Franklin and Porter join him in the field. Better yet for Mansfield, on the eighth orders directed him to report in person to McClellan, who was marching the Army of the Potomac out of Washington to deal with Confederate forces that had crossed the Potomac River into Maryland. It took some time, however, for the order to reach Mansfield. Finally, on September 11, he informed McClellan that he had just received the order and complained that Halleck was now insisting on telegraphing the army commander before he could start out to join him. Mansfield said the delay was not his fault and did not know the cause of it.[33]

September 8, 1862, was an eventful day for Mansfield. In addition to his work with the court of inquiry and the orders being issued for him to report to McClellan, he also met with Secretary of the Treasury Chase. Mansfield proposed to Chase that elements from his former command be brought up from Suffolk to bolster the Army of the Potomac, mostly troops constituting Brig. Gen. Max Weber's brigade. (This was soon done, and Weber's troops would be added to Brig. Gen. William B. French's division of the II Corps shortly before Antietam.) He also complained bitterly of his treatment by other officers and expressed his wish for active service. "I was a good deal affected by the manifest patriotism and desire to do something for his country manifested by the old General," Chase wrote afterward, "and could not help wishing he were younger, and thinking that, perhaps, after all, it would have been better to trust him."[34]

Because of the delay in informing him of his assignment, Mansfield did not depart Washington until McClellan's army was in Frederick, Maryland, on September 13. He hurried to the front and caught up with the army there and, to what could have only been to his great delight, received orders to assume command of the corps formerly commanded by Maj. Gen. Nathaniel Banks on September 15.[35]

McClellan had earlier ordered Banks to remain in Washington and take charge of the defenses of the city. Thus at that moment, the senior division commander of Banks's corps, originally designated the II Corps, Army of Virginia, was exercising command. This was Brig. Gen. Alpheus Williams, a capable leader but not a professionally trained soldier. Thus, as he reorganized the army on the march, McClellan had been seeking a new permanent leader for the corps. He initially ordered Maj. Gen. John Sedgwick from the II Corps to replace Banks. Sedgwick, however, objected to the order on the grounds that he wanted to stay with his division. Although no doubt disappointed at this response, McClellan promptly rescinded the order, giving Mansfield the opportunity for command.[36]

The general's excitement at his posting to the Army of the Potomac was tempered, though, with some trepidation. Before leaving Washington on September 13, he wrote to several people important in his life. Especially notable among these was Sylvanus Thayer, the great West Point superintendent who had done so much for the professionalization of the officer corps that shaped Mansfield's life and was still on duty with the Corps of Engineers, whom he told, "if I never see you again, I have not forgotten your inestimable favors to me." Among his actions upon assuming corps command was the appointment of his son, Lt. Samuel Mansfield, a recent West Point graduate, to his staff as chief engineer and aide-de-camp. "Fill your pockets with sandwiches," he jauntily wrote Samuel, "and follow me." That Mansfield had on his mind and reached out to both the "father of the military academy" and one of the school's newest graduates upon reaching what he must have recognized as probably the culmination of his long career—the assumption of a major field command—is certainly rich with symbolism.[37]

After receiving his formal appointment from McClellan, Mansfield made his way to Middletown, Maryland, on September 15, accompanied by an aide, Capt. Clarence Dyer of Connecticut, and an African American servant, and assumed command of the XII Corps, Army of the Potomac. He quickly located and took over from Williams, whose first impression was that the general was "a most veteran looking officer with head as white as snow."[38]

WHAT EXACTLY DID MANSFIELD inherit as the new corps commander? How might he expect the XII Corps to perform based on its condition, personnel, and temper? He did not have much time to find out. The history of Banks's former command offered little grounds for optimism. It had been organized in early 1862, given the mission of occupying and holding the lower Shenandoah Valley, and initially designated the V Corps, with two divisions. During the Valley Campaign of early 1862, Banks's men fought well at Kernstown on March 23, winning a tactical victory over Maj. Gen. Thomas J. "Stonewall" Jackson's troops. When Jackson outmaneuvered Banks in May, Williams's division fought well on May 25 to protect the rest of the corps. Nonetheless, the men enjoyed few successes and were subjected to the humiliation of having their commander derisively called "Commissary Banks" by Confederates because of the regularity with which they captured supplies from his command. Incorporated in late June into Pope's command and redesignated the II Corps, Army of Virginia, Banks's men had fought their last large engagement before Antietam at Cedar Mountain on August 9. There they fought well, delivering a blow so strong that Jackson was compelled at one point to personally rally his men. In the end, though, they were forced from the field, having suffered nearly 2,400 casualties. The corps also lost division commander Brig. Gen. Christopher C. Auger, who was replaced by Brig. Gen. George S. Greene, one of the few active field commanders who was older than Mansfield.[39]

The unit passed the Second Manassas Campaign guarding stores and thus marched into Maryland having not seen any significant action in nearly a month, with their reputation as losers still intact and their numbers severely depleted. Williams wrote of his old brigade in the aftermath of Second Manassas: "The three regiments are here yet in name, but instead of 3,000 men they number altogether less than 400 men present! Not a field officer or adjutant is here! Of 102 officers not over 20 are left to be present! Instead of hopeful and confident feelings we are all depressed with losses and disasters." He complained, "For over three weeks we have been scarcely a day without marching—for at least seven days without rations."[40] Williams later elaborated on the condition of the XII Corps in discussions with Ezra Carman, who commanded a regiment in his division and became the official historian of Antietam National Battlefield in 1894. "The three months campaign under Gen. Pope," he recounted, "especially the large loss of field and company commanders . . . followed by a month's marching, countermarching skirmishing and fighting from the Rapidan to the Potomac, without regular rations and without tents had left the command much demoralized and in want of everything for a new campaign."[41]

In addition, the XII Corps was the smallest corps in the Army of the Potomac and consisted of only two divisions. Although McClellan put its strength at Antietam as 10,126 men, Generals Williams and Greene would report much smaller numbers actually engaged. Williams put the number of men from his division at 4,735, while Greene's division engaged with only 2,504 soldiers, with only four batteries of artillery added; an aggregate number of 7,631 for the entire corps.[42]

FURTHER EXACERBATING PROBLEMS in the XII Corps was McClellan's decision to assign it five brand new regiments. Even though the corps would commit twenty-two regiments to battle on September 17, these five regiments of men who had only recently enlisted—the 124th, 125th, and 128th Pennsylvania; 13th New Jersey; and 107th New York—in fact constituted the *majority* of the troops Mansfield would lead onto the field at Antietam. In fact, while the addition of new units was a problem that plagued every command in the Army of the Potomac in September 1862 (one brigade that fought as part of the II Corps was composed entirely of new regiments), more were assigned to the XII Corps than to any other.[43]

Other serious problems beset Mansfield's new command. Both Mansfield and Williams were untried commanding a corps in battle, but they were not alone. Two other men untried in this position would take part in the battle at Antietam: Maj. Gen. Joseph Hooker (I Corps) and Brig. Gen. Jacob Cox (IX Corps). In addition, Greene had no experience commanding a division in battle, and the shuffling of command assignments later necessitated by Mansfield's wounding would lead to untried leaders at the brigade level too. So when Williams assumed command of the corps in battle, he had to work with two subordinates were new to division command. On the morning of September 17, Williams, with a division, and only two with brigades, Brig. Gen. Samuel Crawford and Col. George Gordon, had experience at their jobs. This was the command structure Mansfield inherited and would have to depend upon for success.[44] Amazingly, by the end of September 17, no brigade or division in the XII Corps would be under the command of the man who had charge of it at daybreak. Nonetheless, the fact that the corps had not been engaged at Second Manassas ensured that McClellan would include it among those he would lead into action in Maryland. Moreover, its problems were by no means unique among units in the Army of the Potomac.

Only three (Sumner, Porter, and Franklin) of the six corps commanders in McClellan's army had experience commanding a corps in battle. Only nine of the seventeen Union division commanders engaged at Antietam had previous experience at that level of command, while an astounding forty-four of sixty-two Union brigades were led by men new to that level of command. Nearly 19 percent of McClellan's soldiers at Antietam had been in the army two months or less. Of the 189 regiments in the Federal army, nearly 30 had never been in action at all. A few of these had been in the service for a year or more, stationed in quiet areas, but most were recently recruited. Not all soldiers exposed to combat for the first time performed poorly at Antietam, indeed, some performed quite well, such as the members of the 132d Pennsylvania. But number of new units did not do so well, perhaps the most famous of these being the 16th Connecticut, which broke and ran from the critical position it held at the Otto cornfield during the afternoon's fighting. This problem certainly hampered efficient service and was more critical on offensive operations than defensive. In all, though, it seems that these problems were higher proportionally in the XII Corps than in the army as a whole. Moreover, Mansfield's new command had not had the opportunity to participate in the morale-boosting victory at South Mountain on September 14.

MANSFIELD FORMALLY ASSUMED command of the XII Corps on the morning of September 15 near Turner's Gap, where the National Road crossed South Mountain between Middletown and Boonsboro. In a bitter fight the previous day, the Federals had wrested command of the gap from the Confederates and

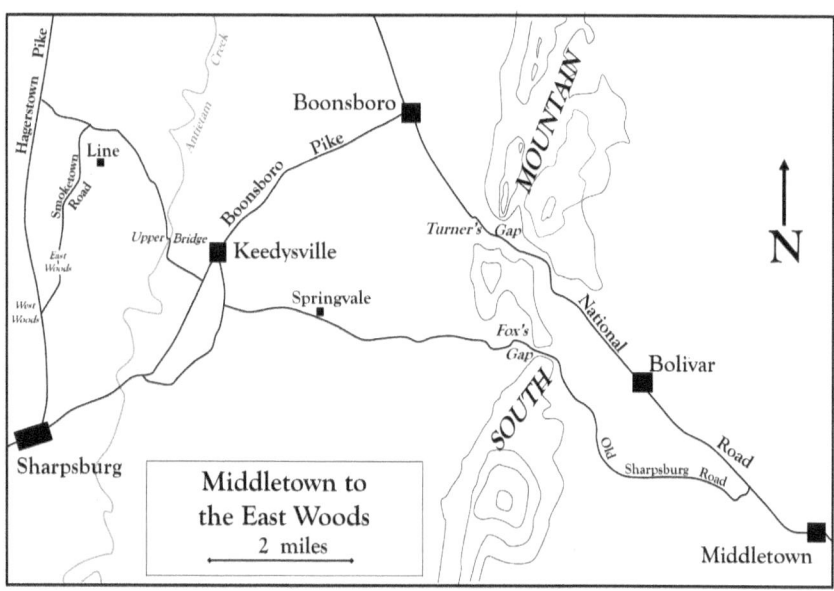

that morning were poised to push on to pursue the Army of Northern Virginia as it retreated toward Sharpsburg. After following Hooker's and Sumner's corps through the gap, Mansfield received orders to bivouac his men in an area called Springvale near Nicodemus Mill, which placed them about three miles from Turner's Gap. Williams spent the night of September 15–16 in the Nicodemus house and took up his pen to give his wife his impressions of the new corps commander. "[He] had a nervous temperament," wrote Williams, "and a very impatient manner." While marching the next day, Mansfield began the process of acquainting himself with his troops. A surgeon in the 107th New York, one of the new regiments, was struck by the scene of the general tending to a soldier overcome by the heat and recommending to the doctor to "bathe his head with water." While this incident shows a commendable compassion for his men, it might also be interpreted as the act of a new commander who has not yet developed the habit of refraining from tending to matters more properly delegated to subordinates.[45]

One reason Mansfield may have found himself delving into relatively minor issues is limited staff resources. One of the most critical first steps any successful commander must undertake is assembling an effective personal staff. Although the general had taken an important step in this regard by contacting his son Samuel and inviting him to join his staff, Lieutenant Mansfield had not arrived yet when his father took the field. Consequently, when General Mansfield rode out of Washington, he did so accompanied only by his assistant adjutant general, Clarence H. Dyer, and a cook. To assist his new subordinate, McClellan generously sent one of his own staff officers, Capt. James W. Forsyth, to XII Corps headquarters. Given the tremendous challenges Mansfield faced, though, a single aide was hardly adequate. Indeed, it is suggestive that not one of these three men were with Mansfield when he was shot.[46]

Before Mansfield arrived on the scene, McClellan had assigned the XII Corps to a two-corps wing commanded by Maj. Gen. Edwin V. Sumner. In the pursuit from Turner's Gap, a division from Sumner's II Corps commanded by Brig. Gen. Israel Richardson led the march from Turner's Gap to Boonsboro and then to the banks of Antietam Creek on September 15. Hooker's corps, which had belonged to the wing of the army commanded by Maj. Gen. Ambrose Burnside, followed, with the rest of Sumner's corps coming behind and Mansfield's command bringing up the rear. (Because his two corps were physically separated as a consequence of the fighting at South Mountain, McClellan issued orders suspending Burnside's wing command on September 15.) When Richardson's division reached the Antietam and found the Confederates in a strong position on the opposite side on Sharpsburg Heights, it deployed north of the road linking Boonsboro and Sharpsburg. Hooker then positioned his command to the right of Richardson, soon after joined by the rest of the II Corps. To the left of Richardson, Porter's V and Burnside's IX Corps took up positions south of the Boonsboro Pike. The XII Corps became the army's reserve.[47]

The following day Mansfield moved his command forward from Nicodemus Mill to a field just west of the small hamlet of Keedysville. Meanwhile, McClellan decided to send Hooker's corps across the Antietam, with an eye on having it operate against the Confederate left north of Sharpsburg. As Hooker crossed the creek, he appealed to McClellan for reinforcements. McClellan responded by ordering Sumner to send Mansfield in support, with the clear understanding that XII Corps thereafter would be subject to Hooker's orders. The army commander then also directed Sumner to have the II Corps ready to move to Hooker's assistance the next morning. McClellan would not commit Sumner and his corps to battle on September 17, though, until events warranted. There is little doubt that he much preferred to have management of Mansfield's command and affairs north of Sharpsburg generally in Hooker's hands rather than Sumner's, which undoubtedly contributed to his decision to wait before deciding how to use the II Corps.[48]

It was late in the evening of September 16 when orders reached Mansfield to take his corps across the Antietam and assist Hooker. Marching at night (and a rainy one too, making the move all the more difficult), the corps crossed Antietam Creek at the Upper (Hitt) Bridge and followed the path of Hooker's troops to the Smoketown Road, which it reached about a mile north of I Corps's position. Williams told his wife that Mansfield was in the lead during the march and that he had trouble keeping up with the old general on rough roads in darkness. The men finally bivouacked on the farm of George Line, lying down fully dressed and sleeping in the light rainfall. Williams reported the time they reached this site as being near 2:00 A.M. Lt. John Gould later recalled that Mansfield slept under a blanket, while Williams complained that his commander kept waking him throughout the night with new directions. Williams also recalled the new regiments were very difficult to direct as they "knew absolutely nothing of maneuvering."[49]

As random picket firing sparked through the night, all realized there would be heavy fighting in the morning. Yet there is no evidence of Hooker making any effort to contact Mansfield directly to discuss what the plan for the next day might be, probably because poor visibility made gathering intelligence about the terrain and the disposition of the enemy extremely difficult and any certain planning before morning unwise. Nor is there evidence of Mansfield making contact with Hooker in order to get instructions. Nonetheless, it seems fairly clear that Hooker clearly understood the older man was subordinate to his orders, as he later reported, "Mansfield's corps, at my request, had been sent to my support, and as soon as all my reserves were engaged I ordered him forward."[50]

When the fighting began early on September 17, however, Hooker appears to have been so focused on the heavy and somewhat confusing engagement his own three divisions found themselves fighting that he was unable or unwilling to give much thought to what directions Mansfield might require once he did arrive on the field. As a consequence, the troubled XII Corps would arrive on the field with its new commander having only the vaguest directions as to what would be expected of him and little sense about the overall plan of battle. Nor is there evidence of anyone seeing fit to provide the general with specific information about the terrain or enemy dispositions once he arrived on the field. All these factors, not surprisingly, led to a very problematic situation that morning.[51]

The opening cannonade at dawn prompted Mansfield to put his troops under arms. Having neither undressed nor stacked arms, the men had slept in the formation of column by companies. Upon receiving orders to move to the field, Mansfield directed his command to march by divisions, brigades, and regiments, with no intermixing or straggling permitted and a rear guard well posted to enforce his orders. He called for the artillery to be placed in the column as he designated, and the ammunition wagons, ambulances, baggage, and commissary trains to follow in that order. (Again, these are the sorts of details that would usually be delegated to staff, but in light of the limited assets Mansfield had in this regard, it is not surprising that he felt compelled to deal with these matters personally.) Once satisfied that all of this was in order, the general then proceeded to ride ahead of his command to view the fighting, halting his horse at the break between the North and East Woods.[52]

Behind him, the men of the XII Corps, with Williams's division in the lead, marched south along the Smoketown Road toward the firing in a column-by-division formation. This placed the two center companies of each regiment side by side in front, with the other eight companies paired behind them to make a column two companies wide and five ranks deep. The advance was "slow and tedious," according to Williams, with frequent halts ordered by Mansfield, no doubt to ensure to the maximum extent possible that he had his command tightly in hand. Williams argued for the regiments to deploy into wide lines of battle, which would have further slowed the march but presented less of a target for Confederate artillery and enabled the men to engage the enemy more effectively. Mansfield denied the request, though, and when Crawford, the lead brigade's commander, began deploying without orders, he reformed them to column by divisions.[53]

Although his death precluded his providing an explanation for why he managed his command in this way, the motives behind Mansfield's thinking are not hard to discern. In addition to the normal impulse to try to exercise as tight a control over one's command that any officer tasked with leading men on a Civil War battlefield possessed—which was invariably greater in their first engagement—there was the fact that Mansfield was making his debut as a battle commander at the level of corps command, at or near what may well have been the worst part of the worst battlefield of the entire war, with a large percentage of green troops, and doing all of this over broken, wooded terrain. Moreover, the general carried with him decades of service in the Regular Army, which while not without its benefits, also no doubt had the effect of accustoming him to insisting on high standards of order and discipline in the handling of troops as well as skepticism that these could be met by volunteer troops, especially green ones, without close supervision.[54]

As his men began to reach the field that morning, Mansfield received orders from Hooker to form Crawford's brigade and move three green regiments to the west so they could take up a position with the Hagerstown Pike on its right and form a line behind the elements of Hooker's badly battered I Corps that were on that part of the field. Other units from Williams's division, meanwhile, received directions to move to the left. Williams complied, placing a new regiment, the 124th Pennsylvania, on the right, soon followed by the 125th Pennsylvania. Mansfield led the 128th Pennsylvania and three veteran regiments forward, planning to form them on the left of the previous two. There was a general perception that I Corps was on the verge of giving way due to the arrival of Confederate reinforcements on that section of the field, and XII Corps was there to bolster them.[55]

Evidently, Mansfield quickly became dissatisfied with the performance of the new regiments, and indeed several accounts describe disorganization being rampant. Not long after this deployment took place, Michael J. Hawley, a corporal in the 46th Pennsylvania, recalled hearing a frustrated Mansfield direct Williams to "bring up your old troops and take back these Pennsylvania cattle!"[56] It was around this time that one of Williams's veteran regiments, the 10th Maine, was moving south along the Smoketown Road and began receiving fire from Confederates in the southern end of the East Woods. Without orders, the regiment deployed into line and, using a fence line for cover, opened fire against their adversaries. Mansfield, from a position to their right and rear, heard the firing and decided to ride in front of the regiment and order them to cease fire, believing they were firing into other Union troops. The general was not alone in this misperception, for there is evidence that this was the impression held by several other officers then on the scene, and thus it is understandable that Mansfield ordered the Maine men to cease firing. It was at this time that he was shot in the chest and carried to the rear with a punctured lung. He was then put in an ambulance and taken to the Line Farm, where he had slept the previous night.[57]

Mansfield remained lucid through much of the day and was attended initially by Surgeon Patrick H. Flood of the 107th New York, who remembered the general saying, "For God's sake do all you can for me and stop the bleeding." Captain Dyer joined his commander and reported him conversing freely through the twenty-four hours he lived after his wounding, although "under the influence of opiates." The staff officer also recalled the presence of other surgeons in attendance and that, as Mansfield weakened, he became less coherent. On the morning of September 18, a surgeon told the general that he could not live. Mansfield replied, "It is God's will, it is all right." He died a few minutes after 8:00 A.M. His body was taken thereafter to his home in Middletown, Connecticut. There a large memorial service was held, with many touching eulogies delivered, including one by Gov. William A. Buckingham. Rev. Jeremiah Taylor, in summing up Mansfield's life, described his extensive record of service to the country over the years and predicted, "His name will go down in the coming ages of our national history, commemorated with Wolfe, Williams, and Warren, who fell in the earlier struggles of our national liberty, and with Lyon, Reno, and Kearney, and a host of others whose bones lie beside our country's alter today."[58]

Thomas G. Clemens

OBVIOUSLY, HISTORY HAS NOT followed Taylor's lead in how it has remembered Joseph K. F. Mansfield; indeed, it has been perhaps a bit unjust. Mansfield's potential as a corps commander remained unproven. His command of troops for the brief time he exercised it did not show any great brilliance or daring, but under the circumstances, it is difficult to find much to censure. He had serious—and eminently justifiable—reservations concerning the efficacy of the new troops in his command, which was reflected in his decision to keep them in massed formations because they were the easiest way for raw recruits to maneuver. Given the reservations expressed by General Williams regarding their ability, this may indeed have been the best method for advancing the green troops with celerity on September 17. Mansfield's mistake about the identity of the enemy and his orders to cease fire were by no means unreasonable given the situation and his instructions from Hooker to bolster the I Corps as it prepared to fall back through his line. Lacking detailed information from anyone regarding the situation or adequate staff to which to delegate such responsibilities, Mansfield properly took it on himself to ride ahead of his command to do his own reconnaissance and survey the situation before committing his troops to battle. In the short time after he left his point of observation north of the East Woods, the situation in the southern end of the woods changed dramatically, though this was not immediately perceptible. Elements from Brig. Gen. John Bell Hood's Division of Confederates charged into the East Woods and opened fire on the 10th Maine, to which they responded before Mansfield approached. His understanding of the situation did not include these new developments, thus his confusion was eminently understandable.[59]

After Mansfield's wounding, the XII Corps fought well at Sharpsburg. After the general was hit, Williams once again took command of the corps, and Crawford assumed command of his division, which helped restore a deteriorating situation in the Miller Cornfield. For his part, Greene led his small division down the Smoketown Road and, after clearing the Cornfield of Confederates, managed to achieve a temporary lodgment in the West Woods. Crawford at this time not only exerted pressure on the Confederates at the Miller Cornfield, which facilitated Greene's advance, but also helped repulse several enemy advances. The arrival of Sumner's II Corps on the field around 9:00 A.M. allowed Williams's men some respite, but elements from some XII Corps regiments would be actively engaged the rest of the day, performing much better than Mansfield or anyone else had any reasonable right to expect, given the units' many problems. Although the men fell back a couple times, they never did so in panic.

After the battle, Williams wrote a message to Sumner, who upon personally reaching the field assumed command as the senior officer in the north part of the Union line. In Williams's words, he warned that his corps was "greatly broken, its loss has been great, but its [illegible] mainly owing to the fact that more than half its numbers are of *new regiments*, that have [illegible] but will come together in a day or so—the old regiments were very small—many not over 100 men strong—I find collected this evening in Crawford's Brigade about 500 men, in Gordon's Brigade about 350. In Greene's Division not over 500."[60]

Understrength, with new commanders, and laboring under shortfalls in supplies, equipment, and morale, the XII Corps fought and sustained huge casualties at Antietam, yet for the most part the men held their ground. Like much of McClellan's army, they were not entirely fit for offensive operations but did their part nevertheless, suffering severely in terms of casualties. Of the roughly 7,500 men committed to the battle, the XII Corps suffered 1,746 casualties, roughly 23 percent of those engaged. Their loss of leadership was heavy. Not only was Mansfield mortally wounded, so was Col. William B. Goodrich, commander of a brigade in Greene's division. Col. Hector Tyndale, commander of another of Greene's brigades, and Brigadier General Crawford, elevated to division command, were also wounded.[61]

The leadership and combat-experience problems in the XII Corps existed before Mansfield arrived and were not ones that could be remedied in a mere two days amid an active campaign that would produce the bloodiest day of battle in American military history. The difficulties experienced by the corps were in this regard reflective of problems throughout the Army of the Potomac in Maryland. While McClellan may have possessed numerical superiority over the Confederates, a lack of experience in the ranks and turmoil in the leadership, issues that contrasted sharply with Lee's army, mitigated a great deal of that advantage. When the dying Mansfield was informed of Hooker's wounding, he uttered a phrase that undoubtedly passed through many a mind in the hastily organized Army of the Potomac at Antietam, "Too bad, too bad, poor fellows, poor fellows!"[62] Like many men in that army in September 1862, Mansfield no doubt went to his death believing that, for his service and dedication to duty in the uniform of the Republic, he merited better circumstances in which to show what he could do and better treatment during the first year and a half of the Civil War from the government under whose flag he served.

NOTES

1. Statement of John M. Gould, Dec. 2, 1862, Middlesex County Historical Society, Middletown, Conn. (hereafter cited as MCHS), copy in the Mansfield Files, Antietam National Battlefield Library, Sharpsburg, Md.

2. See John M. Priest, *Antietam: The Soldier's Battle* (Shippensburg, Pa.: White Mane, 1989); Stephen W. Sears, *Landscape Turned Red: The Battle of Antietam* (New York: Ticknor and Fields, 1983); James M. McPherson *Crossroads of Freedom: Antietam, the Battle That Changed the Course of the Civil War* (New York: Oxford University Press, 2002); and Francis W. Palfrey, *The Antietam and Fredericksburg* (New York: Charles Scribner's Sons, 1882). Also see Frederick Tilberg, *Antietam* (Washington, D.C.: National Park Service, 1960), which also only mentions the general's death.

3. "Joseph K. F. Mansfield," in *Heroes and Martyrs: Notable Men of the Time: Biographical Sketches of the Military and Naval Heroes, Statesmen, and Orators Distinguished in the American Crisis of 1861–62*, ed. Frank Moore (New York: G. P. Putnam, 1862) 135–38; Jeremiah Taylor, comp., *Memorial of Gen. J. K. F. Mansfield, United States Army, Who Fell in Battle at Sharpsburg, Md., Sept. 17, 1862* (Boston: T. R. Marvin and Son, 1862), 28, 39–40, 66; Mansfield Memorial, Sept. 25, 1862, MCHS; Francis Heitman, *Historical Register and Dictionary of the United States Army from Its Organization September 29, 1789, to March 2, 1903* (Washington, D.C.: Government Printing Office, 1903), 688; letters of Jared Mansfield, West Point Application Files, Adjutant General's Office, RG 92, National Archives and Records Administration, Washington, D.C. (hereafter cited as NARA). A profile of Mansfield's life and military career can also be found in "Joseph K. F. Mansfield," U.S. Mexican War: The Zachary Taylor Campsite in Corpus Christi, 1845–1846, Corpus Christi Public Libraries, http://www.cclibraries.com/local_history../MexicanWar/mansfieldjkf.htm (accessed July 24, 2009) (hereafter cited as "Joseph K. F. Mansfield," CCPL).

4. Sidney Forman, *West Point: A History of the United States Military Academy* (New York: Columbia University Press, 1950), 38–45; James L. Morrison Jr., *The Best School in the World: West Point, the Pre–Civil War Years, 1833–66* (Kent, Ohio: Kent State University Press, 1986), 3–5.

5. The best study of the antebellum army and its professionalization is William B. Skelton, *An American Profession of Arms: The Army Officer Corps, 1784–1861* (Lawrence: University Press of Kansas, 1992).

6. "Joseph K. F. Mansfield," CCPL; Emory M. Thomas, *Robert E. Lee: A Biography* (New York: W. W. Norton, 1996), 57–63.

7. "Joseph K. F. Mansfield," CCPL; "Joseph K. F. Mansfield," in *Heroes and Martyrs*, 135–36; Mansfield Memorial; Heitman, *Historical Register and Dictionary*, 688; Mansfield family tombstones, Indian Hills Cemetery, Middletown, Conn.

8. General Taylor's report, May 3, 1864, cited in Edward D. Mansfield, *The Mexican War: A History of Its Origin, and a Detailed Account of the Victories which Terminated in the Surrender of the*

Capital; with the Official Despatches of the Generals (New York: A. S. Barnes, 1849), 34; Heitman, *Historical Register and Dictionary*, 688; "Joseph K. F. Mansfield," in Moore, *Heroes and Martyrs*, 136–37; Oliver Otis Howard, *General Taylor* (New York: D. Appleton, 1892), 158; John S. D. Eisenhower, *So Far from God: The U.S. War with Mexico, 1846–1848* (New York: Random House, 1989), 127–43. Edward Mansfield, Joseph's cousin, graduated fourth in the West Point class of 1818 but refused a commission and became a noted historian and author. After Joseph's death he composed an obituary for the *Cincinnati Gazette* that was republished in Taylor, *Memorial of Gen. J. K. F. Mansfield*, 65–67. "For self-possession and cool courage," one early account of Buena Vista declared, "Major Mansfield ... was unequaled on the field." H. Montgomery, *The Life of Major General Zachary Taylor, Twelfth President of the United States* (1847; Auburn, Ala.: Derby, Miller, 1850), 274. This assessment of Mansfield's performance is echoed in the most recent account of Taylor's operations in Mexico, which offers an unflattering portrait of Mansfield's personality but lauds his performance of his duties, declaring him "indisputably effective under Taylor as an engineer, and exceptionally brave under fire." Felice Flanery Lewis, *Trailing Clouds of Glory: Zachary Taylor's Mexican War Campaign and His Emerging Civil War Leaders* (Tuscaloosa: University of Alabama Press, 2010), 56–57, 142–46, 198.

9. McClellan to his mother, Feb. 4, 5, 1847, in *The Mexican War Diary and Correspondence of George B. McClellan*, ed. Thomas W. Cutrer (Baton Rouge: Louisiana State University Press, 2009), 67; "Joseph K. F. Mansfield," CCPL; Richard M. Breithaupt Jr., *Aztec Club of 1847, Military Society of the Mexican War, Sesquicentennial History, 1847–1997* (Los Angeles: Published under the Auspices of the Society, 1998), 1282. The Aztec Club was organized by Regular Army officers who served in Mexico, further hinting at the creation of a corporate mentality among them, one of political scientist Samuel Huntington's characteristics of a profession. Huntington, *The Soldier and the State: The Theory and Politics of Civil-Military Relations* (Cambridge, Mass.: Harvard University Press, 1957), 10, 16–18.

10. The tensions between regulars and volunteers are effectively documented in Richard Bruce Winders, *Mr. Polk's Army: The American Military Experience in the Mexican War* (College Station: Texas A&M Press, 1997), 51–65, 72–87, 196–200.

11. "Joseph K. F. Mansfield," CCPL; "Joseph K. F. Mansfield," in Moore, *Heroes and Martyrs*, 135–36.

12. Heitman, *Historical Register and Dictionary*, 688; David A. Clary and Joseph W. A. Whitehorne, *The Inspectors General of the United States Army, 1777–1903* (Washington, D.C.: Office of the Inspector General and Center for Military History, 1987), 191; William J. Cooper Jr., *Jefferson Davis: American* (New York: Knopf, 2000), 133–56, 244–60.

13. The feud between Davis and Scott is well chronicled in Allan Peskin, *Winfield Scott and the Profession of Arms* (Kent, Ohio: Kent State University Press, 2003), 218–24; and Cooper, *Jefferson Davis*, 252–54.

14. Joseph K. F. Mansfield, *Mansfield on the Condition of Western Forts, 1853–54*, ed. Robert W. Frazer (Norman: University of Oklahoma Press, 1963), 69.

15. Ibid., 185–86, 198–219.

16. Jerry Thompson, *Texas & New Mexico on the Eve of the Civil War: The Mansfield & Johnston Inspections, 1859–1861* (Albuquerque: University of New Mexico Press, 2001), 5, 169–79; E. B. Long,

with Barbara Long, *The Civil War Day by Day: An Almanac, 1861–1865* (Garden City, N.Y.: Doubleday, 1971), 31.

17. Thompson, *Texas & New Mexico on the Eve of the Civil War*, 182; Long, *Civil War Day by Day*, 38.

18. U.S. War Department, *The War of the Rebellion: A Compilation of the Official Records of the Union and Confederate Armies*, 70 vols. in 128 parts (Washington, D.C.: Government Printing Office, 1880–1901), 2:607 (hereafter cited as *OR;* all references are to series 1 unless otherwise noted).

19. Ibid., 618–19.

20. Adjutant's General Office, *Official Army Register for 1862* (Washington, D.C.: Government Printing Office, 1862), 3; John H. Eicher and David J. Eicher, *Civil War High Commands* (Stanford, Calif.: Stanford University Press, 2001), 363; "Joseph K. F. Mansfield," CCPL. Preceding Mansfield in seniority were John E. Wool, William S. Harney, and Edwin Sumner. His command in Washington at the brevet rank was established in Adjutant General's Office, Special Order No. 126, May 6, 1861. His transfer from Washington to Camp Hamilton near Fort Monroe in October was directed in General Order No. 25, Oct. 2, 1861, Head Quarters Department of Virginia. He assumed the command on October 15. Joseph Mansfield, Compiled Military Service Record, NARA. A presidential memorandum titled "Appointments of Major Generals," dated on or about May 14, 1861, initially listed Mansfield, along with McClellan, for promotion to major general. Mansfield's name was then crossed out. Abraham Lincoln, *The Collected Works of Abraham Lincoln*, ed. Roy P. Basler, 9 vols. (New Brunswick, N.J.: Rutgers University Press, 1953–55), 4:370.

21. *OR*, 2:41–42.

22. *Official Army Register for 1862*, 3; Ezra Warner, *Generals in Blue: Lives of the Union Commanders* (1964; Baton Rouge: Louisiana State University, 1984), 298.

23. Comparisons are made from Heitman, *Historical Register and Dictionary*. For example, see Keyes to Marcy, Apr. 9, 1862, *OR*, 11(3):85. Even a subordinate and critic who described Mansfield as nervous and impatient proclaimed him an "an officer of acknowledged gallantry." Alpheus S. Williams, *From the Cannon's Mouth: The Civil War Letters of General Alpheus S. Williams*, ed. Milo M. Quaife (Detroit: Wayne State University Press and Detroit Historical Society, 1959), 125.

24. *OR*, 4:566, 595, 626–27; McClellan to his wife, July 27, 1861, in *The Civil War Papers of George B. McClellan: Selected Correspondence, 1860–1865*, ed. Stephen W. Sears (New York: Ticknor and Fields, 1989), 70; Mansfield to Louisa Mansfield, Jan. 24, 1862, Mansfield Papers, MCHS (Mansfield added in this same letter that McClellan was "conceited" and "likely to burst from self esteem"); Margaret Leech, *Reveille in Washington, 1861–1865* (1941; New York: Carroll and Graf, 1991), 200; Mansfield, Compiled Military Service Record. In his memoirs McClellan recalled being appointed to a command that consisted of "the Department of Northeast Virginia, under McDowell . . . and the Department of Washington, under Mansfield. . . . Neither of these officers seemed pleased with the new arrangement, more particularly Mansfield." George B. McClellan, *McClellan's Own Story: The War for the Union, the Soldiers Who Fought It, the Civilians Who Directed It, and His Relations to It and to Them*, ed. William C. Prime (New York: Charles L. Webster, 1887), 67. Mansfield was initially ordered to the Department of the Pacific, but the order was changed, sending him to report to General Wool at Fort Monroe. *OR*, 50(1):645.

25. *OR*, 4:566, 595, 625–27, Mansfield, Compiled Military Service Record.

26. Mansfield's report, Mar. 10, 1862, *OR*, 9:4. Mansfield's brigade as of January 31, 1862, was the 20th Massachusetts and the 1st, 2d, 7th, and 11th New York Regiments. Ibid., 15. By what authority he was issuing orders to other regiments, as his report indicates he did during this time, is unclear. Mansfield also demonstrated a willingness to cozy up to influential politicians by letting them know that his sympathies rested with them on the slavery issue. In early 1862 he wrote to Sen. Zachariah Chandler, a leading antislavery Republican and one of the most influential members of the powerful Joint Committee on the Conduct of the War, declaring: "Now is the time to clear the army of all poor Brigadier Generals. . . . In the first place no appointment should be confirmed where a fugitive slave has been sent into the enemies [lines] by order of our officers. When I was in command and in Washington I would never suffer it. . . . I am in favor of abolishing slavery in the District but just . . . a little delay here would be politic." Mansfield to Chandler, Jan. 21, 1862, Zachariah Chandler Papers, Manuscript Division, Library of Congress, Washington, D.C.

27. McClellan to Stanton, Mar. 14, 1862, *OR*, 5:755.

28. Ethan S. Rafuse, *McClellan's War: The Failure of Moderation in the Struggle for the Union* (Bloomington: Indiana University Press, 2005), 191–92.

29. The problems with Wool, McClellan, and the issue of seniority in command appointments are discussed in Russel H. Beatie, *Army of the Potomac: McClellan's First Campaign, March–May 1862* (New York: Savas Beatie, 2007), 193–268.

30. Mansfield to Wool, Apr. 24, 1862, Mansfield Papers, U.S. Military Academy, West Point, N.Y.; Wool's report, *OR*, 11(1):634.

31. Joseph B. Carr, "Operations of 1861 about Fort Monroe," in *Battles and Leaders of the Civil War*, ed. Robert U. Johnson and Clarence C. Buel, 4 vols. (New York: Century, 1887–88), 2:152; Eicher and Eicher, *Civil War High Commands*, 363; Frederick H. Dyer, *A Compendium of the War of the Rebellion Compiled and Arranged from Official Records of the Federal and Confederate Armies, Reports of the Adjutant Generals of the Several States, the Army Registers, and Other Reliable Documents and Sources* (Des Moines, Iowa: Dyer, 1908), 330–31. A report on troops in the Department of Virginia on August 31, 1862, shows Mansfield commanding at Suffolk, with Brig. Gen. Max Weber's brigade of five infantry regiments, two regiments of cavalry, and one battery of artillery under his authority. This hardly constituted a division in the usual sense of the word. *OR*, 18:377.

32. *OR*, 18:385–86.

33. Lt. Col. Richard B. Irwin, "The Case of Fitz John Porter," *Battles and Leaders*, 2:696–97; *OR*, 18:387. The order was issued after Mansfield had departed Suffolk on September 5 for duty on the court. Ibid., 4:496.

34. Salmon P. Chase, *Inside Lincoln's Cabinet: The Civil War Diaries of Salmon P. Chase*, ed. David Donald (New York: Longmans, Green, 1954), 125–27; George B. McClellan (Sr.) Papers, Reel 31, doc. 16020, Manuscript Division, Library of Congress, Washington, D.C.

35. A special order dated September 15 assigned him to the XII Corps. *OR*, 19(2):297.

36. Headquarters, Defenses of Washington, General Order No. 1, Sept. 8, 1862, *OR*, 19(2):214; John Gibbon, *Personal Recollections of the Civil War* (New York: G. P. Putnam and Sons, 1928), 72–73; *OR*, 19(2):283. For a good discussion of Williams and the operations of the XII Corps in Mary-

land prior to Mansfield's arrival, see Ezra Carman, *The Maryland Campaign of September 1862*, 2 vols., ed. Thomas G. Clemens (El Dorado Hills, Calif.: Savas Beatie, 2010–12), 1:150, 160–62, 168–71, 175, 179, 188, 197, 279–80, 288–90, 368, 370–71, 403–4, 411.

37. Mansfield to Sylvanus Thayer, Sept. 11, 1862, Mansfield Papers, MCHS; Mansfield to Samuel Mansfield, Sept. 12, 1862, ibid. Mansfield also encountered Gideon Welles, secretary of the navy and a fellow Connecticut native, during this time. He later recalled the general saying, "We may never meet again." Gideon Welles, *Diary of Gideon Welles: Secretary of the Navy under Lincoln and Johnson*, ed. Howard K. Beale, 3 vols. (New York: W. W. Norton, 1960), 1:140.

38. Capt. Clarence Dyer, "General Mansfield's Last Hours," Oct. 10, 1862, Mansfield Files, Antietam National Battlefield, Sharpsburg, Md.; Williams, *From the Cannon's Mouth*, 123.

39. Mark Mayo Boatner III, *Civil War Dictionary* (New York: David McKay, 1959), 456–67, 936–97, 102; Carman, *Maryland Campaign*, 2:112–13. Further details on the operations of Banks's command in the spring and summer of 1862 can be found in Peter Cozzens, *Shenandoah 1862: Stonewall Jackson's Valley Campaign* (Chapel Hill: University of North Carolina Press, 2008); and Robert K. Krick, *Stonewall Jackson at Cedar Mountain* (Chapel Hill: University of North Carolina Press, 1990).

40. Williams, *From the Cannon's Mouth*, 111, 119.

41. "From Gen. A. S. Williams Mss," in Ezra Carman's handwriting, Ezra Carman Papers, Manuscript Division, New York Public Library, New York.

42. *OR*, 19(1):67; Carman, *Maryland Campaign*, 2:583–84.

43. D. Scott Hartwig, "Who Would Not Be a Soldier? The Volunteers of 1862 in the Maryland Campaign," in *The Antietam Campaign*, ed. Gary W. Gallagher (Chapel Hill: University of North Carolina, 1999), 164. This statement excludes Brig. Gen. Andrew Humphreys's division of the V Corps, which was almost completely new troops, but only arrived after the battle.

44. *OR*, 19(1):474–78, 504.

45. Williams, *From the Cannon's Mouth*, 125; P. H. Flood, surgeon, 107th New York Volunteer Infantry, to Mrs. Mansfield, Apr. 18, 1863, Mansfield File, Antietam National Battlefield Library, typescript.

46. Clarence H. Dyer to John M. Gould, July 29, 1891, Antietam Collection, Dartmouth College, Hanover, N.H.; James W. Forsyth to "My dear Sir," Sept. 23, 1876, ibid.

47. *OR*, 19(2):297.

48. Carman, *Maryland Campaign*, 2:24, 27–30, 43. For a more positive take on Sumner and his conduct during the Maryland Campaign, see Marion V. Armstrong Jr., *Unfurl Those Colors! McClellan, Sumner, & the Second Army Corps in the Antietam Campaign* (Tuscaloosa: University of Alabama Press, 2008).

49. McClellan's report, *OR*, 19(1):5–6; Hooker's report, ibid., 217–18; Williams's report, ibid., 475; Crawford's report, ibid., 484; Williams, *From the Cannon's Mouth*, 124–25; John M. Gould, *Joseph K. Mansfield Brigadier General of the U.S. Army, a Narrative of the Events Connected with His Mortal Wounding at Antietam, September 17, 1862* (Portland, Maine: S. Berry, 1895; repr., Civil War Library, Austin, Tex., 2000), 5–6.

50. Hooker's testimony, Mar. 11, 1863, in U.S. Congress, *Report of the Joint Committee on the Conduct of the War*, 3 vols. (Washington, D.C.: Government Printing Office, 1863), 1:581. The ques-

tion of why Hooker did not wait for Mansfield's arrival before making his attack has recently been addressed by Ethan S. Rafuse, who surmises that when the I Corps commander "decided to attack, the battle had already begun in the East Woods and there was no point in letting this go on in isolation.... Hooker probably anticipated that Mansfield's command would arrive on the field at a point in time when the results of the I Corps's attacks were evident, and intended to let the situation at that point determine how he would employ the XII Corps." Rafuse, *Antietam, South Mountain, and Harpers Ferry: A Battlefield Guide* (Lincoln: University of Nebraska Press, 2008), 34.

51. That Mansfield, and indeed the Union cause in general, might have been better served at Antietam by Hooker leaving minor tactical details to his subordinates so he could focus his attention on the overall situation is a possibility that seems to have eluded the otherwise perceptive Ezra Carman, who wrote approvingly of Hooker's being "exceedingly active that morning, giving personal direction to the movement of every regiment, brigade, and division, and the positioning of every battery, and at all times was at the extreme front under fire.... He was everywhere present and everywhere his presence was an inspiration." *Maryland Campaign*, 2:97–98, 112.

52. Williams, *From the Cannon's Mouth*, 125; [Alpheus S. Williams], "Battle of Antietam," n.d., unsigned typescript, Carman Papers; Carman, *Maryland Campaign*, 2:113.

53. Williams, *From the Cannon's Mouth*, 125; [Williams], "Battle of Antietam."

54. Carman, *Maryland Campaign*, 2:112.

55. [Williams], "Battle of Antietam"; Carman, *Maryland Campaign*, 2:115–17.

56. Michael J. Hawley to Maj. John M. Gould, Jan. 24, 1892, John M. Gould Collection, Dartmouth College, Hanover, N.H.

57. Gould, *Joseph K. Mansfield*, 8, 10–11; Dyer, "General Mansfield's Last Hours." A huge dispute erupted in the postwar years about where Mansfield was shot, by whom, and which soldiers helped him to the ambulance. Gould of the 10th Maine spent from 1891 to 1894 researching the issue. Many soldiers of the 125th Pennsylvania wrote, insisting it was their regiment that witnessed his wounding and carried him from the field. Carman devotes two pages of his study to this issue. Suffice it to say, although Mansfield's death is the most well-known aspect of his life, it is tangential to this discussion, and the author is wary of dissecting a dispute so hotly contested by so many eyewitnesses. Carman, *Maryland Campaign*, 2:166–67.

58. *Memorial of Genl. J. K. F. Mansfield*, 57.

59. Gould, *Joseph K. Mansfield*, 16–17; [Williams], "Battle of Antietam."

60. Alpheus Williams to Edwin Sumner, Sept. 17, 1862, RG 393, pt. 4, entry 45, NARA.

61. *OR*, 19(1):198–99.

62. Dyer, "General Mansfield's Last Hours."

An "Acting Major General"
Charles Champion Gilbert at Perryville

KENNETH W. NOE

On September 29, 1862, a general in the U.S. Army shot another to death in the lobby of the finest hotel in Louisville, Kentucky. The assailant was Brig. Gen. Jefferson C. Davis, an Indianan who believed that the victim, Maj. Gen. William C. Nelson, had called his fellow Hoosiers cowardly, backwoods trash. Nicknamed "Bull" for his massive frame, booming voice, and aggressive personality, Nelson was a former naval officer and family friend of Abraham Lincoln's as well as one of the president's point men in their native Kentucky during the long, tense summer of neutrality in 1861. He fought at Shiloh as a division commander in Maj. Gen. Don Carlos Buell's Army of the Ohio and most recently had arrived in time to command the ill-fated Army of Kentucky during the latter stages of its crushing defeat at Richmond, Kentucky. It was there that Nelson allegedly first insulted Indiana soldiers and, according to wild (and erroneous) camp gossip, even beheaded one or two. When Davis arrived in Louisville after the battle, the two men clashed almost immediately. Egged on by associates that notably included Indiana governor Oliver Morton, the feud festered until it finally ended in gunfire.[1]

Nelson's murder proved to be only the latest blow in 1862 to what was becoming a cancerous command structure in Buell's troubled army. After Shiloh and the fall of Corinth, Maj. Gen. Henry W. Halleck had sent Buell and his army eastward across the northern counties of Alabama with the mission of taking the vital railroad junctions near Chattanooga, Tennessee. He marched reluctantly at best, convinced that Halleck's operational vision was flawed and that it made more sense instead to advance via the more developed logistical base at Nashville. When a severe drought caused water levels to drop in the Tennessee River, Buell turned to regional railroads for supplies, only to see those lines cut repeatedly by Confederate cavalry. By the time the dusty advance ground to a halt southwest of the city in July 1862, the general faced the additional problem of Confederate reinforcements arriving ahead of him. These belonged to Gen. Braxton Bragg's Army of the Mississippi, which had ridden the rails from Tupelo to Chattanooga by way of Mobile and Atlanta. Enough was enough. When Bragg began to push troops north across the Tennessee River, Buell assumed that a major Confederate advance against Nashville was underway. Immediately, and prematurely as it turned out, he fell back to that city, rejecting advice from Maj. Gen. George Thomas and others to choose a position where he could stand and fight.

When Bragg bypassed Nashville and angled instead toward Kentucky, Buell again decided to retreat. Nashville was only the southern junction of a supply line that ran along the Louisville and Nashville Railroad back to the Ohio River. Accordingly, Buell decided to march to Louisville. Hungry, thirsty, embarrassed, and angry, his men staggered northward. Already convinced that their general was too soft on Southerners, many now concluded that he was a traitor as well, one who not only refused to fight when given the opportunity but also, according to camp gossip, snuggled up under a blanket every night with Bragg. On September 25, when the first units entered Louisville, the soldiers could not help but express pride in their stamina and sacrifice. After all, they believed, that they had beaten Bragg in the "great foot race" to Louisville. Still, the army continued to seethe with hatred toward its commanding officer and his favorites. Small wonder that they almost universally rejoiced when news arrived that Davis had killed Nelson, one of Buell's truly loyal subordinates.[2]

On September 29, the day Nelson died, Buell faced additional problems. At a recent public dinner, several officers and Louisville worthies had made toasts that endorsed Maj. Gen. Alexander McDowell McCook of Ohio as Buell's replacement. McCook, who had served under Buell for months, did little to dissuade his supporters. At the same time, Maj. Gen. Horatio Wright, the recently appointed commander of the Department of the Ohio in Cincinnati, also began to angle for the field command. Civilian critics of Buell, most notably Governor Morton, kept up a steady torrent of abuse as well. Worse, midwestern Republican leaders were actively working through their political connections in Washington to secure Buell's ouster as the fall 1862 elections approached, complaining of his lack of military success since Shiloh, soft war ideals, and membership in the Democratic Party. In response to this pressure, on September 24 Lincoln, Halleck, and Secretary of War Edwin Stanton had finally issued orders that relieved Buell of command and replaced him with Thomas. When the orders arrived in Louisville on that chaotic September 29, however, Thomas refused the command, citing Buell's preparations for an impending movement against Bragg's forces at Bardstown. Anxious to deny his own culpability, Halleck had no choice but to suspend the orders until after Buell and Bragg met in the field.[3]

Buell thus retained command, but only tenuously. With the ground reeling treacherously beneath his feet, he realized that only a solid victory over Bragg in the coming days would save him. Unfortunately, due to Buell's personality, all the pressure on him only served to increase his usual tendency toward perfectionism and hesitancy. Unable to fully rely upon those around him, he also gravitated toward favorites as he reorganized his army on September 29. Joining his veterans in Louisville had been a division from Ulysses S. Grant's army, successful, bloodied veterans of the March 1862 battle of Pea Ridge, as well as thousands of raw recruits who had been rushed to Louisville to defend the city in the event of attack. Buell's immediate task was to quickly integrate the new and old units into an effective fighting force. With two exceptions, he placed one raw regiment and three veteran regiments in each brigade. He then combined the resulting brigades into three corps, with Thomas installed as a powerless second in command. To lead I Corps and II Corps, he turned to the two men whose seniority made them obvious choices, McCook and Maj. Gen. Thomas L. Crittenden. Both generals had served competently if not exceptionally under Buell in previous months, and despite the many vocal McCook boosters, Buell had no concerns about either undermining his authority. Crittenden was also the son of Kentucky's popular U.S. senator, John J. Crittenden.[4]

Choosing a commander for III Corps proved a tougher task. Buell had intended to award it to his friend Nelson, but now he lay dead. With the gunman also out of the running, the most obvious alternate choice left was Brig. Gen. Albin F. Schoepf, like Davis one of three division commanders Buell had intended for the corps. Schoepf certainly had respectable credentials. Born in Poland, he was a graduate of the Austrian military academy, a former captain in the Austrian army, and a veteran of the unsuccessful Hungarian Revolution of 1848. When the rebellion collapsed, Schoepf fled first to the Ottoman Empire, then to America. In Washington he came under the wing of Joseph Holt, the Kentucky politician and later secretary of war in James Buchanan's cabinet and Lincoln's judge advocate general. Schoepf subsequently spent much of the first year of the war under Thomas's immediate command in Kentucky.

Schoepf's links to Thomas and Holt were bad enough in Buell's eyes, but what really blocked the Austrian from corps command was the two men's intense personal hatred for each other. At Corinth Buell had taken the side of Schoepf's brigade commanders when they complained about him. Schoepf angrily responded by alleging that Buell's conciliatory policies toward Southern white civilians were products of disloyalty to the Union cause. The feud escalated until August 1862, when Buell ordered Schoepf's arrest after he rode through the latter's lines unchallenged by sentries. Making matters worse that night, Schoepf's friend and subordinate Speed S. Fry pulled a gun on Buell. The immediate conflict was resolved, but Scheopf and Fry were convinced that Buell had plotted to disgrace them publically and quietly sought coconspirators to help them find a way to deprive him of command.

In this light, rejecting Schoepf as a candidate for corps command was perhaps a logical decision, but it left Buell with a very short list from which to work. Jeremiah Boyle, the military governor of Kentucky whom Buell had penciled in as the corps' third divisional commander, was loyal enough but had proven to be overly anxious. Indeed, a series of nervous telegrams to Washington had already placed Boyle on the wrong side of the president. Brig. Gen. Robert B. Mitchell and the newly promoted Brig. Gen. Philip Sheridan were competent commanders but also relative unknowns who only recently had joined the army. Later events suggest that already they could not get along with Buell in any case.[5] Accordingly, Buell made a crucial choice on that fateful day, one that could only make sense within the dysfunctional upper echelon of the Army of the Ohio. He gave III Corps to his loyal friend, Charles Champion Gilbert.

Even before assuming corps command, Gilbert's once-promising career had taken an odd turn in Kentucky. Born in Ohio, the forty-year-old was a member of the celebrated West Point class of 1846 and a Mexican War veteran who had served extensively on the southwestern frontier as a staff officer and also briefly taught at West Point. After the war began, Captain Gilbert received a serious wound leading a company of regulars at the Battle of Wilson's Creek in August 1861. After recovering from his injury, he joined Buell's army in Nashville as its inspector general; served at Shiloh, where he was brevetted to the rank of major in the Regular Army for heroism; and then remained in that position until he went with Nelson to Kentucky, again in the role of inspector general. In the immediate aftermath of the debacle at Richmond, with Nelson wounded and brigade commanders Charles Cruft and James S. Jackson so mentally exhausted that they were unwilling to take charge of the retreat from Lexington to Louisville, General Wright turned desperately to Gilbert. The only problem was rank; Gilbert was still a captain in the Regular Army and thus could hardly give orders to colonels and brigadier generals. Without the authority to do so, Wright immediately resolved the problem—in his mind anyway—by promoting Gilbert to the rank of "acting major general." (Lincoln eventually approved Gilbert's promotion, though only to the rank of brigadier general of volunteers.) Gilbert relished both the stars he would soon affix to the shoulders of a new major general's coat and the task at hand. He drove the survivors of Richmond back to Louisville in what some participants came to call the "Hell-March," and they thoroughly resented him for it. Wright, however, pronounced himself so pleased with Gilbert's performance that he gave him command of all Union forces in Louisville and south down the Louisville and Nashville Railroad, superseding the authority of the perpetually shaky Boyle.[6]

Once in command, Gilbert established and supervised a wearying pace of drill, both for the men he brought back to Louisville and for the new recruits pouring daily into the city to protect it. Curiously, though, he neglected constructing defenses, and only after Nelson took command in the city did the men tardily turn to digging entrenchments. At the same time, Gilbert also played a supporting, off-stage role in one of the stranger episodes of the war. Marching north from Tennessee, Bragg's army besieged the 4,000-man garrison at Munfordville, Kentucky. When the Confederates demanded surrender, newly arrived post commander Col. Cyrus Dunham initially responded with defiance, requested time to hold a council of war, and then wired Louisville for instructions. Incredibly, Gilbert's response was to fire Dunham on the spot and hand the decision to surrender to the garrison's previous commander, a former Indiana businessman, Col. John T. Wilder. Famously, the inexperienced Wilder requested a tour of Bragg's stronger army, counting guns along the way, before agreeing to surrender.[7]

This was the man to whom Buell gave III Corps, an officer who had never commanded a unit in the field larger than a company. Not surprisingly, Gilbert's appointment immediately caused consternation among his subordinates. Sheridan, in particular, refused to serve any longer under both Gilbert and Boyle, leading Buell to give him Boyle's intended division as a partial sop. Gilbert's major enemy, however, turned out to be himself. In many ways, he continued to act as Buell's inspector general.[8] F. W. Keil of the 35th Ohio remembered that

Gilbert immediately became known "for 'nosing' through baggage wagons to see what effects officers and men placed in them."[9] Making matters worse, he also immediately displayed a terrible temper. Unlike many successful Civil War commanders, including several of his classmates, Gilbert did not evince a consciousness of the differences between volunteers and regulars. He immediately treated all with the firm discipline of the Old Army. On the very day of his appointment, the men of the 10th Indiana and 10th Kentucky staged a "rumpus" when they were not paid. Angry, they shoved their bayonetted rifles into the ground and demanded their money. As their colonels and brigade commander, Brig. Gen. Speed Fry, tried to talk sense to them, Gilbert rode up. The temptation to show up Fry, a Kentucky judge before the war who had led volunteers in Mexico as well as one of Buell's leading antagonists, proved irresistible. According to a soldier in the Indiana regiment, Gilbert "began a tirade of profanity and abuse, and finally ordered Battery C [1st Ohio Light Artillery] to unlimber and throw a few charges of canister into the two regiments and 'blow them to ———.'" The battery summarily refused, leaving Gilbert "boiling over, ripping, raring mad." Happily, Thomas eventually arrived on the scene and defused the situation.[10] Gilbert remained furious, though. The next day he ordered all the men in III Corps "to stand to arms every morning from 3 o'clock until daylight." Brigade and division commanders additionally were to circle their commands every half hour in order to make sure that the order was obeyed. In twenty-four hours Gilbert had proven himself a petty martinet willing to blast two of his regiments to kingdom come and, accordingly, quickly earned the enmity of the volunteers in his corps.[11]

On the following day, October 1, Buell's army marched out of Louisville. Two divisions marched eastward toward the state capital at Frankfort in hopes of misleading Bragg as to Federal intentions. The bulk of the army, in contrast, headed southeast, using three separate roads in order to maximize access to water and forage amid a devastating drought. Whether out of friendship or concern, Buell rode with Gilbert. For the men marching in stifling dust clouds without adequate water or enough food, the next few days proved exhausting and demoralizing. Unit cohesion fell apart as soldiers staggered along or else fell out of line. By October 6, III Corps in particular had started to unravel, largely due to the lack of water and grueling pace but also in part to its commander's continued hectoring. Following Buell's instructions to the letter, Gilbert ordered his men not to forage for food or trespass on civilian property. According to several soldiers, he spent much of his time riding among them, personally enforcing those orders and repeatedly threatening their lives.[12]

The soldier-historians of the 36th Illinois, for example, described how Gilbert actually ordered his escort to open fire on a company that had wandered into an apple orchard. "The order was scarcely uttered," they continued, "when every man by the wayside sprang to his feet, seized his musket, and the ramming of cartridges and click of gun-locks was fearfully ominous, and warned the escort to desist from putting the order into execution." The show of defiance cowed the escort but not Gilbert, who now demanded to see "the officer in command of these miscreants." The company commander replied with a threat of his own, telling his corps commander that "one word from me will call the boys out of that orchard a d—d sight sooner than you can shoot them out; and should it come to that, I have the honor to assure you, General, that my boys never allow themselves to be outdone in this shooting business." As he had done earlier, Gilbert immediately backed down, not wishing to be shot by his own men, but later from a place of safety, he placed the entire regiment under arrest.[13]

A number of similarly petty incidents followed, though not all involved enlisted men. Gilbert aroused Sheridan's smoldering ire by scrimping on rations even as he wrote him fawning notes, and the general annoyed another subordinate when he commandeered a rare pool of water solely for himself and his staff, going so far as to place guards around it to keep common soldiers away. The situation worsened as the march proceeded. Encountering on the evening of October 6 a sleeping group of men from the 10th Indiana, the same regiment of Fry's command that he had tangled with in Louisville, Gilbert cursed them for not rising to salute him as he rode past. When a company commander demanded to know who Gilbert was, the general responded by taking away his sword and having him arrested. Not finished, he then harangued the regiment's colonel and demanded the regimental colors. That was too much for these volunteers. In response, the color bearer "gave him a cursing and told him if he polluted the colors by touching them he would kill him." Other men joined in the harangue, one fired his weapon without incident, and at the same time another bayoneted the general's mount. "The horse reared and plunged," a soldier remembered, "and nearly threw Gilbert off—and they went off in a gallop." Left to themselves, several of the Hoosiers promptly pledged to kill Gilbert during the expected battle if they had a chance.[14] Again, Gilbert rode away from an uncomfortable situation he himself had created. Morale in III Corps sank. On the following day, it was Buell who encountered some men from the 75th Illinois foraging in a garden. Another angry confrontation followed, and when one soldier grabbed Buell's bridle, the horse bucked and threw the general to the ground. Unable to sit or ride, Buell spent the rest of the day in an ambulance.[15]

That night, as III Corps bedded down along the Springfield Pike three miles west of the town of Perryville, as a number of officers, including Schoepf, Fry, and Brig. Gen. James Steedman met to plot Buell's removal, the army commander weighed his options. A brisk cavalry battle during the day revealed that the Federals had caught up with the Confederates. Perryville itself, as the hub of the local road network as well as a place thought to have water, was valuable in its own right. With this information in hand, Buell worked until well after midnight crafting a plan that would have all three of his corps converge on the

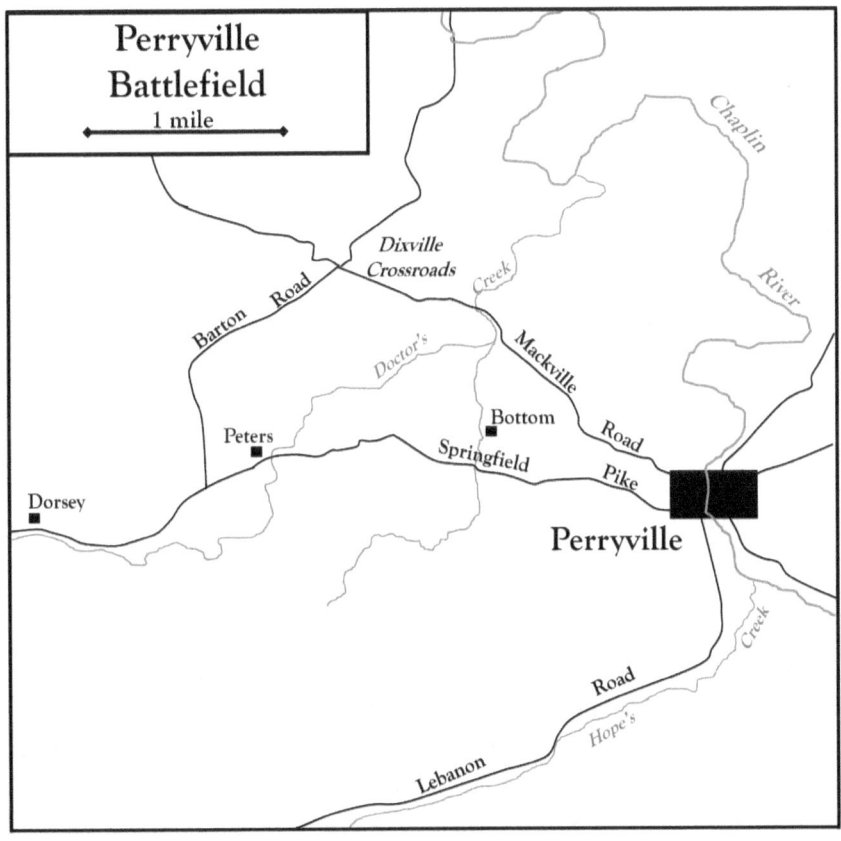

enemy simultaneously in the morning: I Corps to the north along the Mackville Road, III Corps up the Springfield Pike, and II Corps from the southwest along the Lebanon Road. As it turned out, the plan was too ambitious for the weary army; I Corps and II Corps remained far from their jumping-off positions well after dawn. Buell decided to call off the assault and wait until the following morning, confident that the Confederates would still be there.[16]

Meanwhile, fighting broke out unexpectedly on the Springfield Pike. Soldiers had reported pools of water to the east, between two hills known by locals as Peters Hill and, closer to town, Bottom Hill. Unfortunately, Confederate troops had been seen earlier on the former eminence. After midnight Buell ordered Fry to confirm the rumors. Once the enemy presence was confirmed, Buell ordered Gilbert to send a brigade forward to occupy Peters Hill and secure the water. Gilbert handed the assignment to Sheridan, who in turn ordered Col. Daniel McCook's brigade forward before dawn. The Confederates of Brig. Gen. St. John R. Liddell's brigade, occupying both hills, contested the advance. As morning dawned, the fight drew in more and more troops. Slowly and doggedly, Sheridan's Federals pushed the Confederates off of both hills. At about 10:00 A.M., as Sheridan prepared to pursue the enemy, Gilbert arrived on Peters Hill and discovered it unoccupied. Aware that Buell had delayed the planned general assault, he immediately ordered Sheridan to fall back there, go on the defensive, and wait until he received orders to resume his advance. Unaware that the Confederate high command also had decided to break off the fighting, Sheridan reluctantly complied and set his men to digging rifle pits.

The Confederates were having command problems of their own. Bragg had not been with his army, having left Maj. Gen. Leonidas Polk in charge while he met with Maj. Gen. Edmund Kirby Smith in the state capitol and watched the installation of Kentucky's Confederate governor. On October 7 Polk and Maj. Gen. William J. Hardee had determined to attack the enemy force pursuing them. On the morning of the eighth, however, the ferocity of the fighting along Sheridan's front convinced Polk to fall back on the defensive. Bragg arrived in Perryville just as the Bottom Hill fighting ended, and an angry confrontation ensued. Convinced that Buell and most of his army were away to the north, he ordered an attack on the Federal column. At 2:00 P.M., after more confusion and a relatively bloodless artillery barrage, the confused Confederates finally launched an assault against I Corps on the Mackville Road.

For several hours they hammered McCook's corps backward. I Corps found itself on its own. Although many of Gilbert's troops clearly could see the fighting to their left, they did not engage. At headquarters, an injured Buell was blissfully unaware of the engagement thanks to a sound-dampening "acoustic shadow" that resulted from the combination of the field's rolling hills and wind direction. He thus spent much of the day in his cot reading a book. No orders would come from him. Meanwhile, Gilbert, at headquarters with Buell instead of with his men, continued to pester Sheridan with orders to stay put. For his part, Sheridan expected a serious assault on his lines momentarily and bore down awaiting it. His worries seemed to come true at around 3:30 P.M., when a small Confederate brigade appeared to the east moving toward his position. The outnumbered Confederates of Col. Samuel Powell's brigade, unaware of Sheridan's presence on Peters Hill, had marched out to take what they believed to be the battery anchoring the Union right. Powell's men proved no match for two Union divisions as well as elements of II Corps and fell back toward town in what became a rout.

Sheridan hesitated to pursue, but fellow division commander Brig. Gen. Robert Mitchell proved eager for the task. Mitchell's men summarily drove the enemy back into the streets of Perryville. Although the sun was sinking and a fresh Confederate brigade waited in Perryville, a spirited attack promised to not only secure the town but might also block Bragg's escape route south.[17] In the end, all that stood between Mitchell and such an attack was his corps commander. Gilbert had remained with Buell most of the day, both men dismissing the occasional blasts of gunfire they heard as nothing more than the wasteful actions of nervous artillerymen. Buell's serene overconfidence was about to have a regrettable effect on his most dependent subordinate. At about 4:15 P.M. Gilbert rode to the front. Why he did so, however, remains murky. Writing for a popular audience in the 1880s, he claimed that when he first heard the sound of gunfire from Peters Hill, he realized immediately that there was a battle in progress and set off at a gallop for his command. Reports submitted by others during the war itself contradict this claim. A II Corps staff officer, for instance, later testified in an official inquiry into Buell's conduct that when he encountered Gilbert on the road that day, the latter dismissed I Corps's fighting as of little consequence and assured him that the gunfire represented nothing more than a few nervous gun crews attached to the Federal cavalry.[18] For his part,

Thomas remembered a note from Gilbert to Thomas Crittenden written about that time explaining that Gilbert "had met some little resistance himself, but was then camping his troops for the night."[19] In fact, the actual note was even more damning. Gilbert had written that his "children were all quiet and by sunset he would have them all in bed, nicely tucked up, as we used to do in Corinth."[20] It strains credulity to believe that the man who scribbled that note understood the situation at the front any better than Buell and his staff back at headquarters.

It was only when Gilbert neared the scene of fighting that the truth reached him through a dizzying array of voices—and he still largely refused to accept what he heard and saw. First, he encountered Capt. Horace N. Fisher, a I Corps staff officer, who had ridden after the general to seek reinforcements. Describing himself in third person, as he typically did in his postwar writings, Gilbert owned up to his confusion and especially that he was unaware I Corps had advanced since the morning and now had almost retreated back to its originally assigned position; that is, he found McCook's corps exactly where he expected it to be. Thus, he "received the astounding report . . . with much abatement. That a battle could rage for two hours or more on high ground like that, and nobody in camp hear it, was not to be credited at once. . . . The situation was difficult of realization. McCook's command was reported from all quarters as suffering defeat, and yet it appeared to General Gilbert to be fighting in front of the line of battle, an odd place for a beaten wing of an army to be still fighting."[21]

Almost immediately another staff officer reached Gilbert, this time from Sheridan. He reported that Powell's attack had taken place even as Federal guns opened up to the front. Suddenly terrified that his own command was in danger, Gilbert immediately forgot about Fisher and instead ordered Schoepf forward to reinforce Sheridan and Mitchell. He then took off cross-country to his left to catch up with Schoepf's division. Encountering Col. Michael Gooding's stationary brigade of Mitchell's division, Gilbert promptly ordered it to the front as well. At this point, however, yet another McCook aide arrived asking for support. He later reported that the general still would not believe that I Corps was in real jeopardy and refused to do anything until Sheridan had repulsed the enemy. There Gilbert remained, in the rear, unwilling either to ride on to Sheridan's front or observe firsthand the situation of I Corps on his left. Only when the gunfire at the front died down did he act at last in regard to I Corps, recalling Gooding's brigade despite the closer presence of another brigade and dispatching it to the left.[22]

Gooding had not been gone long when a third messenger arrived, this time from army headquarters. Not satisfied with Gilbert's response, Fisher had galloped off in search of direct orders from the commanding general. Like Gilbert, Buell simply could not believe that his army had been in action for three hours and concluded that both Fisher and McCook had overreacted. Indeed, he sent Fisher back to McCook with a message that he "probably" would send help. Several minutes later, however, Buell decided that to be safe, he would dispatch Maj. J. M. Wright to Gilbert with orders to send two brigades from Schoepf's division to the assistance of I Corps. To his surprise, Wright found Gilbert still worried about his own lines and unwilling to comply. Fearing renewed Confederate attacks against his front, he argued instead that he had already sent one of Mitchell's brigades and thus was only required by Buell's order to dispatch one more, not two. Adding that he was anxious to be of assistance, he told Major Wright that he could choose the brigade he wanted. A chagrined Wright dashed off to find Schoepf, who immediately sent forward Steedman's brigade. While all of this was happening, Gilbert dispatched an aide of his own with verbal orders to Mitchell, mandating that he pull back into line next to Sheridan. Furious and unimpressed with Gilbert's staff as well, Mitchell refused to give up his position in town until he received the directive in writing. The aide rode away, only to return awhile later with a note from Gilbert restating the command. Even then Mitchell only partially complied, pulling back one brigade but leaving another on the edge of town.[23]

After dark, with the timely assistance of Gooding's brigade and the noisy, threatening approach of Steedman, a battered I Corps held the vital Dixville Crossroads. Later that night, finally aware of what he faced, Bragg retreated, first to his meagerly supplied base at Camp Breckinridge to the east, then toward Cumberland Gap and Tennessee. Meanwhile, still hesitant to credit reports of the previous day's events, Buell ordered his army forward on the morning of October 9 in his planned grand attack. Finding only the retreating tail of the Confederate army, the Federals lurched into town and halted. In the days that followed, Buell would direct what was at best a half-hearted pursuit of Bragg. Still unwilling to take his army into the hills of eastern Kentucky, he repeatedly balked at conducting a vigorous pursuit, defied orders from Washington, and instead made plans to return to Nashville. Lincoln finally fired him at the end of the month, replacing him with Maj. Gen. William Starke Rosecrans. Almost immediately, Rosecrans replaced Gilbert with Thomas.[24]

Buell's problems were not over, however. In November Secretary of War Stanton ordered Halleck to convene a military commission to investigate Buell's conduct and loyalty. The commission, composed of six officers, including for a time Schoepf, met in Cincinnati. Not surprisingly, the verdict was unfavorable. Although the commission members concluded that Buell was neither a traitor nor too conciliatory toward Southern civilians, they did condemn his generalship throughout the campaign. Included in their findings was strong criticism of Gilbert, both for not acting quickly to support McCook and for denying assistance once he was aware of the situation. One immediate result was that the Senate refused to confirm Gilbert's recent appointment to brigadier general of volunteers. In March 1863 the former corps commander reverted to the regular rank of captain. Promoted the following July, but only to the rank of major with a brevet to the rank of colonel, Gilbert spent the rest of the war in Hartford, Connecticut, far from the fighting, serving as assistant provost marshal. Following Appomattox, he quietly returned to the frontier for another two decades and rebuilt his career there, rising eventually to the rank of colonel. Away from often querulous volunteer soldiers, he once again thrived in the Regular Army. Gilbert retired in 1886, just after he began contributing articles to various publications in which he sought to justify his actions at Perryville. He convinced few readers. In their memoirs and regimental histories, the men who had served under Gilbert so briefly condemned him for decades, skewering him almost as badly as they did Buell. Gilbert died in Baltimore in 1903 but was buried in Louisville, his wife's hometown. Ironically, his grave is near the site of the old Federal entrenchments and not far from where, at the zenith of his Civil War career, he supervised the defense of the city in the early autumn of 1862.[25]

In retrospect, Charles Champion Gilbert initially seems to represent a striking example of abject failure in Civil War corps command. Hindsight allows one to see his many flaws in high relief. Gilbert nursed petty grudges and sometimes forgot that he was no longer an inspector general but rather the commander of a corps. He never adjusted to leading volunteers and treated men who had been civilians a year before as if they were veterans of the Old Army. Determined to enforce official regulations and his sponsor's soft-war policies to the letter, he thus proved unable to cultivate the loyalty of the men under his command, with his actions almost seeming to be deliberately counterproductive. On the battlefield at Perryville, the former captain's lack of experience, initiative, and calm were evident. At several points on October 8, his stubborn adherence to a plan that already had collapsed, combined with his near-panicked determination to safeguard his corps whatever the cost to the larger army at a time when his unit's position actually was secure, led him to throw down roadblocks to a potential war-changing victory. Bragg might never have escaped Perryville had Gilbert allowed Mitchell to take the town, and the war might have ended much differently and more quickly.

Gilbert thus provides a textbook case of how not to direct a corps. Yet in fairness he was hardly the first rookie commander of large bodies of troops to perform badly. At Perryville Gilbert had been in corps command for a week. We will never know if, like so many others, he could have learned from his errors and done better on another field. Buell's position was itself too insecure to protect his new protégé for more than a few days or give him the opportunity to grow into his position. Nor can Gilbert's poor performance be viewed fairly in isolation. His real failings on the road to Perryville and subsequent oblivion still were as much symptoms as anything else, visible manifestations of a virulent cancer that was poisoning the high command of the Army of the Ohio. His questionable promotion to acting major general only happened in the first place because he was willing to accept responsibility and act decisively when Brigadier Generals Cruft and Jackson refused to do so at Richmond. At a decisive moment Gilbert had saved a fighting force when its other commanders wilted. His ascension to corps command likewise would not have been possible without the remarkable murder of one general at the hands of another, the constant scheming of other generals to unseat their commanding officer, and above all, that commander's harried determination to place familiarity and loyalty above experience and proven competence in the face of the enemy—all of which took place at a crucial moment when the general in chief and president had fully demonstrated their lack of confidence in Buell. Gilbert badly bungled his responsibilities to be sure, but only because fellow soldiers such as Cruft, Jackson, Davis, Nelson, Schoepf, Wright, and Buell already had failed at theirs.

In a recent study of the men in Buell's army, historian Gerald Prokopowicz echoes Correlli Barnett's earlier work on World War I armies when he likens a Civil War army to a dinosaur, "a killing machine with powerful muscles and a tiny brain." Its strengths, Prokopowicz concludes, were in its companies and regiments, not in its generals. In an army with a notably "dim" brain such as the Army of the Ohio, there would always be enough blame to go around. Gilbert can only be judged in that context.[26]

NOTES

1. The standard account is now Kirk C. Jenkins, "A Shooting in the Galt House: The Death of General William Nelson," *Civil War History* 43 (June 1997): 101–18.

2. I discuss all of this in more detail in Kenneth W. Noe, *Perryville: This Grand Havoc of Battle* (Lexington: University Press of Kentucky, 2001), 43–93. For a thorough discussion of problems within the Army of the Ohio's command structure, see Gerald J. Prokopowicz, *All for the Regiment: The Army of the Ohio, 1861–1862* (Chapel Hill: University of North Carolina Press, 2001).

3. U.S. War Department, *The War of the Rebellion: A Compilation of the Official Records of the Union and Confederate Armies*, 70 vols. in 128 parts (Washington, D.C.: Government Printing Office, 1880–1901), ser. 1, 16(1):232–33, 16(2):360, 421, 530, 538–39, 546, 549–51, 555, 557–58 (hereafter cited as *OR;* all references are to series 1 unless otherwise noted); Noe, *Perryville,* 92, 93–94.

4. *OR,* 16(1):49, 89, 99, 107, 126, 134, 184–85, 188–89; Albion W. Tourgee, *The Story of a Thousand, Being a History of the Service of the 105th Ohio Volunteer Infantry, in the War for the Union from August 21, 1862, to June 6, 1865* (Buffalo, N.Y.: S. McGerald and Son, 1896), 86–87, 89–91, 101–2. For Buell's personality, see Stephen D. Engle, *Don Carlos Buell: Most Promising of All* (Chapel Hill: University of North Carolina Press, 1999).

5. *OR,* 16(1):134–35, 138, 234, 285, 376, 377, 382, 542–45, 576–77, 594–95, 598–99, 16(2):336, 337, 344, 348, 351, 352–53, 355, 357, 359–60, 365–66, 373, 558–59, 560; Ezra Warner, *Generals in Blue: Lives of the Union Commanders* (Baton Rouge: Louisiana State University Press, 1964), 424–25; Noe, *Perryville,* 81–82, 97–98.

6. *OR,* 16(1):372, 375, 376, 693, 16(2):474, 477, 491; Joseph K. Marshall, *Civil War Diary of Joseph K. Marshall,* ed. W. Louis Phillips (Columbus, Ohio: By the editor, 1982), 1; Julius B. Work, diary, 2–3, Civil War Miscellaneous Collection, U.S. Army Military History Institute, Carlisle, Pa.; Warner, *Generals in Blue,* 173–74; Noe, *Perryville,* 83–85; William Garrett Piston and Richard W. Hatcher III, *Wilson's Creek: The Second Battle of the Civil War and the Men Who Fought It* (Chapel Hill: University of North Carolina Press, 2000), 182, 186, 193, 198, 209; Prokopowicz, *All for the Regiment,* 155.

7. *OR,* 16(1):209–10, 962, 966, 968–71; Thomas Lawrence Connelly, *Army of the Heartland: The Army of Tennessee, 1861–1862* (Baton Rouge: Louisiana State University Press, 1967), 229; Arndt M. Stickles, *Simon Bolivar Buckner: Borderland Knight* (Chapel Hill: University of North Carolina Press, 1940), 200–204.

8. *OR,* 16(1):92, 372, 384; Phillip H. Sheridan, *Personal Memoirs of P. H. Sheridan. General United States Army,* vol. 1 (New York: Charles L. Webster, 1888), 189–90.

9. F. W. Keil, *Thirty-Fifth Ohio: A Narrative of Service from August 1861 to 1864* (Fort Wayne, Ind.: Archer, Housch, 1894), 96. Prokopowicz first made the point regarding Gilbert's marked inexperience with field command. *All for the Regiment,* 155.

10. James Birney Shaw, *History of the Tenth Regiment Indiana Volunteer Infantry, Three Months and Three Years Organization* (Lafayette, Ind.: Burt-Haywood, 1912), 171.

11. General Orders No. 3, III Corps, Army of Louisville, Sept. 30, 1862, Charles C. Gilbert File, Perryville State Historic Site, Perryville, Ky.

12. *OR,* 16(1):89, 525, 665, 16(2):560–61; Noe, *Perryville,* 112–23.

13. L. G. Bennett and William M. Haigh, *History of the Thirty-Sixth Regiment Illinois Volunteers, during the War of the Rebellion* (Aurora, Ill.: Knickerbocker and Hodder, 1876), 240–41.

14. Shaw, *Tenth Regiment*, 171–72; Prokopowicz, *All for the Regiment*, 182.

15. J. W. Sheaffer, "Battle of Perryville," *National Tribune*, Apr. 24, 1890, 4; James Robert Chumney Jr., "Don Carlos Buell: Gentleman General" (Ph.D. diss., Rice University, 1964), 168–69.

16. *OR*, 16(1):49–50, 124–25, 134–36, 221–22, 16(2):580–81.

17. I discuss this in more detail in Noe, *Perryville*, 143–287.

18. *OR*, 16(1):277, 1072; Charles C. Gilbert, "On the Field at Perryville," in *Battles and Leaders of the Civil War*, ed. Robert U. Johnson and Clarence C. Buel, 4 vols. (New York: Century, 1887–88; repr., Edison, N.J.: Castle, 1995), 3:57–58.

19. *OR*, 16(1):187.

20. Ibid., 557.

21. Charles Champion Gilbert, "Bragg's Invasion of Kentucky," *Southern Bivouac* 1 n.s. (Jan. 1886): 468.

22. Gilbert, "On the Field at Perryville," 57–58; *OR*, 16(1):1072–73; Gilbert, "Bragg's Invasion of Kentucky," 467–69.

23. Gilbert, "On the Field at Perryville," 48; *OR*, 16(1):50–51, 94, 95, 97, 277, 655, 1025, 1073, 1075; E. L. Davison, *Autobiography of E. L. Davison* (N.p., 1901), 48; Keil, *Thirty-Fifth Ohio*, 99, J. M. Wright, "A Glimpse of Perryville," *Southern Bivouac* 1 (Aug. 1885): 151.

24. See Noe, *Perryville*, 319–43; Prokopowicz, *All for the Regiment*, 187.

25. *OR*, 16(1):5–11, 20; John H. Eicher and David J. Eicher, *Civil War High Commands* (Stanford, Calif.: Stanford University Press, 2001), 598; Warner, *Generals in Blue*, 174.

26. Prokopowicz, *All for the Regiment*, 5–6 (quotes), 166, 184; Correlli Barnett, *The Swordbearers: Supreme Command in the First World War* (1963; London: Cassell, 2000), 68.

"The Longest and Clearest Head of Any General Officer"

George Gordon Meade as Corps Commander, December 1862–June 1863

CHRISTOPHER S. STOWE

Even before the outset of civil war in 1861, the Willard Hotel in Washington, D.C., had established itself as a choice setting to observe the comings and goings of major players in American public affairs. Located two blocks from the White House along Pennsylvania Avenue, Willard's—as it was widely known—had by early 1863 become the social and political center of a nation at war. Interested citizens and soldiers and their myriad interests swarmed its rollicking main lobby and dining hall to spark conversation and broker deals, often to the distraction of its prominent military guests. Among the principals present at Willard's as 1863 dawned was Maj. Gen. George Gordon Meade, the newly minted commander of the Army of the Potomac's V Corps. Meade, uncomfortable with public throngs and the capital's atmosphere of intrigue, sought to keep a modest profile as he dined there with members of his staff while en route from his Philadelphia home to the army's winter encampment near Falmouth, Virginia. No matter: observers noted twin stars upon the somewhat obscure officer's shoulder straps. An aide-de-camp to the general "overheard two gents talking" amid the noise, Meade wrote his wife, Margaretta, after his visit, "one of whom said what Maj. Genl. is that, to which the other replied Meade. 'Who is he' said the first[,] 'I never saw him before.' No that is very likely," responded the other, "for he is one of our fighting Generals, is always in the field & does not spend his time in Washn. hotels."[1]

A battle-tested and capable soldier, Meade had earned the respect, if not always the adulation, of most officers who served with him from 1861 to 1863. And within six months of his winter repast at Willard's, the outwardly unassuming (but privately ambitious) Pennsylvanian found himself at the head of the Army of the Potomac. Interestingly, Meade's rise probably owed more to his ability to negotiate the army's noxious political climate and maintain a level of professional detachment in a time of transformational war aims than to his performance as a "fighting general." Though in tacit agreement with much of the conciliatory operational approach embraced by the mass of the Union high command during the first half of the war, his public silence amid military and political turmoil spoke volumes to those in camp and Washington who had cultivated an atmosphere of such bad feeling that, by early 1863, it had begun to destabilize the army's command and undermine its efficiency. Moreover, Meade's desire to steer clear of controversy illuminates both the strengths and weaknesses inherent to the strain of idealism in civil-military relations as practiced by the bulk of West Point–trained officers in nineteenth-century America. This convergence of socio-political and professional values played a critical role in informing Meade's decision-making processes and shaping his command relationships as his reputation grew from Fredericksburg to the Chancellorsville crossroads and beyond.

THE MOOD AT FALMOUTH differed markedly from the lively air at Willard's. Defeat along the Rappahannock River on December 13, 1862, had shaken the soldiers' confidence in their leadership—military and civilian—and ultimately in the army itself as an instrument of national policy. The Union command had managed operations at Fredericksburg with a conspicuous lack of skill, launching piecemeal assaults from Prospect Hill to Marye's Heights that achieved only slaughter in the face of Confederate musketry, shot, and shell. Recriminations began within an army that had since its earliest days found factionalism to be a fundamental component of its organizational culture. Not surprisingly, the principal target of complaint was its embattled head, Maj. Gen. Ambrose E. Burnside. A favorite of Pres. Abraham Lincoln, the amiable "Burn" had doubted his own ability to lead the Army of the Potomac when appointed to its command in November. Subsequent events proved his self-assessment correct. Within a fortnight of the Fredericksburg disaster, grumblings among disillusioned subordinates had erupted into a thinly concealed "revolt of the generals." Conservative officers associated with the army's much-beloved first commander, Maj. Gen. George B. McClellan, complained in personal interviews with Lincoln and others of Burnside's incapacity, while Maj. Gen. Joseph Hooker, one of Burnside's most strident critics and an emerging favorite of the Radical Republican bloc in Washington, suggested the nation's deliverance could come only at the hand of a military dictator. Morale correspondingly plummeted throughout the ranks. "The recent battle was only a murder, for which [Maj. Gen. Henry W. Halleck] and A. E. Burnside are responsible," wrote Lt. Eugene Carter of the 8th U.S. Infantry. "I had hoped better things of a Republican Administration," wrote another soldier, "but our Lincoln, though sincere is too easily led by others, and [Secretary of State William H.] Seward, the soundest man in the cabinet, is too cautious. The rest of the cabinet ought to be drawn up in line and shot by a file of [Horace] Greeley's Negroes. We must have McClellan in command and send the old fogies home."[2]

It was against this background of disquiet that Meade saw his star begin a rapid ascent. He had shown valor in commanding his division of Pennsylvania Reserves at Fredericksburg and had been lobbying discreetly but determinedly since the autumn of 1862 for a major-general's commission—the kind of tangible recognition he believed due an officer possessing his record and ability. Indeed, with twenty years' service prior to 1861, Meade joined his contemporaries in the scramble for rank and distinction that was the inevitable product of large-scale mobilization and war. "One thing . . . I am willing to admit," he advised his wife a month after the Battle of Antietam, Maryland, in September 1862, "is [that] I consider myself as good as most of my neighbors and without great vanity, may say I believe myself to be better than some who are much higher." Meade's elevation to permanent corps command after Fredericksburg promised to test both his combat skill and political acumen. It was a challenge that the studious, bespectacled Pennsylvanian embraced.[3]

Born to a prominent Philadelphia family in Cádiz, Spain, on the last day of 1815, Meade from his early manhood attended to careerist impulses with a muted intensity. Socialized to maintain a vaunted status among his contemporaries as an end almost unto itself, he embraced throughout his life a cultural philosophy, common among upper classes of the era, that promoted the ascendancy of those whose social attainments and occupational talents fitted them to rule rationally for the good of the whole. In choosing the career of a soldier, Meade sought to achieve the stability and reputation so esteemed by American elites; in so doing, he might acquire the qualities essential to leadership in what members of his class perceived to be a hierarchical society.[4]

The U.S. Military Academy played a critical role in the shaping of Meade's outlook as an officer and a man. Patterns of professional socialization established at West Point stressed systematic learning, status, and order—qualities at variance with the egalitarian, at times brawling, character of public affairs during the Age of Jackson. Moreover, antebellum West Point conditioned officers to place their allegiance with the army and nation rather than any particular political faction. Recognizing the national mission entrusted to its graduates, West Point emphasized hierarchical values and thus contributed to the development of an officer corps that was at once loyal to the state and scornful of emotive political displays. The end product was a genteel, moderate, and relatively apolitical cadre who viewed the military and political spheres as separate civic functions. In this atmosphere officers argued throughout the era that civilian interference worked against successful operations in peace and war. The business of soldiering, they believed, should instead be left to dispassionate military professionals who placed duty and vocation above partisan concerns. The typical army officer of the era, then, performed a trust for which he had sworn a solemn oath to execute objectively, viewed himself as beholden to civil authority (which he nevertheless viewed with skepticism), and avoided larger questions touching public policy or, worse still, partisan politics.[5]

Despite possessing a jaded view of the nation's political leadership, Meade, always a careerist, expected tangible rewards from those whom he held at arm's length. In pursuing his goals the Pennsylvanian strove to project a modest, if not diffident, image, one that befit a member of his class and profession in an era noted for producing and celebrating unpretentious civic heroes. This practice served the general well by endearing him to those who might exert some control over his professional fortunes. Still, his studied reserve remains a somewhat overstated character feature within the literature, for it masked a very real sense of private aspiration and self-interest typical to nineteenth-century American males.[6]

The course of his career offered innumerable lessons on how to pursue "properly" professional goals. During the war with Mexico, Meade, then a lieutenant in the Corps of Topographical Engineers, looked with revulsion upon officers who sought to gain recognition through appeals to the public press. He voiced his disapproval in letters home, noting that cliques had arisen because published accounts exaggerated the performance of one officer or another during the army's operations. "Instances of individual valor which were never known before . . . came here in the papers, extraordinary feats performed by persons who were never near the reputed scene of action, and all kinds of lies & absurdities have been sent forth." Though no less ambitious than his comrades, Meade felt it was inappropriate to approach the press in an effort to sustain or bolster his image. Learning his lesson from the actions of others, he typically avoided pursuing visibly his careerist goals. His own efforts instead would be more subdued, reflecting the presumed character of a member of the American gentry.[7]

With the coming of civil war in 1861, Meade's conception of military professionalism, coupled with his Northern sensibilities, dictated his decision to uphold the Republic. "I cordially agree with you in earnest prayers that a merciful Providence would so guide the hearts of the rulers on both sides as to terminate this unnatural contest," he wrote a friend in 1861. "But, as for myself, I have ever held it to be my duty to uphold and maintain the Constitution and resist the disruption of this government. With this opinion I hold the other side responsible for the existing condition of affairs." Yet like most Northern-born, West Point–trained commanders during the conflict's early months, Meade favored a conciliatory approach designed to hasten the return of "sensible" Southerners back into their "natural" position within the Federal union. "If we ever expect to be *re-united*," he lectured his wife early in 1862, "we should deport ourselves more like the afflicted parent who is compelled to chastise his erring child, and who performs the duty with a *sad heart*."[8] Most revealing were Meade's statements about what he perceived to be the war's partisan turn. The conflict, the general averred to a Michigan acquaintance, had been transformed by radical politicians into a contest touching chattel slavery. Its effects, Meade reasoned, might damage any hope of reunion between the sections. "If it be proclaimed, and *adhered* to, that the real object of the war is the suppression of the rebellion ... by a proper conduct of the war, we could carry our point ... provided the door was left open for them to yield without sacrificing all their material interests. The cause of anxiety, however, now is that the object of the war will be perverted to the destruction of slavery, and, to the expectation of more fully accomplishing this, the removing of competent officers in its conduct, and the substitution of ignorant fanatics who have no qualifications to recommend them, but a fiendish hatred to gratify."[9]

These and others were the private thoughts Meade expressed to family members and associates. He was not among the vocal dissenters to Lincoln's preliminary Emancipation Proclamation, issued just five days after Antietam in September 1862. Indeed, the general had by that time reconciled himself to the war's hard turn, even if he did not altogether welcome it. "Either one extreme or the other will have to come to pass," he wrote Margaretta. "The day for *compromise*, for a brotherly reconciliation[,] for the old *Union* in reality as well as name, has passed away, and the struggle must be continued till one side or the other is exhausted & willing to give up."[10]

Throughout his career, Meade viewed himself not as a policymaker but as a public servant beholden to obey orders regardless of his personal feelings or impulses. His ability to adapt to and accept changes taking place in the Federal war effort, coupled with a demonstrated combat ability at the brigade and division levels, ensured his continued participation in active military operations. Wisely endeavoring to distance himself from the army's factious political culture, the general focused his energies on operational concerns while largely avoiding—in the spirit of a public-minded, disinterested professional—unconcealed talk that might be construed to be of a "partisan complexion." Meade made up his mind that the Union's prime consideration was to marshal onto the field such numbers as were necessary to combat and subdue the armed capacity of the Rebels. "Not a single exertion on our part should be relaxed," he would write early in 1863. "We might as well make up our minds to the fact that our only hope of peace is in the complete *over-powering* of the military force of the South."[11]

How that might be accomplished was a complicated question, though. The military situation in Virginia appeared nothing short of grim to the generals who, under the stewardship and influence of the soldier-engineer McClellan, formed the dominant faction within the Army of the Potomac. At the heart of the matter was a disagreement between professionals like Meade and civilians over how best to marshal military resources. Schooled in the rudiments of nineteenth-century warfare at West Point and in Mexico and appreciating the growing primacy of defensive tactics as the Civil War progressed, the engineer-generals argued the preferred method to take advantage of the Union's clear material strength was to maneuver on the comparatively secure Chesapeake–James/York River line. From there Federal forces could advance westward toward the Confederate center of gravity at Richmond, Virginia, engaging and overwhelming its covering elements in the process. If unable to find success in a single grand stroke, however, Meade and his brother officers had no qualms resorting to siege operations against an enemy unable to counter the Union's nearly boundless logistics. As far as Richmond was concerned, Meade felt that it "need not & ought not be attacked at all.... [T]he proper mode to reduce it is to take possession of the great lines of railroad leading to it from the South & Southwest, cut these & stop any supplies going there, and their army will be compelled to evacuate it & meet us on ground we select ourselves." The engineers' method, at once sensible, controlled, and cognizant of military realities as they stood in the 1860s, promised the best chance to gain victory without the terrible cost in life and resources so abhorrent to the sensibilities of "scientific" soldiers.[12]

The plan met with derision from Radical Republican politicians, among others, whose approach to war was as explicit as it was simple. To them, the best way to defeat the Confederacy was to find its field armies and fight them in climactic battles wherever they stood. Possessing no patience for "soft" siege operations, Radical politicos and newspaper editors gave voice to popular concerns that McClellan and his ilk lacked the requisite will to carry out the war in its appropriate spirit. Lincoln too, appreciating these demands in what he had aptly termed "a People's contest," harbored misgivings, not only recognizing the popular disdain for scientific warfare but also realizing that the Federal capital at Washington, if left uncovered, might be rendered vulnerable. McClellan's subsequent failure along the James River and before Richmond during the 1862 Peninsula Campaign provided critics the ammunition they needed to renounce the engineers' plan, and with the ascent of Henry Halleck to the position of general in chief in July 1862, a new operational approach was put into place, one that exacerbated the growing disconnect in Federal civil-military relations in the East.[13]

Over the next half year, Halleck rewrote the rules for war in Virginia, an adjustment that reflected concerns for the safety of Washington, grudging respect for Confederate Gen. Robert E. Lee's fighting capacity, and awareness of the popular clamor for immediate results. Though Halleck, like McClellan and Meade a trained military engineer, acknowledged the Peninsula route as the most advantageous line of operations against the Confederates in Virginia, the likelihood that any future movement might result in a prolonged siege of Richmond eliminated the Rebel capital as a principal military target. The "headquarters doctrine" he and Lincoln developed called instead for the Army of the Potomac to keep the enemy at bay (in other words, away from Washington), all the while pressing its commanders to deal Lee's legions a setback if the opportunity presented itself. Other goals, such as undermining Confederate supplies and logistics, would take a back seat to securing the capital and meeting the threat posed by the Army of Northern Virginia.[14]

As a blueprint for victory, Meade and others perceived its military flaws. Because the safety of the Federal capital was of overriding consequence to national morale, the plan offered the Army of the Potomac little unfettered movement in its efforts to defeat Lee. It forced the army, if assuming the offensive, to butt its head overland against awaiting Confederates posted behind a succession of rivers across its path. Moreover, the Federals would be compelled to draw supplies from the Virginia railroad network, growing weaker as they crept south and enabling the enemy to retire at will toward its own base in Richmond. For Meade, only partisan politics could have dealt the army such a disadvantageous hand. "Halleck under Washington influence has been trying to force operations on this line," he explained to Margaretta. "[The Orange and Alexandria Railroad] has but one track . . . , and the known capacity of this road is insufficient by 1/3 to carry the daily supplies required for this army. This fact to an ordinarily intelligent mind, unbiased by ridiculous fears for the safety of Washington, ought to be conclusive. I must confess," he concluded, "[that] this interference by politicians with military men . . . make[s] me very doubtful of the future."[15]

Meade's record during the Seven Days' Battles (where he suffered severe wounds at the Battle of Glendale), Second Bull Run, and the Maryland Campaign (in which, at Antietam, he temporarily led the I Corps upon the wounding of its commander, Joseph Hooker) indicated emerging combat ability. His service, which earned plaudits from superiors, was to him a clear confirmation of his readiness for permanent command at the corps level. Once recovered from his injuries, Meade set his sights on gaining a level of command equal to his ambition and sense of ability; in this effort he utilized the avenues open to him, keeping military and civil authorities aware of his accomplishments and discreetly seeking favors from his wife's family and friends.[16] The promotion of a junior officer, the politically connected amateur soldier Brig. Gen. Daniel A. Butterfield, to the V Corps command as a result of Burnside's comprehensive late November "grand division" reorganization gave Meade—now the senior division commander in the Army of the Potomac—additional impetus to pursue his preference. In a November 23 visit to army headquarters, Meade half-teasingly remarked to Burnside that he "had come to pick a crow." Assured by a gracious commanding general that the slight was unintentional, Meade left the meeting outwardly soothed, but he continued to fret as Butterfield remained in place. December finally brought him a measure of satisfaction. News arrived early in the month that he had been nominated for major general, while his leadership at Fredericksburg on December 13 had caught the attention of those whose good opinion mattered. Two days before Christmas, Meade received command of the V Corps, displacing the unlucky Butterfield. "All [Burnside] regretted now was that I had not been in command of it [at Fredericksburg]," he wrote afterward. "More than this I could not ask."[17]

The V Corps possessed perhaps the finest combat reputation in the Army of the Potomac. Formed by McClellan in May 1862 to find a place for favored subordinate Fitz John Porter, the corps had played a major role in nearly all the army's contests, suffering grievous losses but covering itself with honor. Meade, attached temporarily to the corps with his brigade of Pennsylvania Reserves during the Seven Days, had during that time made a positive impression upon its soldiers. "[His] fighting qualities . . . on previous fields of battle made themselves very apparent," wrote the corps's official historian, "so that he was warmly welcomed, and at once possessed the full confidence of the officers and men." The corps notably included the army's two-brigade contingent of U.S. infantry, which added an aura of professionalism that set it apart from others. Its senior leadership was also first rate. Its division commanders were stellar combat officer Brig. Gen. Andrew Atkinson Humphreys, pugnacious Brig. Gen. Charles Griffin, and stolid Brig. Gen. George Sykes, all of whom would ascend to corps command before the war was over. Still, its standing suffered in the eyes of many observers within and outside the army as a consequence of its affiliation with Porter, who in January 1863 was cashiered from the service for conduct during the Second Manassas Campaign that fueled suspicions that he placed his loyalty to McClellan above his loyalty to the Union cause. Indeed, to those Radicals who viewed any manifestation of conservatism—operational or political—as a public danger, the V Corps seemed emblematic of a ruinous military policy. The November appointment of the Republican-affiliated Butterfield was a move calculated in part to reflect the nascent hard-war approach and alter the West Point–trained engineer coterie's perceived stranglehold upon the army's culture. In superseding Butterfield one month later, Meade, aligned with the McClellan faction and its views, found himself acquiring potential and real enemies along with his newfound status.[18]

The most dangerous of these would-be foes was perhaps Major General Hooker. "Fighting Joe" had complained to Burnside of the change atop the V Corps (which composed half of Hooker's grand division), citing its occurrence "in the midst of active operations" as well as Butterfield's creditable performance during the battle of Fredericksburg. To Secretary of War Edwin M. Stanton, Hooker was more blunt. "In no army except that of the United States are such atrocities committed," the general complained, a veiled hit at Burnside, whose job Hooker coveted. Omitting that Meade had performed to his eminent satisfaction during the Maryland Campaign, Hooker added, "I have now entire strangers in command of the 5th Corps." Here was the rub. A strong friendship had developed between Hooker and Butterfield. Together, Butterfield, exceptionally skilled in managing civilian opinion, and Hooker, as scheming an officer as has ever worn an army uniform, had by December 1862 formed the nucleus of an emergent anti-McClellan (and largely, if not entirely, pro-Republican) bloc within the army that was inimical to its engineer clique. As 1863 opened, the Hooker-Butterfield faction saw professional opportunity in what looked to be a transformation within the army's command structure. Meade's own ascension appeared to diminish somewhat any hopes for it to come to full fruition.[19] Butterfield, every bit as career minded as his replacement, was as angry as Hooker on being relieved from corps command. "Have I any friends in Washington?" he beseeched Michigan Sen. Zachariah Chandler, a known Meade antagonist and member of the influential (and feared) Joint Committee on the Conduct of the War. "I have never asked for anything I do not think I ought to," Butterfield continued to Chandler. "I can not refrain from letting my friends know that *action on their part may secure me the justice in an assignment to command this corps with the rank that is my due.*"[20]

It did not help that the army was approaching something of a command crisis, a consequence of repeated operational failure and clamor for accountability, fanned further by intramural and political rivalry. In addition to Hooker, who had done little to conceal his personal and professional hostility toward Burnside after Fredericksburg, Maj. Gens. William B. Franklin and William F. Smith, two of the most ardent McClellanites still with the army, bypassed their commander to propose to Lincoln a return the Peninsula as the most practical way to gain a decisive victory. Meanwhile, engineer-general John Newton and erstwhile Democratic Party politician John Cochrane, both officers in Smith's VI Corps, sought—and were granted—a private interview with the president on December 30. Here, they painted a depressing canvas for Lincoln of an army deflated by defeat and rife with talk against its commander. Lincoln responded to all of this by directing Burnside to hold off on commencing another general movement against Lee, which the commander had done that very day, the preliminaries of which involved elements of Meade's corps. Then too, members of the Joint Committee on the Conduct of the War showed up at army headquarters looking to push a more aggressive agenda and seeking scapegoats for Fredericksburg among the engineer clique. Meade was not summoned to provide testimony before the assemblage, but camp rumor reached his ear that one of the committee's Radicals, Pennsylvania Rep. John Covode, was prepared to "raise a howl" after returning from his Rappahannock sojourn, "[intimating that] it would not be against Burnside."[21] Such was the Army of the Potomac as it and the new commander of the V Corps settled into an unhappy winter encampment.

In such a contentious setting, it was impossible for Meade to remain completely the military idealist, the disinterested soldier. Moreover, the general's post-Fredericksburg prestige and position atop the V Corps guaranteed that his opinion would be courted not only by peers but by those in Washington as well. Called before the joint committee in the spring of 1863, Meade provided testimony before its powerful chairman, Ohio Sen. Benjamin F. Wade. "My conversations with ... Wade satisfied me that Franklin was to be made responsible for the failure at Fredericksburgh, and the committee are calling all the testimony they can procure to substantiate this theory of theirs," he wrote Margaretta afterward. "I sometimes feel very nervous about my position, they are knocking over Generals at such a rate.... [N]o man is safe ... & no one can tell when he may be pitched overboard."[22] Perhaps this unease contributed to a desire to express publicly his views. In response to an invitation to appear at the New York Loyal National League's meeting celebrating the anniversary of Fort Sumter, the general offered a moderate's assessment of the war effort, noting with approval the league's encompassing message of Union over the divisive tone of more partisan appeals:

> My views, which you ask for, are very brief and simple. They are, that it is, and should be the undoubting and unhesitating duty of every citizen of the Republic to give his whole energies, and to contribute all the means in his power, to the determined prosecution of the war, until the integrity of the government is re-established and its supremacy acknowledged. Deprecating as useless all discussion as to the cause of the war, the fact of its existence, and the necessity for its continuance, should alone occupy us. For its successful prosecution and termination, I am clearly of the opinion there is only required union and harmony among ourselves, and the bringing to bear men and means proportionate to the power and resources of the country. For the

purpose of securing union and harmony, I know of no measure better calculated than the organization of your National Loyal League. Its broad and simple platform is one to which citizens of all parties can readily subscribe; and I have no doubt its effects will be most salutary in proving, to those who are in arms to subvert the government, that, whatever differences of opinion may exist on minor points, upon the main point of there being but one Government and one flag, we are determined and united.[23]

More-martial concerns occupied the corps commander's attention as the winter chill set in. Burnside, beleaguered by professional and political intrigues from all sides yet eager always to act, decided again to try his luck in battle with Lee. Instead of attempting a direct crossing of the Rappahannock at Fredericksburg, this time the bulk of the Army of the Potomac aimed to force passage of the river near Banks's Ford above the town to draw the Rebels away from their formidable entrenchments. If Burnside marched swiftly after crossing the river on the morning of January 21, 1863, he might sever Lee's communications with Richmond and force his nemesis to confront the Federals on terrain of their own choosing. The plan's merits notwithstanding, officers and soldiers throughout the army predicted doom. Protests against Burnside reached an alarming pitch. Meade chose not to indulge in such natter, though his operational objections to the Rappahannock line were by now known to at least some. In fact, he was as much in favor of immediate action as any within the army's high command despite the constraints hung upon it. "I agreed [in discussions] with Franklin that the *James* River was our proper & only base," he explained to Margaretta, "but as they determined in Washn. we should not go there, I thought rather than stand still we ought to attempt a practicable tho' less desirable line.... So you see I am among the *fire-eaters* and may perhaps jeopardize my quiet reputation by being too decided. But the fact is I am tired of this playing war *without risks*." Of the army's chances he was more sanguine than most. "If this programme is carried out, I believe we shall be successful.... The weather is cold but fine. The army are in good condition tho' there are those who insist that its morale is not good but of this I see no signs."[24]

If any reservations lingered within Meade's mind, they were those born of self-doubt. Though his performances as a division commander had earned him plaudits, never before had he exercised command over 15,000 men in a major operation. The thought of it left him feeling daunted on January 15, five days before the march was to commence. "It is hard to say what I want," he confessed after riding along the Rappahannock, inspecting possible crossing places and reflecting upon the campaign at hand. "As a Corps commander I ought to want to move at once & have a chance in my new position. At the same time the responsibility, and the interests at stake in the issue, make me sometimes a little nervous & perfectly willing to have the movement postponed."[25]

January 20 dawned cold and threatening. Hooker's Center Grand Division formed the vanguard of Burnside's developing turning movement. That day Meade's corps mirrored the army as a whole in making fine time marching to its designated jump-off position a half mile short of Banks's Ford. Pontoon bridges were to be constructed above the ford overnight to carry the V and III Corps across the Rappahannock on the twenty-first and onto the open plateau beyond. Franklin's Left Grand Division, composed of the I and VI Corps, was to cross a mile below Hooker, while Maj. Gen. Edwin V. Sumner's Right Grand Division trailed Franklin's and Hooker's columns. Downstream from Fredericksburg, elements of Maj. Gen. Franz Sigel's Grand Reserve Division would conduct desultory demonstrations aiming to fix the Army of Northern Virginia in place while the march progressed.[26]

Unfortunately, it began to rain—heavily—that evening starting around 8:00 P.M. By midnight the precipitation had started to freeze, driven sideways by a howling gale. Hooker's and Franklin's men shivered in their temporary camps near the ford in a night as cheerless as any in the army's existence. The next day saw no letup in the weather; the pontoon train, expected to arrive at the Rappahannock in time to allow a 7:30 A.M. crossing, could make no progress in the thickening Virginia ooze, holding up all combat and support elements in its path. Burnside's chief engineer, though hopeful that the pontoons might span the river on the twenty-second, advised against continuing the campaign, the movement having long since been discovered by Confederates along the southern bank. Finally, facing still-unrelenting bad weather and growing odds against success, Burnside drafted orders on the twenty-second suspending the campaign. The army began a slow march to Falmouth the next day to dry out and consider its fate.[27]

"I never felt so disappointed & sorry for any one in my life as I did for Burnside," Meade wrote Margaretta on January 23 as the V Corps slogged its way back to camp, laboring to corduroy roads for the mired artillery and trains in what was termed in short order the "Mud March." "He really seems to have even the elements against him. I told him warmly when I saw him how sorry I felt, and that I had almost rather have lost a limb than that the storm should have occurred." Burnside admitted to his empathetic subaltern that the weather's ferocity was perhaps just as well, given the uncooperative attitude of other officers. For some time, he had been awake to the fact that his operational course was opposed by key subordinates, "among them Generals in high command who openly rejoiced at the storm & the obstacle it presented." With the campaign in tatters and the prospect of extended winter quarters before him, Burnside deemed it high time to make a stand against army intrigue. The Army of the Potomac's commander could not control the heavens, but that evening he made his way to Washington determined to leash the officers whom he felt stood against him.[28]

Burnside aimed at both the Hooker and engineer/McClellan axes of dissent in his General Orders Number 8, which he presented personally to Lincoln for the latter's approval—with an accompanying resignation letter—the next day. Hooker, singled out uncompromisingly in the document as "a man unfit to hold an important commission during a crisis like the present, when so much patience, charity, confidence, and patriotism are due from every soldier in the field," must, Burnside insisted, be dismissed from the service altogether. The orders, when coupled with the resignation letter and frank discussion with the president, gave the meeting the decided air of an ultimatum, which is what it was: either the malcontents or Burnside would have to go. Lincoln, attentive to the military and political consequences of either course and mindful of Burnside's performance and its deleterious effect upon army morale, finally decided to accept his general's resignation on the twenty-fifth. McClellan acolytes Franklin and Smith were ordered to depart the Army of the Potomac that same day. Its new commander would be Joseph Hooker.[29]

Meade, like many in the army, took time to reflect on the disappointing tenure of the likeable but overmatched Burnside. Unlike many, though, his musings were evenhanded and devoid of rancor. "With all my respect & I may almost say affection for Burnside for he has been most kind & considerate towards me," he penned Margaretta on a snowy twenty-sixth, "I can not shut my eyes to the fact that he was not equal to the command of so large an army." Acknowledging Burnside's qualities, namely "determination & nerve," the Pennsylvanian concluded that he "wanted knowledge & judgement, and was deficient in the enlarged mental capacity which is essential in a commander." Perhaps most damaging to Burnside in gaining the confidence of his officers and men, Meade maintained, were his own transparent claims of impostership. Expressed as they were at the outset of his tenure, they encouraged like opinion among subordinates and in the end "greatly weakened his position."[30]

Joe Hooker was hobbled by no such feelings of self-doubt. The Massachusetts native's ascendance to command, if not predetermined, had received plenty of support since the fall of 1862 from important Radicals and their newspaper-editor proxies. Together they had flocked around the outspoken general while he recuperated in Washington from his Antietam wound. Fighting Joe, a onetime conservative, made known a burgeoning radicalism calculated (in part) to boost his prospects for advancement. The wave of pro-Hooker sentiment that washed over official Washington, as might be expected, was not so warmly received among the Army of the Potomac's principal generals. They had endured enough of Fighting Joe's knack for self-promotion and uneven personal habits to preclude their embracing the command change—even if it offered the prospect of improvement from the Burnside regime. Most galling to them was Hooker's keenness to engage in partisan intrigue. By courting Republican favor, the new commander estranged many within the army's conservative (and, ideally at least, apolitical) core. Meade, though possessing what he described as "a more favorable" opinion of Hooker "than any other of the old regular officers," had long recognized this trait in his chief. "Hooker is a *democrat* & an *anti-abolitionist*—that is to say he *was*," he wrote Margaretta a month after Antietam, when rumors of Fighting Joe succeeding to the army's command first began to simmer. "What he will be, when the command of the army is held out to him, is more than anyone can tell, because I fear he is open to temptation, and liable to be induced by flattery." Ever philosophical, Meade turned then to consider the boundaries of the general's military talent. Recognizing that Hooker "is a *very good soldier*—capital Gen'l for an army corps," the Pennsylvanian, revealing his hand as the engineer-general that he was, questioned whether he possessed the self-control and calculation necessary to succeed in wielding a host of over one hundred thousand men, "as he is apt to think the only thing to be done is *pitch in & fight*." To his eldest son, John Sergeant Meade, the general was more direct, offering Hooker the somewhat backhanded compliment, "If fighting ... is all that is necessary to make a General, he will certainly distinguish himself."[31]

But Hooker did distinguish himself in the weeks after assuming the army's top spot, displaying the kind of deft—and unexpected—managerial touch not seen since the salad days of McClellan. Indeed, he shook his host of the melancholy that had gripped it since November, improving soldier rations and camp sanitation; holding myriad drills, inspections, and reviews; and extending much-welcomed furloughs for the rank and file. The man he handpicked to serve as his chief of staff, Dan Butterfield, devised corps identification badges to enable rapid battlefield unit identification (the V Corps badge was the Maltese cross); for now, they served a more critical function in solidifying a nascent élan among the entire command. Structural reforms followed too: Hooker discarded Burnside's grand-division scheme (which had added an additional layer of command and control to what had already proven to be a ponderous tactical organization), created an independent corps of cavalry better to combat the renowned Confederate mounted arm, and perhaps most significantly, formed the Bureau of Military Information that enhanced greatly the army's ability to tally the enemy's numbers and discern its movements and intent.[32]

Meade supported some of these organizational changes. Despite initially being elevated to the command of the Center Grand Division as a result of the army shakeup, the Pennsylvanian preferred his place atop the V Corps, calling the grand-division arrangement "purely an invention of Burnside's, and ... not I think ... a good one." Any amount of trust in Hooker's executive talent continued to be tempered, however, by the commander's reputed character flaws and penchant for collusion. Though downplaying in letters to Margaretta persistent charges of drunkenness against Hooker, Meade, writing nimbly, noted that "the danger he runs is of subjecting himself to bad influences, such as *Dan Butterfield & Dan Sickles*, who being intellectually more clever than Hooker & leading him to believe they are very influential, will obtain an injurious ascendancy over him & insensibly affect his conduct." Of the "two Dans," whose dodgy and imperious reputations were recognized armywide, Meade was less than generous. "Such *gents* as ... *Sickles* & ... *Butterfield* are not the persons I should select as my intimates, however worthy & superior they may be." He perceptively (and presciently) worried that the ill effects of a Hooker-Butterfield-Sickles alliance might outweigh any operational or organizational benefits it might produce. Faultfinding talk within the high command had, in truth and as Lincoln himself predicted, abated little as Hooker and his staff made preparations for a spring campaign.[33]

Throughout the early months of 1863, the V Corps maintained its sprawling encampment south of Potomac Creek at Stoneman's Switch along the Richmond, Fredericksburg, and Potomac Railroad. During the lull, Meade, perhaps gripped by the ennui of camp life, worried anew about his relative position in the officer corps. Upon learning that certain generals had sought to backdate their volunteer commissions to leverage their careers better, Meade worked to do the same, asking Secretary of War Stanton to date his major general's rank from September 14, 1862—the date of the Battle of South Mountain. Receiving no response, he began to explore his options within the regular service. Soon, he saw some hope. The president, while on a five-day visit to the army early in April, had informed Hooker that a then-vacant brigadier slot in the Regular Army could be awarded on the basis of what happened in the next fight; the leading candidates included Meade. Encouraged by this, the general took inventive, if not inspired, steps to advance his cause. Attending a series of presidential reviews with Mr. and Mrs. Lincoln, Meade engaged the First Lady in polite conversation and, playing upon the chief executive's taste for coarse humor, "ventured to tell the President one or two dirty jokes," noting prosaically to Margaretta, "I think I have made decided progress in his affections."[34]

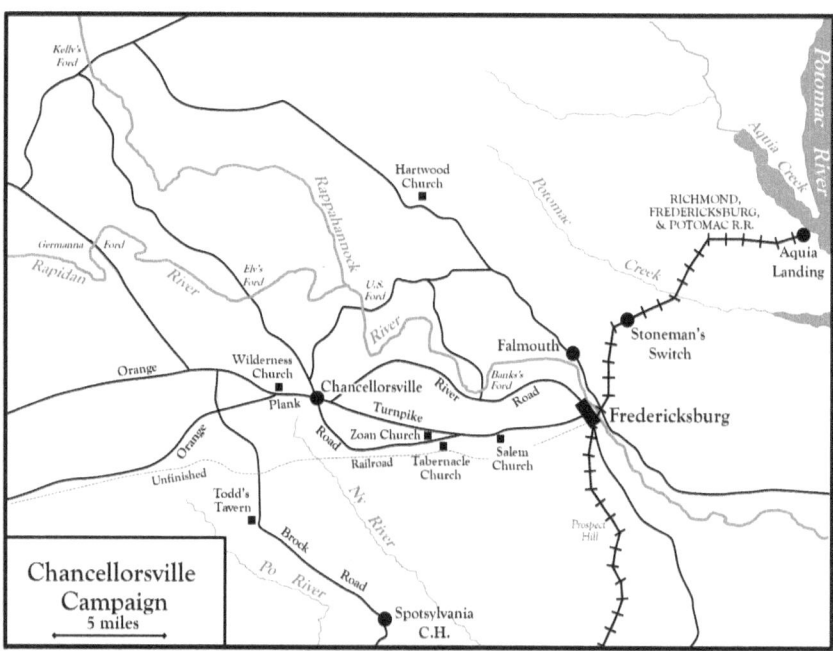

Lincoln had little time for Meade's clumsy ribaldry, for he and Hooker were engaged in serious discussions concerning the army's next offensive. The president was desperate for a victory to shore up the Union's languishing military fortunes, which had by early 1863 eroded public support for the administration and its hard-war policy. Abiding by Halleck's headquarters doctrine and its dictum that Lee's host remain the Army of the Potomac's sole objective, Lincoln emphatically called the continuing James-or-Rappahannock-line debate "a contest about nothing." With his communications advantage, Hooker should, the president believed, "harass and menace" Lee where he stood along the Rappahannock, avoiding Burnside's December folly "of attacking him in his entrenchments." Hooker, mindful of his commander's intent, crafted a plan that was far more comprehensive than Burnside's in January. Seeking like his predecessor to turn Lee's Fredericksburg works, he chose to send most of his cavalry corps, commanded by Maj. Gen. George Stoneman, far to the left and rear of the Army of Northern Virginia in an effort to stymie Confederate communications and, in the event of a Rebel withdrawal toward Richmond, check their retreat. Meanwhile, a "flying column" of three infantry corps—including Meade's—would cross the Rappahannock at Kelly's Ford, located some twenty-five miles above Falmouth, cross that river's southern tributary, the Rapidan, and moving east, turn the Confederate outposts as they covered United States and Banks's Fords. Three more corps under Maj. Gen. John Sedgwick aimed to fix Lee's main body in front of the town, while still another one, Maj. Gen. Darius N. Couch's II Corps, would operate between the scattered Union wings and react to contingencies as they transpired. Hooker, after enduring delays from spring rains and crafting revisions to the plan, made ready to strike Lee as the month drew to a close.[35]

Fearing treachery from every corner, civilian or military, Hooker kept his plans close to the vest. The implications of the silence at headquarters troubled Meade, who after four months in command, still had not led his corps into battle. "[Hooker] is remarkably reticent of his *information*," the general complained to his wife. "I really know nothing of what he intends to do or when or where he proposes doing any thing." Acknowledging the obvious merits of military secrecy, Meade maintained nonetheless that "it may be carried too far & important plans may be frustrated by subordinates, from their ignorance of how much depended on their share of work." A perusal of the joint committee's just-published Fredericksburg report hardened this view. The December contest along the Rappahannock had "turned on a mis-apprehension," claimed Meade, with "Burnside thinking he was saying & ordering one thing and Franklin understanding another." He feared Hooker was laying the foundation for another such episode. "All I ask & pray for is to be told explicitly & clearly what I am expected to do, and then I shall try to the best of my ability to accomplish the task set before me." Worries aside, Meade trusted that the army, its morale now "better than it ever was," might yet accomplish great things. "Look out for *Fighting Joe's* army," he teased Margaretta, whose spirits had sunk in recent weeks, "[and] the grand reaction in our favor."[36]

The V Corps began its march late in the morning on April 27, stepping off several hours behind the XI and XII Corps, whose columns formed the vanguard of Hooker's strike force. The three corps, chosen for their task because their camps were situated farthest from Lee's prying sentinels south of the Rappahannock, were to move stealthily and speedily, unencumbered by the bulk of their artillery and trains. Still, for Meade's men, the hike was laborious. Burdened by knapsacks filled with eight days' rations and laden with personal effects, the rank and file struggled to make time on a cool and gray Monday. In short order they jettisoned along the route an array of accoutrements, including overcoats, blankets, and tent halves. A steady, though not heavy rain added to the general discomfort and may have reminded some of the Mud March. But there would no repeat of January. Meade reached his destination, Hartwood Presbyterian Church, by early evening, the men fatigued but in good spirits. Providence smiled upon the soldiers as they set to making campfires and bedded down for the night.[37]

Satisfied with his work so far, Meade mounted his favorite war horse, Old Baldy, the next day and rode with his command toward Kelly's Ford, twelve miles distant from Hartwood. Along the route he was accompanied briefly by Hooker, who had joined the column to provide supervision and inspiration. Despite rain, the commander's plan worked with an almost clocklike precision. Lead elements of Maj. Gen. Oliver O. Howard's XI Corps crossed the Rappahannock near Kelly's on the evening of the twenty-eighth, followed over the next twelve hours by the remainder of the turning force. Arriving at the Kelly's Ford pontoon bridges, Meade rode at nearly a full gallop among the troops, who rose to cheer their general "until the sound made the hearts of all beat tumultuously." Sensing the drama in the moment, the Pennsylvanian stood in his stirrups and doffed his forage cap, "giving no outward sign of pleasure at the reception, though he afterward said that the memory of that day would never be forgotten."[38]

By Wednesday at 5:00 P.M., two divisions of Meade's corps—Humphreys's command was left behind to escort ammunition and pontoon trains from Kelly's—prepared to wade the Rapidan at Ely's Ford. Peering over his spectacles at an infantry lieutenant during a crossing made hazardous by a swift current and a rocky, slippery bed, Meade asked the subaltern nonchalantly if the water was cold. The young officer replied affirmatively, commenting that the soaked men would suffer a hard night unless they were permitted to build fires for warmth. "Hang it, Sir," Meade retorted. "Don't you know this is a secret movement? We must have no big fires." Contemplating matters a moment further, the general relented, remarking that he could not see how fires were to be avoided in such dank conditions. Indeed, the soldiers slept hard "amidst huge fires" that night, rising the next morning "ready and eager for any movement."[39]

Once on the south bank of the Rapidan, matters were certain to come to a head against an enemy awakening to Union designs. XII Corps commander Maj. Gen. Henry W. Slocum, who directed the advance wing after Hooker departed for Falmouth on the twenty-ninth, was ordered to push his and Howard's corps forward from Germanna Ford, five miles up the Rapidan from Ely's, toward the Chancellorsville crossroads and a rendezvous with Meade. Once there, Slocum would "endeavor to advance at all hazards, securing a position on the [Orange] Plank road and uncovering Banks's Ford." If the column encountered heavy Confederate resistance, Hooker instructed the wing commander to hold his position, as "you will have nearly 40,000 men, which is more than [Lee] can spare to send against you." Chancellorsville, located ten miles west of Fredericksburg at the intersection of the Orange Turnpike and Plank Road, was the key. Hooker stressed that no time be lost in seizing the critical juncture. "From that moment," he said of its capture, "all will be ours."[40]

It was no simple march from Ely's Ford to Chancellorsville. After wading the Rapidan, the V Corps entered the gloomy, forbidding Virginia Wilderness, a seventy-square-mile swath of tangled secondary growth and underbrush possessing few farm fields or clearings suitable for the touch-of-elbow linear tactics of the day. Those who navigated it did so sluggishly and with reasonable fear of what might lurk ahead. So it was for Meade. His orders for April 30 included instructions to secure United States Ford, located on the Rappahannock north of the Chancellorsville clearing, to facilitate transit and communication between the army's scattered wings. Sending ahead two squadrons of his small cavalry contingent to scout the route, the general soon acted upon flawed intelligence, detailing Sykes's division to overpower what turned out to be an imaginary Confederate brigade guarding the ford. Nonetheless, the head of Meade's column, after sundry skirmishing with enemy infantry, reached the Chancellor House by midday. The general's staff commandeered the imposing, two-and-one-half-story brick home, informing the widow Frances Chancellor that it would be Hooker's headquarters before long. Unintimidated by the Yankee presence, "quite a bevy of ladies in light, dressy, attractive spring costumes . . . scolded audibly and reviled bitterly" the gathering Federal host, and they were straightaway banished to a single room at the rear of house. Meade, giving little thought to the protestations of the Chancellor women, pressed cavalry and a brigade of infantry ahead to locate the elusive Confederates and possibly reach Banks's Ford too. In short order Brig. Gen. James Barnes reported a strong enemy force deployed astride the Orange Turnpike some two miles east of the crossroads. Barnes, Meade's oldest subordinate commander at age sixty-one, requested help for his men to push the recalcitrant Rebels aside.[41]

The military situation was yet unclear to Meade after four days of campaigning. Still receiving no operational plan from Hooker, his instincts nonetheless told him to press an advantage already gained. He could barely contain his delight as Slocum arrived at Chancellorsville in midafternoon to assume command of the reunited column. "This is splendid, Slocum," cried the Philadelphian. "Hurrah for Old Joe! We're on Lee's flank and he doesn't know it. You take the Plank Road toward Fredericksburg, and I'll take the Pike, or *vice versa*, as you prefer, and we will get out of this Wilderness." Slocum's response stopped him cold. "My orders are to assume command on arriving at this point, and to take up a line of battle here, and not to move forward without further orders." Visibly deflated by the news, Meade issued instructions pulling Barnes's brigade back toward the crossroads. His generals on the scene were dumbstruck and at once offered their protests. Barnes's division commander, the tetchy Charles Griffin, was so convinced he could seize the Rebel position just east of Mott's Run that he, in an expletive-laden rant, offered to resign his commission should an attempt to do so prove a failure.[42]

Hooker arrived at Chancellorsville by nightfall to take personal charge of the situation. Following behind Fighting Joe were two divisions of Couch's command; expected on the morrow was Sickles's III Corps. Hooker would have within the course of the next day some 70,000 soldiers and thirty-two batteries of artillery on hand to deal with Lee. The mood at the crossroads was jovial, perhaps even unseemly in its optimism. General Orders No. 47 expressed the prevailing sentiment memorably, declaring "that the operations of the last three days have determined that our enemy must either ingloriously fly, or come out from behind his defenses and give us battle on our own ground, where certain destruction awaits him." The missive played well with many in the rank and file, but to Meade the outcome seemed hardly a sure thing. "We are across the river & have out-manoeuvered the enemy," he penned Margaretta, ending his note with figurative as well as literal significance: "[W]e are not yet out of the woods."[43]

The next day saw a column of just under 30,000 soldiers set to trudge toward a broad, open ridge located south of Banks's Ford crowned by the Zoan Baptist and Tabernacle Methodist Churches—the same plateau that had eluded Burnside's grasp months before. Meade's corps would advance along two avenues. Griffin's division was to pass through the Wilderness along the narrow River Road nearly to Banks's Ford, then turn south to link with Sykes's regulars, who would march straight east along the Orange Turnpike to Zoan. Humphreys's trailing division of nine-month enlistees, arriving at Chancellorsville at 7:00 A.M. after escorting the corps trains, was first earmarked to follow Sykes, but last-minute instructions placed it behind Griffin. Farther south, Slocum's XII Corps would move east along the Orange Plank Road, which paralleled the turnpike between Chancellorsville and the plateau, halting near the Tabernacle Church. Hooker expected trifling opposition, trusting reports that the bulk of the Rebel army was still glued to Sedgwick's force at Fredericksburg. Once secure upon the plateau, Hooker likely would assume a defensive posture, meeting his enemy with a killing advantage in numbers and firepower. Fighting Joe would dare Lee, outnumbered two to one and with enemies looming upon both flanks, either to attack him in the kind of set-piece battle tailored to Federal strengths in manpower, weaponry, and logistics, or withdraw south toward Richmond.

Hooker's written orders for Meade, finally issued at around 10:00 A.M. after a stifling morning fog had dissipated, designated a position "midway between Mott's and Colin's [Golin] Runs" as the V Corps's goal. From there, the Pennsylvanian could unmask Banks's Ford, further improving communication between the separated wings of the army as they moved to close upon the enemy. Meade accompanied Griffin's and Humphreys's divisions along the River Road; his presence with the northern column reflected the primacy of its mission within Hooker's larger operational scheme as well as probable concern for its security in the furrowed and forested riverside terrain. Few within the army that day, least of all Hooker, considered the contingency that Lee might seek to deny the Federals possession of the Zoan ridge. Unfortunately, by the time the Yankees began moving on May 1, the plateau had long since been occupied by Confederate divisions commanded by Maj. Gens. Richard H. Anderson and Lafayette McLaws. More help was on the way. Nearly all of Lt. Gen. Thomas J. "Stonewall" Jackson's corps, some 33,000 men in all, had broken camp near Fredericksburg at first light and was on the march to join Anderson and McLaws. Hooker had moved upon his objective exactly one day too late.[44]

Meade moved without incident toward Banks's Ford. His march took him progressively away from Sykes's column as the River Road followed the Rappahannock's meandering course, and soon he lost contact with his lone division on the turnpike. By midday the muted peals of musketry and thud of cannon fire could be heard in the distance through the forest: Jackson had—quite unexpectedly—struck both Sykes and Slocum as their commands lurched eastward. Unsure of his detached division's precise location, Meade sent skirmishers south to establish contact with the regulars, but they failed to push aside a Confederate cavalry screen along the Old Mine Road. Meanwhile, the Philadelphian continued on as ordered, riding past Duerson's Mill and ahead to the Decker Farm overlooking the ford. There his lead regiments turned south toward the plateau and the sound of the guns while engineers and work details prepared to span the river. Meade was at last nearly free of the Wilderness and onto open ground when a message from headquarters arrived directing the corps back to the Chancellorsville crossroads. Maj. James C. Biddle, the general's aide-de-camp, brought the unhappy news to Charles Griffin. The fiery lead division commander, now denied battle twice in successive days, met the directive "with a look of disgust," recalled Biddle. "Call that a position?" he asked the aide. "Here I can defy any force the enemy can bring against me." The order stood. The corps, mirroring the army as a whole, began to retire in haste to its location occupied the night before.[45]

Recent scholarship has been kind to Hooker in assessing his generalship on May 1, 1863, and their points contain merit. To be sure, the general's oft-stated preponderance in numbers was more apparent than real on this day, for Jackson possessed a sizeable manpower edge at the point of contact just west of the Zoan/Tabernacle plateau. Hooker, privy to operational information that was inaccessible to his subordinates, knew this. Moreover, each Union column was out of supporting distance of the other when Jackson struck, militating against success when opposed by a united (and aggressive) foe. Indeed, Sykes's division, in its brisk turnpike fight that afternobn, found both its flanks overlapped and endangered when the withdrawal order arrived. So it was too for Slocum on the Plank Road. Finally, neither element engaged had yet emerged from the Wilderness; the ground they occupied, situated far below the heights Hooker so coveted, possessed little intrinsic tactical value. Still, it can be claimed with equal weight that it was no worse ground—and probably a good deal better— than that at Chancellorsville and that Hooker's retreat affected adversely the morale of many in the army who saw no reason to shy away from a fight that day. Fighting Joe's detractors were (and remain) many; few forgave the commander for, they argued, squandering four days' hard marching and nearly flawless operational execution by the officers and soldiers of the Army of the Potomac. Among the disheartened was Meade, who at one time felt cause to doubt his commander's prudence in the face of battle. Assembled at the crossroads that evening with Gens. Sykes, Couch, and Winfield S. Hancock, the onetime army topographer exclaimed with not a little indignation as his men set to building earthworks: "My God, if we can't hold the top of a hill, we certainly cannot hold the bottom of it!" The general was so disenchanted with the Chancellorsville position (and with Hooker's continued failure to provide guidance to his corps commanders) that he, along with Dan Sickles, visited the army's chief engineer, Brig. Gen. Gouverneur K. Warren, and pressed the latter to assume "as a staff officer of the Commanding General . . . the responsibility of giving the necessary instructions to meet the great emergency of the case." Warren declined, claiming correctly that such a course exceeded his command authority. With that, a sullen Meade returned to his corps.[46]

The general, assigned the eastern flank of the army's defensive cordon, placed his three divisions on line at 3:00 A.M., extending northeast to the Rappahannock from a point one thousand yards above Chancellorsville along the Mineral Spring Road. Crowning a ridgeline that overlooked the course of Mine (or Mineral Spring) Creek, tied to the river on its left, and shrouded along nearly its entire two-mile front by woods, the position had much to recommend it for defense. Here the V Corps lay for almost the entire day of May 2, "strengthening the position by the construction of rifle-pits . . . [and] abatis." Meade, his confidence apparently restored since his meeting with Warren, doubted now that he would receive an attack. Indeed, the position was, according to a staff officer serving with Griffin, rendered quite as good as that at Malvern Hill. "Our position here is so splendid," Capt. Richard Auchmuty wrote his mother, "that as much as I like to have battle postponed, I wish the rebs would come on."[47]

Meanwhile, Lee considered his next move. Desiring to maintain the initiative that had passed to him on May 1, the Confederate chieftain discovered that any attempt to envelop the Federal left in order to sever Hooker's line of communication with the Rappahannock would run into Meade's formidable works, which glistened by midmorning with twenty-eight cannon. Similarly, an assault on Hooker's center at Chancellorsville promised little but futility. Faced with few viable offensive options east of the crossroads, Lee determined instead to commit most of his available manpower—just over 30,000 soldiers—to a wide flanking movement around Hooker's weakly anchored right located deep in the Wilderness, leaving a token force to counter the Federals in his front. The risky endeavor would demand miles of hard marching and consume the entire day, but it held the most hope for Lee as he sought to isolate the Army of the Potomac from its river fords. He entrusted its execution to Jackson.[48]

Jackson conducted his march with as much boldness and exactitude as Hooker's turning movement days before, and his effort was in the end much more lethal. At about 5:45 P.M. the Confederate attack crashed into the poorly placed regiments of Howard's XI Corps three miles west of Chancellorsville along the Orange Turnpike. Crumbling under the weight of the assault, hundreds of its soldiers fled to the rear in confusion. Awakened to the severity of the situation, the Union high command took measures to stem the Federal reverse along the turnpike, restore the integrity of its line, and protect its communications with United States Ford. Meade too recognized the danger; though far from the scene of the disaster and without direction from army headquarters, he dispatched Sykes's regulars to the Ely's Ford Road, facing its regiments south and west in line of battle. By doing so, he reestablished, however tenuously, the army's right and covered its source of supply. "This was done in an incredibly short period of time," recalled James Biddle, and shaped the course of the Yankee defense for the remainder of the campaign.[49]

The sounds of battle resounded through the forest with sunrise on May 3 as the Confederate attack renewed with even more ferocity. Led by Maj. Gen. James E. B. Stuart after Jackson had been wounded the night before, it aimed to drive Hooker from the defensive lines the latter had ably cobbled in the wake of the XI Corps's collapse. For Meade, who possessed more offensive designs than his commander, the day was simply one of frustration. With the entire V Corps in place along the Ely's Ford Road, he heard the sounds of battle ebbing across his front. The Rebels presented their left tantalizingly to the Philadelphian as they charged eastward against the Federals' Chancellorsville works, fairly inviting a crushing flank attack. No authorization came from headquarters permitting such a move (though Hooker had intimated overnight to others that this was at least on his mind), so Meade sat largely inert as the morning wore on, dispatching only Brig. Gen. Erastus B. Tyler's brigade of Humphreys's division to aid elements of the II Corps as they struggled to retain the Yankee line west of the crossroads. Chafing from the inactivity, he instructed his inspector general, Lt. Col. Alexander S. Webb, to scout the wooded terrain ahead in search of a suitable line of attack. Webb returned with a favorable report and urged that the attempt be made at once. With that, the general rode, Webb in tow, the short distance to the army's new headquarters at the Oscar Bullock House for a visit with Hooker.[50]

Meade, grasping Webb's right arm tightly, entered Hooker's tent and stated the case: the opportunity for a decisive counterattack existed if the V and Maj. Gen. John Reynolds's I Corps (which had arrived on the field late the day previous) could be granted the chance to sweep the Rebel forces from the north. Most of its brigades, when combining the two organizations, had yet to be engaged during the campaign; yet Hooker would have none of Meade's proposal. The army commander, having been knocked briefly unconscious an hour before by the effects of Confederate artillery fire, no longer possessed a hint of his fêted offensive spirit. Debilitated from the concussion—a pillar of the Chancellor House had fallen squarely upon his right side—and lying upon his back, Hooker instead dictated that the V Corps remain on the defensive and admonished his subordinate for ordering Tyler into the fray. Unrelenting, Meade begged Hooker with renewed feeling. "I have never known any one so vehemently to advise an attack upon the field of battle," Webb would recall the event, yet the command stood. "I tried all I could," Meade wrote Margaretta five days later, "but I was *over-ruled* & censured." Leaving the tent, the crestfallen officers saw renewed hope when Couch, the army's senior corps commander, arrived to consult with Hooker. But his meeting went no better. The injured army commander temporarily turned over leadership to his subordinate but allowed Couch no discretion: he was to withdraw to predetermined defensive positions closer to United States Ford.[51]

The six infantry corps took up a strong perimeter conforming partly to the works Meade had erected and occupied since May 2, with V Corps infantry and artillery providing some cover for the withdrawal. Fighting the lingering effects of his injury and unnerved by the intensity of Lee's assaults, Hooker awaited news from Sedgwick's Fredericksburg front, hoping that "Uncle John" might help rescue the army's fortunes. But Sedgwick and his VI Corps, after carrying the heights overlooking the town near noon on May 3, encountered stout resistance and was stopped cold by Lee the next day at the Salem Baptist Church, seven miles east of the new Union line. Fighting Joe considered on May 4 whether or not to attack the enemy in his front and rush to Sedgwick's aid, while an anxious Meade could hear the roar of artillery along the Orange Turnpike, surmising that Lee "was trying & must succeed in crushing" the isolated VI Corps. Limited in what he could do by himself, the Philadelphian sent a heavy probe in the form of Col. James McQuade's brigade to test the Rebel defenses in front of the Ely's Ford Road. There would, however, be no more offensive moves that day, tentative or otherwise. At midnight Hooker summoned his available corps commanders to his tent. He appeared finally ready to seek their input and counsel, posing to them the question of either remaining south of the river to resume operations or to withdraw to the safety of the camps at Falmouth.[52]

Hooker made clear his desire to retreat at the start of the meeting, citing the administration's concern for the safety of Washington and doubts over both the army's ability to resume the campaign in the Wilderness and the quality of some of its troops. It seemed clear to Meade afterward that Hooker's mind was well made up, but the commander, accompanied by Butterfield, exited the tent to permit the generals some freedom of discussion. Meade, Reynolds, and Howard voted to hold the army's position and continue the contest. Couch demurred, stating years later that he would fight only if he "could designate the point of attack"—a hit at Hooker's leadership. Sickles, with an attorney's flair, championed his commander's views. "As a soldier," wrote James Biddle,

"[Sickles] advised . . . not to fall back, but as Washington was in danger as a politician he advised [Hooker] to fall back." Meade, according to one witness, countered that "if those were the motives which influenced this army, he did not see why we had crossed the river at all. He advised fighting . . . and relying on our strength to risk a great blow, feeling confident in our cause." Hooker, after reentering, upheld the minority: the Army of the Potomac would retire north of the river. A disgusted Reynolds stalked out of the tent, muttering to no one in particular, "What was the use of calling us together at this time of night when he intended to retreat anyhow?" Fighting Joe shared in the gloom, remarking to Meade later that "he was ready to turn over to me the [army] that he had enough of it and almost wished he had never been born."[53]

It was Meade's men who had opened the Battle of Chancellorsville, and those wearing the Maltese cross would bear responsibility for covering the army's retreat. This task they executed flawlessly throughout a rainy and dismal May 5–6. Meade rode along his lines above United States Ford, steadying his men as they gazed south into the woods toward an unseen enemy. The heavy showers, starting at about 4:00 P.M., soaked man and beast and rendered small arms nearly useless. Reaching the position of one regiment, the general spied its men firing their limited supply of percussion caps in order to dry the soaked nipples on their muskets' cap locks. "What the devil are you doing?" he inquired, irritated by the men's apparent wanton waste. A soldier remarked wryly that they were seeing how many caps it took to make wet gunpowder go off. "Why don't you draw your bullets and reload them?" asked the general. "So we will when we get more wormers," the soldier replied, to the laughter of his comrades. Meade, softened by the infantryman's riposte, thought better of reproaching the unit. "Never mind, my men. If the rebs come up before you are ready, stand firm and give them the bayonet." Lt. George F. Williams, later the managing editor of the *New-York Times*, recalled afterward that "[Meade] could not have given us advice more in accord with our feelings at that moment, and the anecdote made many friends for 'four-eyed George,' as the boys were even then beginning to call him."[54]

The retreat, punctuated as it was by incessant rain, tested everyone's nerves, from the lowliest enlisted soldier to Hooker himself. Indeed, the commander departed for the Rappahannock's north bank and sanctuary, leaving his corps generals to feel, perhaps with some merit, that they were left to fend for themselves. By 9:00 P.M. the pontoon bridges over which the soldiers crossed had been so damaged by rising floodwaters that Hooker ordered the movement suspended for one to two hours. Meade, now isolated but aggressive withal, rejoiced in this turn of fortune. "What an act of Providence!" he shouted to his brother corps commanders gathered at his headquarters—perhaps he might do some proper fighting after all. Signaling across the river to Hooker at midnight that Couch, exercising command authority on the south bank, had called off the operation for the night on account of the still-shaky spans, Meade prepared to defend his position. In this view he had an ally in Reynolds, who promised to "remain . . . and if there is any battle to be fought we will fight it together." But Hooker's response cooled any remaining ardor in George Meade. At 1:20 A.M. on May 6, the commander put a stop to what historian Stephen W. Sears called "another revolt of the generals, this time at the tactical level." He ordered the withdrawal to be carried out as planned.[55]

Recriminations started immediately after the army settled back into its camps. Though recent studies suggest that the rank and file suffered far less from demoralization than after Fredericksburg, talk against Hooker among his corps generals was pronounced. Meade, as was his custom, let few of his opinions be known outside his inner circle of family and friends. He said nothing of Hooker while meeting with Lincoln and Halleck during their whistle-stop encounter with leadership on May 7 and kept a safe distance from a senatorial delegation, friendly to Hooker, that poked around Falmouth shortly thereafter. His personal thoughts were, as ever, evenhanded, albeit critical. "All I can say is that Hooker disappointed the army & myself," he explained to Margaretta, "in failing to show the nerve & coup d'oeil at the critical moment, which all had given him credit for when he arrived." The general saw Hooker's experience as "proof of what a sense of responsibility will do to modify a person's character, and should be a warning to all of us, to be very cautious how we criticize our neighbors, or predict what we would do ourselves. . . . I am sorry for Hooker because I like him & my relations have always been agreeable with him; but I can not shut my eyes to the fact that he has on this occasion missed a brilliant opportunity."[56]

Others were more severe. Couch refused categorically to serve again under Fighting Joe and, visiting the president, sought appointment outside the Army of the Potomac unless Hooker was removed. He allegedly recommended that Meade assume command. Slocum took an extreme tack: he sought to gather enough support among the army's generals to oust Hooker and replace him with another man. That man, he believed, might well be Meade. The Philadelphian had impressed the officer cadre with his consistently aggressive demeanor at Chancellorsville and his continual, indeed impassioned, efforts to brace his commander's nerves. "Gen. Meade is in my opinion the first man in the army," staffer and Meade loyalist James Biddle enthused. "He has shown to be possessed of more mind than any [other] General." Alexander Webb was more fervent in his praise. "[Meade] advised the attacks which were not made & which would have gained the day. He asked to be allowed to attack with his corps supported by Reynolds. It was refused. He advised not to fall back. . . . Yes, he is splendid." In short order Slocum, Couch, and Sedgwick notified their junior that they would subordinate themselves to him if he were to take the army's reins. But Slocum needed Meade's acceptance and commitment to see his scheme through. Would he join the emerging cabal against the army chief?[57]

The general remained diffident, noting that "Hooker has one great advantage over his predecessors, in not having any intriguer among his subordinate Generals, who are working like beavers to get him out & themselves in." Meade would not now become that intriguer. He resisted those who pressed him in the matter. When *New-York Tribune* correspondent George W. Smalley explained to the general that his rise to command was "the wish of the army, or a great part of [it]," Meade responded with quiet firmness, "I don't know that I ought to listen to you." Spurning Slocum's plot, he offered instead to present his views to Lincoln if asked to do so. Meade was grateful for the expressions of confidence from his colleagues, and he certainly doubted Hooker's command capacity, but his ambitions did not extend beyond leadership of a corps. "I think I know myself & am sincere when I say I do not desire the command," he explained to his wife. Besides, "having no political influence, being no intriguer & indeed un-ambitious of the distinction it is hardly probable I shall be called on to accept or decline." If only to silence persistent talk of his candidacy, Meade expressed a preference, lukewarm to be sure, to see Hooker stay where he was. "I should be sorry to see him removed," he wrote his wife, "unless a decidedly better man is substituted."[58]

It was perhaps inevitable that the general would let his guard down, despite his desire to remain above the fray. Pennsylvania governor Andrew G. Curtin, arriving a week after the battle to gauge the pulse of Keystone State officers, sought an audience with Meade. Disheartened with the results of Chancellorsville, Curtin poured out his unhappiness to the general, who did as much as he could "to put [Curtin] in better spirits." Meade also expressed opinions that he might better have reserved for Margaretta alone. Regrettably for the general, Curtin related these views to friends in Washington, concluding on his own that Meade, along with Reynolds, had lost "entire faith" in the ability of the army commander. The news reached Hooker, who, wide awake after being warned by Lincoln earlier that "some corps and division commanders are not giving you their entire confidence," then went to Meade's headquarters to demand an explanation. The general stood up manfully to Hooker, claiming that he "had no right to complain of my expressing my views to others, which he was aware I had expressed to him at the time [of the battle]." To this point Hooker would grudgingly concede. "I feel mortified & angered," Meade vented in a letter home, "that Gov. Curtin should have taken advantage of a private conversation to [place me] in a false position with [Hooker]." Yet the damage was done.[59]

Neither, it might be said, was Hooker. Enraged by a *New York Herald* report that four of the corps commanders had opposed his decision to withdraw, Hooker decided to try to pin responsibility for the retreat upon Meade and Reynolds. Storming again into Meade's tent, he charged the V Corps commander of advising him to retreat during the May 4 council of war. "[Hooker] said that I had expressed the opinion that it was impracticable to withdraw the army & therefore I had favored an advance, and as he *knew* it was perfectly practicable to withdraw, he did not consider my opinion as being in favor of an advance." Dumbfounded as much by Hooker's logic as he was Sickles's argument during the council itself, Meade responded that he would deny the charge and seek the corroboration of others for his version of the story. The Philadelphian, his legendary seismic temper bursting forth, lost all soldierly restraint during the altercation and "damned Hooker very freely," causing members of his staff, fearing an impending court-martial if their general continued his tirade, to scurry for cover. "I am sorry to tell you I am at open war with Hooker," Meade would lament to Margaretta, noting that the "entente cordiale" that had so characterized their command relationship "is destroyed." The episode "was very painful & embarrassing" for him, yet it was not unexpected. "I have always feared the time would come when this would be inevitable with Hooker; for I knew no one would be permitted to stand in his way." Meade would act fast to safeguard his reputation. "The fact is, he now finds he has committed a grave error, which at the time he was prepared to assume the responsibility of, but now desires to cast it off on to the shoulders of others; but I rather think he will be mistaken."[60]

On May 22 Meade sent a circular letter to Reynolds, Couch, Sickles, Howard, Butterfield, and Warren, asking them to "state your recollections of what I said" during the council "and the impression it made upon you at the time." Reynolds recalled Meade as speaking "decidedly in favor of an advance on Fredericksburg at daylight [on May 5]; that you considered this army too long ... subservient to the safety of Washington, and you threw that out of the question altogether." Howard and Warren affirmed that he had counseled the offensive, while Sickles, loyal always to Hooker, replied with care to his V Corps counterpart. Though acknowledging that Meade advised attack at the outset of the meeting, Sickles maintained that the general's views over time "yielded somewhat to other considerations." These included the administration's mandate to protect Washington, the "hazards of a general engagement," shortfalls in supplies, and the "consequences to the North which would follow disaster to this army." After Hooker returned to the gathering, Meade accepted without reservation, wrote Sickles, the wisdom of his commander's course. "[M]y impression was that your original preferences appeared to have been surrendered to the clear conviction of the commanding general of the necessity which dictated his return to the north bank of the Rappahannock, and his unhesitating confidence in the practicability of withdrawing the army." Sickles's rejoinder effectively promised Meade that, if he chose to pursue the matter further, he would face a robust challenge from Fighting Joe and his clique.[61]

The imbroglio fizzled, perhaps thankfully for Meade, because larger considerations came again to dominate the army's attention. Lee, seeking to regain the operational initiative in the eastern theater, aimed now to turn Hooker from his Rappahannock post and move north into Maryland and Pennsylvania. On June 3 the Confederate offensive began. Hooker responded with skill, using the army as a shield against a possible thrust toward the capital in line with strictures placed upon him by Halleck. Still, Lincoln desired more from his army than simply to defend Washington. Indeed, he saw Lee's move north as a better opportunity to inflict damage on the Confederate army than by battling along the Rappahannock. With the head of Lee's column in Maryland by mid-month, far from its base and with the Potomac River to its back, never in the president's estimation had the Army of the Potomac been more favorably positioned to deal the Rebels a decisive blow. But Hooker agonized over enemy intent and lashed out against Halleck's operational constraints, forcing Lincoln to seriously consider his removal from command. By June 27, matters came to a head when a frustrated Hooker submitted a letter of resignation to Halleck, forcing the president's hand.[62]

As tension grew between Hooker and Washington, Meade, despite being on irretrievably distant terms with his own commander, carried out his orders conscientiously and without public comment or complaint. The rift between Hooker and his corps generals actually changed little in their dealings, for Fighting Joe still failed to pull them into his trust when formulating his plans. This did nothing to promote unity of effort as battle loomed north of the Potomac. "I am as much in the dark as to proposed plans, here on the ground, as you are in Philada," Meade complained to Margaretta from Northern Virginia late in June. "This is what Joe Hooker thinks profound sagacity, keeping his corps commanders, who are to execute his plans, in total ignorance of them, until they are developed in the execution of orders." Indeed, the Army of the Potomac's command milieu in June 1863 was so toxic as to discourage almost any rational officer from seeking to control its operations. Committed to a disadvantageous line of maneuver, so the engineer-generals argued, and riven by resentments political and military, it promised more hardship than glory for those called upon to lead it. Meade, figuring the time for speculation and rumor had passed with the enemy deep in the Keystone State, attempted on June 25 again to assure his wife—and perhaps himself—that the command would not fall upon him. "I do not stand . . . any chance because I have no friends political or others who press or advance my claims or pretensions. . . . Besides I have not the vanity to think my capacity to be so pre-eminent and I know there are plenty of others equally as competent as myself. . . . But do you know I think *your* ambition is being roused and that you are beginning to be bitten with the dazzling prospect of having for a husband a commanding General of an army. How is this?"[63]

In the predawn hours of June 28, 1863, Meade received in his tent a visitor from the War Department who bore an order from President Lincoln naming him to the command of the Army of the Potomac.[64]

MEADE'S SIX-MONTH CLIMB from divisional to corps to army leadership came at perhaps the most politically contentious period in the Army of the Potomac's nearly four-year history. Shifting war aims, compounded by twin defeats along the Rappahannock, deepened what was already bitter conflict within the high command. Meade's grasp of these realities was informed by over two decades in army service; his antebellum experience had taught him proper codes of conduct when pursuing his own career aspirations. This knowledge, along with a creditable battlefield record, assisted him as he rose to command the V Corps. Yet when rumored for the army's highest post, the general, noting its political aspects, believed himself to be out of real consideration precisely *because* of his desire to appear unfettered. But in this deprecating self-assessment, Meade missed the mark in an important way. His very reluctance to engage publicly in partisan intrigue (itself a hallmark of a military culture that subordinated outward self-promotion and political displays in favor of the national interest) made him as much a viable contender for the command as did his battlefield performance. Though in private agreement with much of the conservative program espoused by the army's leadership during the first half of the war, Meade's silence spoke volumes to a Washington wearied by the political schemes and unbidden sophistries of overtly ambitious generals.

More critical in explaining Meade's rise was his ability to win over brother officers with his approach to the Army of the Potomac's operational challenges. Though agreeing with other engineer-generals that the Virginia overland route promised little chance for decisive victory against an opponent as skilled as R. E. Lee, he concluded that inaction on whichever line the army was committed would do nothing but hasten strategic defeat for the Federal cause. For this reason alone, Meade called instead to test the fortunes of war, knowing that victorious campaigning was as much due to contingency as a sound operational course. To be sure, those generals not associated with the army's McClellan faction could not agree with what the engineers had to offer in the way of waging war, but this group never made up the dominant element within the command and was nearly neutered with Hooker's demise. This, when coupled with Meade's stridence for the offensive at Chancellorsville, vaulted him to the top of his comrades' list when they contemplated a new commander in the wake of Fighting Joe's reverse in the Virginia Wilderness. Believing after Chancellorsville that Meade possessed "the longest and clearest head of any general officer in this army," I Corps artillery chief Col. Charles S. Wainwright spoke for many of the army's senior officers on June 28 when he noted in his journal, "the appointment is very favourably received."[65]

Yet there were limitations, indeed drawbacks, inherent to Meade's approach to politics and war. Attempting—with and without success—to avoid involvement in national strategic concerns, the general, like many officers before and since, expected his civilian masters to reciprocate in deferring operational control in wartime to those politically disinterested, trained professionals like himself who presumably understood best how to conduct "purely military" matters. Once assuming army command, however, Meade found that such a course was unattainable within the climate of a modern, people's war. With criticism of his generalship continuing to mount after his victory at Gettysburg, Pennsylvania, he considered any amount of official impatience with him to be the product of unreasonable hopes, foolish emotions, and above all, partisan impulses. "This is exactly what I expected," Meade wrote Margaretta after the close of the Gettysburg Campaign. "[It] has been the history of all my predecessors, and I clearly saw that in time their fate would be mine." Though more successful on the battlefield than his predecessors in command of the Army of the Potomac, it was not Meade's fortune to direct it to its final triumph. This reality owed itself in part to a practiced form of political/military idealism that was overcome upon the arrival in March 1864 of Lt. Gen. Ulysses S. Grant.[66]

NOTES

1. George Gordon Meade (hereafter referred to as GGM) to Margaretta Sergeant Meade (hereafter referred to as MSM), Jan. 13, 1863, George Gordon Meade Collection, Historical Society of Pennsylvania, Philadelphia (hereafter referred to as HSP). On the Willard Hotel, see Ernest B. Furguson, *Freedom Rising: Washington in the Civil War* (New York: Alfred A. Knopf, 2004), 14, 45–46, 108–10; and Margaret Leech, *Reveille in Washington, 1860–1865* (New York: Harper and Brothers, 1941), 8–9. In 1858 Meade proclaimed Washington "a most painful & disagreeable place to be in. The intriguers & machinations for the advancement of personal interests, the selfishness & cold-heartedness that is there daily & hourly exhibited, is humiliating in the extreme to all who have any sense of self respect, or who desires to have a good opinion of his fellows." GGM to Macomb, Mar. 11, 1858, Papers of Col. John N. Macomb, 1857–77, Correspondence, June 1857–May 1862, RG 77, Papers of Engineer Officers and Others, 1803–1907, National Archives and Records Administration, Washington, D.C. (hereafter referred to as NARA).

2. Robert Goldthwaite Carter, *Four Brothers in Blue; or Sunshine and Shadows of the War of the Rebellion: A Story of the Great Civil War from Bull Run to Appomattox* (Washington, D.C.: Gibson Brothers, 1913), 210–11; Robert S. Robertson to James S. Coon, Jan. 9, 1863, R. S. Robertson Letters, Fredericksburg and Spotsylvania National Military Park, Fredericksburg, Va. (hereafter referred to

as FSNMP). For discussion of the Federal army after Fredericksburg, see A. Wilson Greene, "Morale, Maneuver, and Mud: The Army of the Potomac, December 16, 1862–January 26, 1863," in *The Fredericksburg Campaign: Decision on the Rappahannock*, ed. Gary W. Gallagher (Chapel Hill: University of North Carolina Press, 1995), 171–92; Stephen W. Sears, *Chancellorsville* (Boston: Houghton Mifflin, 1996), 1–25; George C. Rable, *Fredericksburg! Fredericksburg!* (Chapel Hill: University of North Carolina Press, 2002), 389–402; Daniel E. Sutherland, *Fredericksburg and Chancellorsville: The Dare Mark Campaign* (Lincoln: University of Nebraska Press, 1998), 84–88; Francis Augustín O'Reilly, *The Fredericksburg Campaign: Winter War on the Rappahannock* (Baton Rouge: Louisiana State University Press, 2003), 468–73, 495–97; and John J. Hennessy, "I Dread the Spring: The Army of the Potomac Prepares for the Overland Campaign," in *The Wilderness Campaign*, ed. Gary W. Gallagher (Chapel Hill: University of North Carolina Press, 1997), 70–71. A sympathetic view of Burnside's performance at Fredericksburg is provided in William Marvel, *Burnside* (Chapel Hill: University of North Carolina Press, 1991), 171–73, 200–12.

3. GGM to MSM, Oct. 29, 1862, Meade Collection. For Meade's desire to obtain rank as a major general of volunteers, see GGM to MSM, Sept. 5, 8, 18, 20, 23, 27, 29, Oct. 1, 12, 16, 25, 28, Nov. 3, 7, 8, 9, 14, 20, 22, 24, 25, 30, Dec. 2, 3, 1862, ibid.; and GGM to John Sergeant Meade, Oct. 11, 1862, ibid. Excellent studies of nineteenth-century officer ambition include Marcus Cunliffe, *Soldiers and Civilians: The Martial Spirit in America, 1775–1865* (Boston: Little, Brown, 1968), 135–44, 295–334; William B. Skelton, *An American Profession of Arms: The Army Officer Corps, 1784–1861* (Lawrence: University Press of Kansas, 1992), 193–202, 283–94; Samuel J. Watson, "Professionalism, Social Attitudes, and Civil-Military Accountability in the United States Army Officer Corps, 1815–1846" (Ph.D. diss., Rice University, 1996), 1316–22, 1326, 1334, 1336; Watson, "Manifest Destiny and Military Professionalism: Junior U.S. Army Officers' Attitudes toward War with Mexico, 1844–1846," *Southwest Historical Quarterly* 99, no. 4 (1996): 471, 489–90; and Edward M. Coffman, *The Old Army: A Portrait of the American Army in Peacetime, 1784–1898* (New York: Oxford University Press, 1986), 66–69.

4. On the Meade family and the general's early development, see Christopher S. Stowe, "A Philadelphia Gentleman: The Cultural, Institutional, and Political Socialization of George Gordon Meade" (Ph.D. diss., University of Toledo, 2005), 24–66.

5. Cunliffe, *Soldiers and Civilians*, 289–92, 295–96, 300–301; Coffman, *Old Army*, 87–88, 90–91; Skelton, *American Profession of Arms*, 140, 169–70, 177–79; 282–87, 295–97; Thomas J. Goss, *The War within the Union High Command: Politics and Generalship during the Civil War* (Lawrence: University Press of Kansas, 2003), 147–64; Watson, "Professionalism, Social Attitudes, and Civil-Military Accountability," 723, 725–54; Watson, "Flexible Gender Roles during the Market Revolution: Family, Friendship, Marriage, and Masculinity among U.S. Army Officers, 1815–1846," *Journal of Social History* 29, no. 1 (1995): 83–85.

6. The public spirit of self-denial, so prominent among American officers during the era, is examined in Cunliffe, *Soldiers and Civilians*, 413–14. Studies of ambition and nineteenth-century manhood include E. Anthony Rotundo, *American Manhood: Transformations in American Masculinity from the Revolution to the Modern Era* (New York: Basic Books, 1983), 1–4, 14–20; David G. Pugh, *Sons of Liberty: The Masculine Mind in Nineteenth-Century America* (Westport, Conn.: Greenwood, 1982), 3–43; and Amy S. Greenberg, *Manifest Manhood and the Antebellum American Empire* (New

York: Cambridge University Press, 2005). Perhaps Meade's most famous display of humility was his March 1864 offer to Lt. Gen. Ulysses S. Grant to step down from command of the Army of the Potomac in favor of the national interest. The gesture impressed Grant, who later declared: "This incident gave me even a more favorable opinion of Meade than did his great victory at Gettysburg." Ulysses S. Grant, *Personal Memoirs of U. S. Grant*, 2 vols. (New York: Charles L. Webster, 1885–86), 2:117.

    7. GGM to MSM, July 9, 1846, Meade Collection; Skelton, *American Profession of Arms*, 289–90; Skelton, "Officers and Politicians," 33–34; Skelton, "The Army Officer as Organization Man," in *Soldiers and Civilians: The U.S. Army and the American People*, ed. Garry D. Ryan and Timothy K. Nenninger (Washington, D.C.: National Archives and Records Administration, 1987), 65–66; Stow Persons, *The Decline of American Gentility* (New York: Columbia University Press, 1973), 29–50, 65.

    8. GGM to Joshua Barney, Sept. 7, 1861, Meade Collection; GGM to MSM, Feb. 23, 1862, ibid.; Mark Grimsley, *The Hard Hand of War: Union Military Policy toward Southern Civilians, 1861–1865* (New York: Cambridge University Press, 1995), 1–95. Meade's antebellum outlook mirrored that of many officers then in Federal service. For examples, see John F. Marszalek, *Sherman: A Soldier's Passion for Order* (New York: Free Press, 1993), xv–xvi, 132–39; Ethan S. Rafuse, *McClellan's War: The Failure of Moderation in the Struggle for the Union* (Bloomington: Indiana University Press, 2005), passim; Stephen D. Engle, *Don Carlos Buell: Most Promising of All* (Chapel Hill: University of North Carolina Press, 1999), 66–67; and Mark A. Snell, *From First to Last: The Life of Major General William B. Franklin* (New York: Fordham University Press, 2002), 51–52. On the Civil War as "family struggle," see Reid Mitchell, *The Vacant Chair: The Northern Soldier Leaves Home* (New York: Oxford University Press, 1993), 115–33.

    9. GGM to MSM, Nov. 24, Dec. 12, 1861, Jan. 26, Feb. 9, 1862, Meade Collection; *Detroit Free Press*, Feb. 22, 1862. On the move toward a more radicalized war in 1862, see Grimsley, *Hard Hand of War*, 132–33.

    10. GGM to MSM, Oct. 1, Nov. 7, 1862, Meade Collection. For Meade's acceptance of the "hard war" policy, see Stowe, "Philadelphia Gentleman," 210–15.

    11. GGM to MSM, Apr. 18, 22, 1863, Meade Collection. Excellent analysis of Meade's place within the Army of the Potomac's often-contentious political structure is provided in Hennessy, "I Dread the Spring," 68. Ethan S. Rafuse notes also that Meade's comparatively anonymous position as a brigade and division commander during much of 1862 enabled him to evade the kind of political scrutiny cast upon higher-level leaders within that army, especially those who, like the Pennsylvanian, possessed moderate-to-conservative political leanings. See Rafuse, *George Gordon Meade and the War in the East* (Abilene, Tex.: McWhiney Foundation, 2003), 47, 56.

    12. GGM to MSM, Nov. 22, 1863, Meade Collection; Herman Hattaway and Archer Jones, *How the North Won: A Military History of the Civil War* (Urbana: University of Illinois Press, 1983), 145, 332–33, 465–67; Rafuse, *George Gordon Meade and the War in the East*, 27–30; Joseph L. Harsh, "Lincoln's Tarnished Brass: Conservative Strategies and the Attempt to Fight the Early Civil War as a Limited War," in *The Confederate High Command & Related Topics: The 1988 Deep Delta Civil War Symposium: Themes in Honor of T. Harry Williams*, ed. Roman J. Heleniak and Lawrence L. Hewitt (Shippensburg, Pa.: White Mane, 1990), 124–41; Carol Reardon, *With a Sword in One Hand and Jomini in the Other: The Problem of Military Thought in the Civil War North* (Chapel Hill: Uni-

versity of North Carolina Press, 2012), 17–53. On the historical adherence to scientific principles as a means to understand and wage war, see Antoine Bousquet, *The Scientific Way of Warfare: Order and Chaos on the Battlefields of Modernity* (New York: Columbia University Press, 2009), 9–91.

13. Abraham Lincoln, "Message to Congress in Special Session," July 4, 1861, in *The Collected Works of Abraham Lincoln*, ed. Roy P. Basler, 9 vols. (New Brunswick, N.J.: Rutgers University Press, 1953–55), 4:438; Hattaway and Jones, *How the North Won*, 286–90, 328–37; Rafuse, *George Gordon Meade and the War in the East*, 30; Reardon, *With a Sword in One Hand*, 55–88.

14. Hattaway and Jones, *How the North Won*, 333–37; Rafuse, *George Gordon Meade and the War in the East*, 31, 37.

15. GGM to MSM, Nov. 13, 1862, Meade Collection; Hattaway and Jones, *How the North Won*, 416–17n12, 467; Rafuse, *George Gordon Meade and the War in the East*, 28–29.

16. GGM to MSM, Aug. 21, 24, Sept. 3, 4, 5, 6, 8, 12, 1862, Meade Collection. General-officer esteem for Meade can be found in George B. McClellan, *McClellan's Own Story: The War for the Union, the Soldiers Who Fought It, the Civilians Who Directed It, and His Relations to It and to Them*, ed. William C. Prime (New York: Charles L. Webster, 1887), 140; U.S. War Department, *The War of the Rebellion: A Compilation of the Official Records of the Union and Confederate Armies*, 70 vols. in 128 parts (Washington, D.C.: Government Printing Office, 1880–1901), ser. 1, 11(2):226, 12(2):235 (hereafter cited as *OR*; all references are to series 1 unless otherwise noted). For details of Meade's wounding, see Physician's Affidavit of Anthony E. Stocker, Nov. 7, 1885, RG 15, Records of the Veterans' Administration, NARA. For detailed secondary accounts of Meade's actions during the Seven Days' Battles, see Freeman Cleaves, *Meade of Gettysburg* (Norman: University of Oklahoma Press, 1960), 63–69; and George Gordon Meade, ed., *The Life and Letters of George Gordon Meade, Major-General United States Army*, 2 vols. (New York: Charles Scribner's Sons, 1913), 1:279–99. On Meade at Second Bull Run and in the Maryland Campaign, see Cleaves, *Meade of Gettysburg*, 73–74, 74–80; and Stephen W. Sears, *Landscape Turned Red: The Battle of Antietam* (New York: Ticknor and Fields, 1983), 136–39, 176, 184, 201–7, 272. On Margaretta Meade's role in assisting her husband obtain military appointments, see Stowe, "Philadelphia Gentleman," 47, 210–11.

17. GGM to MSM, Nov. 20, 24, 25, 28, 30, Dec. 2, 3, 5, 6, 9, 10, 16, 17, 20, 23, 1862, Meade Collection; Cortlandt Parker to Edwin M. Stanton, Nov. 18, 1862, RG 94, Records of the Adjutant General's Office, M-1395, 11 ACP 1885, Letters Received by the Appointment, Commission, and Personal Branch, Adjutant General's Office, 1871–94, Fiche ACP 000144, NARA; *OR*, 21:879, 887; Stephen R. Taaffe, *Commanding the Army of the Potomac* (Lawrence: University Press of Kansas, 2006), 65–67. An aide to William Franklin (commander of the Left Grand Division, to which Meade's division, known as the Pennsylvania Reserves, was attached) declared after Fredericksburg that "Meade went in by God and he went in like a gentleman. There was not a braver or cooler man on the field." George Meade [son of GGM] to MSM, Dec. 21, 1862, Meade Collection. On Meade's actions at Fredericksburg, see especially O'Reilly, *Fredericksburg Campaign*, 138–40, 141–46, 149–58, 164–87, 196–210, 215–38. For Meade's Fredericksburg report, see *OR*, 21:509–13. In addition to Butterfield, George Stoneman, Orlando Bolivar Willcox, and Julius Stahel each received command of infantry corps over Meade as part of Burnside's reshuffling.

18. Rafuse, *George Gordon Meade and the War in the East*, 54–56; William H. Powell, *The Fifth Army Corps (Army of the Potomac): A Record of Operations during the Civil War in the United States*

of America, 1861–1865 (New York: G. P. Putnam's Sons, 1896), 36, 41–44, 404; John J. Eicher and David J. Eicher, *Civil War High Commands* (Stanford, Calif.: Stanford University Press, 2001), 859; Taaffe, *Commanding the Army of the Potomac*, 59.

19. GGM to MSM, Dec. 17, 26, 28, 1862, Meade Collection; Hooker to Stanton, Dec. 28, 1862, Edwin McMasters Stanton Papers, Manuscript Division, Library of Congress, Washington, D.C. (hereafter cited as LC); Sutherland, *Fredericksburg and Chancellorsville*, 74. For Hooker's earlier praise of Meade, see Hooker to Halleck, Oct. 21, 1862, RG 94, M-1395, 11 ACP 1885, Letters Received by the Appointment, Commission, and Personal Branch, Adjutant General's Office, 1871–94, Fiche ACP 000144. Hooker lauded the Pennsylvanian as "eminently distinguished for his skill and great gallantry.... No officer of the 1st Corps should have precedence in preferment [to the rank of major general]." A member of the Hooker clique, Maj. Gen. Abner Doubleday, when testifying before the Joint Committee on the Conduct of the War in 1864, lamented the "great deal of favoritism in the Army of the Potomac. No man who is an anti-slavery man or an anti-McClellan man can expect decent treatment in that army as at present constituted." U.S. Congress, *Report of the Joint Committee on the Conduct of the War, at the Second Session Thirty-Eighth Congress. Army of the Potomac. Battle of Petersburg* (Washington, D.C.: Government Printing Office, 1865), 311 (hereafter cited as *RJCCW, Petersburg*).

20. Butterfield to Chandler, Dec. 25, 1862, Zachariah Chandler Papers, Manuscript Division, LC. See also Butterfield to Frederick W. Seward, Dec. 24, 1862, Stanton Papers. Butterfield's farewell address to the V Corps, in which he alludes coldly to his successor, is in *OR*, 21:882. Chandler's animus toward Meade stemmed from the Pennsylvanian's refusal to attend a Union rally in Detroit, Michigan, where the latter was stationed in the days following the surrender of the Federal garrison at Fort Sumter. Feeling that army personnel were subject only to the orders of War Department officials (and not the whims of an impassioned and emotional crowd), Meade's action reflected a spirit of moderation, if not outright conservatism, wholly typical of those within his profession. Even so, and perhaps inevitably in the period following Sumter, his open refusal engendered suspicion among a number of Michigan and national Radical officeholders, including Chandler, who would for the remainder of the war question Meade's loyalty. See Meade, *Life and Letters*, 1:215; and *Detroit Free Press*, Apr. 19, 21, 1861. On the Joint Committee on the Conduct of the War and Chandler's dominant role on it, see Bruce Tap, *Over Lincoln's Shoulder: The Joint Committee on the Conduct of the War* (Lawrence: University Press of Kansas, 1998).

21. GGM to MSM, Dec. 20, 1862, Jan. 2, 1863, Meade Collection; *OR*, 21:868–70, 894–96, 897, 898–99, 900–902, 922–23; Greene, "Morale, Maneuver, and Mud," 179–87; Tap, *Over Lincoln's Shoulder*, 146, 150–59; Sutherland, *Fredericksburg and Chancellorsville*, 84; Rable, *Fredericksburg! Fredericksburg!* 349–50, 390–91; Marsena R. Patrick, *Inside Lincoln's Army: The Diary of Marsena Rudolph Patrick, Provost Marshal General, Army of the Potomac*, ed. David S. Sparks (New York: Thomas Yoseloff, 1964), 200–204. The most careful student of the army's post-Fredericksburg funk, A. Wilson Greene, has found "the ... significance of Lincoln's exchange of views with [Burnside's lieutenants lay in] the revelation of an atmosphere that encouraged subordinate officers to debate ... strategy with the commander in chief without first consulting the commander of the army." "Morale, Maneuver, and Mud," 180.

George Gordon Meade as Corps Commander, December 1862–June 1863

22. GGM to MSM, Dec. 20, 1862, Jan. 2, Mar. 17, 19, 1863, Meade Collection; U.S. Congress, *Report of the Joint Committee on the Conduct of the War. Part I. Army of the Potomac* (Washington, D.C.: Government Printing Office, 1863), 690–93; Tap, *Over Lincoln's Shoulder*, 143–44, 146, 159–61, 162–63; Sutherland, *Fredericksburg and Chancellorsville*, 107, Greene, "Morale, Maneuver, and Mud," 179–80. On Franklin's travails before the joint committee, see Snell, *From First to Last*, 227–62.

23. Loyal National League, *Opinions of Prominent Men Concerning the Great Questions of the Times. Expressed in Their Letters to the Loyal National League, on Occasion of the Great Mass Meeting of the League and Other Loyalists at Union Square, New York, on the Anniversary of Sumter* (New York: C. S. Westcott, 1863), 25–26; letter reprinted in *New-York Times*, July 11, 1863. See also GGM to MSM, Apr. 22, 1863, Meade Collection. Other officers associated with the Army of the Potomac who affirmed their loyalty in letters to the league were generals Hooker, Irvin McDowell, George Stoneman, Silas Casey, John F. Reynolds, Carl Schurz, and James S. Wadsworth.

24. GGM to MSM, Jan. 2, 18, 1863, Meade Collection; *OR*, 21:78–79, 916–18; Greene, "Morale, Maneuver, and Mud," 195–98. See also Charles S. Wainwright, *A Diary of Battle: The Personal Journals of Colonel Charles S. Wainwright, 1861–1865*, ed. Allan Nevins (New York: Harcourt, Brace, and World, 1962), 157–58.

25. GGM to MSM, Jan. 15, 1863, Meade Collection; *OR*, 21:987. Brig. Gen. William Thomas Harbaugh Brooks, a division commander in the VI Corps, had told Meade privately in December 1862 that "he had rather see [Meade] at the head of the army than any other officer here," while Franklin had "strenuously urged" upon Burnside immediately after Fredericksburg "not to let [Meade] leave the army." GGM to MSM, Dec. 20, 23, 1862, Meade Collection. For Franklin's and Reynolds's take on Meade's Fredericksburg performance, see *OR*, 21:448–52, 452–56.

26. *OR*, 21:78–81, 127, 752–53, 986; Greene, "Morale, Maneuver, and Mud," 195–97, 99.

27. *OR*, 21:68–69, 753–54, 989–91, 994; Greene, "Morale, Maneuver, and Mud," 199–203; Sutherland, *Fredericksburg and Chancellorsville*, 90–91; GGM to MSM, Jan. 23, 1863, Meade Collection.

28. GGM to MSM, Jan. 23, 1863; Greene, "Morale, Maneuver, and Mud," 206–9; Rable, *Fredericksburg! Fredericksburg!* 418–22; Sutherland, *Fredericksburg and Chancellorsville*, 91–92. One soldier in Meade's corps found humor in the affair. "And such sport as we had! . . . You would have laughed to see us build those roads. Each regiment would march off to some fence and make a grand charge on it and then march off each with a rail on his shoulder. We realized that day at least, that we were in the Army of 'honest Abe' the railsplitter." Nichols to Father, Jan. 25, 1863, George Hale Nichols Papers, James A. Schoff Civil War Collection, William L. Clements Library, University of Michigan, Ann Arbor.

29. *OR*, 21:998–99, 1004–5, 25(2):3; Greene, "Morale, Maneuver, and Mud," 207–11; Rable, *Fredericksburg! Fredericksburg!* 421–23. Sumner too was relieved from duty with the army upon his own request. War Department clerk Charles F. Benjamin later suggested that Meade was then under consideration for the army's command. Halleck, though, in a contemporary letter, denied outright that Lincoln discussed the matter of Burnside's relief and Hooker's appointment with anyone. See Charles F. Benjamin, "Hooker's Appointment and Removal," in *Battles and Leaders of the Civil War*, ed. Robert U. Johnson and Clarence C. Buel, 4 vols. (New York: Century, 1887–88), 3:239–40; *OR*,

21:1009. An excellent examination of Benjamin's claim is in Greene, "Morale, Maneuver, and Mud," 210–11.

30. GGM to MSM, Jan. 26, 1863, Meade Collection.

31. *OR*, 25(2):4; Walter H. Hebert, *Fighting Joe Hooker* (Indianapolis: Bobbs-Merrill, 1944), 147–49; Sutherland, *Fredericksburg and Chancellorsville*, 93–96; Sears, *Chancellorsville*, 59–61; John J. Hennessy, "We Shall Make Richmond Howl: The Army of the Potomac on the Eve of Chancellorsville," in *Chancellorsville: The Battle and Its Aftermath*, ed. Gary W. Gallagher (Chapel Hill: University of North Carolina Press, 1996), 7–9; GGM to John Sergeant Meade, Oct. 11, 1862, Meade Collection. For a similar cautious assessment of Hooker, see Stephen M. Weld, *War Diary and Letters of Stephen Minot Weld, 1861–1865* (1912; repr., Boston: Massachusetts Historical Society, 1979), 185. After Antietam, Meade recognized that "Hooker's taking command . . . [would] undoubtedly be for my interests"—the general had been Meade's immediate superior within the I Corps—but could not "say I think it will be for the interest either of the army or the cause." GGM to MSM, Oct. 12, 16, 1862, Jan. 26, 1863, Meade Collection.

32. *RJCCW, Petersburg*, 112–13; Richard C. Halsey to Keck, Mar. 10, 1863, Josiah Edmund King Papers, Schoff Civil War Collection; Hebert, *Fighting Joe Hooker*, 172–81; *OR*, 25(2):6, 11–12, 51–52, 57–59, 119–22, 137–38, 149, 152; Edwin C. Fishel, *The Secret War for the Union: The Untold Story of Military Intelligence in the Civil War* (Boston: Houghton Mifflin, 1996), 287–300; Sears, *Chancellorsville*, 67–82; Sutherland, *Fredericksburg and Chancellorsville*, 97–107. John Hennessy flatly terms Hooker's order abolishing the grand-division arrangement "a step backward for the Army of the Potomac," citing the organization of those armies in Virginia that won successes (Lee's in late 1862 and early 1863 and Grant's and Meade's army from 1864 to Appomattox) as proof of the merits of a compact command consisting of two-to-four corps-sized combat elements. While this assessment on its surface has merit—Hennessy claims rightly that managing eight corps proved too much for any single commander to handle during the war—the grand division, in adding an intermediate administrative and operational tier between corps and army headquarters, invited problems in conveying effectively a commander's intent to lower echelons and adversely affected tactical-decision cycles, as an examination of the Prospect Hill fight at Fredericksburg suggests. "We Shall Make Richmond Howl," 9–14.

33. GGM to MSM, Jan. 26, 28, Feb. 6, 13, Mar. 13, Apr. 12, 1863, Meade Collection; *OR*, 25(2):3. Meade's aide-de-camp James C. Biddle, likely parroting the sentiments of his commander, also distrusted Hooker's character. See Biddle to Gertrude, Apr. 24, 1863, James Cornell Biddle Papers, HSP. On Sickles, see especially James A. Hessler, *Sickles at Gettysburg: The Controversial Civil War General Who Committed Murder, Abandoned Little Round Top, and Declared Himself the Hero of Gettysburg* (New York: Savas Beatie, 2009). Butterfield lacks a modern biography. An uncritical account by his widow is Julia Lorrilard Butterfield, ed., *A Biographical Memorial of General Daniel A. Butterfield, including Many Addresses and Military Writings* (New York: Grafton, 1904). For contemporary criticism of Butterfield, see Patrick, *Inside Lincoln's Army*, 209–70.

34. GGM to MSM, Jan. 28, 30, Feb 1, 3, 13, 15, 27, Mar. 1, 7, 9, 12, 13, 19, 24, Apr. 9, 11, 1863, Meade Collection; GGM to Stanton, Jan. 29, 1863, RG 94, M-1395, 11 ACP 1885, Letters Received by the Appointment, Commission, and Personal Branch, Adjutant General's Office, 1871–94, Fiche ACP 000144.

George Gordon Meade as Corps Commander, December 1862–June 1863

35. Lincoln, *Collected Works*, 6:164–65, 189–90; *OR*, 25(2):199–200, 204, 213, 214, 244, 255–56, 262–63, 266–67, 268; John J. Bigelow Jr., *The Campaign of Chancellorsville: A Strategic and Tactical Study* (New Haven, Conn.: Yale University Press, 1910), 138–41, 142–56, 160–69, 173–75; Sutherland, *Fredericksburg and Chancellorsville*, 127–28, 129–30; Sears, *Chancellorsville*, 114–24, 128–32, 136–41.

36. GGM to MSM, Mar. 4, 7, Apr. 9, 12, 17, 18, 26, 1863, Meade Collection; Lincoln, *Collected Works*, 6:190; *OR*, 25(2):256–57; *RJCCW, Petersburg*, 118; Bigelow, *Campaign of Chancellorsville*, 140–41, 162, 181; Sutherland, *Fredericksburg and Chancellorsville*, 129, 131, 133; Sears, *Chancellorsville*, 133–35.

37. *OR*, 25(1):505, 525, 545, 25(2):203–4, 255–56, 262–63, 269, 486–91; Sears, *Chancellorsville*, 141–45; Sutherland, *Fredericksburg and Chancellorsville*, 133; Bigelow, *Campaign of Chancellorsville*, 136, 174–82 passim.

38. William L. Aughinbaugh, journal, May 28, 1863, Schoff Civil War Collection; *New-York Times*, Nov. 10, 1872; *OR*, 25(1):505, 525, 545, 25(2):273–75; Sears, *Chancellorsville*, 165–66; Sutherland, *Fredericksburg and Chancellorsville*, 134; Bigelow, *Campaign of Chancellorsville*, 194–200 passim.

39. *New-York Times*, Nov. 10, 1872; *OR*, 25(1):505–6, 525; 545; 25(2):273–75, 292–93; GGM to Hooker, May 30, 1863, Military Papers of Joseph Hooker, Box 14, Folder G, Huntington Library, San Marino, Calif.; Sears, *Chancellorsville*, 145–50, 161–62, 165–66; Sutherland, *Fredericksburg and Chancellorsville*, 134; Bigelow, *Campaign of Chancellorsville*, 184–87.

40. *OR*, 25(2):274, 292–93; Sutherland, *Fredericksburg and Chancellorsville*, 134–35; Sears, *Chancellorsville*, 167–68, 172; Bigelow, *Campaign of Chancellorsville*, 207–11.

41. *OR*, 25(1):506, 514–15; Ulric Dahlgren to Joseph Hooker, Apr. 30, 1863, Military Papers of Joseph Hooker, Box 13, Folder A; The Survivors' Association, *History of the Corn Exchange Regiment: 118th Pennsylvania Volunteers* (Philadelphia: J. L. Smith, 1888), 171; Sutherland, *Fredericksburg and Chancellorsville*, 135–36; Sears, *Chancellorsville*, 175–81; Bigelow, *Campaign of Chancellorsville*, 216–21.

42. GGM quoted in Richard Meade Bache, *Life of General George Gordon Meade, Commander of the Army of the Potomac* (Philadelphia: Henry T. Coates, 1897), 260; *OR*, 25(1):507, 515, 669, 25(2):304, 305; Alexander S. Webb, "Meade at Chancellorsville," *Papers of the Military Historical Society of Massachusetts*, 14 vols. (Boston: Military Historical Society of Massachusetts, 1895–1918), 3:228–29; Survivors' Association, *History of the Corn Exchange Regiment*, 173–74.

43. *OR*, 25(1):171; GGM to MSM, Apr. 30, 1863, Meade Collection; Sears, *Chancellorsville*, 186–87, 191–92; Sutherland, *Fredericksburg and Chancellorsville*, 139–41; Bigelow, *Campaign of Chancellorsville*, 223, 235–36, 240.

44. *OR*, 25(1):507, 525, 546, 25(2):292–93, 324, 334; Sears, *Chancellorsville*, 197–202; Sutherland, *Fredericksburg and Chancellorsville*, 138–39, 141–42; Bigelow, *Campaign of Chancellorsville*, 237–43.

45. *OR*, 25(2):507; Webb, "Meade at Chancellorsville," 229; Sears, *Chancellorsville*, 202–13; Sutherland, *Fredericksburg and Chancellorsville*, 141–46; Bigelow, *Campaign of Chancellorsville*, 243–44, 245–51.

46. Francis A. Walker, *The History of the Second Army Corps in the Army of the Potomac* (New York: Charles Scribner's Sons, 1887), 224; Sears, *Chancellorsville*, 212–13; Fishel, *Secret War for the Union*, 391; Gouverneur K. Warren to Daniel E. Sickles, Feb. 15, 1875, Gouverneur Kemble Warren Papers, New York State Library, Albany.

47. Richard T. Auchmuty, *Letters of Richard Tylden Auchmuty, Fifth Corps, Army of the Potomac*, ed. Ellen S. Auchmuty (Privately printed, n.d.), 86–87; *OR*, 25(1):507; Sears, *Chancellorsville*, 226,

235–38; Sutherland, *Chancellorsville and Fredericksburg*, 146; Bigelow, *Campaign of Chancellorsville*, 258–62, 269–70.

48. *OR*, 25(1):797–98; Sears, *Chancellorsville*, 228–35; Sutherland, *Chancellorsville and Gettysburg*, 148–49; Bigelow, *Campaign of Chancellorsville*, 256, 262–65.

49. *OR*, 25(1):507; Webb, "Meade at Chancellorsville," 229; Sears, *Chancellorsville*, 236–49, 252–81 passim, 284–87; Sutherland, *Fredericksburg and Chancellorsville*, 149–57; Bigelow, *Campaign of Chancellorsville*, 295–315 passim.

50. *OR*, 25(1):507–8; Webb, "Meade at Chancellorsville," 222, 226, 231; Sears, *Chancellorsville*, 302–3, 341–36, 339–47, 357–58; Sutherland, *Fredericksburg and Chancellorsville*, 160–64; Bigelow, *Campaign of Chancellorsville*, 339–62 passim, 364.

51. Webb, "Meade at Chancellorsville," 222, 226, 231; GGM to MSM, May 8, 1863, Meade Collection; James C. Biddle to Gertrude, May 9, 12, 1863, Biddle Papers; Darius N. Couch, "The Chancellorsville Campaign," in *Battles and Leaders*, 3:169–70; Sears, *Chancellorsville*, 336–37, 357–58; Sutherland, *Fredericksburg and Chancellorsville*, 164; Bigelow, *Campaign of Chancellorsville*, 362–64, 366–67.

52. GGM to MSM, May 20, 1863, Meade Collection; *OR*, 25(1):508, 512, 518, 547–48, 555; Webb, "Meade at Chancellorsville," 234; Sears, *Chancellorsville*, 359–420 passim; Sutherland, *Fredericksburg and Chancellorsville*, 164–76; Bigelow, *Campaign of Chancellorsville*, 367–419 passim.

53. GGM to MSM, May 8, 12, 19, 1863, Meade Collection; James C. Biddle to Gertrude, May 9, 12, 17, 1863, Biddle Papers; Couch, "Chancellorsville Campaign," 171; Sears, *Chancellorsville*, 421–22; Sutherland, *Fredericksburg and Chancellorsville*, 176; Bigelow, *Campaign of Chancellorsville*, 419–20. Sickles had a change of heart the next morning, advising his commander to remain south of the Rappahannock. "You can stay here as long as you please," he attempted to brace Hooker, counseling him to "[s]uggest to the President the earliest possible advance by Dix, Foster, Rosecrans, Burnside, Grant, & Banks." Daniel E. Sickles to Joseph Hooker, May 5, 1863, Military Papers of Joseph Hooker, Box 14, Folder E.

54. *New-York Times*, Nov. 10, 1872; Sears, *Chancellorsville*, 426–27; Sutherland, *Fredericksburg and Chancellorsville*, 178; Bigelow, *Campaign of Chancellorsville*, 422, 427.

55. Webb, "Meade at Chancellorsville," 234–36; Wainwright, *Diary of Battle*, 200; GGM to Hooker, May 5, 1863, Military Papers of Joseph Hooker, Box 14, Folder E; Couch, "Chancellorsville Campaign," 171; Sears, *Chancellorsville*, 428–30; Sutherland, *Fredericksburg and Chancellorsville*, 178–79; Bigelow, *Campaign of Chancellorsville*, 427–32.

56. GGM to MSM, May 10, 12, 20, 23, 1863, Meade Collection; Sears, *Chancellorsville*, 431–36; Sutherland, *Fredericksburg and Chancellorsville*, 184–87; Hennessy, "We Shall Make Richmond Howl," 25; Taaffe, *Commanding the Army of the Potomac*, 101–4.

57. GGM to MSM, May, 8, 10, 20, 1863, Meade Collection; Biddle to Gertrude, May 7, 1863, Biddle Papers; Alexander S. Webb to Robert Webb, n.d., Alexander Stewart Webb Papers, Yale University Library, copy at FSNMP; Sears, *Chancellorsville*, 435–36; Sutherland, *Fredericksburg and Chancellorsville*, 187; Taaffe, *Commanding the Army of the Potomac*, 102–3.

58. GGM to MSM, May 8, 10, 20, 23, 1863, Meade Collection; George W. Smalley, *Anglo-American Memories* (New York: G. P. Putnam's Sons, 1911), 159–60; Sears, *Chancellorsville*, 435; Sutherland, *Fredericksburg and Chancellorsville*, 187.

59. GGM to MSM, May 12, 15, 1863, Meade Collection; James C. Biddle to Gertrude, May 20, 1863, Biddle Papers; Taaffe, *Commanding the Army of the Potomac*, 103. Curtin later denied that he had "understood . . . that [Meade] had lost all confidence in Hooker" and assured the general that he had not aired the claim to anyone. The Philadelphian accepted the governor's words for what they were worth, yet had no doubt that Curtin "said a great deal more than he was authorized to say, or ought to have repeated." GGM to MSM, May 25, 1863, Meade Collection.

60. GGM to MSM, May 19, 1863, Meade Collection; Wainwright, *Diary of Battle*, 219.

61. GGM to MSM, May 25, 26, 1863, Meade Collection; *OR*, 25(1):510–12.

62. GGM to MSM, June 11, 25, 1863, Meade Collection; Lincoln to Hooker, June 16, 1863, in *Collected Works of Abraham Lincoln*, 6:281. The scholarship detailing the early phases of Lee's great raid into Pennsylvania is immense. Two esteemed secondary accounts are Stephen W. Sears, *Gettysburg* (Boston: Houghton Mifflin, 2003), 1–121; and Edwin B. Coddington, *The Gettysburg Campaign: A Study in Command* (New York: Charles Scribner's Sons, 1968), 3–133 passim.

63. GGM to MSM, June 25, 1863, Meade Collection.

64. *OR*, 27(1):61; GGM to MSM, June 29, 1863, Meade Collection; Benjamin, "Hooker's Appointment and Removal," 241–43; Meade, *Life and Letters*, 2: 1–2.

65. Wainwright, *Diary of Battle*, 227.

66. GGM to MSM, July 16, 1863, Meade Collection. On Meade's post-Gettysburg pessimism and continuing military idealism, see especially Hattaway and Jones, *How the North Won*, 465–73; and Brooks D. Simpson, *Abraham Lincoln, the Gettysburg Campaign, and the War in the East, 1861–1863* (Gettysburg, Pa.: Farnsworth Military Impressions, 1998). On Grant's civil-military views, see Simpson, *Let Us Have Peace: Ulysses S. Grant and the Politics of War and Reconstruction, 1861–1868* (Chapel Hill: University of North Carolina Press, 1991), xvi.

Grant's Junior Lieutenant
James B. McPherson and the Vicksburg Campaign, 1863

STEVEN E. WOODWORTH

It was an eminently satisfied Maj. Gen. James McPherson who sat his horse at the fork of the Jackson and Graveyard Roads just east of Vicksburg, Mississippi. To the west along the opposite ridge, silhouetted by the setting sun, stood the fortifications of Vicksburg, toward which McPherson, with the keen interest of a military engineer, had just been squinting. Now, however, his eyes were on the troops marching up the Jackson Road and filing left onto the Graveyard Road toward their assigned position in the center of the lines that Maj. Gen. Ulysses S. Grant was rapidly throwing around the Confederate fortress city. These were the men of McPherson's own XVII Corps. In the past eighteen days, they had marched more than one hundred miles through enemy territory and fought two battles, both victorious. In the speed of their advance, alongside Grant's other two corps, they had outrun their supplies, and few of the men marching past McPherson had had anything to eat that day.

Now they were approaching the goal of their campaign, one of the most heavily fortified cities on the continent, held by desperate, vengeance-minded troops who had nowhere left to retreat. As McPherson well knew, most of his men could guess that they would be asked to assault those fortifications within the next few days. Yet they swung along the dirt road to the jaunty strains of "The Girl I Left behind Me," played by a regimental band somewhere in the back of the column, and as they caught sight of their corps commander beside the road ahead, they burst out in a roar of celebration. As McPherson watched the cheering men march by, tossing their hats in the air, a staff officer noticed that there were tears in the corps commander's eyes.[1]

McPherson was a general who enjoyed the affection of not only his troops but also his army commander, and he returned both warmly. The trust and friendship between him and Grant, as well as the confidence and affection of his troops, facilitated the smooth functioning of the Army of the Tennessee's command system. It stood in stark contrast to the command relations on the other side of the lines, where hostility and distrust between Confederate army commander Lt. Gen. John C. Pemberton and his top subordinates Brig. Gen. John Bowen, Brig. Gen. Lloyd Tilghman, and Maj. Gen. William W. Loring was so intense as to lead to outright defiance and betrayal in ways that had significantly affected the outcomes of two battles in the past few weeks. That kind of thing would not happen in McPherson's XVII Corps of Grant's Army of the Tennessee.

Yet McPherson was relatively new to corps command and had perhaps less confidence in himself than Grant or the rank and file had in him. Young for a major general at only thirty-four years of age, McPherson was highly competent but sometimes exercised his authority in a hesitant, tentative manner, though he steadily grew in confidence and ability.

MCPHERSON WAS BORN on November 14, 1828, near Clyde, Ohio, in the northwestern part of the state. His father was a farmer and blacksmith, but the family came to experience economic difficulty due to his father's illness and untimely death. Young James left home at the age of thirteen to clerk in a store six miles away in Green Springs and helped support his mother and three younger siblings. The boy was well liked in Green Springs, and his employer allowed him to attend school each winter. When the opportunity offered of attending the U.S. Military Academy at West Point, he brushed up his learning with a couple of terms at Norwalk Academy and then handily passed the entrance examination in 1849. McPherson enrolled at the military academy a few months short of this twenty-first birthday, making him one of the oldest among the cadets. He graduated first in the West Point class of 1853.

His high class standing placed McPherson in the army's Corps of Engineers after graduation. He then spent a year as an instructor of engineering at West Point. This was followed by seven years engaged in the construction of fortifications protecting the harbors of New York, Philadelphia, and San Francisco. When the Civil War broke out in 1861, McPherson sought and obtained transfer from California to the East. Shortly thereafter, he was appointed to the staff of Maj. Gen. Henry W. Halleck, commander of Union forces in the Mississippi Valley. McPherson was not only intelligent but also suave, handsome, and friendly. In his new job he proved efficient and was well liked by his superior and peers, rising rapidly in rank from captain to lieutenant colonel.

In early 1862 Halleck assigned McPherson to temporary duty on the staff of then–Brigadier General Grant. He did so to ensure both that Grant had the assistance of a highly competent engineer officer for his coming campaign along the Tennessee and Cumberland Rivers and to serve Halleck as a "listening post" inside Grant's headquarters. Halleck wanted inside reports as to whether Grant, who had gained an unfortunate reputation for drink in the prewar army, was staying on the wagon. McPherson served as chief engineer on the general's staff during the February 1862 campaign against Forts Henry and Donelson and was able to assure Halleck of Grant's continuing sobriety.[2]

Thereafter, McPherson remained on Grant's staff, serving in that capacity at the Battle of Shiloh in April 1862. As Grant's star rose, so did McPherson's, and the young staff officer continued to advance even while his commander was in eclipse after Shiloh due to Halleck's jealously and public criticism of his performance at that battle. On May 15 McPherson was promoted to the rank of brigadier general of volunteers, and a little more than two weeks later Halleck appointed him military superintendent of railroads for the District of West Tennessee. McPherson served in that capacity throughout the summer and into the fall of 1862, while Halleck departed for Washington to assume overall command of Union armies and Grant took over command in the Mississippi Valley. That fall Confederate forces took the offensive, and a Rebel army under Maj. Gen. Earl Van Dorn marched against Union forces occupying the critical railroad town of Corinth, Mississippi. Grant responded by placing McPherson in command of two brigades and directing him to reinforce Maj. Gen. William S. Rosecrans's command at Corinth. McPherson moved quickly but arrived too late to take part in the battle. He did, however, pursue the retreating Confederate army, with his aggressiveness in stark contrast to Rosecrans's lethargy after the battle. Grant saw to it that McPherson's subsequent promotion to major general of volunteers dated October 8, 1862, the final day of the Battle of Corinth.

When Grant began his first major campaign against Vicksburg at the end of October, he gave McPherson command of the center column of his army as it advanced southward into Mississippi along the line of the Mississippi Central Railroad. Making use of his abundant experience as a staff officer, McPherson handled his multidivision command well, but since the Confederate army commander in Mississippi, Lieutenant General Pemberton, chose to retreat rather than give battle, the campaign did not pose an especially severe test of his abilities. After Confederate cavalry raiders cut Grant's supply line, he retreated back into West Tennessee. During this campaign along the Mississippi Central, no legal basis existed for the subdivision of the Union army into separate corps, but as soon as the War Department authorized such reorganization, Grant, on January 11, 1863, assigned McPherson to command of the newly created XVII Corps.

That new appointment was more or less simultaneous with the beginning of Grant's long winter encampment along the west bank of the Mississippi just above Vicksburg. Throughout the winter months of 1863, Grant and his sub-

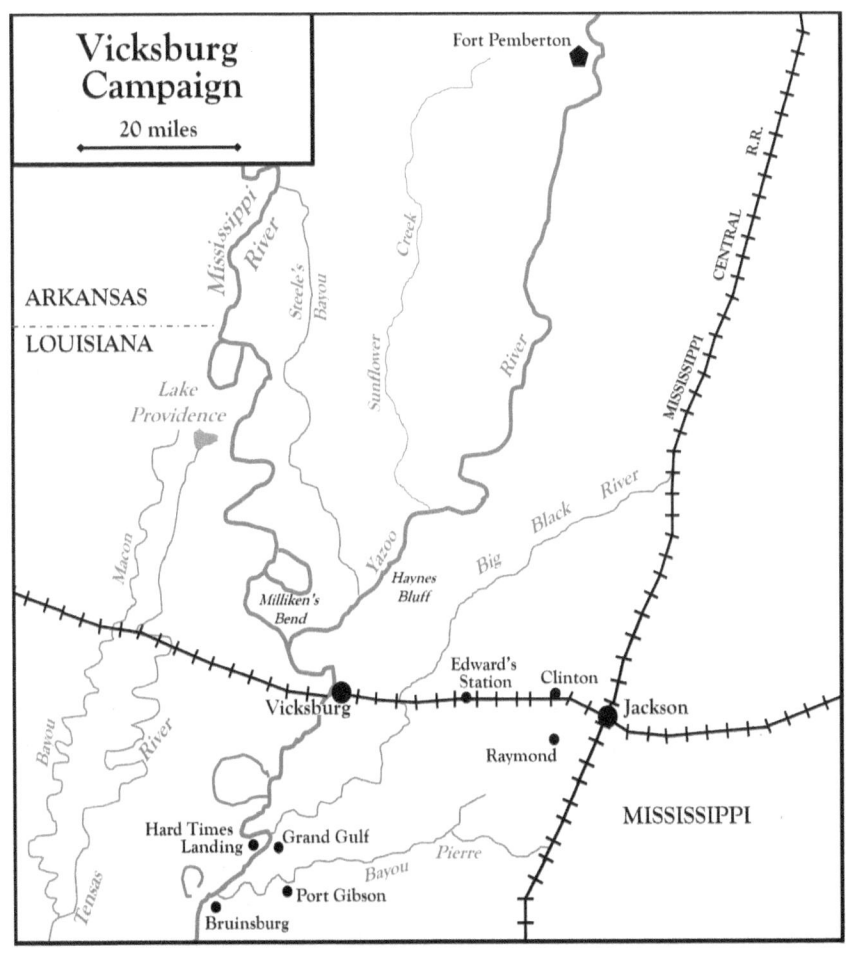

ordinates sought a way to get the army into a position to approach Vicksburg via the interior plateau of Mississippi. In practical terms, this meant finding a way for the navy's gunboats and the army's leased transport steamboats to reach either the Yazoo River above the Confederate batteries at Haynes Bluff or the Mississippi River below the Confederate batteries at Vicksburg and Grand Gulf. Each of the three corps of Grant's field army, the XIII, XV, and XVII, encamped in a different location along the Louisiana shore and had different potential routes to explore or develop, all aimed at opening boat access to the desired stretches of river. Maj. Gen. William T. Sherman's XV Corps encamped at Young's Point, closest to Vicksburg, and worked on a canal there. It also provided troops to support a naval expedition up Sunflower Creek. Maj. Gen. John A. McClernand's XIII Corps encamped a few miles farther north at Milliken's Bend and found a role in the campaign by exploring the west-bank land route the army eventually used, moving along the natural levees among the bayous on the Louisiana side to reach a position below Vicksburg from which forces might be ferried to the Mississippi shore with access to the interior plateau, provided boats could somehow be gotten onto that stretch of the river.

Meanwhile, Grant posted McPherson's XVII Corps at Lake Providence, Louisiana, fifty miles north of Vicksburg. It was the northernmost of the encampments and the one farthest from Vicksburg itself. The reason for encamping there was that the location seemed to offer the prospect of opening a waterway that would lead from the Mississippi at Lake Providence, through a series of bayous in the interior of Louisiana, to the Red River, which emptied into the Mississippi well below Grand Gulf. If the waterway could be opened, it would put steamboats where Grant needed them and allow the army to bypass Vicksburg.

Lake Providence was an oxbow bend of the Mississippi that the river's channel had cut off many years before. Silt had built up at both ends of the bend, which was now separated from the river by the width of the natural levee, about a mile and a half. The crescent-shaped lake was usually as smooth as glass and almost as clear, its banks lined with live oak, cypress, and magnolia as well as several impressive plantations and the little village of Providence. Arriving with his troops during the month of February 1863, McPherson made his headquarters in Bellagio Plantation, the property of Confederate senator Edward Sparrow. His regiments found pleasant campsites in the area and fared much better than Sherman's and McClernand's troops in their muddy, semi-inundated campgrounds at Young's Point and Milliken's Bend.[3]

Assessing the engineering task at hand, McPherson saw that it would be little trouble connecting the Mississippi to the lake. At that time of year, the river's surface was eight feet higher than the lake, so a small ditch dug between them would introduce a torrent of river water that would quickly gouge a channel adequate for the largest steamboats while also, unfortunately, inundating the village of Providence and much of the surrounding countryside.

The real challenge would come beyond the lake, in getting from Bayou Baxter to Bayou Macon and from there to the Tensas River. The route led through a cypress swamp, and the trees would have to be cut off low enough to allow boats to pass over the stumps. That could be more easily done before the Mississippi River raised the water level in the lake and surrounding area by eight feet. To facilitate tree removal, McPherson had his men move a small steam tugboat from the river to the lake, using block and tackle to drag it over the levee and down the main street of Providence. The boat, which McPherson named the *J. A. Rawlins* in honor of Grant's chief of staff, took ten days to make the mile-and-a-half journey. Once in the lake, the *Rawlins* was used for reconnaissance into Bayou Baxter to the edge of the cypress swamp, confirming that the trees were definitely the chief obstacle to the passage of boats. McPherson put his men to work felling the trees. "Boys stand on rafts in the water to chop and saw," an Illinois soldier explained in a letter home. Once the trees were down, the men used long ropes to drag them out of the intended channel.[4]

As the work progressed, McPherson became concerned that the cypress stumps might still prove a prohibitive hazard to boats, even after the levee had been cut and the water level raised. So he hatched an alternative plan. In theory, cutting the levee at a point several miles north of Lake Providence, near the Arkansas line, would result in the flooding of a large area of low-lying farmland west of the lake. Then it would be possible to bypass both Bayou Baxter and the cypress swamp by steaming the transports and gunboats straight across to Bayou Macon via the flooded cotton fields. He tried it, but the results were less than satisfactory. When his men cut the manmade levee, the Mississippi gushed through and did indeed inundate the farmlands west of Lake Providence. Unfortunately however, the waters did not attain sufficient depth to accommodate even the shallow-draft vessels in the Union fleet. Though not deep enough to float gunboats or transports across the cotton fields, the water flowed into Bayou Macon and raised its level to the point that it began flowing backward into Bayou Baxter, which in turn reversed its course and flowed into

Lake Providence. The resulting rise in water level put an end to the tree-clearing operations in the cypress swamp.[5]

Grant stopped by at Lake Providence from time to time to inspect the progress of the work. In early March he took a ride on the *Rawlins,* along with McPherson and both their staffs, down the lake and into Bayou Baxter as far as the route was clear. He was not optimistic. Even if the vessels could get through the cypress swamp, Grant predicted that it would be all too easy for the Confederates to find ways to block their progress on the Tensas or the Red. Still, McPherson was eager to keep trying, and Grant permitted him.[6]

The engineer-general's next scheme was to cut the artificial levee at Lake Providence. By this time, the melting snows of the Ohio and Missouri Valleys had raised the river's surface to a level twelve feet above that of the lake. In theory, letting the waters of the Mississippi flow freely into the lake was bound to raise the water level sufficiently to carry boats over the stumps in the cypress swamp or over the cotton fields or both. After having his troops move their camps to higher ground or, in the cases of some units, to steamboats moored in the river, McPherson put a large fatigue detail to work on the levee late on the afternoon of March 16. They dug two parallel ditches about fifty feet apart, each four feet wide and just deep enough to allow the river water to begin running through them and cascading out on the side toward the lake. By the next morning, as planned, the rushing water had merged and widened the two ditches into a single roaring cataract two hundred feet wide. Onlookers guessed the depth of the inrushing water to be somewhere between eight and twenty feet. No one felt inclined to attempt an exact measurement.[7]

This crevasse did raise the level of Lake Providence. In fact, it flooded the town, and some of the few residents who had not fled weeks before claimed that it would inundate seven counties of northeastern Louisiana. What the water did not do was provide enough depth over the cypress stumps or the cotton stubble to carry the gunboats or transports. Even then, as McPherson reported to Grant, with the use of a sawing machine for cutting another twelve or fifteen stumps below the surface, and with a dredge to clear out a shoal at the entrance of Bayou Macon, it would be possible to establish a channel useable for boats with drafts of up to six feet. By that time, however, the army commander had decided on other methods for accomplishing his purposes. Grant's assignment of McPherson to the job at Lake Providence had probably been based on his deep respect for his fellow Ohioan and for engineer officers in general.

Although McPherson's keen mind had not been able to come up with a solution for the difficult problem of hydrology at the lake, his standing with Grant remained undiminished, and he and his corps were soon on their way to take part in the next scheme for getting at Vicksburg.[8]

The next phase of Grant's campaign to take Vicksburg would bring McPherson a new set of challenges. His first duty as a de-facto corps commander during Grant's Mississippi Central campaign in December 1862 had given him experience moving his troops without significant contact with the enemy. His month encamped at Lake Providence had brought further administrative duties as well as an engineering project of the sort with which he was already experienced, though one arguably far more difficult than any he had ever before attempted. The next phase of the campaign would bring McPherson his first experience as a corps commander in combat.

Grant had decided to march his army down the west bank of the Mississippi, ask RAdm. David Dixon Porter to run elements of his gunboat fleet directly past the Vicksburg and Grand Gulf batteries, and then use the vessels, along with any transports he could run past the batteries, to cross his army from Louisiana to Mississippi somewhere well south of Vicksburg, where his troops could quickly reach the interior plateau. Because the road down the west bank started at Milliken's Bend, where the XIII Corps was encamped, Grant assigned McClernand's command the task of leading the way. In addition to marching, this entailed corduroying the road where it was too muddy for wagons and artillery, replacing bridges the Rebels had destroyed, and finding detours around areas that were underwater due to the very high stage of the river. The route wound this way and that, following the natural levees of various bayous and back channels of the river, to arrive at Hard Times Landing, about forty direct miles below Vicksburg.

Grant assigned McPherson and his XVII Corps to follow immediately behind the XIII, while Sherman and his XV Corps brought up the rear after staging a diversion north of Vicksburg. McPherson's place in the middle of the Union column was in keeping with his status as the least experienced of Grant's principal subordinates. Even McClernand, a political general of sometimes questionable judgment, had experience commanding a division in battle at both Fort Donelson and Shiloh, something lacking from McPherson's otherwise impressive résumé.

The lead division of the XVII Corps reached Hard Times on the evening of April 29 and the next morning began embarking on steamboats for the trip across the river. McPherson's troops landed right behind McClernand's and followed them on the march inland, up onto the plateau overlooking the river. Somewhat to the surprise of the Federals, from Grant down to the soldiers in the ranks, they encountered no Confederates. But as the march into the interior continued through the night, McClernand's lead troops began to encounter resistance and halted four miles short of the town of Port Gibson around 2:00 A.M. The Battle of Port Gibson got properly underway at dawn. McClernand's men did most of the fighting on the Union side, slowly driving the Confederates back through a landscape that was a maze of steep, winding, brush-choked ravines. The combat took place primarily along the axes of two parallel roads several miles apart, both of which led to Port Gibson.

When McPherson's lead division reached the battlefield that afternoon, Grant dispatched one of its brigades on the right fork, where McClernand was personally directing the fighting of three of his own divisions, and another brigade on the left fork to reinforce the detached division of Brig. Gen. Peter J. Osterhaus. McPherson and division commander Maj. Gen. John A. Logan both accompanied this brigade on the left and together supervised its deployment alongside Osterhaus. Shortly thereafter the Confederates retreated, abandoning Port Gibson. McPherson's first experience commanding a corps in battle thus consisted of overseeing the deployment of a single brigade, assisted by the commander of the brigade itself and the commander of the division to which it belonged.[9]

The following day McPherson's corps marched in pursuit of the retreating Confederates. Grant briefly traveled with McPherson's headquarters before taking a detour to visit the abandoned Confederate stronghold at Grand Gulf. The XVII Corps continued to Hankinson's Ferry, on the south bank of the Big Black River, where it halted on orders from Grant. After several days at Hankinson's Ferry resting and allowing Sherman and the army's supply wagons to catch up, the march resumed on May 7, continuing toward the northeast in the general direction of Jackson, Mississippi. McPherson's corps at first had the Union left, parallel and close to the Big Black. This led to occasional light skirmishing with Confederates on the opposite bank. Grant later directed McPherson to veer farther to the right, crossing to the east side of McClernand's corps. Sherman's XV Corps, which had been last to cross the Mississippi, continued to bring up the rear. During this part of the campaign, Grant rode with Sherman.

The fact that he did not consistently make his headquarters with the relatively inexperienced McPherson suggests the high degree of confidence he had in his young subordinate.[10]

More than two hundred supply wagons were constantly shuttling back and forth between the new Union base at Grand Gulf and the rear of the advancing columns, but they could not keep the men adequately fed. For the remainder of their nourishment, the soldiers relied on the long-standing military practice of foraging. With thousands of armed men involved in confiscating food from civilians, it was a short step for some of them to slide over into the outright plundering of personal effects. To stop or at least curtail this abuse, McPherson issued strict orders against such thieving on pain of severe punishment.[11]

On May 12 the XVII Corps continued its march northeastward, now forming the right wing of the Union advance and moving in the general direction of Jackson. Grant hoped to seize and then break Mississippi's main east–west railroad at or near the state capital and then advance on Vicksburg directly from the east. The weather had turned hot and oppressively humid, though dry. Consequently, water sources were an important consideration in the planning of marches. McPherson's plan for this day was to cover the eleven miles from the Roach farm, where the corps had access to the water of Tallahala Creek, to the town of Raymond, where numerous wells would supply the needs of man and beast. In order to avoid the worst of the heat, he made sure his men broke camp and took to the road by 3:30 A.M.[12]

Despite the early start, McPherson's corps found itself by midmorning marching in brutal sun, heat, and humidity. The dust on the road "came to the shoe top," according to a major in an Iowa regiment, and as the men shuffled through it, it rose in dense yellow clouds. An atmospheric inversion layer held the choking dust in a dense bank relatively close to the ground, engulfing the sweating, coughing troops. To minimize the density of dust their men would have to march through, brigade and division commanders lengthened the intervals between their units and the column stretched out.[13]

Confederate skirmishers had harassed the column's screening cavalry throughout most of the march but at midmorning began to put up resistance heavy enough that the horse soldiers could no longer brush them aside. Logan's division marched at the head of the column this day, and its commander ordered his lead brigade commander, Brig. Gen. Elias S. Dennis, to deploy an infantry skirmish line to drive back the Rebels and allow the corps to continue its march. Dennis deployed two regiments, one on either side of the road, in a line that stretched some three-quarters of a mile in all. This proved impractical, however, as the terrain on either side of the road was covered with dense thickets, and the long skirmish line struggled to maintain its alignment as the soldiers fought not against Rebels but rather against the underbrush.

This went on for some time. One of the soldiers struggling his way through the brush thought it was two hours, though it was almost certainly much less than that. Then Logan adjusted Dennis's deployment by pulling most of the two regiments back onto the road and leaving only a few companies in a much shorter skirmish line flanking the road. Thus somewhat less encumbered, the column advanced more rapidly until a little after ten o'clock, when the skirmishers finally broke out of the woods and brambles and into an open field. Continuing across with little if any opposition, the men topped a gentle ridge and descended into the shallow valley of Fourteen Mile Creek, two miles from Raymond. The column followed closely behind, and on reaching the creek, either Logan or McPherson ordered a halt for rest and water. Dennis's brigade deployed along the near bank of the shallow creek, then stacked arms.[14]

While the men drank and rested in the shade of the trees lining the creek, McPherson surveyed the valley from the ridge back in the open field. Weighing the situation, he decided that the Confederates would probably make a strong stand on the ridge on the opposite side of the valley, between Fourteen Mile Creek and the town of Raymond. To push them out of the way, he wanted the rest of Logan's and all of Brig. Gen. Marcellus Crocker's division, which was next in the column. He sent orders back down the column to get the supply wagons out of the road and pass these units to the front. This would take time given the strung-out condition of the column, and there was nothing to do but wait. McPherson ordered a section of the 8th Michigan Battery to deploy on the road just short of the creek crossing and then let its captain send the battery's horses to water in the creek while the rest of Dennis's brigade continued to wait and rest under the trees.[15]

All were surprised when the roar of artillery fire and an outburst of heavy musketry announced the onset of a Confederate attack. Brig. Gen. John Gregg had brought his oversized Rebel brigade of some 3,000 men out from Jackson and moved up to attack McPherson's column in the belief that it was only a small flank guard of a brigade or less. Since his brigade was twice the size of its average Union counterpart, Gregg believed that he had the opportunity to crush the enemy force advancing toward Raymond. While the 7th Texas and 3d Tennessee attacked the Federals in front along Fourteen Mile Creek, Gregg planned to have the rest of his brigade swing to the left, around the Union right flank.[16]

Just before the assault struck his position, McPherson had sent orders to reinforce the skirmish line with another regiment. Logan had relayed the order to Dennis, who had directed the 20th Ohio to advance for that purpose. Attempting to carry out the order even as the Confederates hit, the Ohioans moved forward into the bed of shallow Fourteen Mile Creek. Unable to advance any farther into the teeth of the Rebel onslaught, they took shelter behind its far bank. The other regiments of Dennis's brigade fell back a short distance when Gregg's men struck, so nearly the whole weight of the 7th Texas's assault fell on the 20th Ohio, which held on grimly in its natural entrenchment.[17]

McPherson ordered Brig. Gen. John E. Smith's brigade to move forward and support Dennis's right. As that unit attempted to deploy along the creek bottom to the right of the road, Smith's men encountered dense thickets and uneven terrain that caused their regiments to lose contact with each other. Consequently, several were unable to engage the enemy initially, and the 3d Tennessee's full attack fell on the 23d Indiana and the 20th Illinois. The section of Union artillery in the road was also firing, but the inversion layer held the clouds of smoke low, where it mixed with the rising clouds of dust kicked up by the muzzle blasts. Aiming could be only approximate.

Prevented by terrain, foliage, and atmosphere from observing the combat that had suddenly engulfed his two lead brigades, McPherson could do little but send staff officers galloping back down the column with orders to rush the rest of the corps forward as rapidly as possible. Warned by scouts of Gregg's flanking column to the east, McPherson deployed his next brigade, Brig. Gen. John D. Stevenson's, in the open field east of the road and facing to the right (east). This proved to be a wise decision, the best McPherson made during the battle. Deterred by the sight of Stevenson's line, the flanking column drew back without launching its attack.[18]

With that, along with the stubborn fighting of the 20th Ohio and 20th Illinois, the tide of battle turned. Gregg's only chance had been to collapse the head of the Union column quickly and then defeat its units one by one as they came panting and staggering forward through the heat and dust. As the front stabilized, the rest of Dennis's and Smith's regiments moved up and got into the fight. With the Confederate flanking column withdrawing, McPherson was able to shift some of Stevenson's regiments into the creek bottom to join the fight there as well. Finally, Col. John B. Sanborn's brigade, the lead unit of Crocker's division, came up. McPherson promptly committed it to the battle as well, along with the 8th Illinois Infantry, which had been detached from train guard and double-quicked forward. Once the Union weight of numbers made itself felt, the battle was all but over, and Gregg beat a hasty retreat.[19]

In his first battle as a corps commander, McPherson had been caught by surprise—which he subsequently neglected to mention in his report. His column had been strung out in such a way that his lead brigades had been compelled to fight alone for some time, and the action had taken place in an environment that temporarily negated some of his advantage in numbers. But though expecting no attack, McPherson had, with his habitual attention to detail, positioned the section of the 8th Michigan Battery wisely while its horses were to be watered so that when the Confederate attack struck, the gunners were able to lend their fire to the defense. McPherson reacted superbly to the Rebel onslaught, remaining cool, calling up reinforcements, and deploying Stevenson's brigade to counter the Confederates' attempted flanking movement. The last of these was also a dividend of his wise decision to deploy scouts, cavalry videttes, and infantry skirmishers in front and on either flank of his column. This reconnaissance screen had warned him of the initial enemy presence on the road ahead, and the surprise that opened the battle had not been Gregg's presence but rather the fact that he acted in a way McPherson had not expected.

Grant had been riding with Sherman that day. Informed of the fight at Raymond, he recognized that Gregg's attack had to have been launched from Jackson. More convinced than ever that the Mississippi capital had to be neutralized, he sent orders to his corps commanders that evening, directing Sherman and McPherson to move against Jackson while McClernand feinted against Pemberton's Confederate army, which was then at Edward's Station, about halfway between Vicksburg and Jackson. In compliance with these new orders, McPherson's corps marched eight miles on May 13 to reach the town of Clinton, ten miles west of Jackson on the Southern Railroad of Mississippi, the line that connected Vicksburg to the state capital. The general immediately had his men start tearing up the tracks.[20]

Grant's orders for May 14 called for McPherson to approach Jackson from the west while Sherman advanced toward the city from the southwest. The day dawned under lowering skies and a steady rain that had been falling most of the night. The column slogged and waded along roads that had overnight become deeper in mud than they had been in dust the day before as a weather front brought one thunderstorm cell after another across central Mississippi. McPherson's men encountered Confederate skirmishers about two miles from Jackson. Soon thereafter, they came under artillery fire, which indicated that the Rebels were going to make a serious stand in front of the town. Simultaneously, Sherman's advanced units engaged Confederate defenders on the south side of Jackson. Both corps deployed for battle. Their lines did not connect, but Grant, who was riding with Sherman again, was confident that either corps could, if necessary, defeat the entire enemy force at Jackson.[21]

McPherson's conduct of his end of the brief battle for the Mississippi state capital rewarded his commander's confidence. He deployed two divisions under Confederate artillery fire in the plowed fields on either side of the Clinton Road. He then had the men lie down while skirmishers moved forward to determine the exact location and extent of the Rebel position. With that task complete and the heavy downpour easing up a little, McPherson ordered his troops to move forward. They advanced steadily until they were within half a mile of the Confederate line. Then McPherson ordered them to fix bayonets and charge at the double quick. The line swept forward, the men yelling "like Indians." For a time, the Rebels stood their ground, inflicting about three hundred casualties, but McPherson's line overlapped the Confederates on both ends, and the defenders soon fled.[22]

Sherman's men entered the city from the south at about the same time. Together the two corps took possession and set about the task of destroying targets of military importance in Jackson such as factories, railroads, depots, and the like. That afternoon Grant met with Sherman and McPherson to discuss the army's next move. He had learned that Gen. Joseph E. Johnston, overall commander of Confederate forces in Mississippi, had sent an order to Pemberton directing him to attack the Union army near Clinton while Johnston attacked from the other side. Grant now knew from the direction of Johnston's retreat that he would not be able to carry out his role in this plan—Pemberton's army would be on its own marching east from Vicksburg. Grant ordered Sherman to keep his corps in Jackson for another day to complete the work of neutralizing the city as a Confederate base. Meanwhile, he would take McPherson's corps and move west at 5:00 A.M. the next morning to join McClernand and deal with Pemberton.[23]

At 5:00 A.M. on May 16, two railroad employees entered Grant's camp bearing word that Pemberton's army was near Edward's Station, several miles farther west. The general sent the available portion of his own army marching west to meet Pemberton on three parallel roads. Two divisions, totaling five brigades, took the southerly Raymond Road. Two more, under McClernand's direct command and totaling four brigades, advanced on the appropriately named Middle Road, while three divisions, totaling eight brigades, marched under McPherson's direct command on the Jackson Road, the northerly of the three routes. The three columns would be well within supporting distance of each other so that no one column was in danger of having to fight a battle alone. The lead units of all three began marching at about 6:00 A.M.[24]

Skirmishers in front of each of the columns encountered Confederates a little more than an hour later, six miles east of Edward's Station and about one mile east of the point where the Jackson and Middle Roads converged. McPherson promptly sent a message back to Grant, who was still at the camp near Bolton, informing him of this development and suggesting that he come to the front. Hurrying forward on the Jackson Road, Grant joined his lieutenant on the battlefield around 7:30 A.M. Union skirmishers had by this time driven their Confederate counterparts back onto the enemy's main body. Pemberton, though, had possession of the dominant terrain feature in the area. About half a mile short of the crossroads where two of the roads met, the Jackson Road, which here ran north and south, passed over a bald hill named after the local landowners, the Champion family. Pemberton had deployed one of his divisions on the hill, facing north down the Jackson Road, and his other two divisions along a ridge that ran south from Champion Hill, their line facing east, toward McClernand's approaching troops on the Middle and Raymond Roads.[25]

Grant issued orders for the deployment of the two divisions on the Jackson Road. The first was the two-brigade command of Brig. Gen. Alvin P. Hovey. Part of the XIII Corps, Hovey's division would on this day be operating with the XVII. Grant deployed these two brigades on either side of the Jackson Road. He had McPherson deploy the next division, Logan's, so as to extend Hovey's line to the right (west), opposite a ridge that sloped down from Champion Hill toward Baker's Creek. The Confederates were simultaneously extending their own line along that ridge. The commander of a Georgia brigade assigned to that task thought he saw an opportunity to snatch some of the cannon Grant was deploying and led his men on a charge down the hill toward Logan's position. The Confederates had underestimated the degree to which those men were prepared to receive the attack. Logan had one brigade, Smith's, already in line, with Stevenson's moving up on the right. Aided by the fire of the coveted guns themselves, Smith handily repulsed the Confederate assault.[26]

With Grant directing the overall shape of the battle along the Jackson Road, McPherson busied himself overseeing the deployment of Logan's division—in effect, acting the part of a division commander himself. He directed Stevenson's brigade, on the right of the line, to advance into a patch of woods whence it could deliver an enfilading fire into the flank of any further Confederate attempt to attack Smith's brigade and the Union artillery. As Stevenson's men moved into position, McPherson and Logan rode from left to right along Smith's line. Both were highly popular officers, and the men cheered them enthusiastically. "Give them Jesse, boys," shouted McPherson, "Give them Jesse." Logan, who was already becoming a legend in the army for his ability to inspire troops in battle, was more verbose and launched into a fiery harangue. When they reached Smith's right flank, McPherson continued on to Stevenson's position, but Logan turned back to ride Smith's line again, shouting further encouragement to the men.[27]

About the time McPherson reached Stevenson's position, the Confederates on Champion Hill did indeed launch a second assault aimed at Smith. With the keen eye of a military engineer, McPherson saw that Stevenson's brigade was, as he had anticipated, perfectly positioned to deliver a devastating fire into the attackers once they got a little closer. He therefore ordered Smith's men to hold their fire and wait. As the Confederates advanced, Stevenson's troops became impatient. Many were shouting, "Let us fire," and "Let us advance." A few fired without orders. Then McPherson saw Smith's brigade begin to advance, having been ordered forward by the headstrong Logan. That removed the prospect of enfilading the attackers, and McPherson ordered Stevenson's brigade to join the counterattack.[28]

The attacking force he had hoped to enfilade was the 23d Alabama, which was making a decidedly ill-advised foray. The Alabamians turned and ran before the onslaught of Logan's division, which then pursued them up the slope of the ridge extending west from Champion Hill. The remainder of the Confederates on that section of the ridge were not able to mount an effective defense. Meanwhile, more or less simultaneously with Logan's advance, Hovey's division charged against Champion Hill itself, routing the defending troops of

Maj. Gen. Carter L. Stevenson's division. On the far right of the entire Union line, General Stevenson's brigade had an especially easy time of it. Since their position entirely overlapped the Confederate left flank, they met little resistance, passed on over the ridge, and struck two batteries of artillery that Pemberton had positioned on the next ridge to try to support his left flank. These they overran, capturing seven guns. The Federals finally halted astride the Jackson Road, which they had regained after its bend to the west. They were thus squarely between Pemberton's army and its primary escape route via the Jackson Road bridge over Baker's Creek.[29]

This would have brought a response from Pemberton were he not busy dealing with other problems. Hovey's division, advancing simultaneously with Logan's, had driven the Confederates off Champion Hill and now moved to seize the crossroads of the Middle and Jackson Roads. Pemberton launched a counterattack against Hovey and drove him back over the hill, shifting the tide of battle. To counter this development, McPherson had few resources. The second of his divisions on the road, Crocker's, was arriving while the battle was in progress. He distributed the various regiments of its first brigade, that of Colonel Sanborn, as reinforcements to various sectors of Hovey's line in response to urgent calls for reinforcements as that division fought to stave off Pemberton's counterattack. The next brigade, Col. George B. Boomer's, McPherson committed as a unit, sending it straight down the Jackson Road and up the slope of Champion Hill. Passing Hovey's fleeing troops, the brigade found itself facing the onslaught of Bowen's division and had to fall back fighting down the north slope of the hill.[30]

Shortly before the crisis had developed on Champion Hill, Grant rode to the Union right to check on the status of Stevenson's brigade. There he met Logan. Neither general recognized the significance of Stevenson's position astride the Jackson Road between Pemberton's army and Baker's Creek. When word reached Grant of the collapse of Hovey's division, he ordered Stevenson to pull out of his position and march to shore up the line north of the hill. Before these regiments could arrive, however, the situation had stabilized. McPherson committed Crocker's third brigade, Col. Samuel E. Holmes's, and it together with Boomer's command stalled the by-now overextended Confederate attack. Logan, meanwhile, led his two remaining brigades in swinging to the left to take the Confederate attackers in flank and rear. By that time, Hovey's division had rallied and now joined Crocker's in driving Bowen's Confederates back over

Champion Hill. The added pressure of Logan's flank attack turned the Rebel retreat into a rout.[31]

Grant quickly realized that Stevenson's brigade was no longer needed in the Champion Hill sector of the battlefield and countermarched it back to its former position, where it joined what had by that time become a general Union advance along the entire front, which drove the Confederate army off the field in a more or less disorderly retreat. Pemberton escaped by the narrowest of margins thanks to his military engineers, who during the course of the battle had succeeded in building a bridge over Baker's Creek well south of the Jackson Road bridge, which had been his only viable line of retreat when the fighting started. With Grant's troops firmly in control of Jackson Road from Champion Hill all the way to Stevenson's position much closer to the creek, Pemberton used this alternate bridge, ending the day's fighting.

The Battle of Champion Hill, a much larger affair than Port Gibson, Raymond, or Jackson, was McPherson's first major battle as a corps commander, though it was a limited experience in that respect. Three Union divisions fought the entire battle, and with Grant present, McPherson had less to do than would ordinarily have been the case for a corps commander in battle. Nonetheless, his tactical instincts and eye for terrain had both proven excellent. His placement of Stevenson's brigade beyond the Confederate flank was wise, and his plan to enfilade the next Confederate attack would no doubt have worked well. Yet the fact that some of Stevenson's men had fired their rifles prematurely, even while McPherson was present with the brigade, suggests that although his men loved him, they did not yet have the desirable degree of respect for him. Logan possessed more of the men's confidence, and it was he who had preempted McPherson's plan by launching Smith's brigade prematurely. Grant had acquiesced in this, ordering Hovey forward at about the same time. Though the advance had been spectacularly successful, it also became overextended and vulnerable to counterattack. The course of battle would probably have been smoother for the Union if, as McPherson seemed to prefer, the Federals had waited until Crocker's division was all up before beginning the attack. Once the crisis came, though, McPherson had handled his limited resources as well as anyone could have.

Following Champion Hill, Grant's army marched west toward Vicksburg. After its hard fight, McPherson's corps followed behind McClernand's, which save for Hovey's detached division had not taken part in the battle. While the XIII Corps fought the small battle of Big Black Bridge the following day, McPherson's men swung north and built makeshift bridges over the Big Black eight miles upstream. Continuing to follow Pemberton's retreating army, Grant's troops arrived outside Vicksburg and filed into position around the town's defenses on the evening of May 18. While taking his first look at the defensive works, McPherson was cheered by his passing troops.[32]

The next day Grant launched an all-out assault on Vicksburg, hoping to take advantage of the momentum he had gained by the victories at Champion Hill and Big Black Bridge. The results were disappointing. The terrain around the city was a tangle of sinuous steep-sided ridges separated by deep ravines choked with brush. Without adequate time for reconnaissance and preparation, the assault was uncoordinated, confused, and partial. Still hoping to avoid a prolonged siege, Grant decided to try again on May 22, by which time, presumably, preparations for a coordinated attack would be complete, and his army could bring its full force to bear against the Rebel defenses.

Within his assigned sector of the front, McPherson chose to aim his heaviest effort against the most powerful Confederate defenses, the Great Redoubt and the Third Louisiana Redan. Questionable as it might have seemed to attack directly into the enemy's strength, McPherson had good reasons for the decision. The two powerful earthworks flanked the point at which the Jackson Road entered the Confederate lines. Leading into Vicksburg, they ran along the crests of the most open and direct ridges. Any other routes of approach would have entailed struggling through ravines and approaching the defenses up very steep slopes. While some of McPherson's units would attack across that difficult terrain with the goal of holding the defenders there in position, his hope was that the heavy assault along the road would overwhelm the Confederates in the two strongpoints. In theory, a reinforced line of skirmishers would force the defenders to keep their heads down while the assault column charged forward. In practice, this proved unsuccessful as the Confederates inflicted heavy casualties on the advancing Federals.[33]

The charging troops nevertheless succeeded in reaching the ditch in front of the earthworks, but once there they found the scaling ladders they had made the night before (at the rate of two per company) were too short to reach the parapet. The attack stalled. The men hung on grimly in their advanced positions because that was safer than retreating under heavy fire. They eventually made their way back to Union lines after nightfall. Immediate responsibility for the construction of the ladders seems to have rested on Brigadier General Stevenson, though Logan and McPherson would also share whatever blame there was to be apportioned. In fact, it was difficult to judge the height of the Confederate parapet from the opposite ridge and impossible to determine accurately the depth of the ditch that fronted it. Preparation time had been minimal, thus the odds of success poor.[34]

After the failure of the May 22 assault, the Army of the Tennessee settled down to lay siege to Vicksburg. All three of Grant's corps carried on active sapping operations in their sectors, and approach trenches snaked their way up the bluffs, edging ever closer to the Confederate fortifications. In McPherson's sector the main line of approach was once again along the ridge that carried the Jackson Road and aimed at the Great Redoubt and the Third Louisiana Redan. Again the task fell primarily to Logan's division. McPherson assigned his chief engineer, Capt. Andrew Hickenlooper, to supervise the siege operations along this axis. Under Hickenlooper's direction, the troops dug approach trenches and planted a heavily fortified artillery position within 130 yards of the Confederate parapet. Continuing to drive his sap closer to the defenses, the captain reached a position almost at the foot of the outer slope of the redan's earthwork.

Next, Hickenlooper selected a special team of thirty-six experienced coal miners to tunnel under the fort and place a 2,200-pound charge of gunpowder. At 1:00 P.M. on June 25, he was able to report to McPherson that the mine was ready for detonation. McPherson and Grant had been preparing for this day for some time. Logan's division would attack through the gap that would be opened when the mine blew. Meanwhile, Grant alerted the rest of the army to stand by to fire on the Rebel lines with every available weapon and be ready to feign infantry assaults at any point from which the Confederates seemed to be shifting troops for reinforcement of the Jackson Road sector. Grant and his staff took position to view the explosion and assault from the advanced Union battery just 130 yards from the Third Louisiana Redan.[35]

The planned explosion shook the lines at 3:30 that afternoon, blowing a corner of the redan into the air, and the attack went as scheduled. Unfortunately, the assaulting troops found the Confederates, hearing the sound of tunneling beneath their feet and guessing its import, had withdrawn most of their troops from the site and placed them behind a breastwork they had built across the previously open rear of the redan. Throughout the remainder of that day and that night, units of McPherson's corps, relieving each other in shifts, fought stubbornly to take the breastwork. Logan, from whose division most of the attacking troops came, wanted to call off the attack and withdraw his troops from the crater, later complaining that his superiors insisted on continued attempts to break through. He referred to both McPherson and Grant, but it was the latter who insisted on keeping up the fight in the crater. McPherson, whether he agreed or disagreed with his commander's decision, was reduced merely to transmitting his orders. Late in the afternoon of June 26, Grant gave up and ordered the troops to dig in as close to the new Rebel works as possible and resume the war of the spade.[36]

With McPherson's approval, Hickenlooper began another tunnel the next day. Starting from a new entrenched position in the middle of the crater, he had his men tunnel under a part of the redan that was still intact and held by the Confederates. By June 30 this new shaft was complete and ready, but a Confederate countermine was very close. McPherson sought permission to detonate the mine at once rather than let the Rebels possibly break into it and disrupt it. Grant agreed, and a second blast collapsed much of what had remained of the redan. This time no infantry assault was planned or intended, and McPherson merely followed up the blast with an artillery bombardment that inflicted additional casualties on Confederate reinforcements who rushed to the sector to counter the expected Union assault.[37]

Three days later the guns fell silent and surrender negotiations opened. McPherson took a key role in them by persuading Grant to accept the idea of paroling the captured garrison rather than demanding unconditional surrender and sending all of the Confederates north as prisoners of war. On July 4 Pemberton surrendered. Grant designated Logan's men to be the first Union troops to march into the city, honoring the division's hard fighting at the crater nine days earlier. McPherson had his staff officers fly the national colors of the XVII Corps from the Vicksburg courthouse cupola. Thus ended the young general's first extended field campaign as a corps commander.[38]

JAMES B. MCPHERSON HAD performed creditably in his first major campaign as a senior commander. Despite the enormous importance and extended nature of the operations that culminated in the capture of Vicksburg, though, they provided a remarkably limited amount of experience for the general and did not subject him to the most severe of tests. McPherson had had little to do at the Battle of Port Gibson. At Raymond he had enjoyed a massive superiority in numbers, once he got his troops up, and after the first surprise, he reacted well and soon took control of the situation. At Jackson McPherson again enjoyed a heavy advantage in numbers, thanks to Grant's operational skill, and in contrast to Raymond, he faced an unaggressive opponent. Champion Hill was a very hard-fought battle, but Grant directed the action personally, leaving McPherson relatively little to do. Even at the fight at the Third Louisiana Redan, Grant had been well to the front, personally directing the action and determining how long the attack should be maintained.

None of this is to suggest that McPherson had performed poorly or that he was anything else but highly impressive and promising. On top of that, his good relations with Grant and with his fellow corps commanders helped promote cordial cooperation within the Army of the Tennessee, in stark contrast to the case of his fellow corps commander John McClernand, whose inability to lay aside political posturing had brought him into constant conflict with Grant. McPherson, however, was precisely the type of highly trained professional soldier Grant liked. Thanks in no small part to Grant's skill and wisdom, the demands of the tasks laid on McPherson during the campaign were dramatically less than those placed on, for example, Maj. Gen. Oliver O. Howard, an officer of about the same age who was simultaneously making his two debut campaigns as a corps commander within the Army of the Potomac. In those outings, Chancellorsville and Gettysburg, Howard faced the stiffest imaginable opponents and nearly impossible situations. Whereas Howard's commanders in those two campaigns set him up for failure, Grant during the Vicksburg Campaign provided the support and guidance that a junior corps commander needed in order to achieve success in his first outing.

NOTES

1. William E. Strong, "The Campaign against Vicksburg," in *The Papers of the Military Order of the Loyal Legion*, 56 vols. (various publishers and dates; repr., Wilmington, N.C.: Broadfoot, 1994), 11:329–30 (hereafter cited as *MOLLUS*).

2. Jean Edward Smith, *Grant* (New York: Simon and Schuster, 2001), 173.

3. Abram J. Vanauken Diary, Feb. 3, 7, 12, 13, 1863, Illinois State Historical Library, Springfield; Daniel G. Winegar Diary, Feb. 6 8, 1863, ibid.; Robert Ridge Diary, Feb. 2, 1863, ibid.; Wimer Bed-

ford Reminiscences, Library of Congress, Washington, D.C.; Luther H. Cowan Diary, Feb. 23, 1863, Luther H. Cowan Papers, Wisconsin Historical Society, Madison.

4. U.S. War Department, *The War of the Rebellion: A Compilation of the Official Records of the Union and Confederate Armies*, 70 vols. in 128 parts (Washington, D.C.: Government Printing Office, 1880–1901), ser. 1, 24(1):15–16 (hereafter cited as *OR*; all references are to series 1 unless otherwise noted); Thomas M. Stevenson, *History of the 78th Regiment O.V.V.I: From Its "Muster-In" to Its "Muster-Out;" Comprising Its Organization, Marches, Campaign, Battles, and Skirmishes* (Zanesville, Ohio: Hugh Dunne, 1865), 223–24; Manning F. Force, "Personal Recollections of the Vicksburg Campaign," in *MOLLUS*, 1:293; Allen Morgan Geer, *Civil War Diary of Allen Morgan Geer, Twentieth Regiment, Illinois Volunteers*, ed. Mary Ann Anderson (Denver: Robert C. Appleman, 1977), 80–81; Winegar Diary, Mar. 5, 1863; Ridge Diary, Mar. 4, 1863; James W. Jessee, *Civil War Diaries of James W. Jessee, 1861–1865, Company K, 8th Regiment of Illinois Volunteer Infantry*, ed. William P. LaBounty (Normal, Ill. McLean County Genealogical Society, 1997), chap. 3:11; William W. Belknap, *History of the Fifteenth Regiment, Iowa Veteran Volunteer Infantry* (Keokuk, Iowa: R. B. Ogden and Sons, 1887), 245–46.

5. *OR*, 24(3):76; Stevenson, *History of the 78th Regiment*, 224; Geer, *Civil War Diary*, 81.

6. Ridge Diary, Feb. 24, 1863; Ulysses S. Grant, *Personal Memoirs of U. S. Grant*, 2 vols. (New York: Charles L. Webster, 1885–86), 1:448–49.

7. *OR*, 24(3):98, 110; Cowan Diary, Mar. 16, 1863; Luther H. Cowan to "Dear Harriet," Mar. 17, 1863, Luther H. Cowan Papers, Wisconsin Historical Society, Madison; Winegar Diary, Mar. 19, 1863; Geer, *Civil War Diary*, 82; Stevenson, *History of the 78th Regiment*, 226–27; Belknap, *History of the Fifteenth Regiment*, 245–46; William L. Wade Diary, Mar. 17, 1863, U.S. Army Military History Institute, Carlisle Barracks, Carlisle, Pa.

8. Winegar Diary, Mar. 19, 1863; Luther H. Cowan to "Dear Harriet," Mar. 17, 1863, Cowan Papers; "The Seventeenth Corps," *National Tribune*, May 18, 1893, 1.

9. *OR*, 24(1):48–49.

10. Ibid., 49–50; Grant, *Personal Memoirs*, 1:485–86; Virgil G. Way, comp., *History of the Thirty-Third Regiment Illinois Veteran Volunteer Infantry in the Civil War, 22nd August, 1861, to 7th December, 1865, by General Isaac C. Elliott with Company and Personal Sketches by Other Comrades and Complete Historical Rosters* (Gibson City, Ill.: The [Regimental] Association, 1902), 38; John H. Ferree to "Dear Brother," May 9, 1863, Indiana Historical Society, Indianapolis; Edwin C. Bearss, *The Campaign for Vicksburg*, 3 vols. (Dayton, Ohio: Morningside, 1985–86), 2:409–11; Warren Grabau, *Ninety-Eight Days: A Geographer's View of the Vicksburg Campaign* (Knoxville: University of Tennessee Press, 2000), 168–72.

11. Jessee, *Civil War Diaries*, chap. 3:18.

12. *OR*, 24(1):50, 637; Grabau, *Ninety-Eight Days*, 222; Cowan Diary, May 12, 1863.

13. Grabau, *Ninety-Eight Days*, 223–24.

14. *OR*, 24(1):714; Henry Dwight, "A Soldier's Story," *New York Daily Tribune*, Nov. 21, 1886.

15. *OR*, 24(1):637.

16. Dwight, "Soldier's Story"; *OR*, 24(1):709, 714; Force, "Personal Reminiscences of the Vicksburg Campaign," 1:298–300; Grabau, *Ninety-Eight Days*, 222–24, 229.

17. Dwight, "Soldier's Story"; *OR*, 24(1):637, 714; Force, "Personal Reminiscences of the Vicksburg Campaign," 1:298–300.

18. Grabau, *Ninety-Eight Days*, 231–32; Bearss, *Campaign for Vicksburg*, 2:497–500.

19. *OR*, 24(1):637; Grabau, *Ninety-Eight Days*, 232–34; Bearss, *Campaign for Vicksburg*, 2:500-10.

20. Grant, *Personal Memoirs*, 1:499–504; Ulysses S. Grant, *Papers of Ulysses S. Grant*, ed. John Y. Simon et al., 32 vols. (Carbondale: Southern Illinois University Press, 1967–2012), 8:204–12; Bearss, *Campaign for Vicksburg*, 2:512–14; Edward P. Stanfield to "Dear Father," May 26, 1863, Edward P. Stanfield Papers, Indiana Historical Society, Indianapolis; W. S. Morris, L. D. Hartwell, and J. B. Kuykendall, *History 31st Regiment Illinois Volunteers Organized by John A. Logan*, (1902; repr., Carbondale: Southern Illinois University Press, 1998), 61–62; John Q. A. Campbell, *The Union Must Stand: The Civil War Diary of John Quincy Adams Campbell, Fifth Iowa Volunteer Infantry*, ed. Mark Grimsley and Todd D. Miller (Knoxville: University of Tennessee Press, 2000), 93–94.

21. *OR*, 24(1):638; Grant, *Personal Memoirs*, 1:499–500; Grant, *Papers*, 8:204–8; Bearss, *Campaign for Vicksburg*, 2:512–14.

22. *OR*, 24(1):638–39; Ira Blanchard, *I Marched with Sherman: Civil War Memoirs of the 20th Illinois Volunteer Infantry* (San Francisco: J. D. Huff, 1992), 89–90; Edward P. Stanfield to "Dear Father," May 26, 1863, Stanfield Papers; Joseph J. Huston, "Who Planted the Flag at Jackson, Miss.?" *National Tribune*, Feb. 19, 1885; L. F. Parrish, "At Jackson," *National Tribune*, Aug. 11, 1887, 3.

23. Grant, *Personal Memoirs*, 1:506–9; William T. Sherman, *Memoirs of General W. T. Sherman* (1875; repr., New York: Library of America, 1990), 347; *OR*, 24(1):639.

24. *OR*, 24(1):51; 24(2):59–60; T. J. Williams, "The Battle of Champion's Hill," *MOLLUS*, 5:204; Thomas H. Bringhurst and Frank Swigart, comps., *History of the Forty-Sixth Regiment, Indiana Volunteer Infantry, September, 1861–September, 1865* (Logansport, Ind.: Wilson, Humphreys, 1888), 60.

25. *OR*, 24(1):639; John B. Sanborn, "The Campaign against Vicksburg," *MOLLUS*, 27:131.

26. *OR*, 24(1):640; Grabau, *Ninety-Eight Days*, 287; Jessee, *Civil War Diaries*, chap. 3:20–21.

27. Morris, Hartwell, and Kuykendall, *History 31st Regiment*, 64–65; *OR*, 24(1):647, 24(2):53; Jessee, *Civil War Diaries*, chap. 3:20–21; Force, "Personal Reminiscences of the Vicksburg Campaign," 1: 301–3; Blanchard, *I Marched with Sherman*, 92.

28. Jessee, *Civil War Diaries*, chap. 3:20–21; Grabau, *Ninety-Eight Days*, 288.

29. *OR*, 24(1):640; Morris, Hartwell, and Kuykendall, *History 31st Regiment*, 65; Jessee, *Civil War Diaries*, chap. 3:21; A. J. Floury, "Champion Hills: A Graphic Picture of a Most Exciting Time—Logan's Division at Champion's Hill," *National Tribune*, Sept. 11, 1884, 3; Gould D. Molineaux Diary, May 16, 1863, Special Collections, Augustana College Library, Rock Island, Ill.

30. *OR*, 24(1):642, 24(2):50, 63; Campbell, *Union Must Stand*, 95–98.

31. Grant, *Personal Memoirs*, 1:517; J. B. Harris, "An Incident of Champion Hills," *National Tribune*, July 31, 1884, 3; R. M. Dibel, "Champion's Hill," *National Tribune*, Sept. 11, 1884, 3; Grabau, *Ninety-Eight Days*, 296.

32. Strong, "Campaign against Vicksburg," 11:329–30.

33. *OR*, 24(1):710, 719; Campbell, *Union Must Stand*, 99–100.

34. *OR*, 24(1):710, 719; Jessee, *Civil War Diaries*, chap. 3:22; Molineaux Diary, May 22, 1863;

William L. Shea and Terrence J. Winschel, *Vicksburg Is the Key: The Struggle for the Mississippi River* (Lincoln: University of Nebraska Press, 2003), 149–50; Campbell, *Union Must Stand,* 99–100.

35. Andrew Hickenlooper, "The Vicksburg Mine," *MOLLUS,* 3:539–41; Bearss, *Campaign for Vicksburg,* 3:908–10; Strong, "Campaign against Vicksburg," 11:338; Force, "Personal Recollections of the Vicksburg Campaign," 1:307.

36. Hickenlooper, "Vicksburg Mine," 3:542; Strong, "Campaign against Vicksburg," 11:340; Bearss, *Campaign for Vicksburg,* 3:915–18; Lydia Minturn Post, ed., *Soldiers' Letters, from Camp, Battle-field, and Prison* (New York: Bunce and Huntington, 1865), 263–64; Wilbur Fisk Crummer, *With Grant at Fort Donelson, Shiloh, and Vicksburg, and an appreciation of General U. S. Grant* (Oak Park, Ill.: E. C. Crummer, 1915), 136–42; Lucien B. Crooker, Henry S. Nourse, and John G. Brown, *The Story of the 55th Regiment Illinois Volunteer Infantry in the Civil War, 1861–1865 (Clinton, Mass.: W. J. Coulter,* 1887), 252; William Wiley, *The Civil War Diary of a Common Soldier: William Wiley of the 77th Illinois Infantry,* ed. Terrence J. Winschel (Baton Rouge: Louisiana State University Press, 2001), 50–53; Isaac Jackson, *"Some of the Boys . . .": The Civil War Letters of Isaac Jackson, 1862–1865,* ed. Joseph Orville Jackson (Carbondale: Southern Illinois University Press, 1960), 107–8; William M. Reid Diary, June 25, 1863, Illinois State Historical Library, Springfield; Aurelius Lyman Voorhis Diary, June 25, 1863, Indiana Historical Society, Indianapolis; Nathan G. Dye to "Dear friends," June 26, 1863, Nathan G. Dye Papers, William R. Perkins Library, Duke University, Durham, N.C.; *OR,* 24(2):294.

37. Bearss, *Campaign for Vicksburg,* 3:925–29; W. H. Tunnard, *A Southern Record: The History of the Third Regiment Louisiana Infantry* (1866; repr., Fayetteville: University of Arkansas Press, 1997), 232; Ridge Diary, July 1, 1863; Jessee, *Civil War Diaries,* chap. 3:27; Grant, *Personal Memoirs,* 1:552.

38. *OR,* 24(1):115; Grant, *Personal Memoirs,* 1:559–64; Strong, "Campaign against Vicksburg," 11:349–54.

William B. Franklin and the XIX Corps in the Trans-Mississippi, 1863–64

MARK A. SNELL

Maj. Gen. William B. Franklin is best known as the commander of the Army of the Potomac's VI Corps during the early part of the Civil War and as the scapegoat for the Union disaster at the Battle of Fredericksburg. Yet he also served in the Trans-Mississippi, commanding the XIX Corps during the calamitous Sabine Pass Expedition of 1863 and the ill-fated Red River Campaign of 1864. While he prohibited his men from conducting total war, which placed him out of step at the time with Northern strategy for subduing the rebellion, Franklin's leadership in the Red River Campaign quite possibly saved Maj. Gen. Nathaniel Banks's army from destruction, and his engineering experience gave credibility to a construction experiment that allowed a naval flotilla to escape capture.

Franklin was born in York, Pennsylvania, in 1823. He attended the U.S. Military Academy and graduated first in the class of 1843, the same class in which Ulysses S. Grant graduated twenty-first. Commissioned in the Corps of Topographical Engineers, Franklin saw action during the Mexican War but spent most of his army career overseeing construction projects for the Treasury Department, including a stint as chief engineer of the construction of the U.S. Capitol dome in Washington, D.C. He commanded a brigade during the First Battle of Manassas, a division during the early part of the Peninsula Campaign, and the VI Corps of the Army of the Potomac during the Seven Days' Battles, Second Manassas, and the Maryland Campaign. After Maj. Gen. Ambrose Burnside took command of that army in November 1862, he reorganized it into three "grand divisions," appointing Franklin to command of the Left Grand Division during the Fredericksburg Campaign.

When the Army of the Potomac stormed across the Rappahannock River during the second week of December 1862, Franklin was in command of more than 40,000 men. Although he had expected his own grand division to make the main attack on the southern part of the Confederate defenses, Burnside's late-arriving orders were vague, and Franklin, though instructed to attack "with a division at least," assaulted Lt. Gen. Thomas J. "Stonewall" Jackson's troops with the entire I Corps. Maj. Gen. George Meade's division of Pennsylvanians actually penetrated the Confederate line, but his corps commander, Maj. Gen. John F. Reynolds, did not send reinforcements, and Franklin did not urge him to do so, resulting in a Confederate counterattack and restoration of their position. The Right Grand Division suffered horribly in its futile attacks against Marye's Heights, and the battle ended in a tragic, bloody defeat for the Federal army. Accusations and recriminations followed. In the wake of the battle, two of Franklin's generals, John Newton and John Cochrane, traveled to Washington and complained directly to Pres. Abraham Lincoln about the low morale in the army and Burnside's plans for a renewal of the offensive. Maj. Gen. Joseph Hooker also grumbled, not only to members of the Lincoln administration but to the press as well. Congress's Joint Committee on the Conduct of the War launched an investigation to determine who was at fault for the Fredericksburg fiasco, and it targeted Franklin as the scapegoat.

In January 1863 the Army of the Potomac attempted to move upstream and cross the Rappahannock River in order to position itself on the left flank of the Army of Northern Virginia. Bad weather hampered the operation, and it finally was cancelled. Burnside then departed for Washington to confer with General in Chief Henry Halleck, Secretary of War Edwin Stanton, and President Lincoln. He demanded that Franklin and Hooker be relieved of command, and if not, then he would resign his own position. Lincoln relieved Burnside from command, promoted Hooker to command of the Army of the Potomac, and fired Franklin. About two months later, the joint committee released its report, which blamed Franklin for the Fredericksburg defeat. Meanwhile, the general had relocated to his hometown of York to await further assignment, which finally came at the end of June, when he was ordered to the Department of the Gulf, with headquarters in New Orleans. His new assignment shunted him far away from Washington and the Army of the Potomac to a place where he would be much less of an aggravation to the Lincoln administration, both militarily and politically.[1]

While Franklin prepared to make the journey to his new assignment, several events of national significance occurred. During the first three days of July, the Army of the Potomac, under the command of General Meade (who had replaced Hooker on June 28), soundly defeated the Army of Northern Virginia at the Battle of Gettysburg, thus forcing Gen. Robert E. Lee to abandon his invasion of the North. Then on July 4, the Mississippi River bastion of Vicksburg fell to the forces of Maj. Gen. U. S. Grant. Four days after Vicksburg's capitulation, the Confederate stronghold at Port Hudson, Louisiana, surrendered to the forces of General Banks. As the stretch of the Mississippi River between Vicksburg and Port Hudson was the last section of the river under effective Confederate control, the entire length of the Mississippi now was in Union hands.

The fall of Vicksburg and Port Hudson meant that a new military objective in the western theater must be pursued, and both Grant and Banks thought that Mobile, Alabama, would be the next goal. Political and diplomatic considerations, however, swayed Lincoln instead to order an invasion of Texas. His desire to open that state's fertile cotton-growing region to free labor coupled with concern over France's invasion of Mexico were the main factors in his decision. New England textile interests suffering from the loss of Southern cotton were anxious to see Texas invaded so that a supply of the fluffy white bolls would again make their way into the mills of Massachusetts and Connecticut. Also, despite the long-standing U.S. commitment to hemispheric independence from the Old World, France nevertheless invaded Mexico in 1861. After some early setbacks, the French army scored important victories against the Mexicans in the late spring of 1863, and on June 7 Mexico City fell. Lincoln could ill afford to antagonize the French at this critical stage of the Civil War, but occupation of at least a part of Texas by U.S. troops could forestall any French plans to invade the Lone Star State.[2] Any necessary enforcement of the Monroe Doctrine, though, would have to wait until after the Confederacy was defeated.

The Union general responsible for military operations in this region was the victor of Port Hudson, Nathaniel Prentiss Banks. Forty-seven years of age in 1863, Banks had risen from poverty to become the Republican governor of Massachusetts in 1858. His political clout had gained him a commission as major general of volunteers when the war began, but his military career would be checkered. One of several Union generals defeated by Stonewall Jackson during the 1862 Shenandoah Valley Campaign, Banks almost got his revenge on Jackson a few months later during the Battle of Cedar Mountain. Outnumbered nearly two to one, his men fought stubbornly, but the timely arrival of Confederate reinforcements denied the former governor a victory. Banks then was appointed the commander of the Department of the Gulf, where his most important mission to date had been the reduction of the Port Hudson defenses. Despite heavy losses suffered by his XIX Corps, his forces eventually overwhelmed the Confederate garrison.³ Banks would be Franklin's immediate commander during the latter's stay in the Department of the Gulf.

Franklin had his first meeting with Banks on July 22. "He received me cordially, was very glad to see me, and at once talked of taking a run home to see Mrs. B[anks]," Franklin told his wife, Anna, in a letter written the same day. He dined with the general and his wife that evening. After the repast, Banks informed Franklin that he was thinking about placing at Baton Rouge, under his command, about half of the troops in the Department of the Gulf. Franklin thought that he would enjoy that assignment better than staying in New Orleans, for Baton Rouge's climate was a bit cooler and the citizens he considered nicer. Nevertheless, Franklin was dispirited. "I am convinced now, that I was only sent here to get rid of me," he admitted to Anna. "There are more Generals than are needed, even taking out all those who have gone off."⁴ He was correct on both accounts. Besides Banks, another general who had been banished to the Department of the Gulf was Charles P. Stone, who had been castigated by the joint committee for his defeat at Ball's Bluff in the autumn of 1861, imprisoned, and then released from confinement in the summer of 1862.

Franklin, meanwhile, had been assigned to a board of officers to determine the placement and condition of fortifications on the Mississippi River. He finished this assignment during the first two weeks of August. Although Banks seemed to express confidence in his abilities, Franklin disclosed to his close friend Maj. Gen. William F. "Baldy" Smith, who earlier had commanded a division under Franklin in the VI Corps, that he did not have much faith in Banks. "I find him more ignorant than I supposed he could be," Franklin wrote. Nonetheless, he found most of the general's staff officers "pretty smart" and admitted that Banks had "excellent luck" in his past military operations. The commander's high opinion meant that Franklin hopefully would take over command of a corps.⁵

With the transfer of Maj. Gen. Edward O. C. Ord's XIII Corps to the Department of the Gulf in August, Banks decided to give his own XIX Corps to Franklin, who assumed command on the twentieth. The XIX Corps comprised three infantry divisions and three regiments of cavalry. Franklin was delighted to command a corps again, but as he explained to Smith, the state of affairs in his new outfit "are exceedingly disorganized . . . and I am afraid that there are neither the men or means here to their proper condition." He was glad to be far away from Washington "on account of getting no orders from there, but it is a very bad thing when you want ordnance & quartermaster stores." Under ideal conditions, Franklin would need several months to adjust to his new command and to address logistical and manpower shortfalls. He would have too little time to fix much of anything, for in three weeks Banks would order him to launch an amphibious assault on the Texas coast with the intent of seizing Sabine City, where 40,000 bales of cotton supposedly were stored. The plan also called for this force to march on Beaumont, seize the railroad linking the town with Houston, and use that rail line as his main supply route for an attack on Houston, the ultimate strategic objective of the campaign.[6]

Five days prior to the beginning of the expedition, General Grant arrived in New Orleans and paid Franklin a social visit. The two generals dined together and afterward had a long conversation with the commander of the U.S. Navy's West Gulf Blockading Squadron, Commodore Henry H. Bell, undoubtedly about the upcoming joint operation. Franklin provided very few details to Anna about the visit, but a few months later he divulged to Baldy Smith that Grant was on quite a "bender" for the first two days of his stay in the Crescent City. Franklin confided to his friend that, luckily, Grant fell off his horse, which "stopped the frolic, for he could not walk, and was saved for the time." Franklin reckoned that the reason why the general was reveling so hard was because his wife had not accompanied him. "When I saw Grant in Vicksburg about Aug. 1," he recalled in his letter, "he was perfectly straight & told me that he had drunk nothing during the war. I was as you can imagine somewhat surprised when I saw him in New Orleans. But Mrs. G, a cross-eyed *very* ugly woman was at Vicksburg, and there was no such woman at New Orleans."[7]

Franklin began his Texas operation on Friday afternoon, September 4. To get from New Orleans to the Texas coast, his command would load on transports and steam down the Mississippi to the Gulf of Mexico, then veer west to the mouth of the Sabine River. There, at Sabine Pass, the navy escort of four gunboats was to silence the guns of Fort Griffin, which sat above the river's mud flats. Fort Griffin was a timber-reinforced earthen structure, with three twelve-foot-thick-by-eight-foot-high bastioned walls facing west, south, and east. On the north side (or rear) of the fort was an earthen redoubt measuring four feet high. The gunboats first would have to pass the higher walls of the fort before they could lob shells over the lower wall from the rear. Fort Griffin con-

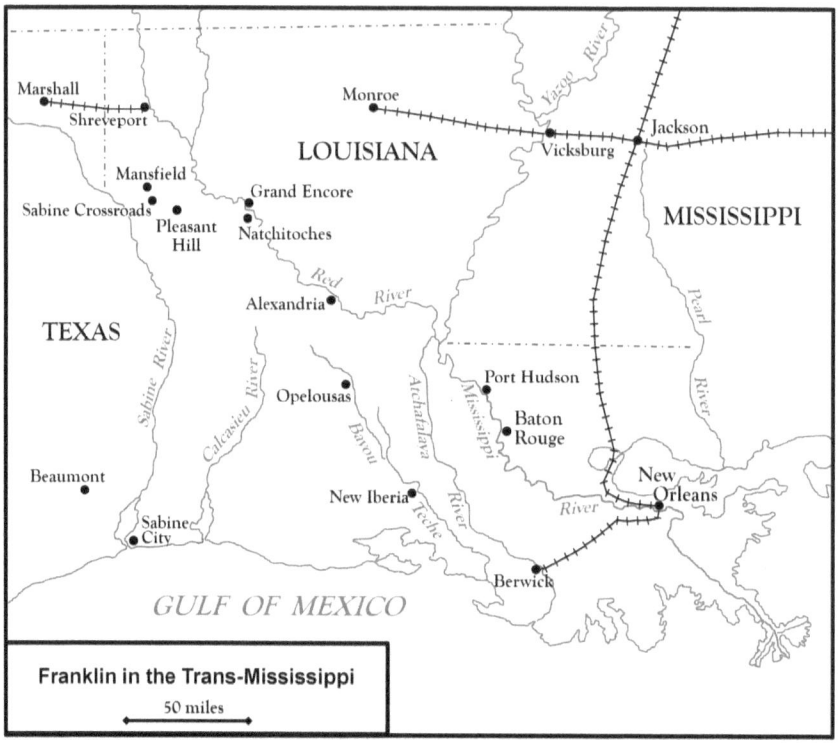

Franklin in the Trans-Mississippi
50 miles

tained two thirty-two-pounder smoothbore cannons, two thirty-two-pounder howitzers, and two twenty-four-pounder smoothbores. Although Franklin did not know it, Griffin's garrison had only forty-seven men commanded by Lt. Dick Dowling, an Irish immigrant and son of a local bar owner.[8]

The Union plan was pretty straightforward, but it required the element of surprise and a considerable bit of coordination between the army and navy if it was to be successful. Brig. Gen. Godfrey Weitzel, an 1855 graduate of West Point and commander of the First Division, XIX Corps, was to depart New Orleans on Friday evening, September 4, with one thousand infantrymen and two artillery batteries loaded on four transports escorted by the gunboat *Arizona;* rendezvous at Berwick Bay with Lt. Cdr. Frederick Crocker (commander of the naval element assigned to the expedition) and the gunboats *Clifton* and *Sachem;* link up with the gunboat *Granite City* still later (which was carrying an experienced pilot who knew Sabine Pass); and then proceed to Sabine Pass, arriving there on Sunday night, September 6. The rest of the XIX Corps was to embark on Friday night and depart shortly thereafter. At first light on September 7, the gunboats were to engage Fort Griffin's batteries while Weitzel landed his division and pinned down the Confederate artillerymen with rifle fire. Once the fort fell, the rest of the XIX Corps would land and move on Beaufort, Texas.[9]

The entire operation turned into a comedy of errors. Weitzel's transports rendezvoused with Crocker as planned and transferred to the three gunboats over a hundred infantrymen to serve as sharpshooters during the assault. From that point on, everything began to go wrong. The rendezvous with the *Granite City* was delayed, and without a knowledgeable pilot, Crocker got lost: he thought he had steamed past Sabine Pass, turned his ships around, and thinking it was the Sabine, arrived off the mouth of the Calcasieu River, which actually was thirty miles to the east. Next, two of Weitzel's transports broke down and required repair before they could continue. By this time, Franklin and the rest of the transports had unknowingly passed Weitzel and Crocker. Consequently, the corps commander arrived at the mouth of the Sabine River first, crossed over the sand bar, and "seeing nothing to indicate the presence of our people, . . . recrossed the bar." Crocker, who now planned to launch the assault on Tuesday morning, had sent a gunboat ahead to catch the rest of the force and stop them from entering the mouth of the river, but it did not arrive in time, for the lead vessels already had begun steaming up the river.[10] Thus, the element of surprise, so crucial to the operation, had been lost.

Despite this setback, Franklin and Crocker were determined to make an attempt to take Fort Griffin. Crocker steamed over the sand bar and made a reconnaissance on Tuesday morning. He found the fort right where he expected it to be, but he also noticed a "cottonclad" gunboat nearby. Crocker called for the other vessels to come in. Franklin ordered them forward, but some of the transports, loaded down with troops and supplies, had difficulty making it over the bar; one transport ran aground and could not be extricated, and its troops were transferred to other ships. Next, Franklin, Crocker, and Weitzel made a reconnaissance of the Texas shore, where the infantry would land. The small boats that carried the officers could get no closer than 125 feet from shore, having struck mudflats that prevented them from going any farther. When the sailors jumped out of the boats, they sank to their knees in mud; Franklin reckoned that soldiers carrying muskets and equipment would have sunk to their waists. The shore was found to be soft marsh, and about 50 feet farther inland was a narrow strip of sand, on which there was a road leading to the fort. It was determined that the only suitable landing site was farther north, closer to the fort, where the bank was almost perpendicular and the water deep enough to allow the transports to run directly alongside of it. Unfortunately, the guns of Fort Griffin completely commanded this location.[11]

The channel leading past the fort divided about 1,000 feet below it, with a reef just two feet beneath the surface separating the channels. Crocker's plan was to send two gunboats (the *Sachem* and *Arizona*) on the eastern side of the reef and take his own gunboat, the *Clifton*, up the other channel, closest to the fort. Once the two boats in the eastern channel began to draw the fort's fire, Crocker would continue up the western channel at full speed and engage the fort with grape and canister at close range. Weitzel and about five hundred infantrymen, with the gunboat *Granite City* in the lead, were to follow behind Crocker and land the troops as soon as the *Clifton* began steaming at full speed. Once on shore the infantry would advance as skirmishers and attempt to drive the Confederate artillerymen away from their guns while the *Clifton* engaged the batteries at close quarters.[12]

The assault began at 3:00 P.M. on Tuesday. Thirty minutes later, when the two gunboats in the eastern channel came into range, the guns of Fort Griffin opened fire. The *Sachem* was disabled almost immediately, taking a shot through its boilers, the steam killing or injuring many of the officers and crew. Then the *Arizona* temporarily ran aground. Meanwhile, Crocker had taken the *Clifton* up the western channel and engaged the Confederate guns at close range. The vessel did not stand a chance, and soon it was disabled and forced to surrender. For some inexplicable reason, the *Granite City* and the transport did not move toward the shore when the *Clifton* began its run. Weitzel, however, reported that he was preparing to put his infantry ashore when he saw the white flag being raised on the *Clifton*, rendering the landing futile. He did not mention in his official report whether the *Granite City* led him to his landing site or not. Franklin reported that when the *Clifton* raised the white flag, both the *Arizona* and the *Granite City* withdrew from the channel and across the sand bar, where once again the *Arizona* ran aground. "A few moments afterward I was ordered to retire," Weitzel wrote, "and then again to go outside and anchor in rear of the [transport ship] Crescent." Crocker and many of his sailors were captured and imprisoned, and many more were killed, wounded, or reported missing. Weitzel reported a minimum of ninety-seven soldiers lost, mostly sharpshooters on the gunboats.[13] The entire operation was a complete fiasco.

The Confederates allowed Crocker to file a report even though he was being held captive. In it he lambasted some of the naval officers for their cowardice, especially the commander of the *Arizona* and the officer who lowered the *Clifton*'s flag, and he questioned why the *Granite City* and Weitzel's transport failed to make the troop landing. "The conduct of the commanders of the *Arizona* and *Granite City* or of my officer who hauled down the flag I am not now called upon to characterize, nor that of General Franklin in failing so utterly to cooperate," he wrote, "but I trust my Government will soon place me in a position to ask an enquiry of the facts." Crocker filed another report in 1865 after he was released from his Confederate prison. Once again he wondered why the army did not live up to its end of the bargain: "The reason why the army failed to cooperate, after having promised so fairly, I have been unable to learn; but it has been since proven to me that if a single movement toward landing troops had been made, the expedition would have proved a success. For two days after the fight there were not more than 300 men at Sabine or within many miles of that place."[14]

Crocker did not know that Weitzel had prepared to land his force and had stopped only when the *Clifton* raised the white flag. With that warship out of action, the amphibious assault was doomed to failure since Fort Griffin's gunners now could concentrate their fire on the infantry. Perhaps a land assault might have carried the day, as Crocker believed, and the disabled Union ships could have been recovered, but it is more likely that any such attack would have been a bloody failure. Once Crocker had been taken prisoner, there was no guarantee that the other naval commanders would have supported the landing. Both the *Granite City* and the *Arizona* already had withdrawn, and there even was some doubt if the gunboats would stay and provide protection for the transports. A few days after the battle, Franklin wrote Anna and told her that he hailed the skipper of the *Arizona* as it was retreating and "asked him if he did not intend to stay & protect the unarmed transports. He replied, 'the field guns of the enemy will be down on you in five minutes!' & then put out as fast as he could."[15]

Franklin was in quite a predicament. Without the support of the gunboats, he could not stay, and he could not land his troops without exposing them to the direct fire of Fort Griffin's guns. In addition, he was running short of drinking water for his men and their animals. He later reported, "There was no time to send to New Orleans to get instructions, and I therefore concluded to recross the bar and return to the mouth of the Mississippi."[16]

Considering that the operation could have turned out even worse than it did, Franklin expressed to Anna that he had "great reason to congratulate myself upon the result." Still, as the ranking officer of the expedition, the general concluded, "I imagine that I shall be blamed for it, but I do not consider myself blamable in the slightest degree; so I do not care a copper what the papers say." A week and a half later, after he had time to reflect, Franklin admitted: "The Sabine Pass expedition was not in my opinion a wise one, but I had to make it, and I consider that we escaped from what at first sight looked like a serious disaster.... I believe I did all that at wise man would have done under the circumstances."[17]

Secretary of the Navy Gideon Welles, however, did not blame Franklin. Instead, he sent a letter of reprimand to Commodore Bell for "the dispatching of three or four small vessels to Sabine Pass to contend, in the narrow and shallow channel, against earthworks." He also disapproved of Bell "placing ... such an expedition under the command of an officer [Crocker] of comparatively little experience in such matters." In conclusion, Welles instructed Bell that "in such movements the Navy in case of failure is always held responsible, and therefore they should not be made without the proper force and material to guard against disaster and secure success, and should be intrusted to officers of much experience and judgment only."[18] Nevertheless, the failed expedition, regardless of who was to blame, would be one more stain on William B. Franklin's already tarnished reputation.

The general and his command returned to New Orleans on September 11. His stay was brief, for within the week he and the XIX Corps were ordered toward Berwick City west of New Orleans. "It is a miserable hole," Franklin complained to his wife, "and with twenty thousand troops in it was perfectly awful." General Banks had determined not to try another thrust up the Sabine, as the earlier attempt had "given notice to the enemy of our purposes," he explained to President Lincoln, "and enabled him to concentrate his forces against us." As a result, he had "directed the movement of the troops across the Berwick Bay, with a view to the overland movement into Texas." Banks expressed some doubt concerning the operation, owing to the fact that almost all of the expedition's supplies would have to be hauled in wagons since the countryside was practically destitute of food and forage.[19]

By September 26 Franklin could tell his wife that his troops were finally on the move, this time to the northwest, in the direction of New Iberia. Pushing up the swampy, alligator-infested Bayou Teche, they immediately ran into problems. "Where we are going," he divulged to Anna, "the enemy sunk obstructions across the Teche, and we must get them out before we can go farther with much comfort.... After we get the obstructions out we will probably go to New Iberia, and whether we strike West or North from there will depend upon circumstances there."[20]

The weather was pleasant through most of September—Franklin called the weather "delightful" and was pleased that his "men were wonderfully healthy—but on the twenty-seventh it began raining and continued through the last week of the month, making the roads muddy and almost impassable. Once the weather cleared, Franklin pushed his column farther to the northwest, keeping his cavalry out in front of the slow-moving infantry and wagons. The troopers skirmished regularly with Confederate cavalry, and on October 4 they "foolishly got into an ambush, and lost one man killed & five wounded. But the rebels ran without making much of a stand," Franklin wrote from his camp about four miles below New Iberia. Overall, however, the general was proud of his command. He informed Anna on October 5 that his "men have behaved very well on this march. There was no marauding & no straggling." He had few kind words for the behavior of the soldiers in the XIII Corps, though: "They have no discipline, are all from the West, and I am afraid that sugar & sweet potatoes have been made to suffer." North and South had been at war nearly thirty months, but Franklin still believed that civilians and their property should not be the targets or the intentional victims of combatants. Despite his opinion of the westerners' discipline (or lack thereof), the general admitted, "They are a hard set, but it is said they will fight well."[21]

Franklin had two infantry divisions of the XIX Corps with him during this campaign, the First and the Third. First Division was commanded by Brigadier General Weitzel, and Third Division was led by Brig. Gen. Cuvier Grover. Franklin also had a cavalry division under the command of Brig. Gen. Albert Lee. With the exception of these troopers, the force was composed of troops primarily from New York and the New England states. "I like my command," Franklin admitted to Anna, "but it is too small. If it were larger, with the same officers and men, I would lief [that is, as soon] have it as any I know.... Grover & Weitzel are my Division commanders and are as good as any that anyone has." The Fourth Division did not take part in this campaign, remaining behind to man the defenses of New Orleans.[22] The detachment of the XIII Corps, under command of Maj. Gen. Cadwallader C. Washburn, also came under Franklin's immediate authority by virtue of his seniority of rank.[23] As a result of this attachment, he was anxious for Banks to come to the field and take overall command. "I wish he would come," Franklin admitted to Anna, "for my position with the 13th Corps is anomalous. I only command them because I rank the General [Washburn] now in the field."[24]

Franklin's force continued its plodding pace northward, brushing aside enemy patrols along the way. Near Carrion Crow Bayou, the Confederates made a spirited assault against Lee's cavalry, and Franklin had to commit an infantry brigade to the fight before forcing the enemy to abandon the field. This sort of hit-and-run combat was "very disgusting work," he wrote on October 16, "and I hope that it soon will be over."[25]

By October 21 Franklin's force was at Opelousas, about fifty miles due west of Baton Rouge. The Federals had been campaigning for over a month and yet had made very little progress. As General Banks explained to the president in a letter dated October 22, "The deficiency of the transportation, the removal of numerous obstructions to navigation on the Teche, and the difficulty of obtaining supplies made it impracticable for us to reach Opelousas until this date." As real as these obstacles were, Franklin had another problem, one that only Banks could solve: other than his continued movement through Louisiana toward Texas, he had no real understanding of his military objectives. On October 26 he admitted to Anna: "I have nothing to tell you of our plans. It would be improper to tell if I knew, but I assure you that I do not know." He did believe that his next move would be toward Alexandria, since that was the direction in which the Confederates had retreated. But operating in this poor region was difficult for the general from a humanitarian point of view. "I am afraid that I am too soft hearted to be a soldier," he wrote. "We have to feed our animals upon the country, and my heart bleeds for these poor people. We take all of their corn leaving only enough for them to scrape along with."[26]

Franklin also made Banks aware of his precarious supply situation. "There is very little forage in the country, and a move somewhere must soon be made," he reported to General Stone, Banks's chief of staff. "The forage question is important, and I think that we must get nearer to New Iberia or the Mississippi River." Further complicating his logistical situation, stormy weather moved in the last week of the month and made the roads difficult to negotiate. Franklin seemed fed up with his situation. Confederate forces under Maj. Gen. Richard Taylor had not yet come out for a stand-up fight, which frustrated him even more. "I respectfully reiterate my request for definite instructions," he demanded of Stone, "believing that I have demonstrated that there is no enemy in front who can be attacked by this expedition, and also that it is impossible to stay here long." As a result, Franklin fell back toward New Iberia, which he supposed would make a better base for his operations. He justified the retrograde later to his wife, telling her that the reasons for the movement were: "1st because we were too far to the front to be certain of feeding ourselves there, 2nd that the enemy had gone to parts unknown, except small guerilla parties which were very annoying, and 3rd the roads about Opelousas were getting awfully bad."[27]

Although problems caused by the weather and the supply system were real enough, Franklin's perception that there was "no enemy in front" or that they "had gone to parts unknown" proved to be erroneous. General Taylor had ordered his cavalry commander, Brig. Gen. Thomas Green, to "pursue and harass the enemy." On November 3 Green caught up with an advance post of Brig. Gen. Stephen B. Burbridge's Fourth Division, XIII Corps at Carrion Crow Bayou. In a three-hour battle, Green inflicted 154 killed and wounded on Burbridge's division while sustaining 125 casualties of his own. In addition, Green's men captured approximately 560 Federals. When Franklin told Anna about the battle, his displeasure with Burbridge was rather evident. Although reinforcements pushed the Confederates off the field "and several miles back...., [Green's attack] was nevertheless a surprise, and I am disgusted with the com[andin]g officer who was Gen Burbridge." Franklin further explained to his wife: "I was nearly a week myself at the very point [as Burbridge] & never feared a surprise the whole time, for the troops were so posted that it was impossible. Now the same commander in the same place is caught in a trap. So you see how our reputations depend upon ignorant subordinates.... You cannot imagine how I have been annoyed by the disorganized state of this command. My whole campaign has been a perfect purgatory." Referring to the recent departure of General Ord on sick leave, Franklin wrote sarcastically: "The troops of Gen. Ord's Corps appear to have sickened him, and I do not much wonder at it. They are good fighting men but have no organization or discipline."[28]

A decade and half later, Taylor wrote of this episode, "Green's pursuit was stopped by the approach of heavy masses of the enemy from the south, who seemed content with the rescue of Burbridge, and they retired at once to the vicinity of New Iberia, fifty miles away."[29] In reality, Franklin already had made the decision to withdraw south; Green's onslaught neither changed the outcome of the campaign nor hastened the Federals' march to a new base of operations.

Franklin's entire Bayou Teche Expedition was, by this time, a moot point anyway. On October 26 General Banks took the Second Division, XIII Corps and several attached regiments and steamed for the southern tip of Texas. By November 2 he was disembarking his troops at Brazos Santiago. "The recent movements in the Teche country," he reported, "and the late attack upon the Sabine [Pass], have drawn all the [Confederate] forces from Western to Eastern Texas. But for this, the landing we have effected would have been impossible." Whether he realized it or not, Franklin and his operation had become a mere diversion. In the meantime, Banks hoped to gain other lodgments on the Texas coast and then intended "to move a portion of the troops under General Franklin . . . to this point." No one was more pleased about such a maneuver than Franklin. Referring to Banks's operation, he announced to Anna, "if it succeeds, as I presume it will, I think we will go there by sea instead of by land, a consummation devoutly to be wished for." But the Teche expedition had worn him down: "I have got awfully tired of campaigning, and I doubt whether any person in the war [is] more anxious than I am to have it over."[30]

Banks made several other unopposed landings on the Texas coast, but he never called for Franklin's troops. His occupation of Texas was restricted to these few small pockets over which his limited forces had established military control. When Franklin learned of the location of the initial landing, he divulged to Anna, "Gen Banks has landed at Brazos Santiago where I always told him that he ought to go." Several months later he admitted to Baldy Smith, "Banks . . . had started for Texas without giving me the slightest intimation as to where he was going, and as his instructions had been carried out, there was nothing left to do but to keep up the delusion that we were bound for Texas too."[31]

Although Banks seemed to feel that he had carried out the intent of Lincoln's orders, General in Chief Halleck was not satisfied with his efforts. Under the impression that the main Union advance into Texas would be along the route of the Red River, he earlier had ordered Maj. Gen. Frederick Steele, a West Point classmate of Franklin's and commander of the Department of Arkansas, to advance southward with his VII Corps and join with Banks's forces on the Red. When Halleck discovered that Franklin's advance had stalled and that Banks had landed forces on the Texas coast, he sent Banks a missive on November 18 in which he warned him about dividing his army in the face of the enemy and advised him that the best line of advance was by Berwick Bay and the Atchafalaya, which connected the Red River with the Gulf. Halleck would continue to pressure him for a campaign up the Red for the next two months.[32]

In the interim, Franklin and his command remained relatively inactive, with the exception of cavalry probes and skirmishes. He expressed to Anna that "this warfare is petty, but it is very annoying to us, as it keeps our cavalry busy and wears out our horses. The enemy runs whenever we approach him with large enough force to fight him." Franklin concluded, "I do not expect any trouble here, but I expect to find them firing upon our boats, picking up stragglers, etc." On November 20 the Federals exacted a bit of revenge for Green's earlier attack when a combined force of cavalry and infantry surprised the 6th Texas Cavalry and captured twelve officers and one hundred enlisted men. The Union soldiers "completely surprised the enemy," Franklin boasted, "taking them all except about twenty who got away.... I hoped to have made a larger haul, but as the enemy would not keep a larger force there, we did the best we could." Then on November 25 his men surprised another Confederate detachment and captured one officer and sixty-eight men while killing or wounding several more.[33]

These limited successes, undertaken in the last days of a campaign that had fizzled out, were of little consequence. The weather was turning colder, and it was frigid enough by the next to last day of November that a basin of water froze in the tent of one of Franklin's staff officers. The sudden drop in temperature was causing the men to suffer, as few had overcoats. Conditions in the Confederate army were even worse, though, prompting General Taylor to request a prisoner exchange. According to Franklin, "Gen Taylor desired us to exchange prisoners man for man, on the ground that our prisoners have no blankets, some of them no shoes, and it will be impossible to alleviate their sufferings this winter." He was willing to negotiate an exchange, but the swap had to be unconditional. He answered Taylor's request "by stating that I will exchange man for man if they will commence the exchange without reference to Regiments or Corps so as to get the officers of negro regiments back. This condition I presume will break up the negotiation." He also proposed sending blankets and clothes to the captured Union soldiers if Taylor would permit it. To Franklin's surprise, the Confederate general agreed to the exchange "without acknowledging the principle that officers of negro regiments are subject to exchange, or without saying anything about it."[34] It seems that the exchange occurred, for in a message to General Stone sent on December 12, Franklin reported, "Taylor writes, by flag of truce received to-day, that part of our prisoners are at Shreveport and part at Tyler, Tex., so that some delay will occur in getting them back."[35]

Although the campaign had drawn to a close, Franklin remained concerned about the conduct of his men while they occupied enemy territory. He related a story to Anna about a Confederate major who, under a flag of truce, complained about Union stragglers who "went to his house, & used insulting language to his wife, and he asked me for written protection." The general told him "that I could not give him protection, but asked him to treat any stragglers of ours found marauding precisely as he would treat any other marauders, that is, shoot them." He then took formal measures to inhibit the misconduct of his soldiers. On December 14 he issued General Orders No. 45, which instructed his men that anyone captured by the Confederates outside the Union picket lines while "straggling, stealing, and robbing, going upon unauthorized expeditions or upon expeditions sent by regimental commanders, without authority and without proper escort," would be given last priority in a prisoner exchange. In addition, he warned them, the command would not receive them on parole from the enemy "under any circumstances." The pronouncement also stated that Franklin had "already informed the commanding officer of the enemy that it is his wish that any soldier of this command found robbing outside our lines should be treated like other robbers." The order applied to everyone in the corps, "but applies more directly to the mounted men, whose conduct in straggling, stealing, and maltreating women is a disgrace to the American soldier."[36]

Although Franklin may have thought he still was fighting a limited war, the harsh discipline he exacted upon his soldiers for looting, pillaging, and unauthorized foraging made him look like a martinet and caused ill feelings toward him from his men. The westerners under his command referred to him as "the old Potomac fossil," while the easterners felt cheated because the officers of the western regiments seemed to turn a blind eye when their soldiers foraged and looted. Those from the East already were being ridiculed by their western counterparts for their relative lack of combat experience, and Franklin's insistence upon military discipline and respect for the rights of Southern civilians caused an even greater divide between the XIX Corps and the western troops. The surgeon of the 114th New York Infantry wrote of the westerners in his memoirs: "They . . . were arrogant braggarts, continually dilating upon their wonderful achievements, and forever depreciating the laudable efforts of others. They said that they had 'come down from Vicksburg for the purpose of showing these paper collar and white glove gents (meaning the Nineteenth Corps) how to fight.' They only wanted 'the wooden nutmeg fellers' to keep out of their way, and *they* would 'finish [the] rebellion in the Gulf Department in short order.' Such remarks, and others still more invidious, wrought an ill state of feeling between the Corps, which often resulted in fisticuff fights." The westerners' confidence and feelings of superiority did little to improve the morale of the entire command, nor did Franklin's "regular army airs" (as one westerner complained) make him very popular with XIX Corps soldiers.[37] Yet despite the dissimilarities between the troops, once the fighting began the men put aside their differences in order to combat their common enemy. They also apparently shared a dislike for Franklin. As 1864 dawned, a harsher type of warfare would accompany it, one that was aimed at the destruction of not only Confederate armies but also the Confederacy's infrastructure and the will of the Southern people to continue the war.

Franklin occupied most of the winter waiting for orders that would reorganize the XIX Corps. Banks, meanwhile, persisted in his belief that the best approach to Texas was by sea, but political considerations would not allow him to continue such operations. President Lincoln desperately wanted Louisiana to be politically reorganized before a reconstructed state government was formed, and as scant progress had been made, he fired off a letter to Banks in which he told the general how disappointed he was that so little had been done to ensure a Unionist victory at the polls. In a subsequent letter, the president noted that Banks was to be the "master of all" political arrangements in the state of Louisiana, thus making the former Massachusetts governor's job a bit easier. The general, an astute politician himself, had hopes of gaining the 1864 Republican presidential nomination and, not wanting to do anything to further tarnish his military reputation, thought it best to carry out the orders of the president lest he find himself relieved of command. General in Chief Halleck had been pressuring Banks since late summer to target Shreveport as an intermediate objective in an overland campaign to invade Texas. Much to his dismay, Banks had resisted his advice, and it would have been impossible to undertake the campaign in January anyway since the Red would not be navigable by the navy's vessels until its annual March rise. The department commander would have two months to concentrate on the Louisiana political scene before he could undertake a spring campaign up the Red River.[38]

A final consideration for Banks was cotton. He had knowledge of large stores of cotton on the upper Red, with even more in southern Arkansas. Seizure of these stocks would provide additional funds for the U.S. Treasury, and wealthy mill interests with a good deal of political clout in Massachusetts were extremely anxious to have a fine supply of fiber come into their textile mills. Thus, on January 23 Banks sent Halleck a letter in which he agreed to begin organizing a Red River campaign.[39]

General Franklin first discussed the campaign plan with his commander on February 24. Later that day he noted in his diary, "He believes in the rise [of the river]—directed me to get ready as soon as possible." Franklin conceded to Anna that he did not think the new expedition would amount to much, "but I have become tired of staying still and shall be glad to move somewhere."[40]

If any campaign was doomed to failure before it even began, it was the expedition up the Red River. The plan called for Banks's force of 17,000 men (XIX Corps and two divisions of XIII Corps) to move overland up the Bayou Teche toward Alexandria. There, it would join with the XVI and XVII Corps from the Army of the Tennessee, which under the protection of a naval armada, already would have steamed down the Mississippi and up the Red, defeating any enemy resistance it encountered until it met up with Banks around March 17. Once the two commands had united, they would push up the Red and attack Shreveport. Meanwhile, General Steele and his VII Corps would move southward from Arkansas (while Banks moved northward) and attack Shreveport from the opposite direction.[41]

Banks would encounter myriad obstacles during the campaign, but his largest problem would be with command and control. General Halleck failed to appoint a single commander to direct the entire operation, which included soldiers from three different military departments and the navy. Although Maj. Gen. William T. Sherman—to whose army the XVI and XVII Corps belonged—would have been the best choice, Banks ranked him, so Sherman chose not to accompany the expedition and sent Brig. Gen. Andrew J. Smith in his stead. Steele was considered for command of the operation, but that decision would have had political ramifications. As Halleck confessed to Sherman once the campaign had gotten under way: "We fully agree that the Departments of Arkansas and the Gulf should be under one commander as soon as the armies come within communicating distance, but the difficulty is to get a suitable commander. General Banks is not competent, and there are so many political objections to superseding him by Steele that it would be useless to ask the president."[42]

The consequence of this dilemma was that the campaign was undertaken in violation of one of the rules of war—unity of command. Even had the operation been under one commander, the problems of communication and coordination between Steele and Banks were monumental. As Lt. Col. Richard B. Irwin, Banks's adjutant general, observed years later, "the two Federal commanders, separated from each other at the start by nearly five hundred miles of hostile territory, could only communicate by the rivers in their rear over a long circuit, lengthening as they approached their common enemy in his central stronghold."[43]

There was one problem of strategic significance that no one anticipated. Once Shreveport was under Union control, the city was to be used as a staging area for an overland invasion of eastern Texas. Shreveport, however, was deep in enemy territory, and the Federals' main artery of supply would be the Red River and a few roads running roughly parallel to it. Further complicating matters, the Red was only navigable during the spring rise. A Union garrison at Shreveport would have to rely on the wagon roads for most of the year. If the flow of supplies were severed, Shreveport either would have to be evacuated or suffer the same fate as Vicksburg's Confederate garrison.

As difficult as *holding* Shreveport may have seemed, just *getting* there would be a complex and arduous assignment. RAdm. David D. Porter's gunboats and ironclads would be able to steam up the Red only if the river rose high enough after the spring rains to allow the keels to clear bottom, and they could return only if the river remained high. Even the attachment of Sherman's troops came with a caveat: they must not go beyond Shreveport, and they must be returned to the Army of the Tennessee no later than April 15, for they were needed for the campaign against Atlanta.[44] Logistics also had to be given serious consideration. The roads were primitive and food and forage were scarce, necessitating long wagon trains to carry provisions as well as ammunition. Then there was the terrain. A reporter who accompanied the expedition later wrote:

> The topography of Virginia has been assigned as a reason for every defeat of the Army of the Potomac; but Virginia is a garden and a meadow, when compared with the low, flat, pine countries that extend form Opelousas . . . to Fort Smith [Arkansas]. . . . I have ridden for fifty miles into the heart of

this pine country, and from the beginning to the end of the journey there was nothing but a dense, impenetrable, interminable forest, traversed by a few narrow roads, with no signs of life or civilization beyond occasional loghouses and half-cleared plantations.... Such a thing as subsisting an army in a country like this could only be achieved when men and horses can be induced to live on pine trees and resin.[45]

In the face of all these obstacles—problems of command and control, communications, logistics, difficult terrain, and the uncertainties of the weather—Henry Halleck was determined that the campaign should proceed. When U. S. Grant replaced Halleck as general in chief in March 1864, he allowed the operation to go forward, not wishing to call it off at so late a date. (Halleck became the U.S. Army's chief of staff.)

Yet no matter how futile the prospects of the campaign may have appeared, Franklin knew it was his duty to get the troops prepared for the upcoming operation. He regularly inspected the XIX Corps's camps—even ordering a medical inspection of his command—and on March 7, in an attempt to streamline his trains, issued orders for all personal baggage to be sent to New Orleans. General Banks would not be present when the march northward was to begin; he was in New Orleans preparing for the inauguration of Louisiana's new "loyal" governor. Franklin, therefore, was placed in temporary command of the column, which included 10,500 soldiers in the two divisions of the XIX Corps; 4,800 troops in the XIII Corps's two divisions, commanded by Brig. Gen. Thomas E. Ransom; and Brigadier General Lee's 4,600-man cavalry division.[46]

Franklin's force was set to begin its northward trek when a violent rainstorm struck on March 8, turning the roads into a quagmire and rendering marching impossible.[47] While he was waiting for the roads to dry, the general issued a stern warning to his troops on March 11. In General Orders No. 25, Franklin decreed strict prohibitions against straggling, looting, and marauding. He asked his officers and soldiers to assist him in the enforcement of this order, reminding them that "warring on an unarmed population is barbarous, and that robbing defenseless women and children and insulting unarmed men will only embitter the war and make enemies where we should make friends."[48]

After several days of waiting, the roads finally dried enough so that Franklin's column could commence its advance. Lee's troopers led the way, departing the town of Franklin on March 13. Moving in the direction of Opelousas and Bayou Boeuf, the horse soldiers arrived in Alexandria six days later. More rain and muddy roads made the march difficult. The infantry and artillery followed along the same 175-mile route, but because of their slower pace, they did not plod into Alexandria until March 24 and 25. Brigadier General Smith and his detachment from the Army of the Tennessee, meanwhile, had arrived in Alexandria on the seventeenth and eighteenth, already having captured Confederate Fort DeRussy on the way. The late arrival of Franklin's columns was inconsequential, however, since the Red River was still was too low to allow Admiral Porter's vessels to navigate the rapids that lay just above Alexandria. It was not until April 3 that the majority of gunboats and troop transports were able to steam upriver.[49]

Franklin's column would not remain long in Alexandria. On March 27 his command—minus Grover's division, left behind to garrison Alexandria—began its march toward Natchitoches, while A. J. Smith's force waited aboard the navy transports. Once the river rose sufficiently after the third, the entire Union force began to concentrate near Natchitoches. Just upriver lay the village of Grand Ecore, where Banks's headquarters ship, the *Black Hawk*, docked. Here, the general made a fateful decision that would alter the outcome of the entire campaign. Until reaching Grand Ecore, the roads generally ran parallel to the Red River, but now the main road to Shreveport headed westward, away from the river. The maps were faulty, and so was the advice of the *Black Hawk*'s pilot, who counseled against crossing the river and having the troops move on Shreveport from a road on the opposite bank, insisting that it would take them at least three days longer to get to their objective. Franklin urged Banks to send out a cavalry reconnaissance to find a better route, one that would allow the army to stay in contact with the navy, whose ships not only provided fire support but also hauled the bulk of supplies.[50]

Time was a commodity of which Banks was running out; in less than two weeks, he would have to return A. J. Smith's command to Sherman. Consequently, he could ill afford to cross the river and take a route that would add several more days to his march, nor could he allow the cavalry to look for another riverside road that may not even exist. Banks thus made the decision to march away from the Red by taking the main road to Shreveport via the hamlet of Pleasant Hill and the town of Mansfield. Unfortunately for the ex-

Massachusetts governor, had he heeded Franklin's advice and permitted Lee's troopers to scout for a better passage, they would have found just such a road about five miles upriver from Grand Ecore.[51]

The decision to take the Shreveport Road meant that the army would have to transfer the bulk of its ammunition and supplies from ship to shore, requiring long wagon trains following immediately in the rear of the troop columns. Because of the lack of suitable roads, the trains would not be able to take alternate routes of advance, a common practice that normally kept the main arteries open for rapid movements of combat forces. Since the cavalry had the mission to be far in front of the slower-moving infantry and artillery—"generally one days' march in advance of the infantry columns," reported Banks's quartermaster—the cavalry's train (about three hundred wagons) would have to stay close behind the horse soldiers rather than far to the rear with the infantry's wagons. All told, about nine hundred wagons accompanied the army.[52]

Franklin and his force left Natchitoches on April 6. "Marched from Natchd. Went as far as Bayou Dupont[,] 17 miles from N[atchitoches]. Encamped there," the general scribbled in his pocket diary. He also wrote a description of the route his force had traveled that day: "Piney woods, sandy, heavy roads the whole day." There were so few clearings in the area that the ammunition train had no place to bivouac and thus had to encamp in the road. According to an officer in the 30th Maine Veteran Volunteers (part of Third Brigade, First Division, XIX Corps), the entire region was "an almost unbroken forest with little water or forage, and traversed by a single road so poor and unworked as to be difficult to travel, and often so narrow as to render it impossible for army wagons to pass each other."[53] If marching through such a remote, heavily wooded area was difficult, fighting in it would be nearly impossible.

Yet a fight was brewing. Major General Taylor and his 7,000-man army had been backpedaling away from Banks's force since the beginning of the campaign. Even Alexandria had been evacuated without a fight. In fact, the steady Confederate withdrawal in the face of the Union advance girded Banks in his decision to take the Shreveport Road and leave the protection of Porter's gunboats. Franklin too had doubts about Taylor's willingness to give battle. On April 6 he wrote Anna from Natchitoches: "This morning we are off for Shreveport, and I think that it may take six or seven days to get there. It is my impression that the enemy does not wish to fight us and will keep out of our way if possible, but then you know they may have other councils."[54]

Taylor indeed had "other councils," even though his superior, Lt. Gen. Edmund Kirby Smith, commander of the Confederate Trans-Mississippi Department, had not wanted to bring on a general engagement. Although Taylor could not hope to fight a battle with his outnumbered force and still gain a victory, he also believed he could not remain idle while the invaders tramped virtually unopposed through his native state. He was not able to convince Smith to let him make a stand, but at least Taylor persuaded him to reinforce his army. By April 6 the Confederate force had grown to 8,800 soldiers, but it still numbered less than half of Banks's total command.[55]

Meanwhile, Franklin and his columns pushed on, arriving at Pleasant Hill on April 7. The cavalry division continued to press ahead of the infantry, but it was encountering stubborn resistance from Taylor's horsemen. Franklin wrote in his diary that Lee's men had been "in front all day, skirmishing severely." He later revealed that the cavalry were out "in front seven or eight miles [beyond Pleasant Hill], skirmishing with the enemy. They found them hard to drive, and the commander [Lee] was daily sending back for infantry to help him, which I would never give him." (Actually, Franklin relented and *did* start an infantry brigade forward, but Lee sent back word that they were not needed after all.) Franklin surmised that if the infantry was committed to the fight, a full-scale battle could erupt; besides, Lee had four regiments of "mounted infantry" that fought dismounted. These regiments, he believed, surely gave the cavalry enough firepower.[56] Given the heavily wooded terrain and the one narrow road to bring up reinforcements, Franklin was not about to let his cavalry commander get sucked into a trap. If Lee got into a pinch, the mobility his troopers enjoyed would enable them to rapidly extricate themselves and fall back on the infantry. The only thing that could get in the way was their cumbersome wagon train.

General Lee realized that in case of a hasty retreat, his ponderous trains would pose a sticky problem. He earlier had asked Franklin if the cavalry's wagons could be placed at the rear of the XIX Corps's marching column, but in front of the infantry's trains. The general refused, telling Lee to watch after his own wagons. Franklin reasoned that if the lengthy cavalry train, several miles long, was placed between the infantry and its own train, it would take too long for the infantrymen to get to their wagons for their daily issue of rations and other supplies.[57] From a logistical perspective, he was correct, but from a tactical viewpoint, allowing the cavalry's trains to remain so far forward could (and did) have dire consequences. Any tactical advantage that the horse soldiers held would be erased if the wagons slowed them and prevented a withdrawal. Franklin apparently believed that Dick Taylor would not give battle until the Federal force reached Shreveport, but he still should have given consideration to this simple request, or at least have ordered Lee to reduce the size of his ponderous train.

During the evening of April 7, General Banks arrived at Pleasant Hill, where Franklin was camped. When Banks found out about Lee's request for infantry support, he overruled the earlier denial and at 11:00 P.M. ordered a brigade forward to report to the cavalry commander by daylight. Franklin in turn ordered General Ransom, commanding the detachment of the XIII Corps, to send one of his brigades to link with the horsemen. When the foot soldiers arrived at daybreak, they and the cavalry immediately engaged the enemy in their front.[58]

The long march from Natchitoches, coupled with an all-day rain on April 7, had hampered the movement of the Federal columns and strung them out between Natchitoches and Pleasant Hill. From the van of the cavalry force to the rear of A. J. Smith's command (which departed Natchitoches on the seventh), the column stretched some thirty-five miles. Franklin determined on April 8 to close up his forces. Lee was directed not to move beyond supporting distance and to keep his wagon train well closed and out of the way of the infantry. Ransom was to bring his command forward about eight miles as was Brig. Gen. William H. Emory with the XIX Corps (Emory temporarily commanded the corps while Franklin commanded the combined force). General Smith, meanwhile, was to make a twenty-mile march, bringing his detachment of Sherman's army to within eight miles of Emory. As one XIX Corps officer noted many years later, "If this order had been carried out, or not interfered with, that night would have found the army in a fairly compact order and able to accept battle when offered."[59]

On the morning of the eighth, Lee's troopers and Col. Frank Emerson's brigade of Brig. Gen. William J. Landram's Fourth Division, XIX Corps steadily pushed the Confederates through the pine forest. Around 10:00 A.M. Franklin received a message from Lee asking for another infantry brigade to *replace* Emerson's command, which was exhausted. The general complied with this request, distinctly understanding that the fresh brigade would take the place of Emerson's brigade, not supplement it; Franklin even sent General Ransom along to make sure that this happened. By noon Lee and Emerson had driven their adversaries back about six miles to a point where the forest abruptly ended a few miles south of the town of Mansfield. In front of Lee was a clearing about 800 yards wide and 1,200 yards long. After scattering the Confederate skirmishers posted in the field, the Federals advanced to a hill in their front. Lee then sent his own skirmishers about a half mile forward to the edge of the forest on the other side of the clearing. What they found was more than they expected: Dick Taylor and his army were prepared to give battle.[60]

Although Banks's army had a more than two-to-one advantage in troops, Taylor knew that the narrow road and thick forest would keep the Federals from bringing their entire force to bear. The Louisianan later wrote, "the vicious dispositions of the enemy made me confident of beating all the force that he could concentrate that day." Boosting his optimism was the knowledge that 4,400 reinforcements were on their way from Arkansas and due to arrive the next day.[61]

Franklin also knew that the terrain favored the enemy, which is why he was so concerned about committing more infantry to the battle. If the Union army was going to fight, he wanted to do it only when the entire force could be brought to bear, not when it was strung out for twenty miles. Banks, however, was of a different opinion. Riding forward to assess the situation, he heard from Lee that his force on the field either must disengage or must receive heavy reinforcement. Banks decided on the latter option, committed the fresh infantry brigade alongside Emerson, and told his assistant adjutant to send the following message back to Franklin: "The enemy are apparently prepared to make a strong stand at this point, and you had better make arrangements to bring up your infantry, and to pass everything on the road. He thinks you had better send back and push up the trains, as manifestly we shall be able to rest here." Several minutes later Franklin received another message, instructing him to get all the infantry forward as rapidly as possible. It was now 3:15 P.M.[62]

Franklin immediately ordered his other XIII Corps division, commanded by Brig. Gen. Robert A. Cameron, to hurry to the battlefield, about five miles away. He and his staff rode forward as well and arrived around 4:15 P.M. Taylor's forces already had succeeded in enveloping Landram's division, causing it to break, so Franklin immediately placed Cameron's division in a defensive position perpendicular to the Shreveport Road, about a quarter mile to the rear of where the battle had commenced and just in front of the cavalry's wagons train. This new line stopped the Confederates for about an hour. Meanwhile, Franklin sent word to General Emory to bring up his division. "The state of things upon my arrival was discouraging," Franklin later reported, "and as the enemy far outnumbered the infantry force, in a short time the infantry broke, after a gallant fight, and went to the rear." The Confederates eventually enveloped both flanks of Cameron's division too. Franklin attempted to steel his troops by his presence. A correspondent of the *New Orleans Era* reported that the general "dashed boldly into the thickest of the fray, cap in hand and cheer[ed] on the men." Just north of a place called Sabine Crossroads (where a road connecting landings on the Sabine and Red Rivers crossed the Shreveport Road), Franklin was trying to rally his troops when a bullet fired by a soldier from Maj. Gen. John G. Walker's Texas Division glanced off of his left leg and struck his horse, which died within the hour.[63]

The Union rout soon became general. The cavalry's wagon train obstructed the road, adding further confusion and panic to the fleeing men and preventing the withdrawal of ten pieces of artillery belonging to the XIII Corps. There still was some hope for the Federals, however. Franklin earlier had instructed Emory "to form his division across the [Shreveport] road in the first good position that he could find." Franklin mounted another horse and was riding to the rear when he found Emory getting ready for the Confederate onslaught at a place called Pleasant Grove. "I found him in the act of forming his line when I arrived, about 2 miles in rear of the field," the general recalled. By now it was 6:00 P.M. Dick Taylor's men had been fighting for most of the day, and the rugged terrain added to their fatigue. Despite these challenges, the Confederates nevertheless slammed into Emory's line. This time the Federals held. Emory screamed at his soldiers, "Men, you must hold this position at all hazards; before the enemy gets past here they must ride over me and my little gray mare." Franklin was quite impressed with his subordinate: "Here he [Emory] was most strenuously attacked by the enemy, who made vigorous charges against his front and flanks. He repelled them all with great loss to the rebels, and remained at night-fall master of the position." During this phase of the battle, Franklin lost a second horse to enemy fire. But the Federals stood their ground until darkness brought an end to the day's fighting. Emory's division then formed the rear guard while the rest of the force slipped away to Pleasant Hill during the night.[64]

The battle was a terrific blow to Banks and his army, and it effectively crushed any hopes of capturing Shreveport and invading Texas. Since Banks had not been able to mass his superior forces, Taylor's little army outnumbered the Federals at all times throughout the fight. The Battle of Sabine Crossroads, as it was called in Union reports (the Confederates called it the Battle of Mansfield), was a costly engagement. Banks lost 113 killed, 581 wounded, and 1,541 missing, for a total of 2,235 casualties out of the 12,000 men engaged, roughly 19 percent of his force. In addition, twenty artillery pieces, more than 150 wagons, and approximately one thousand horses and mules were captured. Taylor fared much better, losing only 1,000 in killed and wounded from his 8,800-man force.[65] As Franklin concluded in a hastily scribbled note to Anna: "We had a terrible fight yesterday, and thank God I am safe. . . . My men behaved admirably, but we were beaten nevertheless." In a subsequent letter he expressed his anger with Banks, blaming him outright for the Union defeat. "The cause of our defeat was the putting forward of a Brigade of Infantry to support the Cavalry," he wrote. "This induced putting forward another, and thus we were drawn into a gen[era]l engagement with most of our Infantry too far to the rear to bring up. It was disgraceful Generalship, and thank God I am not responsible for it."[66]

Banks originally had wanted to bring A. J. Smith forward to Pleasant Grove during the night of April 8, but Franklin and Brig. Gen. William Dwight, Banks's close friend, dissuaded him. Franklin doubted if Smith could arrive by daylight to bolster the force, and even if he did get there in time, the only water supply in the area was under Confederate control. Besides, the XIX Corps already was in full retreat and probably would not stop until it reached Pleasant Hill. So a general withdrawal was ordered, and by 8:30 the next morning, the bulk of Banks's army had consolidated at Pleasant Hill, fifteen miles to the south. A. J. Smith already was there and preparing for action.[67]

Dick Taylor's command, bolstered by the arrival of Brig. Gen. Thomas J. Churchill's 4,000 reinforcements, meanwhile moved toward the Union position. Franklin was a mere bystander during the battle that was to come. With Banks on the field, Franklin no longer exercised command of the force and thus was relegated to an advisory role. Most of Lee's cavalry division, as well as the XIII Corps, now under Cameron's command (Ransom was wounded on April 8), was accompanying the wagon train toward Grand Ecore, leaving Franklin only one division to command.[68] Emory had been acting as corps commander since the overland force departed Alexandria, so Franklin allowed him to continue in this role.

Two brigades of Emory's command were positioned about a half mile north of Pleasant Hill, just east of the Mansfield Road (what the locals called the main road to Shreveport). Dwight's brigade was out front, with Brig. Gen.

James McMillan's brigade just behind it in reserve. To Dwight's left-front and straddling the Mansfield Road was one of Smith's brigades, commanded by Col. William T. Shaw. Emory's remaining brigade, under Col. Lewis Benedict, was about three-eighths of a mile west of McMillan's position, next to a road that forked off of the Mansfield Road and led to the Sabine River. The remainder of Smith's command was in rear of Pleasant Hill, about a mile behind Shaw's forward position. There were several gaps in the Union lines that should have been closed, but none of the generals seemed to notice, though they certainly had plenty of time to make final adjustments.[69] A Philadelphia reporter accompanying the army saw several of the generals standing around prior to the fight and recorded the scene for posterity:

> General Banks, with his light-blue overcoat buttoned closely around his chin, was strolling up and down, occasionally conversing with a member of his staff, or returning the salute of a passing subaltern. Near him was General William B. Franklin, his face as rough and rugged as when he rode through the storms of the Peninsula, the ideal of a bold, daring, imperturbable soldier. There are few braver men than this Charles O'Malley of major-generals. He had two horses shot under him the day before. His face was very calm that morning, and occasionally he pulls his whiskers nervously, as though he scented the battle afar off, and was impatient to be in the midst of the fray. General Charles P. Stone, the chief of staff, a quiet, retiring man, who is regarded, by the few that know him, as one of the finest soldiers of the time, was sitting on a rail smoking cigarettes, and apparently more interested in the puffs of smoke that curled around him than in the noise and bustle that filled the air. There was General Smith, with his bushy, grayish beard, and his eager eye, as it looks through spectacles, giving him the appearance of a schoolmaster.

The chief of artillery was the busiest officer of them all, and along with the entourage of colonels, majors, aides, and orderlies, the group presented a "rather tedious party" that "formed and melted away, and reformed and discussed the battle of the evening before, and the latest news and gossip form New Orleans, and wondered when another mail would come." The correspondent depicted this scene as "weary and tame."[70] Had these officers been more concerned about the placement of their troops than other, less-pressing matters, they undoubtedly would have discovered the dangerous gaps.

A matter of pressing importance that Franklin had discussed with one of his staff officers that day was the predicament faced by Porter's armada if the Red River began to drop. Franklin's chief engineer, Lt. Col. Joseph Bailey, suggested the idea of building a dam at Alexandria to get the ships over the rapids.[71] If the navy was stranded above the rapids, the army either would have to stay and protect the vessels or the fleet would have to be scuttled. Either way would prove disastrous to Union arms. Franklin may not have been the most aggressive general in the Union army, but he was a fine engineer and at least had the presence of mind to be planning ahead for a contingency. But the Federals first would have to get back to the river, and if Richard Taylor had his way, that was not going to happen.

The Battle of Pleasant Hill began at 5:00 P.M., "when a furious attack was made on General Emory's left." During this assault by Churchill's command on Benedict's brigade, Colonel Benedict was killed. "This [Emory's left flank] gave way after a hard fight," Franklin wrote, "and the rebels at once seemed to have position of the whole plain." The Confederates continued to press their advantage, and soon the Union left-center had been destroyed. Now the rest of A. J. Smith's westerners counterattacked, driving the Confederates "from the plain and about 1 1/2 miles along the Mansfield road." Franklin concluded that "the remainder of General Emory's line fought handsomely the remainder of the day, and the enemy was driven back along the whole line with the loss of two guns."[72]

The Federals were lucky. The faulty placement of Shaw's brigade precipitated the Confederate breakthrough, and it was only the quick thinking of A. J. Smith that saved the day. Ludwell Johnson, the eminent historian of the Red River Campaign, concludes that it was "almost impossible to fix responsibility for the Federals' deployment on any individuals." He contends the blame must be shared by Franklin, Smith, Emory, and even Banks's chief of staff, Charles Stone. "Banks of course must bear the lion's share of the blame," Johnson writes, "for he had at least seven hours on April 9 to make his dispositions."[73] Yet as a West Point–trained professional and Banks's second in command, Franklin should have noticed and rectified the problems prior to the fighting, especially since he had all day to make arrangements before Taylor attacked. Certainly, Banks was in overall command, but Franklin had a duty to advise his commander of the proper course of action. It is clear that Franklin was furious at Banks for the way he handled the previous day's fighting, and perhaps this anger—and the pain from his leg wound—clouded his judgment on April 9.

The Battle of Pleasant Hill ended as a tactical Union victory when the Confederates abandoned the field. Taylor had about three hundred more troops than Banks, but the Southerners also suffered 257 more casualties than the Federals. It was one of the few bright spots to which any Union general could point in an otherwise dismal campaign. Pleasant Hill was a close call, but it gave Banks a second wind. He even contemplated another advance on Shreveport, telling General Smith of his plans and sending an order to General Lee to turn the trains around and start them back toward the army. Several of Banks's lieutenants, Franklin included, were opposed to such a move and convinced the general to change his mind. Franklin advised taking the army to Blair's Landing on the Red River. There, the land force could get resupplied under the protection of the navy's gunboats, and it could be reinforced from the troops who had remained with the fleet. The drawback of this was that the army would have to build a pontoon bridge over Bayou Pierre, thus delaying the retrograde and setting the stage for another Confederate attack.[74]

General Dwight, however, recommended going all the way back to Grand Ecore to meet up with the navy, and Banks decided on this option. Franklin probably did not care either way as long as he did not have to fight another battle under Banks's command. Several months later, when he was called before the Joint Committee on the Conduct of the War to testify about the Red River Campaign, Franklin pontificated, "From what I had seen of General Banks's ability to command in the field, I was certain that an operation depending on plenty of troops, rather than upon skill in handling them, was the only one which would have probability of success in his hands."[75]

When A. J. Smith heard of Banks's decision for an immediate withdrawal, he was both surprised and enraged. The commanding general earlier had told him that the army was going to renew its advance on Shreveport, and now just the opposite was happening. Smith remonstrated to Banks and asked him to allow at least enough time to collect the wounded and bury the dead. But Banks explained that there was a dearth of water and supplies and pointed out the extraordinary number of casualties that the command had sustained. Besides, he told his subordinate, the other generals were the ones who suggested the retreat.

Smith then asked if the column might remain until 9:00 A.M. the next day, but Banks would not consider it.[76]

In his despondency Smith went to Franklin. Undoubtedly not aware that the second in command had suggested the retreat, Smith proposed that Franklin place Banks under arrest and then take command of the army. The general was certain that the officers and men from the detachment of Sherman's army would follow him. Franklin allowed Smith to vent his anger. He calmly poured a cup of coffee and then reminded him what he was suggesting. "Smith," Franklin said, "don't you know this is mutiny?" This apparently sobering thought brought the irate general back to his senses, and nothing more was said.[77]

Franklin may not have possessed Smith's fighting spirit, but at least he understood the necessity of logistical support, not to mention the fact that men and beasts require water, and there was none at Pleasant Hill. Yet there were several other good reasons why he was opposed to renewing the offensive. "In the first place," Franklin recalled, "the cavalry all had started to the rear that morning, with the exception of about 500 men. The horses that morning had been out of food for about thirty six hours. There was nothing for them to eat, and there was nothing for the cavalrymen to eat, their trains had all been captured."[78] Under these circumstances, hunger and thirst proved to be more potent inducements than Smith's justifiable emotions.

The retreat to Grand Ecore was completed by April 11. Franklin nevertheless was disgusted with the situation. "Think of my having to expose the lives of my men and my own to bolster up the mistakes & folly of a political General," he groused to Anna in a letter written from Grand Ecore six days later. "We ought now to be in Shreveport, after a successful fight with the enemy. We really are here, and the enemy is better off by the guns & wagons he captured from us, than he was before we came, and probably better concentrated. But I will stop grumbling." Things could have turned out much more disastrously, from Franklin's personal perspective, and he was well aware of it. The bullet that ricocheted off his riding boot could just as well as lodged in his leg. (He did admit, however, that the leg was very stiff and "nearly black and blue below the knee.")[79]

The army waited at Grand Ecore for several days while the navy turned around its vessels and steamed back down the Red, which was getting lower by the day. Confederate cavalry harassed the fleet the whole way, and by the time the boats arrived, they were badly riddled from gunfire. One New York soldier in the XIX Corps recorded in his diary that "the sides of some of the transports are half shot away, and their smoke-stacks look like huge pepper boxes." By April 15 most of the vessels were tied up next to Grand Ecore. With the river so low it became painfully obvious that the navy could no longer support the operation, so Banks decided to return his entire force to Alexandria. In order to strengthen the command, he earlier had ordered forward General Grover's division of the XIX Corps from its occupation duty at Alexandria. Banks also countermanded the orders compelling A. J. Smith's command to be returned to Sherman. The river was so shallow now that the army would be required to protect Porter's fleet, and Banks was not about to allow Smith and his desperately needed soldiers leave him now.[80]

Franklin had hoped that the Confederates would attack now that the blue-clad troops were ensconced in Grand Ecore. "I do wish they would come and have it out severely," he confessed to Anna on April 17. "I have no doubt of the result, and I am sure that the men have no fears. We have fully 20,000 infantry here with plenty of artillery and cavalry, but the enemy does not come." His men, however, were not as cocksure. While inspecting a section of defenses being built by the men of the XIII Corps, Franklin declared: "You don't need any protection. We can whip them easily here." These veterans had been thrashed ten days earlier at Sabine Crossroads, and the defeat still haunted them. One of the western troops replied, "We have been defeated once, and we think we will look out for ourselves." It is not known if Franklin took the comment as a personal affront to his own generalship, or whether he shrugged it off as a commentary on Banks's tactical abilities. Capt. Otis Whitney of the 27th Iowa Infantry seemed to sum up the feelings of many of the westerners. On April 15 he recorded in his diary just how he and his men felt about the eastern generals: "Genl. Banks is blamed by every one as the author of our present uncomfor[t]able position. Genl. Franklin also comes in for a full share & he is considered by all that I have heard speak of him as either a blunder head or a traitor. I have no confidence in either Banks or Franklin."[81]

On April 19 General Banks ordered A. J. Smith and his command to Natchitoches and to take up defensive positions to cover the retreat of the main force. By April 21 the rest of the army was heading southward, under the control and direction of Franklin. Once the main column reached Natchitoches, Smith's troops fell in and constituted the army's rear guard.[82]

Franklin began the march in great pain. A few days earlier his surgeon made an incision in his leg to let it drain. It turned out that the injury was more severe than previously believed, the force of the ball having killed the flesh in the vicinity of impact. The doctor now thought it would be best if the wound "ran freely." The leg continued to give the general problems throughout the retreat, getting so painful that he had to ride in an ambulance.[83]

On April 23 a Confederate cavalry force attempted to prevent the Union column from crossing the Cane River at Monett's Ferry, and after a spirited fight, Emory's troops overwhelmed the Confederates, though at a cost of nearly three hundred casualties compared to only fifty for the Southerners. The Union force promptly built a pontoon bridge over the river and proceeded southward as the retreat continued. Disgruntled by the campaign's lack of success, Smith's men renewed the burning and marauding that had characterized their march thus far, torching just about every house and building they came across and leaving a path of smoldering ruins and homeless families in their wake. The pursuing Confederates were enraged. General Taylor recalled: "We passed the smoking ruins of homesteads, by which stood weeping women and children. ... It was difficult to restrain one's inclination to punish the ruffians engaged in this work, a number of whom were captured; but they asserted, and doubtless with truth, that they were acting under orders."[84]

In his conversations with civilians, Taylor ascertained that Generals Banks and Franklin "and the officers and men of the 19th corps, Eastern troops, exerted themselves to prevent these outrages, and that the perpetrators were the men of General A. J. Smith's command from Sherman's army." Taylor was correct. In keeping with his conservative philosophy—that war should be waged against the enemy's army and not the civilian populace—Franklin issued an order upon his return to Alexandria condemning the "indiscriminate marauding and incendiarism" that accompanied the march from Grand Ecore, acts he deemed "disgraceful to a civilized nation." A preliminary investigation provided no conclusive evidence, so the general authorized a $500 reward for information leading to the arrest and conviction of the guilty parties. The order only substantiated the westerners' collective opinion of Franklin as the "old Potomac fossil." He had become an anachronism in a war that had turned "modern."[85]

The Union column trudged into Alexandria on April 25 and 26. When Franklin finally had time to write to his wife on the twenty-sixth—his first letter to her in nine days—he admitted that "the dreariness [of the retreat] was only equalled by the Peninsula seven days." His wound had worsened, making matters even drearier. Upon arriving in Alexandria, the surgeon examined him and extended the incision he had made about a week earlier. "Of course I am on my back, and will be so for some time," Franklin disclosed to Anna. "The D[octo]rs say two weeks. I am in my tent now, but move to-day into a very comfortable house close by the camp. I know that you are interested in all these details, and I have told you the worst." Though obviously trying to allay her worst fears, he also wanted her to know just how close he had come to being a real casualty. "Is it not disgusting that a mere bruise should have such a result," he wrote. "But I have great reason to be thankful that it is no worse. The thickness of a sheet of paper farther to the left in the passage of the ball would have broken my leg. I shall certainly never dispise thick legged riding boots again."[86]

Although the army had made it safely back to Alexandria, the navy still was struggling to negotiate the low waters of the Red River. Taylor's army also tried to impede their progress by regularly assailing the boats with rifle and artillery fire from the river's banks. As difficult as their current situation may have seemed, Admiral Porter and his sailors undoubtedly would have found themselves in an even worse predicament had it not been for Franklin. According to Porter, back when the army still was at Grand Ecore, "General Franklin came to me ... and asked me if I had been informed that General Banks was going to retreat to Alexandria." Porter told him that the general said it was "his intention to hold this country." Franklin replied that "there was no such intention; orders have already been issued for the army to retire, and I am to conduct the retreat." The admiral was astounded. He sent a high-ranking naval officer to Banks to determine his intentions. For some unknown reason, Banks told the officer "that he had not the faintest idea of leaving."[87]

Porter took Franklin's words at face value, however, and moved his vessels about a mile downriver from Grand Ecore. According to the admiral, "I had a great deal of difficulty in getting them over the sand-bar there; but I got them over just about in time, for another day might have rendered it impossible for me to do so." Despite the receding waters of the Red and the Confederates' continued attacks, the vessels finally were in sight of Alexandria. Porter might have breathed a sigh of relief, but here was yet another obstacle, one that the navy might not be able to overcome: the falls of the Red River.[88]

The Red had become so shallow that even the lightest vessels would not be able to pass over the falls (rapids) without foundering. Franklin had remembered his conversation with Lieutenant Colonel Bailey on the day of Pleasant

Hill, so when the army still was at Grand Ecore, he gave Bailey a letter of introduction to Porter and instructed him to tell the admiral about his plan for a dam to raise the water above the falls. He also told Bailey to convey to Porter that he himself believed the plan was feasible. Finally, Franklin instructed him to ask Porter to confer with Banks at once so that, if Porter agreed with the scheme, the necessary preparations could be made for the dam's construction.[89]

The plan was relatively simple. By using felled trees, sandbags, and quarried stone, Bailey designed a system of timber dams, stone cribs, and bracket dams extending from both sides of the river and meeting in the middle. When the dam was completed and the water behind it rose high enough for the vessels to clear the rocky bottom of the rapids, a section of the dam would be broken and the boats would pass through the opening and over the rapids on a cascade. There actually were two distinct sections of rapids above Alexandria, thus necessitating the construction of two separate dams. If the first dam worked, Bailey's crews would then build the second.[90]

By the time the navy made it to the falls above Alexandria, Porter "found the army in a great state of stampede. I did not see anything to be frightened at myself, but the army was going to clear out at once and go down the river." (It is interesting to note that the only word that Franklin wrote in his pocket diary for April 28—which was about the time that Porter arrived—was "Stampede.") The admiral went ashore, found Banks, and bluntly told him that abandoning the navy at Alexandria "was out of the question; that we must do something to get the fleet down." Bailey seemed to be the navy's only hope, yet there were very few army or navy officers who believed that his idea would work. Porter recalled that when "Colonel Bailey had suggested the building of a dam . . . , they hooted at it, and so did all the engineers."[91]

Porter, however, held General Franklin in high regard. In an April 28 letter to Secretary of the Navy Welles, he called him the best general in Banks's army—and since Franklin believed the dam would work, Porter embraced the plan too. Bailey then went on the twenty-ninth to discuss the plan with Banks and Maj. Gen. David Hunter (who was bearing a message from Grant urging Banks to abandon the current campaign and prepare for one against Mobile). Bailey recalled that although Hunter "had little confidence in its feasibility, he nevertheless thought it better to try the experiment, especially as General Franklin, who is an engineer, advised it." Finally, Banks relented and gave his approval to the project.[92]

But Franklin would not get the opportunity to see the dam built nor witness its successful results, though Bailey made sure that he received at least some measure of the credit. In his official report of the project, Bailey wrote: "To Major-General Franklin, who, previous to the commencement of the work, was the only supporter of my proposition to save the fleet by means of a dam, and whose persevering efforts caused its adoption, I desire to return my grateful thanks. I trust the country will join with the Army of the Gulf and the Mississippi Squadron in awarding to him due praise for his earnest and intelligent efforts in their behalf." Franklin would get no such public praise. Confined to his bed because of his bad leg and annoyed by a constant parade of well-meaning visitors, the general departed Alexandria in a navy gunboat on April 30 and, accompanied by Hunter, returned to New Orleans on convalescent leave.[93] For him, the Red River Campaign was over.

Franklin never received another command. While convalescing, he was summoned by his old classmate, U. S. Grant, to Petersburg, where the Army of the Potomac was attempting to lay siege to the Army of Northern Virginia. Grant was considering giving Franklin another command. But 1864 was a presidential election year, pitting George McClellan against Abraham Lincoln, and promoting a McClellan supporter like Franklin to an important post would not sit well with the administration. On top of that, his lackluster performance with the Army of the Potomac, coupled with the fact that he had just been a corps commander in the defeated Army of the Gulf, did not help his chances. On his trip northward from Petersburg, Franklin's train was captured by Maj. Harry Gilmor's Confederate partisans near the Gunpowder River in Maryland. Though still recuperating from his wound, the general made a daring escape when his captors fell asleep. Nevertheless, he was destined to sit out the rest of the war as a member of a board for retiring officers.

William B. Franklin led a successful postwar career as vice president of Colt's Firearms and was involved in many civic projects in Hartford, Connecticut. He also was appointed president of the National Home for Disabled Volunteer Soldiers, a position he held for twenty years. During the Civil War, however, Franklin never lived up to his potential, yet it seems the experience he gained during his tenure with the Army of the Potomac paid dividends when he commanded the XIX Corps in Louisiana, despite the fact that he clung to his conservative philosophy of warfare like an "old Potomac fossil."

William B. Franklin and the XIX Corps in the Trans-Mississippi, 1863–64

NOTES

1. For background on Franklin's career prior to 1863, see Mark A. Snell, *From First to Last: The Life of Major General William B. Franklin* (New York: Fordham University Press, 2002). This essay is a revision of chapters 14 and 15 of that book.

2. Herman Hattaway and Archer Jones, *How the North Won: A Military History of the Civil War* (Urbana: University of Illinois Press, 1983), 432; Ludwell H. Johnson, *The Red River Campaign: Politics and Cotton in the Civil War*, 2d ed. (Kent, Ohio: Kent State University Press, 1993), 13–16, 33–35.

3. Patricia Faust, ed., *Historical Times Encyclopedia of the Civil War* (New York: Harper and Row, 1986), 38, 121–22, 677.

4. William B. Franklin to Anna Franklin (hereafter cited WBF to AF), July 22, 1863, W. B. Franklin Papers, York County Heritage Trust, York, Penn.

5. WBF to AF, July 26–30, 1863, ibid.; Franklin to Smith, Aug. 3–10, 1863, William Farrar Smith Papers, Vermont Historical Society, Barre. Special Orders No. 183, Headquarters, Department of the Gulf, assigned Franklin to the board, along with Brig. Gens. Charles Stone, William H. Emory, and Godfrey Weitzel and Maj. D. C. Houston, chief of engineers. U.S. War Department, *The War of the Rebellion: A Compilation of the Official Records of the Union and Confederate Armies*, 70 vols. in 128 parts (Washington, D.C.: Government Printing Office, 1880–1901), ser. 1, 26(1):657–58 (hereafter cited as *OR;* all references are to series 1 unless otherwise noted).

6. Headquarters, Department of the Gulf, Special Orders No. 200, Aug. 15, 1863, *OR,* 26(1):684; Headquarters, XIX Corps, General Orders No. 1, Aug. 20, 1863, ibid., 693; Franklin to W. F. Smith, Aug. 18, 1863, Smith Papers; Seymour V. Connor et al., *Battles of Texas* (Waco, Tex.: Texian, 1967), 148–49; Johnson, *Red River Campaign,* 37; Banks to Franklin, Aug 31, 1863, *OR,* 26(1):287.

7. WBF to AF, Sept. 2, 1863, Franklin Papers; WBF to W. F. Smith, Dec. 28, 1863 (emphasis in original), Smith Papers. By December 28 Smith already had been part of Grant's successful campaign to lift the siege of Chattanooga. Franklin was warning his friend about the general's penchant for the bottle and cautioned Smith to "look out for him."

8. *OR,* 26(1):294; Connor et al., *Battles of Texas,* 148–49.

9. *OR,* 26(1):294–98.

10. Ibid., 294–95, 298–300.

11. Ibid., 295; "Second Report of Acting Volunteer Lieutenant Crocker, U.S. Navy, Late Commanding Naval Forces, Edgartown, Mass.," Apr. 21, 1865, U.S. Naval War Records Office, *Official Records of the Union and Confederate Navies in the War of the Rebellion,* 31 vols. (Washington, D.C.: Government Printing Office, 1894–1927), ser. 1, 20:545 (hereafter cited as *ORN;* all references are to series 1 unless otherwise noted).

12. *ORN,* 20:545.

13. *OR,* 26(1):297, 299; *ORN,* 20:545.

14. *OR,* 26(1):301–2; *ORN,* 20:548.

15. WBF to AF, Sept. 12, 1863. Although Franklin did not mention the *Arizona* by name, this remark was attributed to its captain, Acting Master Howard Tibbets, who was the subject of an enquiry into his actions at Sabine Pass. See *ORN,* 20:554.

16. *OR*, 26(1):297.
17. WBF to AF, Sept. 14, 20, 1863, Franklin Papers.
18. *ORN*, 20:538.
19. WBF to AF, Sept. 12, 19, 1863, Franklin Papers; *OR*, 26(1):292.
20. WBF to AF, Sept. 26, 1863, Franklin Papers.
21. WBF to AF, Sept. 26, 29, Oct. 5, 1863, ibid.
22. *OR*, 26(1):334–36, 748–49; WBF to AF, Oct. 12, 1863, Franklin Papers.
23. *OR*, 26(1):334–36. A footnote to this document reads: "On October 20, Major-General Washburn, owing to the illness of Maj. Gen. E. O. C. Ord, assumed command of the Thirteenth Army Corps, but Washburn continued in command of that portion indicated."
24. WBF to AF, Oct. 12, 1863, Franklin Papers.
25. WBF to AF, Oct. 16, 1863, ibid.
26. *OR*, 26(1):292; WBF to AF, Oct. 25, 26, 1863, Franklin Papers.
27. *OR*, 26(1):340–41; WBF to AF, Oct. 26, Nov. 2, 1863, Franklin Papers.
28. *OR*, 26(1):393–95, 359; WBF to AF, Nov. 5, 1863, Franklin Papers.
29. Richard Taylor, *Destruction and Reconstruction: Personal Experiences of the Late War* (New York: D. Appleton, 1879), 150; T. Michael Parrish, *Richard Taylor: Soldier Prince of Dixie* (Chapel Hill: University of North Carolina Press, 1992), 313.
30. *OR*, 26(1):397–98; WBF to AF, Nov. 2, 1863, Franklin Papers.
31. WBF to AF, Nov. 14, 1863, Franklin Papers; Franklin to Smith, Dec. 28, 1863, Smith Papers.
32. Johnson, *Red River Campaign*, 40–41.
33. WBF to AF, Nov. 18, 20, 26, 1863, Franklin Papers.
34. WBF to AF, Nov. 29, 1863, ibid.; Franklin to Stone, Dec., 4, 1863, official-communications journal, ibid. Some of the dispatches and messages in this book are also found in the *Official Records*, but many, including the one cited here, are not.
35. *OR*, 26(1):847–48. No other correspondence relating to the exchange could be found.
36. WBF to AF, Nov. 29, 1863, Franklin Papers; *OR*, 26(1):854–55.
37. Quotes in Philip Cuccia, "'Gorillas' and White-Glove Gents: Union Soldiers in the Red River Campaign"(senior thesis, U.S. Military Academy, 1989), 1, 12. Port Hudson was the only campaign in which the XIX Corps had participated to that point in the war. The soldiers of the XIII Corps, in contrast, were veterans of Shiloh, Corinth, Vicksburg, and other engagements.
38. Johnson, *Red River Campaign*, 40–43, 45–47.
39. Ibid., 47–48.
40. William B. Franklin diary, Feb. 24, 1864, Franklin Papers; WBF to AF, Feb. 24, 1864, ibid.
41. Johnson, *Red River Campaign*, 81–85.
42. *OR*, 32(3):289.
43. Richard B. Irwin, "The Red River Campaign," in *Battles and Leaders of the Civil War*, ed. Robert U. Johnson and Clarence C. Buel, 4 vols. (New York: Century, 1887–88), 4:347.
44. Johnson, *Red River Campaign*, 84.
45. *Philadelphia Press*, Apr. 25, 1864, quoted in J. Cutler Andrews, *The North Reports the Civil War* (Pittsburgh: University of Pittsburgh Press, 1955), 506–7.
46. Franklin diary, Mar. 2–3, 7, 1864; Irwin, "Red River Campaign," 349–50.

47. *OR*, 34(2):544–45. According to Banks, a violent rainstorm struck Franklin, Louisiana, on March 8, placing " the roads in such condition as to make a march impracticable for at least four days." Johnson, *Red River Campaign*, 98.

48. *OR*, 34(2):544, 562.

49. Irwin, "Red River Campaign," 349–50; Franklin diary, Mar. 13–25, 1864.

50. Irwin, "Red River Campaign," 350–51; *OR*, 34(1):198; Johnson, *Red River Campaign*, 113–15.

51. Johnson, *Red River Campaign*, 115.

52. *OR*, 34(1):237.

53. Franklin diary, Apr. 6, 1864; Charles B. Hall, "Notes on the Red River Campaign," in *War Papers Read before the State of Maine, Military Order of the Loyal Legion of the United States* (1898; repr., Wilmington, N.C.: Broadfoot, 1992), 4:268.

54. Parrish, *Richard Taylor*, 324–28, 335; WBF to AF, Apr. 6, 1864, Franklin Papers.

55. Parrish, *Richard Taylor*, 338–39; Robert L. Kerby, *Kirby Smith's Confederacy: The Trans-Mississippi South, 1863–1865* (New York: Columbia University Press, 1972), 302.

56. Franklin diary, Apr. 7, 1864; WBF to AF, Apr. 13, 1862, Franklin Papers; Franklin testimony, Jan. 6, 1865, in U.S. Congress, *Report of the Joint Committee on the Conduct of the War*, 3 vols. (Washington, D.C.: Government Printing Office, 1865), 2:29.

57. Johnson, *Red River Campaign*, 125; Franklin testimony, 2:32.

58. *OR*, 34(1):257.

59. Hall, "Notes on the Red River Campaign," 269.

60. Johnson, *Red River Campaign*, 127–28; *OR*, 34(1):257; WBF to AF, Apr. 13, 1864, Franklin Papers.

61. Taylor, *Destruction and Reconstruction*, 162.

62. Quoted in Johnson, *Red River Campaign*, 129.

63. *OR*, 34(1):257; Johnson, *Red River Campaign*, 136; *New Orleans Era* account in Frank Moore, ed., *The Rebellion Record: A Diary of American Events* (New York: D. Van Nostrand, 1865), 8:555; WBF to AF, Apr. 11, 1864, Franklin Papers; Hall, "Notes on the Red River Campaign," 271; James K. Ewer, *The Third Massachusetts Cavalry in the War for the Union* (Maplewood, Mass.: William J. Perry, 1903), 149–50.

64. Ewer, *Third Massachusetts Cavalry*, 149–50; Emory quoted in Parrish, *Richard Taylor*, 351; *OR*, 34(1):257; WBF to AF, Apr. 11, 1864, Franklin Papers; Johnson, *Red River Campaign*, 136; Hall, "Notes on the Red River Campaign," 271.

65. Johnson, *Red River Campaign*, 140–41. The specific number of Confederate killed, wounded, and missing is not known since the returns were lost during the war.

66. WBF to AF, Apr. 9, 13, 1864, Franklin Papers.

67. *OR*, 34(1):201; Johnson, *Red River Campaign*, 146.

68. Johnson, *Red River Campaign*, 152–54; *OR*, 34(1):268.

69. Johnson, *Red River Campaign*, 147–48.

70. This account appears in Moore, *Rebellion Record*, 8:549.

71. Franklin testimony, 2:33.

72. *OR*, 34(1):258; Johnson, *Red River Campaign*, 158–60.

73. Johnson, *Red River Campaign*, 167.

74. Ibid., 162–63.

75. Franklin quoted in ibid., 163.

76. Ibid., 163–64.

77. Franklin quoted in ibid., 164.

78. Franklin testimony, 2:35.

79. Franklin diary, Apr. 11, 1864; WBF to AF, Apr. 13, 17, 1864, Franklin Papers.

80. Johnson, *Red River Campaign,* 214 (quote), 215–18.

81. WBF to AF, Apr. 17, 1864, Franklin Papers; Franklin and soldier quoted in Johnson, *Red River Campaign,* 217; Whitney quoted in Cuccia, "'Gorillas' and White-Glove Gents," 21.

82. *OR,* 34(3):235.

83. WBF to AF, Apr. 26, 1864, Franklin Papers.

84. Faust, *Encyclopedia of the Civil War,* 111; Johnson, *Red River Campaign,* 224–25, 234; Taylor, *Destruction and Reconstruction,* 193.

85. Taylor, *Destruction and Reconstruction,* 194; *OR,* 34(3):307. The best study of the concept of total war as practiced by Sherman's troops is Mark Grimsley, *The Hard Hand of War: Union Military Policy toward Southern Civilians, 1861–1865* (New York: Cambridge University Press, 1995).

86. WBF to AF, Apr. 26, 1864, Franklin Papers.

87. Porter testimony, Mar. 7, 1865, in U.S. Congress, *Report of the Joint Committee on the Conduct of the War,* 2:278.

88. Ibid., 279.

89. *OR,* 34(1):403.

90. Alvin M. Josephy Jr., *War on the Frontier: The Trans-Mississippi West* (Alexandria, Va.: Time-Life Books, 1986), 68.

91. Porter testimony, Mar. 7, 1865, 2:279; Franklin diary, Apr. 28, 1864.

92. *ORN,* 26:93; *OR,* 34(1):403.

93. *OR,* 34(1):403–4; Franklin diary, Apr. 30, 1864.

"Always 'Fighting Joe'"
Joseph Hooker and the Campaign in North Georgia, May–July 1864

ETHAN S. RAFUSE

"Envious, imperious, and braggart" was how Maj. Gen. William T. Sherman described Maj. Gen. Joseph Hooker in a letter to his wife on July 29, 1864. Hooker had just asked to be relieved from duty with the Army of the Cumberland in protest of Sherman's passing him over for command of the Army of the Tennessee in favor of Maj. Gen. Oliver Otis Howard. Though Hooker had performed commendably as leader of the largest Federal corps to participate in the Atlanta Campaign, Sherman shed no tears over his departure. "Self prevailed with him," he declared, "and knowing him intimately I honestly preferred Howard."[1]

Hooker had come west ten months earlier, looking to regain his place among the leading stars of the Union war effort. To get back in the war after his removal as commander of the Army of the Potomac in June 1863, in September he agreed to lead its two smallest corps when they were sent west after the Union defeat at Chickamauga. During the subsequent operations around Chattanooga that avenged Chickamauga, Hooker got off to a good start. On November 24 he directed a successful attack against Lookout Mountain that became renowned as the "Battle above the Clouds," then led a pursuit of Gen. Braxton Bragg's retreating Confederate army that ended with a sharp action at Ringgold Gap on the twenty-seventh. It certainly appeared that "Fighting Joe" was back in form and fated for bigger things when active campaigning resumed in 1864. The Atlanta Campaign would be his chance.

Unfortunately, almost immediately after his arrival west of the Appalachians, Hooker had also managed to alienate the two men it was becoming dangerous for any officer of ambition in the Union army to offend, Sherman and Ulysses S. Grant. This was unfortunate but not surprising, for Hooker had a particular talent that few could match for developing bad relations with peers and superior officers. It would be fatal for his personal fortunes in 1864.

BORN IN NOVEMBER 1814 in Hadley, Massachusetts, Hooker graduated from the U.S. Military Academy at West Point in 1837 and served with distinction in the Mexican War before leaving the army during the 1850s and settling in California.[2] He volunteered his service to the Union in 1861 and rose quickly, turning in fine combat performances as a division and corps commander in the Army of the Potomac. He also actively and effectively cultivated political support from Republicans in Congress and the Lincoln administration by presenting himself as a fighting general and an alternative to the conservative West Point clique that enjoyed Maj. Gen. George McClellan's patronage within the Army of the Potomac high command.

Hooker did not like the nickname "Fighting Joe," which was attached to him during the first year and a half of the war. "That name has done and is doing me incalculable injury," he complained to a friend who made the mistake of using it to address him. "It makes a person ... think that I am a hot-headed, furious young fellow, accustomed to making furious and needless dashes at the enemy."[3] Still, Hooker's popular image as a fighting general was well deserved. His handsome appearance, fearlessness in combat, and personal charisma appealed to the soldiers he led and gave them confidence in his leadership. "A general fitted by education, by experience, and by the highest qualities of mind and heart, to command men in the great game of war" was how one of Hooker's staff officers described him years later. "He is the finest looking Major General I have seen," one man in Sherman's army proclaimed after his first encounter with Hooker in November 1863, "over 6 feet high—well built—good looking—florid complexion—'Presbyterian whiskers'—and looks 'every inch a soldier.'" "We all have great confidence in Hooker," another man declared a few months later, "and esteem him highly."[4]

Lamentably, Hooker's merits were offset—ultimately too much—by some awful personality traits. A high opinion of his own ability as a general, although largely justified, made him hypercritical of others. He was also utterly without scruple in pursuing his personal and professional ambitions. This combined with a reputation for drinking and womanizing to sow friction with many fellow officers. In his memoirs Grant spoke for many who had crossed swords with Hooker when he declared him "a dangerous man. He was not subordinate to his superiors. He was ambitious to the extent of caring nothing for the rights of others."[5] This image was cemented in many minds by Hooker's conduct during Maj. Gen. Ambrose Burnside's unfortunate tenure in command of the Army of the Potomac.

Working in Hooker's favor was the fact that Abraham Lincoln liked his aggressiveness as a commander and was fond of him personally. This led to his appointment as Burnside's replacement at the head of the Army of the Potomac. Though Hooker revitalized the army and proved himself a commendable operational thinker, his performance at Chancellorsville and response to the Confederate army's move north across the Potomac River afterward disappointed the president. Responding in part to evidence of bitter friction between Hooker and his subordinates, Lincoln removed the general from command of the Army of the Potomac on June 27. The president, though, still believed Hooker's talents could be of use to the Union war effort and was eminently gratified at the general's acceptance in September 1863 of the assignment to command the Army of the Potomac detachment sent west. "Whenever trouble arises," Lincoln remarked, "I can always rely upon Hooker's magnanimity."[6] Burnside and a host of other officers would have undoubtedly found that comment rather curious.

Hooker made the most of his chance, though the change in scenery did not diminish the darker aspects of his personality. "He is in an unfortunate state of mind for one who has to co-operate," one man complained only a few days after the general's arrival on the scene, "fault finding, criticizing, dissatisfied." And what Hooker saw during the operations around Chattanooga did nothing to allay his inclination toward a poor opinion of men fate placed in his path to advancement. "Here there is a total lack of system and administrative ability," he groused to a member of Lincoln's cabinet. "It is felt in all branches of service.... To find an officer capable of doing his duty is a luxury."[7] A few months later he complained to Washington that Brig. Gen. William F. Smith, the Army of the Cumberland's chief engineer and an old enemy from the Army of the Potomac, "had an ascendency over Grant, who is simple-minded." This was evident in what Hooker perceived to be a failed effort at Chattanooga to "shut me out of the fight. Grant's object being to give the éclat to his old army, and Smith's."[8]

As 1864 opened, Hooker had reason for both optimism and pessimism. During the fall and winter of 1863–64, his allies in Washington made a vigorous effort to discredit his successor as Army of the Potomac commander with an eye on restoring Hooker to his former position. This, however, came to naught. Consequently, the general resigned himself to the fact that "with all of the important army commands ... disposed of for the ensuing campaign," his fortune would be made under the command of Sherman, who took command of the Division of the Mississippi upon Grant's elevation to general in chief of all the Union armies in March 1864.[9]

This was not a good development for Hooker, who complained in a letter to the secretary of war that he was "regarded with a great deal of jealousy by those filling high places" and made clear that he had little regard for Sherman, whose efforts at Chattanooga he proclaimed "really deplorable." In the course of a long letter to Secretary of the Treasury Salmon Chase in December 1863, Hooker had offered a thorough recounting of how in his eyes Grant's attempt to make Sherman the hero of Chattanooga failed miserably and prevented his own efforts from achieving all they could. Sherman's struggles at Chattanooga, he proclaimed, were simply a repeat of his earlier failures around Vicksburg in December 1862. "Please remember what I tell you," he warned Chase, "Sherman is an active, energetic officer, but in judgment is as infirm as Burnside. He will never be successful."[10]

It certainly did nothing for Hooker's frame of mind to know that one of Sherman's great patrons in the war had been Maj. Gen. Henry W. Halleck. Both generals had developed a bitter distaste for Hooker when they came into contact with him in California before the war, a time in which, one admirer of Hooker later conceded, he had fallen "into some of the bad habits which follow idleness ... which I have heard his California friends allude to as the process of 'going to the dogs.'" Halleck's disdain only intensified during Hooker's tenure with the Army of the Potomac. Sherman fully shared Halleck's prejudices. "I know Hooker well," he wrote in April 1863, "and tremble to think of his handling 100,000 men.... Let Hooker once advance or move laterally and I fear the result."[11] Closer contact with the general in 1863–64 did nothing to lead Sherman to revise his opinion. Certainly, the conspicuous contrast between Hooker's dramatic victory at Lookout Mountain and Sherman's inability to achieve much in his attacks during the battles for Chattanooga—and the relish with which Hooker brought it to the attention of anyone who would listen—did nothing to put Sherman at ease.

Thus, if Hooker was to realize his hopes for completing his military redemption in 1864, he had a tricky minefield to navigate. He started out about as well as a man of his temperament could despite a perception that, as he later proclaimed, "Grant and Sherman, who were in partnership, gave me the cold shoulder." Hooker accepted a reorganization of Sherman's command that consolidated his quasi-independent force of two small corps into the XX Corps and made it part of the Army of the Cumberland. This placed him under the command of Maj. Gen. George H. Thomas, with whom he would develop a remarkably positive relationship. Hooker was also pleased to get approval to place his chief of staff and close friend, Maj. Gen. Daniel Butterfield, in command of a division in the new corps. At the same time, he was also undoubtedly rankled, although he restricted his complaining to private letters to patrons in Washington, by Maj. Gen. John M. Schofield's receiving command of the Army of the Ohio, which despite its exalted name, was actually one-fourth smaller than Hooker's command.[12]

Although "utterly disgusted" with Grant and Sherman by the time the 1864 campaigns began, Hooker looked forward to the opening of operations. His eagerness was evident in May, when a friend asked him what he considered "the highest form of human enjoyment." Without hesitation, Hooker replied, "campaigning in an enemy's country." The XX Corps would begin the campaign with approximately 25,000 men organized into three divisions commanded by Brig. Gen. Alpheus S. Williams, Brig. Gen. John W. Geary, and Butterfield. And as was his penchant, during the winter of 1863–64, Hooker fully won the affections of the rank and file in his command. "With regard to Hooker," one man advised his family a few weeks before the campaign began, "everybody loves him and to see him as he rides along our lines is only to like him more each time." In a letter to a friend just before operations began in Georgia, the general conveyed both his own supreme confidence about the future and his concerns. "I am regarded," he wrote, "with more jealousy in this new sphere of operations than I ever was in the East. It is not without reason for it is as certain as any future event can be that I shall be regarded as the best soldier in the Army if I am not now. . . . An effort will be made to prevent this, but the result will likely be as futile as the last one. I have never yet seen the time that there was no place for a man willing to fight."[13]

DURING THE FIRST WEEK of May 1864, the great campaign in Georgia began. Hooker's command began moving, along with the other two corps of the Army of the Cumberland, toward formidable Confederate positions on Rocky Face Ridge. "I am off to the front," Hooker advised one of his friends in Congress on May 3, "not that I am looking for any considerable fight but wherever there is one I like to be counted in." For three days, Hooker and his men marched

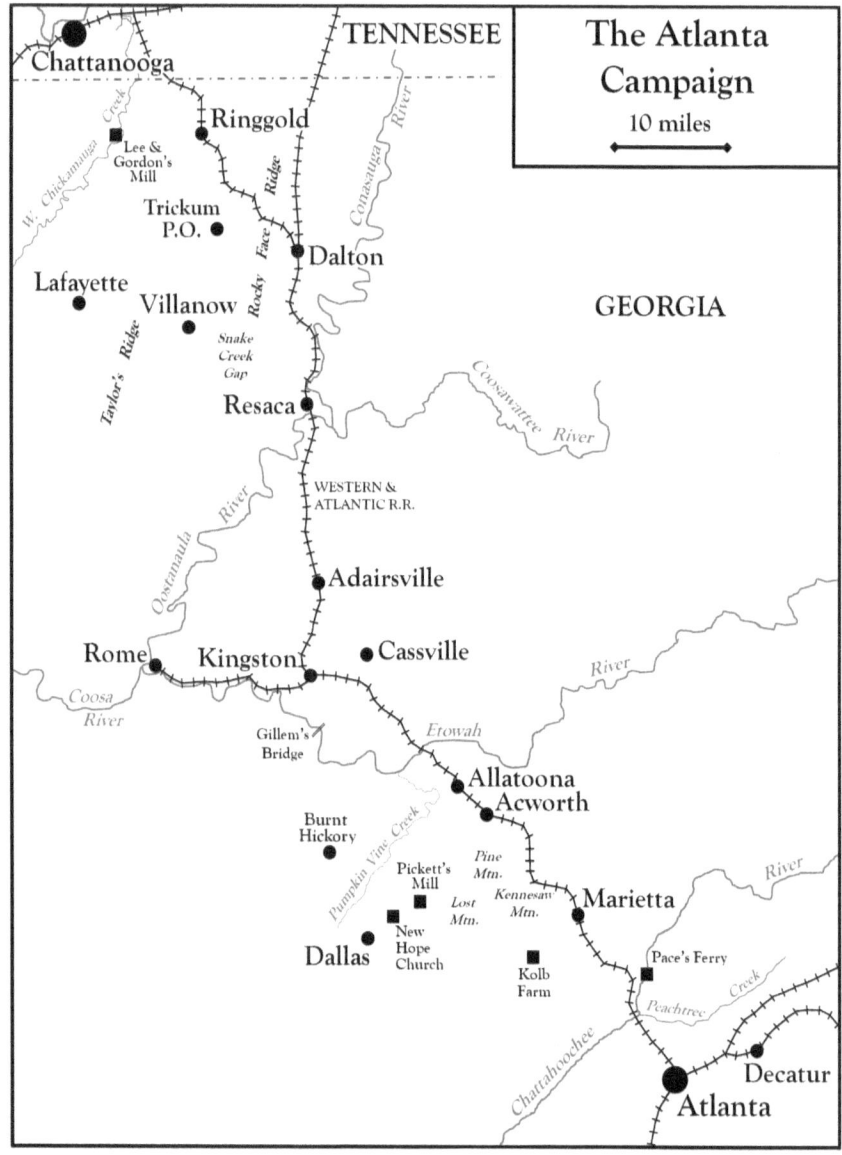

south and eastward through fierce heat, crossing West Chickamauga Creek at Lee and Gordon's Mill. This provided them with an opportunity to see the Chickamauga battleground, after which one man wrote, "never in my life do I want to see such terrible evidence of human destruction as were there visible.... The battle ground at Stones River I used to think was awful, but compared to this, it seems a mere skirmish."[14]

Hooker then pushed through Taylor's Ridge and on May 7 reached a point in Dogwood Valley about five miles from Rocky Face Ridge known as Trickum's Post Office. Hooker's job, along with the rest of the Army of the Cumberland and Army of the Ohio, was to menace the Rebels on Rocky Face Ridge from the west and north. This, Sherman hoped, would enable the Army of the Tennessee, commanded by Maj. Gen. James McPherson, to push unmolested toward Snake Creek Gap, pass through, and operate against Gen. Joseph E. Johnston's line of communications. As the commander of the force on the far right of the Union line facing Rocky Face, Hooker had the additional task of supporting the cavalry division commanded by Brig. Gen. Hugh Judson Kilpatrick, to whom Sherman gave responsibility for covering the gap between McPherson and the rest of the army.[15]

The morning after Hooker's command completed its march to Dogwood Valley, Thomas informed him that Sherman wanted the Army of the Cumberland's other two corps, Maj. Gen. John Palmer's XIV and Maj. Gen. Oliver Otis Howard's IV, along with Schofield's command, to move against Rocky Face Ridge. He directed Hooker to probe Buzzard's Roost and Dug Gaps in the ridge, which was done at the former place by Butterfield's division. Hooker moved forward with that division as it pushed the enemy pickets back to their main line on the ridge. Yet after conducting "a close personal inspection of the enemy's defenses," Hooker concluded that Butterfield's assessment of Buzzard's Roost Gap as a "very ugly place to send troops" was correct. He also directed Geary to "march without delay to seize" Dug Gap, though "with instructions not to make a fight unless to our advantage." Despite these words of caution, Geary attempted to carry the enemy position in the gap but found it too strong to be taken, suffering 357 casualties in bitter fighting with the Rebels.[16]

Nonetheless, Thomas's and Schofield's efforts against Rocky Face Ridge did distract Johnston from McPherson's movements, and during the afternoon of May 8, Hooker was able to notify Thomas that he had learned that "McPherson [was] in Villanow at 2 P.M. moving upon Snake Creek Gap. Hoped to have possession of it to-night." McPherson, however, did not make the most of his opportunity. Upon reaching the gap, he had a relatively clear path to the Western and Atlantic Railroad, Johnston's logistical lifeline, but became nervous about his isolated position and decided not to press forward aggressively toward the railroad at Resaca.[17]

To assist the Army of the Tennessee, on May 9 Sherman directed Thomas to prepare to move the Army of the Cumberland south. Having received a message from McPherson at midmorning that he was "pushing on through Snake Creek Gap" and another in the afternoon that he was "within one mile and a half of Resaca," Hooker instructed Geary to "keep a sharp lookout to-night, as the enemy's communications have been cut." Over the course of the day, however, concern about McPherson's situation grew, and by the time evening arrived, Hooker had received information indicating that the Army of the Tennessee was not in fact at Resaca and from Thomas to "send without delay to-night, one division through Snake Creek Gap" and "hold the other two divisions of your corps in readiness to move in the same direction."[18]

The next day Hooker dispatched Williams's and Butterfield's divisions south in compliance with orders from Thomas, who also instructed him to leave Geary's division where it was until relieved by a division of cavalry. Kilpatrick's troopers and Williams's division reached Snake Creek Gap by the end of the day. Williams then reported to McPherson and received instructions to post two of his brigades at the western entrance to the gap and push one forward to support the Army of the Tennessee in front of Resaca.[19] Although scouts found only scattered Confederate cavalry in his front, McPherson remained nervous that Johnston might fall upon him with overwhelming force. Thus, he decided to continue fortifying his position near Snake Creek Gap, where by the morning of May 13, he had been joined by the rest of Hooker's corps, with Butterfield arriving early on the eleventh and Geary arriving the following day. By then, however, Johnston had abandoned Rocky Face Ridge and fallen back to Resaca, on the night of May 12–13, to establish a strong defensive position.[20]

Although disappointed at McPherson's failure, Sherman immediately directed his forces to move toward Resaca. On May 12 Hooker received directions from Thomas to issue three days' rations and sixty rounds of ammunition to his men and by the following morning "have your corps massed by divisions on the right of the Resaca road at the debouch from General McPherson's entrenchments." He immediately had orders issued in compliance with Thomas's directions and stipulated that when the corps reached the designated position, Williams's division would form its center, with Geary on the left and Butterfield on the right near McPherson's left. As the rest of Sherman's command joined the troops in front of Resaca in the days that followed, Thomas suggested that they make a feint at Resaca and send McPherson's army plus Hooker's corps across the Oostanaula River to turn the Rebel position. Sherman, however, rejected this plan and instead kept his entire army north of the river, facing Resaca.[21]

Following a May 14 assault by elements from the Army of the Ohio that captured some of the enemy's outer works, General Schofield became witness to a scene between Sherman and Hooker that indicated, he later wrote with considerable understatement, "their personal relations were other than the most satisfactory." During the afternoon, Schofield called the army-group commander's attention to a cleared hill that might give him a good view of the Confederate line. By the time Sherman made his way over to the hill, a number of other general officers had joined him, Hooker among them. This attracted the attention of the Confederates, who began firing at the group with artillery. This induced all to leave the area but Hooker and Sherman, less Schofield later suggested because they were brave men, than out of a desire to show up each other. "Striding round the ground," he wrote, "appearing to look at nothing in particular and not conversing with each other ... each waiting for the other to lead off in retreat. After quite a long continuation of this little drama ..., the two great soldiers, as if by some mysterious impulse—for they did not speak a word—simultaneously and slowly strode to the rear, where their horses were held."[22]

Whatever Sherman saw from the hill did not prevent him from positioning his command in such a way that made the unit holding his far left, Maj. Gen. David S. Stanley's division of Howard's corps, vulnerable to an attack on its flank. Late in the afternoon of May 14, Johnston attempted to exploit this by ordering Lt. Gen. John Bell Hood to launch such an assault with his corps. Fortunately, by the time Hood got underway, Howard had already sent a courier to Thomas asking for help. Thomas turned to Hooker and instructed him to send a division to Howard's assistance. Hooker, delighted at the opportunity to get in the fight in a significant way, rode over to Williams's command in such a manner that one of the men knowingly remarked out loud, "Now, you will soon hear from him." Less than a half hour later, Williams's men were moving toward the far left of the Union line, in the words of one man, "on a full run with old Joe Hooker at the head."[23]

Before Hooker could arrive, though, Hood's men slammed into Stanley's position shortly after 5:00 P.M. The overwhelmed Federals quickly surrendered their trenches to the Rebels, who then paused in the face of fire from a single Indiana battery commanded by Capt. Peter Simonson. Just as Hood's men were resuming their attack and appeared ready to overrun Simonson's position, Hooker arrived on the scene. Urged to give the Southerners a taste of "Army of the Potomac fighting," Williams's men then unleashed a ferocious series of volleys that shattered the enemy attack. As Hood's men fell back to their original lines, Hooker itched to follow up Williams's victory but lamented in a message to Thomas's headquarters shortly after midnight that he was unable to do so with only one division on hand.[24]

After the fighting ended, Hooker managed to secure a meeting with Sherman, and shortly thereafter a message was en route to Thomas directing him to "order Hooker and Howard to attack in the morning directly south down upon Resaca." Thomas quickly forwarded the orders to his two subordinates. Hooker then ordered Geary and Butterfield to bring their divisions over to Williams's position north of Resaca. When they arrived, he posted the XX Corps to the left of Howard's corps, with Williams's division on the left, Butterfield's in the center astride the road running north out of Resaca, and Geary's to the right. Schofield's command would support Hooker's left and rear.[25]

By 11:00 A.M. on May 15, Hooker had his men in position and was forming Butterfield's division for the assault against Hood's line. Shortly after 1:00 P.M., Howard began his attack and was greeted with such a fierce fire from the Rebel defenders that it brought the one-armed general's corps to a halt. At around 1:30 Hooker ordered his command forward, with its objective being seizure of what Geary described as "an irregular conglomerate of hills, with spurs running in every direction." If the Federals could get possession of these hills, they would render the Confederate position north of Resaca untenable. Because Williams had been engaged the previous day, Hooker decided to have Geary and Butterfield make the attack with their commands in column for maximum speed and shock effect.[26]

Unfortunately, Geary and Butterfield had to make their charge over thickly wooded, steep, and broken terrain that wreaked havoc on their tightly packed formations. Consequently, except for Brig. Gen. William T. Ward's and Col. John Coburn's brigades of Butterfield's division, which managed to briefly capture a four-gun battery, the Federal attacks lost whatever force their formations were supposed to bring to bear, all in the face of what one of Ward's men declared a "perfect shower of shot, shell, and grape." (Another soldier later recalled with immense satisfaction that when the Federals occupied Resaca a few days later, a letter written by the battery's commander to his family was found that proclaimed "none but Joe Hooker's men would have ... captured his battery.") Thus, the Confederates, holding a position one officer described to his family as "too hot a nest for Yankees at that time," were able to repulse Hooker's attacks. In less than two hours, approximately 1,200 of the 12,000 men Geary and Butterfield had brought to the battlefield were casualties.[27]

Encouraged by his success against Geary and Butterfield, Hood made an attempt to crush the Union left. Hooker, however, had already taken proper defensive precautions, directing Williams to move his division up to a position on a series of hills overlooking the Western and Atlantic Railroad. From there, Williams's men shattered the Confederate attacks with relative ease. "The rascals were evidently astounded," Williams boasted to his daughter a few days later, "and they were tremendously punished."[28]

The night of May 15–16 once again saw the Rebels in retreat. During the battle of May 15, elements from McPherson's army moved around the Confederate left and induced Johnston to fall back toward the town of Cassville in order to preserve his communications. Sherman immediately ordered the rest of his command across the Oostanaula in pursuit, having lost approximately 4,000 casualties in the operations around Resaca.[29]

SHERMAN WASTED LITTLE TIME directing Thomas to get his army moving in pursuit. After taking possession of the Confederate works during the morning of the sixteenth, Hooker assured Thomas's headquarters that he would "push on after them without delay."[30] After crossing the Conasauga River at Fite's Ferry above Resaca, Hooker quickly marched his command, with Geary's division in the lead, to Newton Ferry on the Coosawattee but found the crossing there unusable. Consequently, he moved east a few miles until he reached McClure's Ford and Field's Ferry, where materials were available to construct bridges. The delay this entailed meant that only Geary's infantry could cross the Coosawattee by the end of the day, although Hooker assured Schofield his entire command would be across the following morning. This, however, dashed Sherman's hopes that these forces would be south of the river by nightfall. Schofield, keenly sensitive to the personal friction between Sherman and the XX Corps's commander, made a point that night of making known to his commanding officer his displeasure at this turn of events and who he believed was at fault. Hooker's cause undoubtedly received a boost, however, in Washington when his old friend Dan Sickles, who had been accompanying the XX Corps since the beginning of the campaign, sent a note to Lincoln that same day proclaiming "Hooker's assault yesterday on Hood's intrenched camp, which I was fortunate enough to see . . . will rank among the brilliant achievements of the war."[31]

Unknown to the Federal high command, though, Johnston was at that point putting together a counterstroke that he hoped would redeem Confederate fortunes in Georgia. By falling back from Adairsville to Cassville on two roads, he hoped to induce Sherman to split his command as well. The Confederate commander then hoped to reconcentrate his own army at Cassville while the Federals were still divided and strike an overpowering blow against Sherman's eastern column before the rest of his force could arrive.[32]

Few if any in the Union high command sensed the danger. Like Sherman, most assumed that Johnston would not stop his retreat until he was behind the Etowah River. Hooker managed to get his infantry across the Coosawattee by 10:00 A.M. on the seventeenth but encountered what he described as difficulties "beyond parallel in getting my artillery over." (The effect this had on Schofield's movements prompted another set of complaints from that officer, which led Hooker to reply, "No one can regret the detention more than myself . . . , but artillery can only be crossed with great difficulty and delay," and to suggest that Schofield try instead to "cross . . . [his] corps by the bridges thrown at Resaca" or "send for a pontoon bridge.") As a consequence of these difficulties, Hooker was compelled to go into camp short of where Thomas wanted him to be. Less than two hours after reporting this to army headquarters, Hooker received a response informing him that the Rebels appeared to be in force just outside Adairsville and asking him to "if possible . . . push up a division to-night."[33]

The first evidence Sherman received that Johnston was up to something came on the evening of May 18. That morning Thomas had indeed divided his command, with the IV Corps and the XIV Corps taking the road from Adairsville toward Kingston and the XX Corps marching over Gravelly Plateau toward Kingston and along the road from Adairsville to Cassville—the very route upon which Johnston intended to spring his trap. Hooker promptly complied with orders to have his command on the march at 1:00 P.M., placing Butterfield's division in the lead, followed by Geary's and Williams's commands, and planned at the end of the day to "concentrate my corps within four miles of Kingston."[34]

Shortly after receiving approval of his plan from army headquarters, however, Hooker began receiving troubling information from Butterfield, who at around 3:00 P.M. made contact with the enemy and shortly thereafter was able to identify the force in his front as part of Hood's corps. Shortly after 6:00 P.M. Hooker advised his superiors: "I found myself within about three miles of Cassville, where I was checked by a rebel picket. On my way I captured a rebel soldier just from Cassville, who informed me that since noon to-day [Maj. Gen. W. H. T.] Walker's division had been drawn up in line of battle." Sherman concluded that the general had merely come into contact with a Confederate rear guard, in line with his own assumption that Johnston was in fact at Kingston. Hooker, however, prudently directed his division commanders to issue sixty rounds of ammunition that night and that his ordnance train "be so parked so that if ammunition should be required it can readily be got at."[35]

In the morning of May 19, Butterfield's division resumed its march south. Less than two miles out, the general sent a message to Hooker at 7:30 A.M. reporting that he was encountering "just resistance enough to compel me to advance cautiously and in line." By 1:00 P.M. Butterfield's concern had turned to alarm. Col. James Wood, the commander of his lead brigade, reported that an enemy force had been spotted to the left of the road that seemed much too large to be a mere rear guard. Wood immediately pulled back and began digging in while Butterfield sent two messages to Hooker, reporting: "The enemy came near catching me in a bad position . . . and compelled me to take a defensive position. . . . They are now in my front with two batteries, cavalry, and about twenty regiments of infantry, as counted by those who saw them pass to our right . . . at the double-quick to cut [Wood] off or attack in flank." By 3:00 P.M. Butterfield's anxiety was alleviated by the arrival of Geary's division, which took up a position to his right, and Williams's command, which went into in line to Butterfield's left.[36]

The forces Wood had seen in fact belonged to Hood's corps, which had been positioned east of the road from Adairsville to Cassville so it could pounce on the flank of any Federals who happened to appear in the vicinity. Unfortunately for the Rebels, before Butterfield's command was close enough to fall victim, Johnston's plan had been undone. At midmorning Hood received word of a

Union force advancing toward him from an unexpected direction. This not only led him to cancel the planned attack but also to pull back in order to prevent this unexpected force from getting on his flank and rear.[37]

Not being privy to what was going on in Hood's mind as they took up their positions north of Cassville, Hooker's men watched warily and no doubt with relief as the Confederates withdrew. Hooker then resumed the advance toward Cassville—though with his men in battle line and exercising caution. Finally, his troops reached a point north and west of Cassville where Geary was able to link up with Howard's command. Shortly thereafter, a division from Schofield's command arrived on the scene and took up a position to the left of Hooker's corps. Once his forces were reconcentrated late in the afternoon, Sherman ordered a bombardment of the Confederate line on a ridge on the other side of Cassville that rendered Johnston's position untenable. On the night of May 19–20, Johnston's men left the area and made their way south of the Etowah to new defensive works in the rugged terrain around Allatoona.[38]

SHERMAN SUBSEQUENTLY DECIDED that he would not follow Johnston's retreat directly but would instead attempt a wide turning movement that would take his armies across the Etowah River well west of the railroad. He would then swing around the Army of Tennessee's flank and march his three armies toward Marietta via the crossroads town of Dallas. This, Sherman believed, would compel Johnston to retreat from Allatoona back to Marietta or even across the Chattahoochee River. Hooker's command was to cross the Etowah at Gillem's Bridge, then along with the rest of the Army of the Cumberland, advance directly on Dallas from the north while McPherson swung west to approach the town from that direction. Schofield's job was to reach a position from which his small army could counter any Rebel attempt to make a stab at the Union left and rear.[39]

Late on May 22, army headquarters modified Hooker's orders so that he ended up using a pontoon bridge to cross the Etowah. This did not prevent the general from getting his entire command across the Etowah on the twenty-third, and by the end of the day the XX Corps had reached a point south of Euharlee Creek with little difficulty. Yet the switch in Hooker's crossing site created a problem for Schofield. Delays in the Army of the Ohio's movements caused by this modification first led Schofield to once again write to Sherman to complain: "Understanding from your dispatch of yesterday that you desired General Thomas' army to move first, I have not attempted to interfere with General Hooker's movement. . . . [T]his frequent conflict between General Hooker's orders and mine causes great trouble." The following day Hooker led the Army of the Cumberland's march south, with Brig. Gen. Edward McCook's cavalry division screening its advance, and by nightfall had managed to reach "a little hamlet of five or six log houses" less than ten miles from Dallas known as Burnt Hickory. There, the Federals made camp under what one officer described as a "tremendous storm of thunder, lightning, and rain."[40]

Unfortunately, Johnston picked up evidence of Sherman's intentions almost as soon as the Federal army started moving, and by the morning of May 25 the Confederates had taken up a strong position defending Dallas and a small crossroads just to the east where New Hope Church was located. By doing so, he effectively blocked the road to Marietta.[41] When the Army of the Cumberland resumed its march early on May 25, Hooker's command was once again in the vanguard. Shortly after leaving Burnt Hickory, Geary's lead division reached Owen's Mill on Pumpkinvine Creek around 9:00 A.M. There, Hooker and Geary saw the bridge over the creek ablaze and personally rushed forward with their cavalry escorts to save it. As they began extinguishing the flames, however, they came under fire from an outpost manned by about two dozen Confederates located on a hill on the opposite bank. Hooker responded by ordering a detachment from his escort to ford the creek and drive off the enemy. By the time this had been accomplished, Geary's infantry began arriving at Owen's Mill and went to work repairing the bridge as Thomas arrived on the scene and decided to accompany them the rest of the day. Once the bridge was completed, Geary's division crossed the creek, continuing to set a fast pace that was leaving the rest of the Army of the Cumberland well behind.[42]

Then, shortly after crossing the bridge, Hooker and Geary reached a point where a road leading east that was not on their maps intersected with the one they were taking to Dallas. Surmising that this unknown road also connected to Dallas, Hooker decided to divide his command, with Geary's men taking the new route and the other two divisions staying on the main road. In fact, the former led Geary and Hooker in the direction of New Hope Church, four and a half miles from Dallas, and they soon encountered a considerable force of Rebel skirmishers. They managed to drive them back and capture a few, from whom they learned that they were heading toward New Hope Church and a position occupied by Hood's corps. Fearing an attack on Geary's isolated division, Hooker halted its march and directed his subordinate to push forward skirmishers aggressively, as Geary later wrote, "to deceive the enemy as to our weakness by a show of strength." The rest of the division deployed into line on a ridge and constructed log barricades. Hooker also dispatched messengers to Williams and Butterfield, who at that point were less than two miles from Dallas, directing them to move to Geary's assistance. Fortunately for Hooker, Hood had no intention of attacking at that time. By late afternoon, Williams's and Butterfield's divisions had arrived on the scene, found Geary's men unmolested, and took up positions facing the Rebels.[43]

As this was going on, a staff officer who had gone to army-group headquarters with a report on Hooker's situation found Sherman in a testy mood. "I don't see what they are waiting for in front now," the commanding general complained after scribbling a note for the officer to take to Thomas, "there haven't been twenty rebels there to-day." Shortly thereafter, Hooker learned that Sherman wanted him to "attack violently and secure the position at New Hope Church." Although dubious as to the prospects for a successful attack, he moved to comply with Sherman's orders. He reshuffled his divisions, and as Williams placed his command in the lead, Hooker told him to "push forward and drive the enemy until I found out his force or chased him away."[44]

With Butterfield's division posted to the left, Williams's on the right, and Geary's behind Williams, Hooker directed all three of his subordinates to, as they had at Resaca, form their commands into columns for the attack. When the First Division stepped off to begin the assault shortly after 5:00 P.M., Hooker personally followed the first of its three brigade lines forward to the cheers of his men. "The whole line for a mile or more took it up," a staff officer later recalled, "and drowned the firing with their huzzas." Things initially went well. Williams covered a little over a mile of relatively level but thickly forested ground in good order and easily drove back the Rebel skirmishers. Upon reaching the base of the ridge on which Hood's main line was posted, however, the Federals came under a blistering fire that forced them to halt. As the men recovered from the initial shock of what Williams described as "shot, shell, and canister in murderous volleys" and began exchanging fire with the well-entrenched Confederates, the skies opened up and a terrific thunderstorm began with, wrote one man, "the thunder of heaven's artillery combined with that of man's murderous invention." Recognizing the futility of continuing his attack, Hooker pulled the First Division back. He then consoled Williams by telling him that his advance had been "the most magnificent sight of the war ... [and he had] never seen anything so splendid." Always conscious of the importance of good publicity, Hooker also located an artist from *Harper's Weekly*, who was accompanying the army, and talked him into doing a sketch of Williams's attack.[45]

Word quickly made the rounds within the army that Hooker's encounter with Sherman after what became known as the Battle of New Hope Church was less congenial. As if the repulse of his attack and the loss of more than 650 good men were not enough to blacken his mood that night, Hooker found himself subjected to a lecture from Sherman about how he had waited too long before striking. Unable to restrain himself, Hooker—to the delight of his men when the story made its way around camp—sarcastically conceded that perhaps his commander was right; the delay, he sneered, might have allowed Hood to receive all of fifty more men to assist in the afternoon's battle.[46]

THE DAYS THAT FOLLOWED brought little opportunity for Hooker and his command to do much more than dig and strengthen their trenches, menace the Confederates in their front (Geary described it as a "general daily routine of artillery practice and sharpshooting"), and endure almost daily rains. Finally, after other Federal units had fought indecisive engagements at Pickett's Mill and Dallas, during the first week of June, Sherman abandoned a position that many of his men had come to refer to as the "Hell Hole" by shifting to the left until his forces were once again on the Western and Atlantic Railroad.[47] On June 1 Hooker extracted his three divisions from in front of New Hope Church, moved around the rest of the army, and by the fourth had taken up positions near Pickett's Mill and Allatoona Creek. By June 6 Sherman was once again on the railroad in the vicinity of Acworth; Hooker, despite being furnished with an incorrect map of the area that forced Butterfield to perform measurements of lots and land in order to calculate distances, managed to move his command to a position near the intersection of the Sandtown Road and the Burnt Hickory and Marietta Roads. The XX Corps would occupy this position until the morning of the tenth, by which time the Confederates had also moved back to the railroad and taken up a strong defensive position on a series of hills north of Marietta.[48]

After giving his men a few days to rest and his logisticians a chance to get his railway supply line in order, Sherman resumed his offensive on June 10.

With McPherson's army on the left, Thomas's in the center, and Schofield's on the right, Sherman advanced southward astride the railroad. For once, Hooker's command would not find itself in the lead but instead found itself trailing the other two corps in the Army of the Cumberland.[49]

It did not take long for Sherman, who initially thought the Confederates might have fallen back across the Chattahoochee, to learn from his cavalry that Johnston in fact was posted in a formidable line north of Marietta. The Federal advance was enough, however, to induce the Confederate commander to pull back from a series of advanced posts anchored on Pine Mountain and Lost Mountain during the night of June 15–16 to a strong position anchored on Kennesaw Mountain. During these operations, Hooker's command engaged in almost constant skirmishing with the enemy as they probed their lines and pursued them as they fell back toward Kennesaw Mountain. The general made frequent appearances on the front line throughout these operations, "attended by a single orderly," one man informed his family, "and a calm, placid look is inevitable to him. When he passes the troops he always smiles and looks upon them as a father . . . , and it does one's soul good to hear the rousing cheers which greet him. You never saw him but if you get a likeness of George Washington you will have a better picture of Hooker than any I have seen."[50]

The exception to the relatively low-intensity character of the corps's operations came on the fifteenth. In compliance with orders from army-group headquarters calling for an attempt to "break the enemy's center," Hooker personally directed Geary to make a spirited but ill-advised attack against a strong enemy position on Pine Mountain that afternoon. Meanwhile, a fierce but likewise indecisive fight involving Ward's brigade and an enemy force that Butterfield described as "strong and spiteful" took place near Gilgal Church. In the days that followed, the XX Corps returned to their ongoing skirmishing with the Confederates, which Hooker watched closely enough to feel competent to issue directions to a division commander to "adopt some plan, and build some protection for your sharpshooters . . . , in each case by cutting three logs about eight feet and a half long, eighteen inches in diameter, and placing them in the ground upright like a stockade, with an aperture in the center to fire through."[51]

Despite the progress his army made in May and early June, Sherman was frustrated. "We have had an immense quantity of rain, from June 2 to 14," he informed Grant on the eighteenth, "and now it is raining as though it had no intention ever to stop." He was less bothered with the weather, though, than with Thomas's army. "My chief source of trouble," he complained to Grant, "is with the Army of the Cumberland, which is awful slow. A fresh furrow in a ploughed field will stop the whole column and all begin to intrench. I have again and again tried to impress on Thomas that we must assail and not defend . . . , yet it seems the whole Army of the Cumberland is so habituated to be on the defensive that, from its commander down to its lowest private, I cannot get it out of their heads." Sherman then specifically complained about the delay in launching the attack at New Hope Church on May 25, which he believed threw away one of those "splendid opportunities which never recur in War."[52]

FINALLY, ON JUNE 22, the sun came out, and Sherman felt ready to resume offensive operations. Two days earlier Thomas had repositioned Howard's IV Corps so it would take over Hooker's portion of the line and thus enable the XX Corps to "operate more strongly against the enemy's left flank, and . . . cooperate with and support General Schofield's army, which was nearly two miles distant on the Sandtown road." With this having been accomplished, Sherman decided to pushed Thomas's and Schofield's armies toward Marietta in an attempt to operate against Johnston's left. Commanding the corps on Thomas's right, Hooker was to spearhead the advance, with the Army of the Ohio supporting his right. "If he can get possession of the ground up to Mrs. Kolb's," Sherman advised Thomas, "I wish him to do so."[53]

Hooker directed Williams to advance toward Kolb's Farm near the intersection of the Powder Springs–Marietta Road and the Macland Road. To the First Division's left, Geary pushed forward, with orders from Hooker to drive "away the rebels from some commanding heights about a mile in advance of my center." Once Geary had done this, Hooker anticipated it would allow him to bring up Butterfield's Third Division on the Second Division's left. Meanwhile to the south, Schofield advanced along the Powder Springs–Marietta Road to connect with and cover Hooker's right. At first the advance went well. Hooker's men drove off the skirmishers they encountered with little difficulty, and after reaching the top of what he described as "an important and commanding ridge," Geary halted his command and began digging in. Hooker rode up to the ridge at this time and directed his division commander "to hold the place at every hazard."[54]

Shortly thereafter, Geary's men began to receive artillery fire from the Rebels. Hooker directed Butterfield to move his division forward and form on the

Second Division's left, while by 4:00 P.M. Williams held a position to the right of Geary that enabled him to connect with the Army of the Ohio. Meanwhile, Hooker learned that Johnston had posted two corps just up the Powder Springs–Marietta Road with orders to attack. He immediately ordered all of his men to "throw up breastworks without delay," as did Schofield. From his headquarters at the Kolb house, Hooker also dispatched two messages to Thomas, reporting, "I desire that Geary's and Butterfield's divisions may be relieved by divisions from other corps, in order that my line may be sufficiently contracted to render it safe."[55]

As Hooker's message made its way to Thomas, two regiments that had been sent forward to reconnoiter the dense woods in front of Williams and Schofield sent back reports confirming the presence of a large Confederate force just to the east. This induced Hooker to send another message to Thomas at 4:00 P.M.: "Testimony of prisoners represent that the whole rebel army lies between my immediate front and Marietta and that they are marching in this direction. General Schofield has one division here, and all are at work making their defensive arrangements. My line is too long to make an obstinate defense. In my judgment, Butterfield's and Geary's divisions should be relieved." Upon receiving this message, Thomas rushed over to Hooker's position but saw little evidence to support his subordinate's assessment of the situation. Consequently, he denied the request for assistance at that moment, although he did have an aide say that Howard's and Palmer's corps might be moved toward the XX corps "tomorrow morning, if necessary."[56]

In fact, the three divisions of Hood's corps were in Hooker's front, and their commander had aggressive intentions. About the time Thomas's rejection of Hooker's request left Army of the Cumberland headquarters, the ever-combative Hood, in Hooker's words, "commenced throwing his masses forward with great violence on our right and center." Aided by the thick forest, Col. George Gallup's 14th Kentucky, one of the two regiments Hooker and Schofield had posted ahead of their main lines, managed to put up such a fierce fight, supported by some of Schofield's artillery, that the attack south of the road achieved nothing. On the other side of the road, however, the Confederates surged across relatively open terrain and had an easier time. As what General Williams called "the peculiar yell of the rebel mass" ripped through the air, the Confederates drove back the lone New York regiment posted in front of this section of Hooker's line. Then, however, Union artillery fire ripped into the enemy front and right, tearing huge holes into the Rebel formations, followed by ferocious volleys from Williams's infantry. Together they shattered the attack so decisively that, the division commander later wrote, "after the first half-hour the men considered the whole affair great sport. They would call out to the Rebels... 'What do you think of Joe Hooker's Iron Clads?'" By the time the fighting ended that night, Hooker's men, at a cost of less than 250 casualties, had inflicted over 1,500 on the Rebels, which has inspired historian Albert Castel to proclaim the engagement at Kolb's Farm "more a one-sided slaughter than... a battle."[57]

At midnight Hooker sent a message to Thomas boasting that the enemy had been "spiritedly repulsed, sometimes with his columns hopelessly broken and demoralized. Our artillery did splendid execution among them.... The conduct of my troops throughout the day was sublime." The confidence of the men soared. "Hooker is *the* commander," one soldier proclaimed to a friend two days later. "I wish you could see him when a fight is underway. His enthusiasm is enough in itself to inspire any man."[58]

Casting a significant shadow over the events of June 22 for "*the* commander," however, was yet another reminder of just how low his standing was with Sherman. At the heart of it was an exchange of messages between Hooker and his superiors at the beginning of the fight at Kolb's Farm. At the time, Sherman was about two miles away from the XX Corps's position, and when the sound of artillery fire reached him, he sent a signal message to Hooker: "How are you getting along. Near what house are you?" A few hours later, after the fight was over, he received a reply from Hooker, sent almost immediately upon receipt of Sherman's initial inquiry, that made no mention of Schofield's command: "We have repulsed two heavy attacks and feel confident, our only apprehension being our extreme right flank. Three entire corps are in front of us." Sherman immediately responded: "Schofield was ordered this morning to be on the Powder Springs and Marietta road in close support of your right. Is this not the case? There cannot be three corps in your front. Johnston has but three corps, and I know from personal inspection that a full proportion is now and has been all day on his right and center." Shortly thereafter, Thomas assured Sherman that Schofield was in fact with Hooker and that they had enough force to handle the Confederates. Thomas did not provide him with any sense of exactly who those Rebels were, though, or how many there were in front of Hooker and Schofield. He did confide to Sherman that when "Hooker reported he had the whole rebel army in his front, . . . I thought at the time he was stampeded." Finally, at around midnight, the group commander received a message from Schofield describing the fight at Kolb's Farm and reporting that only Hood's corps had been engaged there.[59]

The next morning Sherman made his way over to the battlefield. Ignoring the fact that he had initiated their direct correspondence the previous afternoon, he chastised Hooker for bypassing Thomas in responding directly to the army-group commander's initial message. Sherman then accused him of deliberately insulting Schofield by ignoring the presence of the Army of the Ohio when he expressed apprehension for "our extreme right flank"—ignoring the fact that Hooker had not expressed concern over *his* right flank but "*our extreme* right flank," meaning the entire army group's. (Schofield later conceded that there could be little misunderstanding of Hooker's message on this point.) Sherman then berated the general for falsely claiming that he was facing all three of Johnston's corps the previous day, even though there was no evidence that Hooker—although manifestly wrong in his assessment of the situation—had deliberately misread the confusing intelligence he received in the course of the day or was in anyway insincere in his reports.[60]

One of Thomas's staff officers later declared that this episode marked the beginning of the "open feud which culminated in Hooker's refusal to serve longer under Sherman." So far in the campaign, the XX Corps had seen the heaviest fighting of any corps (indeed, by late June Geary was expressing concern that "if we keep on, the Division will soon '*be expended on the field of honor*'"), but that seemed to count for nothing with Sherman. Nor did it seem to matter that, in the eyes of that same staff officer, who was in daily contact with Hooker, he "commanded his corps with an energy, courage, vigilance, and success unsurpassed by any commander in the field. . . . [N]o more subordinate or obedient officers served in this army. No matter how unwelcome an order he received or the time he received it, he was the only one who invariably obeyed it promptly, cheerfully, and ungrudgingly."[61]

Hooker's conduct in respect to Sherman, though, was much less commendable than this officer recognized. By the second week of June, the general was openly criticizing Sherman in front of his staff and subordinates. Certainly, Sherman's next big move after Kolb's Farm, an ill-conceived frontal assault on June 27 against a near-impregnable Confederate position on Kennesaw Mountain, did nothing to boost his standing in the eyes of the XX Corps's commander. ("Experimental slaughter" was how one of Hooker's staff officers, undoubtedly echoing the sentiments of his chief at the time, later characterized Sherman's conduct of the battle.) Then, as if Hooker's mood could not get any blacker, on June 29 he lost the services of his closest friend in the army when what Williams described as a "disgusted and tired" Butterfield successfully petitioned for relief from command of his division for health reasons.[62]

UNION OPERATIONS AROUND Kennesaw Mountain ended when elements from the Army of the Ohio began sliding to the west and south. When evidence of this reached Johnston, who realized that the Federals would soon be closer to the Chattahoochee than he was, he ordered a retreat on the night of July 2–3.[63] Both Sherman and Thomas anticipated such a move, and as a consequence the latter issued orders on July 2 to Hooker to "feel him to-night and in the morning at some point in front of your line for the purpose of ascertaining his intentions, and be prepared at daylight to follow him up should he have moved." Thus, when Hooker informed Thomas early on the third that the Confederates had abandoned his front, both Thomas and Sherman were ready to push forward. By the time Thomas informed Sherman at 5:00 A.M. that the enemy was gone, Hooker already had his men on the march toward the Chattahoochee, with Williams's division on the left and Butterfield's former division, now commanded by Brig. Gen. William T. Ward, advancing on the main Powder Springs road, with Geary's command on its right. As the corps passed over the abandoned enemy works, "our hearts were filled with gladness that the foe had been compelled to retire," as one man wrote his family. "As we marched through the awful slaughter pens he had prepared for us, it was enough to appall the bravest.... [W]hat joy our hearts thrilled as we marched through them without the firing of a gun."[64]

Through the morning of July 3, Hooker pushed forward to Marietta, where Thomas concentrated his army around midmorning before continuing the advance, with Hooker's XX Corps on the right, Palmer's XIV Corps in the center along the railroad, and Howard's IV Corps on the left. In Hooker's command Geary continued to move on the right, while Williams's division followed behind Ward on the Turner's Ferry Road. A few miles south of Marietta, however, the Army of the Cumberland began to encounter stiffer resistance than Sherman anticipated, as to his surprise Johnston had taken up a strong, fortified position on the north side of the Chattahoochee. Upon receiving word that the Rebels had constructed formidable works a short distance away, all three of Thomas's corps commanders issued orders directing their units to halt and form into line.[65]

To Hooker's consternation, however, his lead division, with an inebriated Ward at its head, continued marching until they were nearly a mile out in front of the rest of the Army of the Cumberland. Before this resulted in catastrophe, a concerned Hooker reached Ward to find out what the problem was. "Gen. what ails you?" he asked his subordinate, "are you drunk, or are you crazy, or are you fool; what does ail you[?]" Ward was too intoxicated to muster a response and could only, one witness recalled, "leer at him, with his drunken, half shut eyes." After telling Ward that his actions were "the most foolish thing he had ever heard of," Hooker directed Col. John Coburn to take direction of the division "and have his command lie down and keep perfectly still until he could bring up the other divisions to support him." He then instructed Geary and Williams to hurry forward and directed Coburn to push skirmishers forward close to the enemy's advanced works. These actions, one appreciative man in Ward's command wrote two days later, "probably saved [the division] from utter annihilation. . . . [I]f the rebels had not adhered to the tactics they seem to have adopted in this campaign of fighting entirely on the defensive . . . , they might have captured the whole division." By 4:00 P.M., Geary's and Williams's men had arrived and established a solid connection with the corps to the left before the Second Division received directions to swing south to form on the corps's right.[66]

The following day, the Fourth of July, Sherman's command continued moving toward the Chattahoochee, passing over "miles & miles of breastworks." The Federals did not go far before they determined that Johnston had no intention at that point of crossing the river and had posted his army in what Sherman declared "the best line of field intrenchments I have ever seen." In line with orders from corps headquarters to continue pressing the enemy on July 5, that afternoon several of Hooker men reached a ridge from where they were able to catch a clear view of Atlanta. "The sight of the city," Geary later wrote, "gave great encouragement to my men, who, seeing the prize which was to crown the campaign, looked cheerfully forward to its speedy possession."[67]

Declining to attack the Confederates directly, Sherman sent Schofield up the Chattahoochee in an effort to turn Johnston's right. Meanwhile, Hooker received orders to push across Nickajack Creek, hold his force in a concealed position from the enemy, keep an eye on the enemy's pickets, and keep closed up with the rest of the Army of the Cumberland. On July 8 Schofield found an unguarded crossing and began pushing across the river. Johnston had little choice but to fall back across the Chattahoochee, and early on the morning of the tenth, Hooker's command occupied the abandoned works. This retreat, and the lack of any evidence that Johnston had any satisfactory plan to make a fight for Atlanta, was too much for Pres. Jefferson Davis. On July 17 he issued orders relieving the general from command and appointing Hood as his replacement.[68]

Hooker understood as well as anyone that Hood was a bold and determined fighter. In three of the significant engagements Hooker's corps had fought in since May—Resaca, New Hope Church, and Kolb's Farm—it had been Hood's corps they had faced. In two of these cases Hood had attacked, and it could easily be surmised that the change in command presaged a more aggressive defense of Atlanta. It is also hard to miss some of the parallels between Hood's situation now and Hooker's a year and a half earlier. They were each a corps commander who had risen through the ranks due to a reputation for aggressiveness, used political connections to undermine his superior, and then had been placed in independent command for the first time. Would Hood falter when the crunch came as some said Hooker had at Chancellorsville? The answer would come soon enough.

As Davis sorted out the command situation in his Army of Tennessee, Sherman gave his men a few days' rest along the banks of the Chattahoochee. During this time, Williams took the time to boast in a letter home that during the campaign, "our corps has had the fighting share. It seems to me we are always in advance.... When we came from the Potomac, the troops here called us the 'paper collar troops.' Now they call us the 'iron clads.'" For his commander, Williams expressed surprising affection: "He is indeed a strange man, but the men like him as he is always seen when a fight is on.... In truth, the impetuous Joseph, surnamed Hooker, hates to be left behind—is restless, prompt, sometimes impatient, and always 'Fighting Joe.'" A few weeks earlier, an officer in the Third Division had expressed his sentiments in even more enthusiastic terms. "I have almost," he informed his family, "fell in love with 'Old Joe.'"[69]

AFTER A FEW DAYS' REST, Sherman resumed his offensive. He pushed McPherson's and Schofield's armies across the river far out to the left in an attempt to reach and cut the Georgia Railroad. Meanwhile, Thomas's Army of the Cumberland moved along a more direct route from the Chattahoochee toward Atlanta.⁷⁰ On July 17 Hooker led his "iron clads" across the river at Pace's Ferry. They pushed across Nancy's Creek the following day and moved toward Buckhead, after which they took up a position with Palmer's corps to their right and Howard's to their left. At daylight on the nineteenth, the troops moved toward the northern bank of Peachtree Creek in compliance with Sherman's desire that Thomas "press down from the north on Atlanta, holding in strength the line of Peach Tree, but crossing and threatening the enemy at all accessible points." Then, learning skirmishers from the XIV Corps were "hotly engaged," Hooker rushed Geary's division forward to the hills overlooking the creek. He personally supervised the posting of artillery to cover a forced crossing to seize high ground on the opposite bank. Under cover of the guns and a heavy infantry force, the pioneer corps proceeded to construct bridges, which enabled the Second Division to push across the creek and fortify a tête-de-point at the crossing.⁷¹

Meanwhile, Hood learned a gap had opened up between the right of the Army of the Ohio and the Army of the Cumberland. To exploit the situation, Hood decided to let Thomas's men cross Peachtree Creek on July 20, after which he would move into the gap to strike an overpowering blow against their left and drive the Army of the Cumberland into the cul-de-sac formed by the juncture of Peachtree Creek and the Chattahoochee River. Unknown to Hood, on July 19 Sherman, out of concern for Schofield and McPherson, enhanced the prospects for a successful Confederate attack by ordering Thomas to move Howard's IV Corps farther to the left in an attempt to close the gap between the Armies of the Cumberland and Ohio.⁷²

On the morning of July 20, Thomas pushed the rest of Hooker's and Palmer's corps across Peachtree Creek. After the XIV Corps was across, it advanced a mile from the creek and began entrenching, while Hooker moved Williams's division across. After passing through Geary's position, the First Division moved off to the right along a farm road. As this was going on, Hooker directed Ward, whose division crossed the creek at Peachtree Road, to move up to secure the Second Division's left and fill a gap between Howard's corps and Brig. Gen. John Newton's division, which Thomas had held back from Howard's command, which was also across Peachtree Creek. At 10:30 A.M. Thomas, with Hooker at his side, directed Newton to "prepare your command for an advance, and move forward in conjunction with General Hooker's troops." About that time, Geary's men had already begun an advance that would carry them forward about three-quarters of a mile to a ridge along which ran the Collier Road. There they halted while, to their left on the other side of a tributary of Peachtree Creek known as Early's Creek, Newton also reached the ridge, where he halted and directed his troops to fortify their position.[73]

As Newton and Geary advanced, they learned from Confederate prisoners that most, if not all, of Hood's army was in fact nearby and poised to strike. Hooker immediately directed Geary to gather more information and instructed his other two division commanders to push forward skirmishers as quickly as possible in order to fill the gaps between Geary's position and Newton's and Palmer's commands. While awaiting the arrival of the rest of the XX Corps, Geary deployed Col. Charles Candy's and Col. Patrick Jones's brigades, backed by artillery and behind breastworks, on Collier Road ridge while sending a New Jersey regiment a few hundred yards forward as an advanced post. Due to the terrain, Palmer and the commander of his lead division had a hard time seeing what Hooker was doing and consequently spent part of the early afternoon anxiously corresponding with Army of the Cumberland headquarters. This impelled Thomas to inform Hooker; "Palmer reports that he is waiting for your troops to advance before he can move. If this report is correct I wish you to push forward your command at once." At 3:30 P.M. Hooker sharply replied that his lines were in fact in contact with the left of the XIV Corps and that "Palmer can scarcely understand where my line is—or his own, if he makes that statement." In fact, Williams and Ward had not finished moving forward to fill the gaps between Geary and Newton and Palmer. They still had not done so when, at around 4:00 P.M., the Confederates launched a massive attack to open the Battle of Peachtree Creek.[74]

Despite the problematic condition of the Union line, Hood's counterstrike at Peachtree Creek, made en echelon from east to west, fell far short of achieving the Confederate commander's ambitious objectives. From behind their fortifications, Newton's men were able to fight off determined assaults against their front and both flanks. The next echelon of Rebels advanced directly toward the section of the Collier Road ridge between Newton's and Geary's positions. Upon reaching the ridge, they encountered only a two-regiment skirmish line that Ward had pushed forward in an attempt to connect the two divisions' lines. Hood's men drove the Federal skirmishers back but were brought to a halt when the rest of Ward's troops arrived on the scene. "Meeting my line of battle," Ward later wrote, "seemed to completely addle their brains. Their first line broke, mixing up with the second line; they were now in the wildest confusion, firing in all directions, some endeavoring to get away, some undecided what to do, others rushing into our lines." "Now commenced an awful scene," one man informed his family, "the rebels ran in confused masses from us and the very heavens seemed to tremble at the terrible fire we poured into them." The Confederates attempted to rally, but it was no use. As they fled, Ward moved up, connected his flanks with Newton and Geary, and began fortifying his position on the ridge. "I had witnessed the first field fight of the campaign—the only one in which neither party had the shelter of breastworks," one of Ward's men proclaimed afterward, "and I think it must prove to Mr. Hood that the Yankees can fight as well in the field as in breastworks. We only hope he will continue these tactics."[75]

Meanwhile, a brigade of Alabamians and Louisianans overwhelmed Geary's advanced position and began maneuvering against his right. "The appearance of the enemy as they charged upon our front . . . was magnificent," he later wrote. "Pouring out from the woods they advanced in immense brown and gray masses (not lines) with flags and banners, many of them new and beautiful. . . . Rarely has such a sight been presented in battle." Geary's men put up a fierce resistance, but the power of the assault and the fact that it threatened to overlap their flanks quickly aroused intense anxiety. "I was very blue," one man later confessed, "it seemed to me that the day was lost." Then, however, Hooker himself arrived on the ridge with Geary's reserve brigade, "magnificent in appearance, as always, mounted on a splendid horse, looking, as he was, the beau ideal of the soldier of the olden type." "Boys," he told the troops, "I guess we will stop here." Hooker personally rallied them and, as the soldier's account continued, "stop there we did, and reformed and went back with him." Within a few minutes, whatever prospects existed for a Confederate victory on Geary's front were gone.[76]

As Newton, Ward, and Geary became hotly engaged, Williams moved his command forward to take up a position on the Second Division's right. With one brigade on each side of the Howell Mill Road, Williams's men managed to reach their designated position and waited until the Rebels were nearly upon them before unleashing a fierce volley of musketry. A bitter fight at short range exploded in which the Confederate ranks were subjected to brutal Union artillery fire and the determined resistance of the Federal infantry. "Not a regiment was broken or shaken," Williams later crowed. "I cannot too strongly praise the conduct of my division on this occasion." When night fell, Hooker's line remained unbroken, but it had taken nearly 1,700 casualties to sustain it.[77]

Hooker was understandably proud that his corps had put in yet another fine performance, and the following morning he received a warm reception from the men as he rode among them. "Oh, it would have done you good to see the boys cheer him," one soldier informed his family. "His face looked just like a sunbeam. . . . We gave him cheer after cheer and it was carried from regt. to regt. all along the line." When asked where the Confederates he had fought were now, an eminently satisfied Hooker reportedly replied, "some of them were in hell, the rest back in Atlanta." That the events of July 20 had done nothing to bolster the XX Corps's standing or his in the eyes of the army-group commander became evident, however, when Sherman paid a visit to Hooker's headquarters that same day. Upon the general's arrival, Hooker, in the words of one of Thomas's staff officers, "spoke with proper pride of what his men had done, and of his heavy losses in the battle." Sherman expressed his appreciation for the XX Corps's service by dismissively remarking, "Oh, most of 'em will be back in a day or two."[78]

For his part, by the time the Federals reached the Chattahoochee, Hooker was regularly expressing disdain for Sherman and his conduct of the campaign to almost anyone who would listen. Indeed, he was so outspoken that Daniel Butterfield had felt compelled on June 12 to send his friend a letter begging him to exercise restraint in how he talked about Sherman and the other army commanders. "You should not," he warned,

> speak in the presence of others as you did . . . to-day, regarding General Sherman and his operations. You can ill afford to have your proud record as a soldier tarnished with the statement that notwithstanding your vigorous and earnest compliance with all orders, your hard fighting under any and all circumstances, that the weight of your opinions and criticisms, openly expressed to your subordinates, tended to impair confidence in your commanders. . . . I know how hard it is for you to conceal your honest opinions. Your frankness and candor will out with it. These opinions travel as "Hooker's opinions." Your own Staff are impregnated with them, and you will be accused in future by any officer serving under you who may fall under your censure, with verbal insubordination. . . . Understand me, I do not say that your remarks are not justifiable, so far as truthful expression of hon-

est opinion goes, but as carrying weight and repetition among men of lesser capacity, they tend to injure you; they are impolitic; you never were, nor never will be a politic man—of that I am well aware—but you must be more guarded.[79]

There was no way the situation could continue. Hooker, who had seen his own effectiveness as commander of the Army of the Potomac undermined by grousing subordinates, should have known this better than anyone. But he simply could not restrain himself. Nor was Sherman going to extend an olive branch to a subordinate for whom he had nothing but contempt. "From the beginning," one officer later wrote, "General Sherman had shown unrelenting prejudice against [Hooker]; had listened willfully to every piece of gossip about him; had spoken slightingly and sneeringly of his work; and, in every way, done what he could to belittle his service."[80] Not surprisingly, when the opportunity came to provoke a final confrontation, Sherman took full advantage of it.

It came less than a week after Peachtree Creek. On July 22 Hooker's corps and the rest of the Army of the Cumberland pushed forward to occupy the Confederate outer works in order to get close enough to use artillery against Atlanta and keep up the pressure against the Confederates. Sensing the Confederates had only a rear guard standing between him and the town, an eminently sanguine Hooker had one of his staff officers issue an order to the men of the XX Corps. The order noted that the general believed the Rebels would probably abandon Atlanta that evening and proclaimed that it "will be a great compliment to the Twentieth Corps to have it said that it was the first to enter Atlanta."[81]

That same day, however, Hood made clear the fight was anything but over by launching attacks on Union forces north and east of Atlanta. The Federals repulsed them, but in the midst of the fighting, McPherson was killed. Command immediately devolved upon the Army of the Tennessee's senior corps commander, Maj. Gen. John A. Logan, but Sherman did not want a political general like Logan in command of an army. On the basis of seniority, rank, experience, and service in the campaign so far, the obvious alternative was Hooker. Certainly, Hooker believed this to be the case, as did a newspaper correspondent who was accompanying the XX Corps and advised his readers that the question as to who would succeed McPherson was "already mooted.... Hooker is the ranking officer in Sherman's army, and could best fill the vacancy." The only question, as he saw it, was if the general would bring his devoted corps with him to the new command.[82]

Sherman, however, was not about to let the matter of seniority outweigh his intense disdain for Hooker. Shortly after McPherson's death, he asked Howard if he would like command of the Army of the Tennessee. Years later Howard recalled objecting to this offer: "I have a good corps and am satisfied, and as General Hooker is senior to me in rank he might be deeply offended." Sherman made it plain that he did not care. "Hooker has not the moral qualities that I want," he declared, "not those adequate to the command; but if you don't want promotion, there are plenty who do." On July 24 Sherman notified Washington of his wishes, and two days later Howard formally assumed command of the Army of the Tennessee.[83]

If Sherman was hoping to provoke Hooker, he could not have made a better choice to replace McPherson than Howard, whom Hooker later declared "was always a woman among troops. If he was not born in petticoats, he ought to have been." Junior to Hooker in age, experience, and rank, Howard had done little to indicate that he was capable of commanding an army effectively. Moreover, Hooker, with no little justification, placed much of the fault for his defeat at Chancellorsville on the general's failure to heed direct warnings about a potential attack against his position on May 2, 1863. This episode, which Hooker later proclaimed the inevitable result of Howard's "imbecility and want of soldiership," gave the Confederates the opportunity to launch a decisive attack that helped turn what might have been a Union victory into a humiliating defeat.[84] It would have taken an exceptionally high degree of modesty and self-control for Hooker not to object to Sherman's decision. Of course, these were not qualities for which he was noted. To the surprise of almost no one, upon learning of the appointment, Hooker wrote to Thomas to demand relief from duty under Sherman's command. "Justice and self-respect alike," he declared with understandable indignation, "require my removal from an army in which rank and service are ignored."[85]

"Hooker is offended because he thinks he is entitled to the command," an evidently satisfied Sherman informed Washington. "I must be honest and say he is not qualified or suited to it. He talks of quitting. . . . I shall not object." Sherman moved with manifest delight on July 27 to process Hooker's application for relief from duty and authorization to report to Washington, explicitly directing Thomas to "make Hooker resign his post as commander of the Twentieth Corps, that he cannot claim it and occasion delay in filling the vacancy." That same day he asked Washington to order Maj. Gen. Henry Slocum, who had developed an intense hatred for Hooker during earlier service under his command (which was warmly reciprocated), to Georgia to take command of the XX Corps.[86] "Hooker was a fool," Sherman gleefully wrote to Halleck a few weeks later. "Had he staid a couple of weeks he could have marched into Atlanta and claimed all the honors." "Hooker was offended because he was not chosen to succeed McPherson," Sherman later declared in his memoirs, "but his chances were not even considered; indeed, . . . I did feel a sense of relief when he left." For his part, when asked by a reporter to comment on Sherman's memoirs in 1875, Hooker contemptuously replied that he had "no taste for responding to Gen. Sherman's slanders" and that he "had rather be among those maligned by the *Memoirs* than among those commended."[87]

On July 28 Hooker bid farewell to the XX Corps. He thanked the men for their service and told his officers that his decision to leave was motivated by insults and slights by higher ups against him personally and the corps he commanded. This, he told them, he could no longer abide, for he had become greatly attached to the corps and appreciated its hard service throughout the campaign. Indeed, by the time the Atlanta Campaign was over, the XX Corps would count more than 7,400 members dead, wounded, or missing, more than any of the other Federal corps that participated in the campaign.[88]

After speaking to his men, Hooker reviewed the XX Corps for the last time. "Cheers could not keep down the tears," a Massachusetts soldier later recalled, "bronzed old veterans of the corps wept like children; few eyes were dry." "Old Joe has left," another soldier declared afterward, "we are mourning his loss greatly. . . . He was in my opinion the best general in this department and jealousy made Sherman and Thomas use him so that he could not stay under them and he asked to be relieved. Well, this we cannot help, but our best wishes will ever attend the dear old man. . . . [T]he soldiers, who fight battles will always love him." "He was received with great enthusiasm, though any noisy demonstration was forbidden as it would attract the enemy's fire," wrote another of the final review, who proclaimed that although rumored to be "almost a drunkard . . . , he is unquestionably a superior Corps commander, his troops have the most unbounded confidence in him and all are sorry to part with him."[89] "Uncle Joe Hooker has left us," another man wrote, "never has the loss of a Comdr cast such a gloom over troops as now hang over the XX Corps." "If you would write truthful history," one officer declared several years later, "don't go to a bureau clerk in Washington to find out if we, who served at the front, ever lost confidence in Hooker.... [A]sk any of the Twentieth Corps men, who, with sorrowful faces and moistened eyes bade him farewell ... under the walls of Atlanta." Hooker's departure was "much to the regret of the whole division," Williams advised his family a few weeks later. "Hooker has certainly been a superior corps commander ... full of energy, always courteous and pleasant, and has a great faculty of winning the confidence and regard of all ranks. It was a blue day when he left us."[90]

THE REGRETS EXPRESSED by the men of the XX Corps were certainly understandable. During the months he commanded them, Joseph Hooker demonstrated beyond any doubt that he was a brave fighter, capable tactician, and first-rate leader of men. Indeed, Albert Castel, author of the foremost modern study of the Atlanta Campaign, argues that the general "performed excellently during the Atlanta campaign, perhaps better than any other corps commander." Hooker also, however, confirmed once and for all in 1864 that he was not a good soldier. Completely absent from his mental makeup was an ability to understand that Maurice de Saxe's axiom, "After the organization of troops, military discipline is the first matter ..., the soul of armies," not only applied to the men in the ranks but to their officers as well.[91]

One would think that Hooker's own experiences with the Army of the Potomac would have impressed upon him that less-than-cooperative, much less openly critical, subordinates—no matter their individual or collective merits—were a cancer on an army that could not be tolerated for long without severe consequences. Yet his ego either rendered him incapable of seeing this or led him to believe that his merits as a commander and his political connections meant that an exception would have to be made in his case. (Lincoln certainly did him no favors in this regard when he not only did not punish, but actually rewarded, Hooker's behavior toward Burnside.) Consequently, he simply was unable to act with the degree of subordination that was necessary of a corps commander if an army was to operate at maximum effectiveness.

Hooker's conduct is all the more mysterious given that it is hard to see what he could have thought it would accomplish. Sherman was a man of many faults, not the least of which was what Hooker correctly perceived to be a tendency to play favorites among his subordinates and belittle the accomplishments of those outside his special circle. Still, there was no way Hooker could have hoped to win a power struggle with Sherman in 1864. The only way he could have done so was if some disaster befell the Union war effort in Georgia that could be pinned on Sherman's shoulders, which no one who could have helped Hooker had any interest in seeing happen. The political fate of his friends in the Republican Party was so tied to Sherman and Grant in 1864 that there was little chance that they were going to do anything that summer that might create a command crisis in one of the Union's major armies on his behalf. That even after his removal Hooker was unable or unwilling to recognize this was the case is evident in the fact that, during the weeks and months that followed, he could not refrain from disparaging Sherman personally and professionally to officials in Washington.[92]

And so Fighting Joe Hooker's active military career came to an ignominious, but ultimately appropriate end. In September 1864 he assumed command of a department encompassing Illinois, Michigan, Indiana, and Ohio, where his duties consisted mainly of monitoring Copperhead activity in those states and dealing with minor guerrilla raids from across the Ohio River. In his capacity as department commander, in April 1865 Hooker had the honor of leading the funeral procession for President Lincoln in Springfield, Illinois. He remained in the army until 1868 and eventually settled in Long Island, where he died in October 1879.[93]

NOTES

1. Sherman to his wife, July 29, 1864, in *Sherman's Civil War: Selected Correspondence of William T. Sherman, 1860–1865*, ed. Brooks D. Simpson and Jean V. Berlin (Chapel Hill: University of North Carolina Press, 1999), 676.

2. Biographical information on Hooker is drawn mainly from the only modern published study of the general, Walter H. Hebert, *Fighting Joe Hooker* (Indianapolis: Bobbs-Merrill, 1944). In his authoritative study of the Atlanta Campaign, Albert Castel asserts, "There is no good study of Hooker, but then none is possible, owing to the absence of necessary sources." *Decision in the West: The Atlanta Campaign of 1864* (Lawrence: University Press of Kansas, 1992), 580n9. This is a bit too dismissive of Hebert's study, which while not particularly revealing on the Atlanta Campaign, is quite solid overall. Moreover, though Castel identifies a real obstacle the student of Hooker confronts, it is by no means an insurmountable one. While no full report by Hooker can be found in the volume of the *Official Records* devoted to the Atlanta Campaign, it is still possible to piece together what he was doing from documents contained therein and from other sources, including

Castel's work; Richard M. McMurry, "The Atlanta Campaign: December 23, 1863, to July 18, 1864" (Ph.D. diss., Emory University, 1967); and two brief studies of the campaign, McMurry, *Atlanta 1864: Last Chance for the Confederacy* (Lincoln: University of Nebraska Press, 2000); and Stephen Davis, *Atlanta Will Fall: Sherman, Joe Johnston, and the Yankee Heavy Battalions* (Wilmington, Del.: Scholarly Resources, 2001).

3. "Major-General Hooker," *Harper's Weekly,* Feb. 7, 1863; William F. G. Shanks, *Personal Recollections of Distinguished Generals* (New York: Harper and Brothers, 1866), 189–90; William G. DeLuc, *Recollections of a Civil War Quartermaster,* ed. Augustine V. Gardner (St. Paul, Minn.: North Central, 1963), 119.

4. Campbell to Dear Charley, Nov. 21, 1863, in *The Union Must Stand: The Civil War Diary of John Quincy Adams Campbell, Fifth Iowa Volunteer Infantry,* ed. Mark Grimsley and Todd D. Miller (Knoxville: University of Tennessee Press, 2000), 222; Cox to Dear Frank, May 10, 1864, in "'Gone for a Soldier': The Civil War Letters of Charles Harding Cox," ed. Lorna Lutes Sylvester, *Indiana Magazine of History* 68 (Sept. 1972): 197.

5. Ulysses S. Grant, *Personal Memoirs of U. S. Grant* (1885; repr., 2 vols. in 1, Lincoln: University of Nebraska Press, 1996), 657. Hooker fully reciprocated Grant's disdain, proclaiming in an 1872 interview that "Grant has got no more moral sense than a dog." "Fighting Joe Hooker: He Fights the Battle of Chancellorsville over Again," *San Francisco Chronicle,* May 23, 1872.

6. Special Orders No. 427, Sept. 24, 1863, U.S. War Department, *The War of the Rebellion: A Compilation of the Official Records of the Union and Confederate Armies,* 70 vols. in 128 parts (Washington, D.C.: Government Printing Office, 1880–1901), ser. 1, 29(1):151 (hereafter cited as *OR;* all references are to series 1 unless otherwise noted); John Hay, *Inside Lincoln's White House: The Complete Civil War Diary of John Hay,* ed. Michael Burlingame and John R. Turner Ettlinger (Carbondale: Southern Illinois University Press, 1997), 87.

7. *OR,* 31(1):72; Hooker to Chase, Nov. 3, 1863, in *The Salmon P. Chase Papers: Volume 4, Correspondence, April 1863–1864,* ed. John Niven (Kent, Ohio: Kent State University Press, 1997), 170–71.

8. *OR,* 32(2):468. Hooker repeated his criticisms of Grant and Smith in a letter to an influential Michigan senator in May. "Grant will never forgive me for having knocked all his plans into a cocked hat by a single move on Lookout Mountain," he declared. "I discern on the part of the President and Secretary of War to have him exercise to the prejudice of the service his extraordinary course in relation to Schofield and Baldy Smith," he added. "The latter was a cast off from the Army of the Potomac during my command of it for good and sufficient reasons.... He has always been for short marches & no fights." Hooker to Chandler, May 3, 1864, Zachariah Chandler Papers, Manuscript Division, Library of Congress, Washington, D.C., container 3 (hereafter cited as LC). Even Maj. Gen. George Thomas, for whom Hooker eventually developed a degree of admiration, did not escape censure from Hooker and his coterie for his generalship at Chattanooga. DeLuc, *Recollections of a Civil War Quartermaster,* 121–22.

9. *Detroit Post and Tribune, Zachariah Chandler: An Outline Sketch of His Life and Public Services* (Detroit: Post and Tribune, 1880), 244–45; Bruce Tap, *Over Lincoln's Shoulder: The Committee on the Conduct of the War* (Lawrence: University Press of Kansas, 1998), 177–87; Hooker to Wade, Mar. 18, Apr. 2, 1864, Benjamin Franklin Wade Papers, Manuscript Division, LC, container 10; Hebert, *Fighting Joe Hooker,* 269.

10. *OR*, 31(2):340, 32(2):469.

11. William T. Sherman, *Memoirs of General William T. Sherman*, 2 vols. (1875; repr., New York: Da Capo, 1984), 2:86; DeLuc, *Recollections of a Civil War Quartermaster*, 126; John F. Marszalek, *Commander of All Lincoln's Armies: A Life of General Henry W. Halleck* (Cambridge, Mass.: Harvard University Press, 2004), 95, 165–66, 169–75; Shanks, *Personal Recollections of Distinguished Generals*, 169; Sherman to his wife, Apr. 17, 1863, in *Sherman's Civil War*, 452.

12. Thomas B. Van Horne, *The Army of the Cumberland* (1875; repr., New York: Smithmark, 1996), 365; Special Field Orders No. 105, *OR*, 32(3):364–66; Daniel Butterfield, *Address on General Hooker and His Command at Lookout Mountain and Chattanooga* (New York: Exchange Printing, 1896), 5, 10; "Fighting Joe Hooker: He Fights the Battle of Chancellorsville over Again," *San Francisco Chronicle*, May 23, 1872. After the war Hooker proclaimed Thomas "Sherman's superior as a soldier in every sense," and served as one of the pallbearers at Thomas's funeral. "Sherman's Memoirs: Major Gen. Hooker Severely Criticises Them," *New York Times*, May 28, 1875; Brian Steel Wills, *George Henry Thomas: As True as Steel* (Lawrence: University Press of Kansas, 2012), 447.

13. Daniel E. Sickles, *Address Delivered in Boston before the Hooker Association of Massachusetts* (Norwood, Mass.: Norwood, 1911), 25; *OR*, 38(4):17–18; Cram to his mother, Apr. 23, 1864, in *Soldiering with Sherman: Civil War Letters of George F. Cram*, ed. Jennifer Cain Bohrnstedt (DeKalb: Northern Illinois University Press, 2000), 89; Castel, *Decision in the West*, 97.

14. Hooker to Chandler, May 3, 1864, Chandler Papers, container 3; Geary to his wife, May 6, 1864, in *A Politician Goes to War: The Civil War Letters of John White Geary*, ed. William Alan Blair and Bell I. Wiley (University Park: Pennsylvania State University Press, 1995), 170–71; Cram to his mother, May 3, 1864, in *Soldiering with Sherman*, 95.

15. *OR*, 38(1):139–40, 38(2):27, 113–14, 38(4):27–28, 35, 37, 39–40, 44, 45, 46, 56, 58.

16. *OR*, 38(1):140, 38(2):114–17, 38(4):61, 70, 71, 76, 77, 78, 80, 93–95; Geary to his wife, May 1, 1864, in *Politician Goes to War*, 173.

17. *OR*, 38(4):79; Castel, *Decision in the West*, 135, 137–39; McMurry, "Atlanta Campaign," 86–92.

18. *OR*, 38(4):92, 94, 96–97, 104, 105.

19. *OR*, 38(1):140, 38(2):27, 38(4):112–13, 116, 125–26, 129.

20. *OR*, 38(2):117, 38(4):136, 140. One of Hooker's staff officers later recalled, "When Hooker, whose command was following McPherson, saw his error, and that only by intervening between Resaca and Dalton could the enemy be driven from his line of retreat, offered through General Thomas to do the work, asking to be allowed to throw his corps across the line of [the] railroad between Dalton and Resaca, Sherman denied his request for the reason—as I believe—that he would not give Hooker an opportunity to gain the credit that his favorite, McPherson, had failed to secure." DeLuc, *Recollections of a Civil War Quartermaster*, 126; Castel, *Decision in the West*, 142–53.

21. *OR*, 38(4):151, 158, 159, 160–61; Castel, *Decision in the West*, 154–56, 160–61.

22. John M. Schofield, *Forty-Six Years in the Army* (New York: Century, 1897), 140–41. One of Hooker's staff officers witnessed a similar scene a few weeks later, encountering Hooker "with General Sherman, sitting at a table of some kind on which lunch had been served. As I came up I noticed that they had finished eating, and that they had remained sitting when the fire broke out afresh, neither wishing to rise first. I said: 'It looks to me as if one school boy was afraid, and the

other 'dassent.' They both laughed, rose, and together moved away." DeLuc, *Recollections of a Civil War Quartermaster*, 126.

23. Castel, *Decision in the West*, 163–64; McMurry, "Atlanta Campaign," 100–101; *OR*, 38(1):190, 38(4):178; Wallace to his wife, May 21, 1864, in "William Wallace's Civil War Letters: The Atlanta Campaign," ed. John O. Holzhueter, *Wisconsin Magazine of History* 57 (Winter 1973–74): 95.

24. *OR*, 38(1):178, 38(2):28, 38(4):178, 193; Castel, *Decision in the West*, 164–66.

25. *OR*, 38(4):189, 191–92, 193, 199; Henry Stone, "Opening of the Campaign," in *Papers of the Military Historical Society of Massachusetts*, vol. 8, *The Mississippi Valley, Tennessee, Georgia, Alabama, 1861–1864* (1910; repr., Wilmington, N.C.: Broadfoot, 1989), 386–87.

26. *OR*, 38(2):118, 38(4):190–91.

27. *OR*, 38(1):118, 322–23; Reid to his sisters, May 16, 1864, in *The View from Headquarters: Civil War Letters of Harvey Reid*, ed. Frank L. Byrne (Madison: State Historical Society of Wisconsin, 1965), 147–49; Cox to Dear Frank, June 20, 1864, in Sylvester, "Gone for a Soldier," 203; E. B. Fenton, "From the Rapidan to Atlanta," in *The Atlanta Papers*, ed. Sydney C. Kerksis (1893; repr., Dayton, Ohio: Morningside, 1980), 226; Cram to his mother, May 27, 1864, in *Soldiering with Sherman*, 99; Castel, *Decision in the West*, 174–75. After the fighting ended and night had fallen, Geary, on his own initiative, sent forward a party to secure possession and remove from the field the four guns Butterfield's men had briefly captured. Future president Benjamin Harrison, then a colonel, subsequently claimed that his command was the first to seize the cannon.

28. *OR*, 38(2):28–29; Williams to his daughter, May 20, 1864, in *From the Cannon's Mouth: The Civil War Letters of General Alpheus S. Williams*, ed. Milo M. Quaife (1959; repr., Lincoln: University of Nebraska Press, 1995), 308.

29. McMurry, "Atlanta Campaign," 109, 114, 116, 118–19, 123–24; Castel, *Decision in the West*, 178–79.

30. *OR*, 38(4):204.

31. *OR*, 38(1):142, 38(2):29, 121, 324, 38(4):210, 216, 217, 220–21; Geary to his wife, May 1, 18, 1864, in *Politician Goes to War*, 169, 175–76.

32. Castel, *Decision in the West*, 195, 198–200; McMurry, "Atlanta Campaign," 125; William R. Scaife, "Waltz between the Rivers: An Overview of the Atlanta Campaign from the Oostanaula to the Etowah," in *The Campaign for Atlanta & Sherman's March to the Sea, Volumes I & II: Essays on the American Civil War in Georgia, 1864*, ed. Theodore P. Savas and David A. Woodbury (Campbell, CA: Savas Woodbury, 1994), 278–79.

33. *OR*, 38(4):220–21, 227.

34. *OR*, 38(1):142, 38(2):121, 38(4):237, 238.

35. *OR*, 38(4):237, 238, 240, 247.

36. *OR*, 38(2):29, 121–22, 38(4):251, 254.

37. Castel, *Decision in the West*, 200–201; McMurry, "Atlanta Campaign," 126–32; Scaife, "Waltz between the Rivers," 282–86.

38. *OR*, 38(2):29, 122; Castel, *Decision in the West*, 203–6, 208–9; McMurry, "Atlanta Campaign," 135–40, 144.

39. *OR*, 38(4):269, 274, 283, 288–89.

40. *OR*, 38(1):143, 38(4):283, 296; Reid to his sisters, May 29, 1864, in *View from Headquarters*, 154; Williams to his daughter, May 31, 1864, in *From the Cannon's Mouth*, 311–12.

41. McMurry, "Atlanta Campaign," 150–52; Castel, *Decision in the West*, 219, 220–21.

42. *OR*, 38(2):122–23, 38(4):307–8; Henry Stone, "From the Oostenaula to the Chattahoochee," in *Papers of the Military Historical Society of Massachusetts*, vol. 8, *Mississippi Valley, Tennessee, Georgia, Alabama*, 407–8.

43. *OR*, 38(2):29–30, 123; McMurry, "Atlanta Campaign," 153–55; Stephen Pierson, "From Chattanooga to Atlanta in 1864 . . . a Personal Reminiscence," in Kerksis, *Atlanta Papers*, 276–77; Castel, *Decision in the West*, 221–22.

44. *OR*, 38(1):60, 66; Stone, "From the Oostenaula to the Chattanoochee," 409; Samuel H. Hurst, *Journal History of the Seventy-Third Ohio Volunteer Infantry* (Chillicothe, Ohio: n.p., 1866), 130–31; Williams to his daughter, May 31, 1864, in *From the Cannon's Mouth*, 312.

45. *OR*, 38(2):30, 123; DeLuc, *Recollections of a Civil War Quartermaster*, 115; Reid to his sisters, May 29, 1864, in *View from Headquarters*, 154–57; Williams to his daughter, May 31, 1864, in *From the Cannon's Mouth*, 312–13.

46. Castel, *Decision in the West*, 226; Mead to his family, June 4, 1864, in "With Sherman through Georgia and the Carolinas: Letters of a Federal Soldier," ed. James A. Padgett, *Georgia Historical Quarterly* 32 (1948): 293.

47. *OR*, 38(1):66–67, 144–45, 38(2):30, 124–26, 38(4):323, 325, 341–42, 356, 362–63.

48. *OR*, 38(1):147–48, 38(4):385, 394–95, 402–3, 408–9, 418, 420, 421, 435, 428–29, 434; McMurry, "Atlanta Campaign," 181–83; Castel, *Decision in the West*, 258–59, 267.

49. *OR*, 38(4):445–46, 454.

50. Castel, *Decision in the West*, 269, 281, 285; *OR*, 38(4):454–55, 466, 475, 479–80, 481, 483, 498, 519; Cram to his mother, June 15, 1864, in *Soldiering with Sherman*, 104.

51. *OR*, 38(1):148–50, 38(2):126–29, 324–25, 38(4):484, 493–94, 522, 523, 524–25, 526, 536–37, 538; Pierson, "From Chattanooga to Atlanta," 280–81; Reid to his sisters, June 19, 1864, in *View from Headquarters*, 160–62.

52. Sherman to Grant, June 18, 1864, in *Sherman's Civil War*, 654–55.

53. *OR*, 38(4):547, 548, 551, 557–58.

54. *OR*, 38(2):31, 132–33, 38(4):562.

55. *OR*, 38(2):31–32, 133, 38(4):561, 562.

56. *OR*, 38(4):561, 562.

57. *OR*, 38(2): 32, 513–14, 569, 646, 655, 38(4):563; Reid to his sisters, June 24, 1864, in *View from Headquarters*, 163–64; Cram to his mother, June 25, 1864, in *Soldiering with Sherman*, 114–15; Williams to his children, July 10, 1864, in *From the Cannon's Mouth*, 328–29; Castel, *Decision in the West*, 295.

58. *OR*, 38(4):562–63; Robinson to "Friend Hunt," June 24, 1864, quoted in Castel, *Decision in the West*, 299.

59. *OR*, 38(4):558, 559–60, 561, 566.

60. Sherman, *Memoirs*, 2:57–59; Schofield, *Forty-Six Years*, 134–36. Castel offers an authoritative dissection of this entire episode that is decidedly unflattering to Sherman in "Prevaricating through Georgia: Sherman's Memoirs as a Source on the Atlanta Campaign," in *Winning and Losing in the Civil War* (Columbia: University of South Carolina Press, 1996), 104–6. See also McMurry, "Atlanta

Campaign," 205–8. For a take on the matter that is more positive toward Sherman and critical of Hooker, see Earl J. Hess, *Kennesaw Mountain: Sherman, Johnston, and the Atlanta Campaign* (Chapel Hill: University of North Carolina Press, 2012), 32–33, 42–43.

61. Geary to his wife, June 25, 1864, in *Politician Goes to War*, 183; Stone, "From the Oostenaula to the Chattahoochee," 420.

62. Butterfield to Hooker, June 12, 1864, in *A Biographical Memorial of General Daniel Butterfield, including Many Addresses and Military Writings*, ed. Julia Lorrilard Butterfield (New York: Grafton, 1904), 146–48; McMurry, "Atlanta Campaign," 210–21, 328–31; Castel, *Decision in the West*, 301, 303–21; DeLuc, *Recollections of a Civil War Quartermaster*, 116; *OR*, 38(2):326, 38(4):602, 603–4, 614–15; Williams to his daughters, July 15, 1864, in *From the Cannon's Mouth*, 33.

63. Castel, *Decision in the West*, 317–19, 321–22, 327–30; McMurry, "Atlanta Campaign," 228–32.

64. *OR*, 38(1):154, 38(4):31, 135, 38(5):18, 29, 31, 42, 135; Pierson, "From Chattanooga to Atlanta," 283–84; Cram to his mother, July 4, 1864, in *Soldiering with Sherman*, 119–20.

65. *OR*, 38(1):154, 38(2):31, 135; Pierson, "From Chattanooga to Atlanta," 283–84; Cram to his mother, July 4, 1864, in *Soldiering with Sherman*, 119–20.

66. Reid to his sisters, July 5, 1864, in *View from Headquarters*, 165–66, 166n11; Castel, *Decision in the West*, 331; *OR*, 38(2):31, 135. This was not an isolated incident. A few months earlier Ward had been so inebriated that he mismanaged a march, after which one of the men proclaimed him "our drunken old Genl ... whose sheer delight is to swill whiskey, etc. No one respects him and all unite in hoping that he will soon be removed." Cram to his mother, Mar. 6, Apr. 23, 1864, in *Soldiering with Sherman*, 80–81, 89. "The poorest excuse for a Genl I ever saw," declared another man, "he keeps eternally *drunk* and has no confidence placed in him either by his superiors or inferiors." Cox to Dear Frank, May 10, 1864, in Sylvester, "Gone for a Soldier," 198.

67. Mead to his family, July 6, 1864, in Padgett, "With Sherman through Georgia and the Carolinas," 297–98; William T. Sherman, "The Grand Strategy of the Last Year of the War," in *Battles and Leaders of the Civil War*, ed. Robert U. Johnson and Clarence C. Buel, 4 vols. (New York: Century, 1887–88), 4:253; *OR*, 38(2):136, 38(5):53.

68. *OR*, 38(2):155, 515, 38(5):66, 67, 96, 102, 103, 106; Castel, *Decision in the West*, 340–41, 344–47, 352–58, 360–61; McMurry, "Atlanta Campaign," 344–66.

69. Williams to My dear Lew, July 17, 1864, in *From the Cannon's Mouth*, 334–35; Cox to his sister, June 20, 1864, in Sylvester, "Gone for a Soldier," 204.

70. *OR*, 38(5):158, 159, 166, 170.

71. *OR*, 38(1):155–56, 38(2):33, 136–37, 327, 38(5):160, 161, 167, 170–71, 179, 184, 185, 189–90.

72. Castel, *Decision in the West*, 366–68.

73. *OR*, 38(1):202, 38(2):33, 136–37, 327, 38(5):183, 184, 185–86, 190, 199; Albert Castel, "'... The Heavens and the Earth Had Suddenly Come Together': The Battle of Peachtree Creek," in *The Campaign for Atlanta and Sherman's March to the Sea*, ed. Theodore P. Savas and David A. Woodbury (Campbell, Calif.: Savas Woodbury, 1994), 29.

74. *OR*, 38(2):33, 137, 327, 38(5):203, 204.

75. *OR*, 38(1):290–91, 38(2):327–28; George A. Newton, "Battle of Peach Tree Creek," in Kerksis, *Atlanta Papers*, 398–402; Cram to his mother, June 21, 1864, in *Soldiering with Sherman*, 125; Reid to his sisters, July 22, 1864, in *View from Headquarters*, 171–73.

76. *OR*, 38(2):137–41; Pierson, "From Chattanooga to Atlanta," 289–90.

77. *OR*, 38(2):33–34, 141, 329.

78. Cram to his mother, July 24, 1864, in *Soldiering with Sherman*, 127; Newton, "Battle of Peach Tree Creek," 403; Henry Stone, "The Siege and Capture of Atlanta," in *Papers of the Military Historical Society of Massachusetts*, vol. 8, *Mississippi Valley, Tennessee, Georgia, Alabama*, 449.

79. Butterfield to Hooker, June 12, 1864, in *Biographical Memorial of General Daniel Butterfield*, 146–48.

80. Stone, "Siege and Capture of Atlanta," 449.

81. *OR*, 38(1):155–56, 38(5):222–23, 227, 228, 233.

82. Castel, *Decision in the West*, 385–414, 418; Larry J. Daniel, *Days of Glory: The Army of the Cumberland, 1861–1865* (Baton Rouge: Louisiana State University Press, 2004), 417.

83. Oliver O. Howard, "The Battles about Atlanta," *Atlantic Monthly* 38 (Oct. 1876): 395; *OR*, 38(5):240–41, 260, 261, 266, 277.

84. "Fighting Joe Hooker: He Fights the Battle of Chancellorsville over Again," *San Francisco Chronicle*, May 23, 1872; Hooker to Bates, Apr. 2, 1877, Dec. 24, 1878, Samuel Penniman Bates Collection, 1875–79, Box 3, Pennsylvania Historical and Museum Commission, Harrisburg.

85. *OR*, 38(5):273.

86. *OR*, 29(1):156, 38(5):271–72, 273–74, 307.

87. *OR*, 38(5):793; Sherman, *Memoirs*, 2:86; "Sherman's Memoirs: Major Gen. Hooker Severely Criticises Them," *New York Times*, May 28, 1875. In his treatment of the Sherman-Hooker imbroglio, Richard McMurry neatly and succinctly concludes: "Had Hooker not been so proud, he would not have so much resented Howard's selection—but had Hooker not been so proud, he and Sherman might not have been so antagonistic toward each other." "Atlanta Campaign," 331.

88. *OR*, 38(1):145, 152, 158.

89. Adam Underwood, *The Three Years Service of the Thirty-Third Massachusetts Infantry Regiment, 1862–1865* (Boston: A. Williams, 1881), 229; Cram to his mother, July 31, 1864, in *Soldiering with Sherman*, 129; Reid to his sisters, July 30, 1864, in *View from Headquarters*, 175–76.

90. Daniel, *Days of Glory*, 418; Cox to his sister, Aug. 4, 1864, in Sylvester, "Gone for a Soldier," 213; DeLuc, *Recollections of a Civil War Quartermaster*, 115; Williams to his daughter, Aug. 11, 1864, in *From the Cannon's Mouth*, 338.

91. Castel, "Prevaricating through Georgia," 106; Maurice de Saxe, "My Reveries upon the Art of War," in *Roots of Strategy*, ed. and trans. Thomas R. Phillips (Harrisburg, Pa.: Military Service Publishing, 1940), 245.

92. *OR*, 38(5):857; Hooker to Chandler, Dec. 19, 1864, Chandler Papers, container 3.

93. H. Edwin Tremain, *Major-General Joseph Hooker* (Cincinnati: Robert Clarke, 1881), 19–20; Hebert, *Fighting Joe Hooker*, 288–95.

8

Winfield Scott Hancock and the Overland Campaign

BROOKS D. SIMPSON

What makes for a good corps commander? What skills are required to do a good job? How do we assess a corps commander's performance? In truth, the study of the art of command during the American Civil War remains undeveloped as a field of inquiry. All too often generals owe their rating in the popular mind to reputation and results; far less is made of the importance of working with subordinates and superiors, supervising logistics and training, and assembling a competent professional staff. Moreover, given the frequent turnover of corps commanders, especially in the Army of the Potomac, it is difficult to separate an overall assessment from what happened in a handful of battles.[1]

Some of these factors become apparent when it comes to reviewing how Maj. Gen. Winfield Scott Hancock performed as a corps commander. His three stellar days at Gettysburg invariably color perceptions of his subsequent career in corps command. Moreover, the tendency of Lt. Gen. Ulysses S. Grant and Maj. Gen. George G. Meade to rely upon Hancock's II Corps throughout the Overland Campaign naturally leads one to conclude that, because they considered him the best man available for important jobs, he was actually very good at performing them. Moreover, the constant combat of May and June 1864 wore down both Hancock and his men, complicating efforts to evaluate performance under difficult and trying circumstances. Add to this the fact that the Overland Campaign and its constituent battles, while they are the subject of several fine studies, have not received the detailed, loving, and increasingly repetitious attention paid to Gettysburg, and one might conclude that there is much more that one may discover if one looks hard enough.

Brooks D. Simpson

BORN ON FEBRUARY 14, 1824, in Montgomery Square, Pennsylvania, some twenty miles northwest of Philadelphia, Winfield Scott Hancock's very name suggests that he was destined for military greatness. He grew up in nearby Norristown, and it was from there that he traveled to the U.S. Military Academy at West Point, New York, in 1840. Graduating toward the tail end of his class in 1844, he served in the West and participated in the Mexican-American War, joining none other than his namesake's command in the advance against Mexico City. Peacetime saw him shuffle from post to post, including a stint in "Bleeding Kansas," and he was in California when war broke out in 1861. Given command of a brigade in Maj. Gen. George B. McClellan's Army of the Potomac that September, Hancock efficiently executed his responsibilities on the parade ground, in training his officers, and in managing the staff work that went with his position. Singled out by McClellan for his performance at the Battle of Williamsburg in May 1862, he earned the sobriquet "Hancock the Superb." At Antietam that September he assumed command of a division when Maj. Gen. Israel Richardson went down mortally wounded after taking the Sunken Road, then led these troops at Fredericksburg and Chancellorsville. In June 1863 he replaced Maj. Gen. Darius Couch as commander of the II Corps on the eve of what would become known as the Gettysburg Campaign.[2]

Hancock had earned a reputation as one of the finest division commanders in the Army of the Potomac at the time of his elevation to corps command. Looking every inch the soldier, he was as skilled at handling his men on the field as he was personally courageous. As one officer remarked when observing him at Chancellorsville, "General Hancock is in his element and at his best in the midst of a fight."[3] He also showed a fair amount of skill in avoiding much of the infighting that characterized that army. A loyal Democrat, he kept his political views largely to himself, although they were not unknown. He did not neglect burnishing his public image with the press, a concern that would have repercussions at the conclusion of the opening operations against Petersburg in 1864. In short, it looked as if he was ready to embark upon a promising career in corps command, with a bright future before him.

Much is made of Hancock's performance at Gettysburg, and rightly so. Historian Glenn Tucker claims that Hancock "saved the army and the Union on each of the three days at Gettysburg"; fellow Hancock biographer David Jordan proclaims that "Gettysburg was Hancock's field." Certainly, he seemed to be nearly everywhere and yet always at the right place during those three days in July 1863. He helped rally Union forces on Cemetery Ridge on July 1 and approved of the field as a good place to give battle. On July 2 he fed reinforcements to the Union center and left to stave off Confederate efforts to transform their breakthroughs at the Wheatfield, the Peach Orchard, and Cemetery Ridge into preludes to a truly decisive victory for the Army of Northern Virginia on Northern soil. On July 3 he supervised the repulse of the final Confederate assault, demonstrating great personal bravery in so doing. It was one of finest examples of battlefield generalship during the entire conflict.[4]

Lost in this appraisal, however, is that during the fighting at Gettysburg, Hancock did not operate as a corps commander. At first he was simply Army of the Potomac commander Maj. Gen. George G. Meade's envoy, cloaked with important powers to take charge and make an assessment of the situation. During the next two days, Brig. Gen. John Gibbon directed the II Corps while Hancock functioned as an extension of army command. Indeed, to classify him as a wing commander does not adequately encompass his contribution. Yet it should be noted that his role on each day of the battle was largely reactive as he responded to enemy initiatives. He did not engage in offensive operations, complete with reconnaissance, deployment, and planning an attack. In short, while Gettysburg may have proven to be Hancock's finest moment, it did not offer a true test of his abilities as a corps commander.

As he directed units to stem the Confederate tide from a small knoll south of the famed copse of trees on July 3, Hancock fell seriously wounded. A ball had entered his upper thigh after hitting his saddle, so a nail and bits of wood also entered the wound. Removed from the battlefield, he eventually returned home to Norristown to recover, but convalescence proved slow and painful. At first surgeons struggled to extract the ball that had done much of the damage, and the abscess created by the wound continued to drain. Eventually, removal of the ball eased his pain, but the wound refused to heal, and it took time for the general to regain use of his leg.[5]

Months of limited mobility took their toll on the general. He gained a considerable amount of weight, while staff officer Francis A. Walker, a great admirer of his chief, remarked that Hancock's "former activity and elasticity" was permanently diminished as a result of the wound.[6] Given the general's tendency to ride to the scene of battle and take a hands-on approach to managing his men, this was no small matter, for his personal vigor was part of his command style. He would never quite regain the condition that had made him such a sight on so many battlefields. An attempt to return to active duty in December 1863 proved premature, and it was not until March 24, 1864, that he took charge of the II Corps once more.[7]

While Hancock was on the mend, the II Corps fought on. His first successor, Brig. Gen. William Hays, proved unequal to the task before him and failed to command the respect of his subordinates (although that may have been due to the fact that Hancock was a tough act to follow). In August 1863 Maj. Gen. Gouverneur K. Warren took over command. Warren distinguished himself in a sharp action at Bristoe Station that October, but at the end of November, he called a halt to a planned frontal assault against Confederate lines at Mine Run, exasperating Meade. Whether or not he made the right call was an interesting question in the mind of Henry L. Abbott, an officer in the 20th Massachusetts. Perhaps, Abbott speculated, Warren might have taken advantage of an earlier opportunity to advance against the enemy works after breaking the Confederate picket line. "I believe Hancock would have done [so], but Warren, though devilish fond of distinction & notoriety, hasn't a dash of genius, & on the other hand isn't a fool, but a well educated engineer, who can appreciate only the physical advantages & disadvantages & position, & not at all the moral superiority of men who have made up their minds individually to die, but not to run." The implication was that Hancock would have remedied these deficiencies.[8]

By the spring of 1864, the II Corps had also undergone a major transformation. Meade had decided to reassign units of the badly understrength I and III Corps throughout his army, reducing it to three infantry corps (II, V, and VI). The II Corps absorbed what remained of the III Corps, which never quite recovered from the battering it took at Gettysburg. At the same time, the three divisions of the II Corps that fought at Gettysburg were consolidated into two divisions, with brigades shuffled from one division to another and thus finding themselves with new comrades. The implications on unit identity and cohesion might prove telling once the campaign got under way.

The revamped II Corps was now four divisions strong, some 27,000 men in all, although numbers could be deceptive. Many of the soldiers were reaching the end of their enlistment term, and it was a good question as to whether they could be relied upon to give their all with a safe trip home only weeks away. A good number of these men were in the units transferred from the old III Corps, rendering those commands still more problematic when it came to committing them to battle. Moreover, as staff officer and later corps historian

Francis A. Walker would observe, the creation of larger brigades with more regiments did not lead to the commissioning of more brigadier generals. In short, the II Corps of the spring of 1864 was radically different than it had been the previous July.[9]

Only one of the corps's three division commanders at Gettysburg, John Gibbon, retained command of a division. He would be joined by Brig. Gen. Francis C. Barlow, who had been severely wounded at Gettysburg while directing a division of the since-departed XI Corps; Brig. Gen. Gershom Mott, who had seen service as a brigade commander in the III Corps; and Maj. Gen. David Birney, who had headed a division in the III Corps at Gettysburg. It was a mixed lot. Gibbon had proven to be a steady field commander who had at Gettysburg directed the corps for long stretches. Birney was a fairly good fighter as well, although Gibbon openly wondered if Birney would be equal to the task if Hancock remained incapacitated. A success as a brigade commander, Barlow's performance at Gettysburg was shaky, although he remained a favorite with some officers. Mott's career was undistinguished to date, and there was no reason to believe anything different would occur in 1864. Thus the corps Hancock would command in 1864 was not the one he had directed in 1863, and he would have to learn to work with three principal subordinates who were new to him (although he had requested Barlow).[10]

Hancock himself still cut an impressive figure. "He is a tall, soldierly man, with light brown hair and a military heavy jaw," observed Theodore Lyman of Meade's staff, "and has the massive features and the heavy folds round the eye that often mark a man of ability." Indeed, over the next several months, Lyman would take quite a fancy to Hancock, and his vivid pen portraits have helped shape our impression of the general.[11]

On May 4 Hancock's corps crossed the Rapidan River at Ely's Ford, east of where the other three infantry corps in Lt. Gen. Ulysses S. Grant's command would cross at Germanna Ford. Making its way to Chancellorsville, it remained there overnight on the site of the previous May's fighting. The following day the corps headed toward Todd's Tavern, from where it was assumed that it would be positioned to move westward to strike the Confederate right flank along Mine Run. News that Gen. Robert E. Lee's Army of Northern Virginia was on the move to attack the Union columns as they snaked their way south through the Wilderness resulted in a change of plans, with Grant and Army of the Potomac commander Meade deciding to give battle in the thick underbrush and woods west of Chancellorsville. Hancock soon reached the intersection of the Orange Plank Road and the Brock Road and decided first to fortify the Brock Road with a log parapet. This delayed any effort to move west to strike Lt. Gen. Ambrose P. Hill's corps marching east along the Orange Plank Road, but the fieldworks might come in handy should matters not go well down the road.[12]

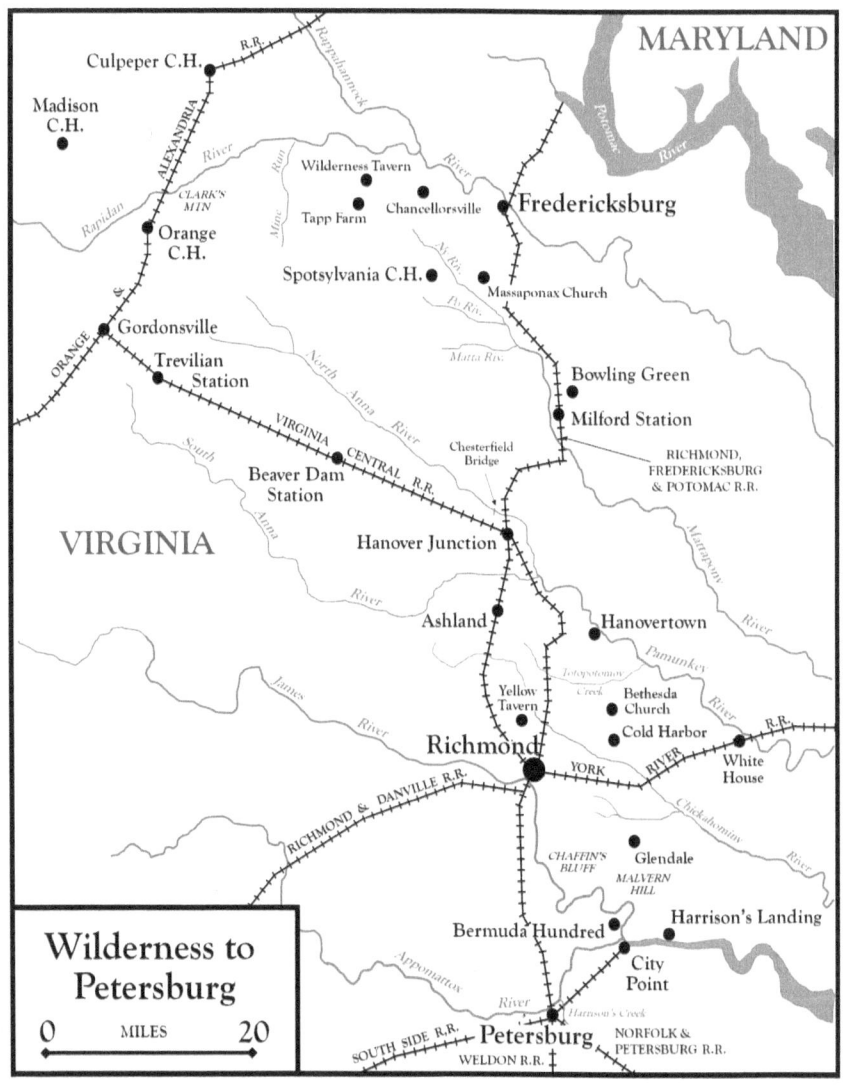

During the afternoon of May 5, Meade ordered Hancock to support VI Corps division commander Brig. Gen. George W. Getty's efforts to drive Hill's Confederates away from the Plank Road, but these orders went astray. It would be left to Getty to spearhead the advance alone. By the time Hancock directed Birney and Mott's divisions to support the attack, it was blunted by lack of coordination. Carrying orders from headquarters, Lyman encountered Hancock "on his fine horse—the *preux* chevalier of this campaign—a glorious soldier, indeed!" What the general had to say was a little less encouraging. He told Lyman to report to the army commander "that it is very hard to bring up troops in this wood, and that only a part of my corps is up, but I will do as well as I can."[13] That was barely enough: within minutes Mott's men came streaming back. It was left to Gibbon's division to stabilize the shaky Union position along the Brock Road. Hancock's decision to prepare defensive works thus proved valuable. As dusk came, Barlow's division arrived and drove the Confederate advance back until darkness halted operations for the day.

Grant and Meade chose Hancock's corps to spearhead the drive on the Confederate right on May 6. Maj. Gen. Ambrose Burnside's IX Corps, a late addition to Grant's command (and independent of the Army of the Potomac due to the fact that Burnside ranked Meade), would support the thrust. That news did not reassure Hancock. He viewed Burnside as undependable and recalled with disgust his tenure as commander of the Army of the Potomac. But the II Corps commander also fumbled in arranging for the attack. He claimed it was his intent to have Barlow's division move from the extreme left to align with Mott's division to lead the assault. Yet neither Gibbon nor Barlow recalled receiving any such orders, and only one of Barlow's brigades joined Mott. The result was a gap in the Union line between Mott and Birney when the Yankees advanced west along the Orange Plank Road, driving Hill's men before them. That initial success proved temporary. When Lt. Gen. James Longstreet's corps arrived in force, it pushed forward into the undetected gap, flanked the Yankees, and drove Hancock's men back all the way to the Brock Road. The field fortifications they had erected on May 5 again proved useful in stopping this Confederate advance; so did the fact that the Confederate effort lagged after friendly fire felled Longstreet. At last Burnside struck, but Hancock, citing confusion and disorganization in his divisions, set aside a suggestion that he support a renewed attack. Instead, he drove off a final Confederate assault that afternoon, although the men in Mott's and Birney's divisions appeared to be rattled.[14]

It was a trying day for Hancock. Burnside had not moved promptly to support the attack. "I knew it!" he had exclaimed upon learning of Burnside's tardiness that morning. "Just what I expected. If he could attack *now*, we would smash A. P. Hill all to pieces!" Moreover, Hancock remained convinced that he had arranged to redeploy Barlow to protect his flank, although it appears that at one point he was well aware that only one brigade had been moved to its new position. But the general overlooked his own confusion once Longstreet struck: in responding to reports of Confederate advances that promised to threaten both flanks, Hancock shifted brigades to and fro, dissipating what remained of his momentum even as units from other corps were attached to his command, complicating matters still more. As Brig. Gen. Alexander S. Webb, one of Hancock's brigade commanders, later noted, along the Union left "each general commanded something not strictly in his command." It was challenging to exercise authority effectively in the thick woods and undergrowth of the Wilderness: it was also evident that Mott's division was not made up of the sort of officers and soldiers that characterized the rest of the II Corps. Nor was Hancock quite up to exercising command with his accustomed vigor. Lyman had come across the general early in the afternoon, and Hancock confessed that he was tired as he asked that they sit down to discuss the situation.[15]

Frustrated as he might have been by the setbacks and missed opportunities of the Wilderness, Hancock could rest content in the knowledge that of the four infantry corps commanders, he had enjoyed the most success. Warren's handling of V Corps on May 5 proved suspect; VI Corps commander Maj. Gen. John Sedgwick nearly encountered disaster on May 6 when an attack at dusk rattled several divisions and nearly caused widespread panic; and Burnside's failure to support Hancock in a timely fashion seemed to confirm the reputation of incompetence he had gained at Antietam and Fredericksburg. Given these impressions, it was natural for Grant and Meade to lean more and more on Hancock, a tendency that would become even more manifest over the next two weeks. But as Webb noted, many of the soldiers in the II Corps "had no longer that confidence in their commanders which had been their best and strongest trait during the past year."[16]

On the evening of May 7, Grant began pulling out of his positions in the Wilderness. He decided to march southeast toward Spotsylvania Court House, passing by Lee's right flank in an effort to seize a road junction that would place him between the Army of Northern Virginia and Richmond, forcing Lee to take the offensive to oust him from that key crossroads. But the Confederates won the race for the road junction, and once more both sides began exchanging blows as Grant looked for a weak point in Lee's lines. Hancock's corps played a featured role in the eleven days of fighting that followed. This was not so much a tribute to the general's skill as it was a sign that neither Grant nor Meade had much faith in the other corps commanders. Warren's disputatious nature angered Meade and frustrated Grant, who at the outset of the campaign would have turned to Warren for army command had something happened to Meade. As Lyman concluded: "Warren is not up to a corps command. As in the Mine Run move, so here, he cannot spread himself over three divisions. . . . [T]he result is partial and ill-concerted and dilatory movements." A sharpshooter's bullet cut down Sedgwick on May 9; it would take some time for his newly promoted replacement, Maj. Gen. Horatio G. Wright, to come up to speed. As for Burnside, although the Rhode Islander resented the fact that Grant had sent staff officer Lt. Col. Cyrus B. Comstock over to keep an eye on him, he did little to shake the impression that he could not be relied upon to do what needed to be done when it came to offensive operations.[17]

Eager to do something, Grant on the ninth directed Hancock to strike at what he presumed to be the left of Lee's line along the Po River. But his impatience proved costly, for he directed Hancock to commence operations prematurely, alerting Lee to his intentions and allowing him to respond before the full force of an organized attack could be felt. Hancock exacerbated this problem when he decided to halt his advance short of crossing the Po a second time—once more caution prevailed. Lee believed that with some luck he might catch and destroy the exposed corps. Making things worse, on May 10 Grant directed Hancock to support another effort to seize Laurel Hill on the Confederate left. In ordering Gibbon and Birney to support that endeavor, Hancock left Barlow's division to fend for itself as a tempting target under the assumption that if the Confederates concentrated against Barlow, they would have to weaken their line elsewhere, including Laurel Hill.[18]

Not much came of these expectations. The Confederate line held at Laurel Hill. Meanwhile, Barlow had to extract himself from an increasingly perilous position under fire, with Hancock doing what he could to rescue the exposed division. Elsewhere, Mott's division was engaged in an ill-managed venture against the Confederate center. His failure helped doom Col. Emory Upton's effort to breach Lee's line to the east, wasting an innovative approach to storming fortified positions. Upton had ordered his men to withhold small-arms fire until they reached their objective so that the charge's momentum would not be slowed by a halt to deliver a volley; once the initial thrust pierced the enemy line, men would fan out left and right to roll up the enemy line. Without proper support, however, the effort was futile.[19]

Hancock had too many things to keep track of during May 9 and 10 to do a good job of supervising any of these operations. The same could not be said for what came next. Convinced that the Confederate line could be broken by a determined assault emulating Upton's methods, Grant designated May 12 as the day that the entire II Corps would smash the Confederate center, a salient that some men called the Mule Shoe. Rain on May 11 and a resulting fog provided some cover but also complicated efforts to reconnoiter the position. Hancock made little effort to remedy that difficulty. While later accounts highlighted the failure of staff officer Comstock to arrive in time to help scout the terrain, several members of Hancock's staff were also not up to the task. As a result, several of the division commanders ventured the opinion that the attack would end in disaster, especially after they found themselves pointed in the general direction of Lee's army.[20]

Thus, it came as some surprise on the foggy morning of May 12 when the advancing Yankees smashed through the Confederate fortifications along the salient. Initial reports were that the assault was an overwhelming success. But Hancock quickly fumbled the effort to exploit the situation as he mindlessly poured more men into the breach until it was too crowded for them to do much. The Confederates rallied and counterattacked, and both sides kept committing men to what was turning into a slugfest in the mud and rain. Eventually, the Confederates constructed a new line of defensive works at the base of the salient and withdrew to that position, limiting the damage inflicted by Hancock's attack. To be sure, other Union corps commanders did not perform well that day. Neither Grant nor Meade did much to supervise the attack personally, leaving it to staff officers to convey orders that reflected a less-than-perfect understanding of the situation at the front.[21]

In the aftermath of the fighting, Hancock reorganized his corps into three divisions. Gone was Mott's command, with its units folded into Birney's division. At the same time, reinforcements arrived in the form of heavy artillery regiments stripped from the Washington defenses and transformed into infantry units. For several days, there was a lull in the fighting for Hancock's men, ending on May 18 when another frontal assault, undertaken by Gibbon's and Barlow's divisions, achieved nothing. As the II Corps shifted toward the left of the Army of the Potomac, a Confederate attack on May 19 struck the raw heavy artillery units, which acquitted themselves well enough in their first battle.[22]

The first two weeks of campaigning had proved trying for Hancock. The Gettysburg wound continued to pain him, so much so that when possible, he abandoned riding a horse for a trip in a wagon. The general's weight gain during his hiatus also contributed to his eroding stamina.[23] Nevertheless, Grant and Meade continued to rely upon him to take the lead in important operations. Warren remained out of favor at army headquarters, in part because he had a tendency to question orders rather than implement them. Wright, who was wounded (though not seriously) on May 12, was still struggling to acquaint himself with his new responsibilities. As for Burnside, Grant and Meade were losing patience with his subpar performance, and it was increasingly evident that an awkward chain of command that had Grant issuing orders to Burnside directly rather than through Meade simply was not working well. In contrast, Grant had recommended Hancock for promotion to major general in the Regular Army, a sign of just how much he appreciated his performance.

Relying upon Hancock to deliver the telling blow was understandable, but it had its consequences. It meant that the II Corps would suffer a disproportionate number of casualties, including officers. It called upon Hancock to do more at a time when he found that, physically, he could not do as much and to operate even more effectively as a corps commander when it appeared that both he and his staff were still trying to learn on the job. At some point this reliance would become overreliance. But that would continue to be the case so long as Grant and Meade found themselves frustrated with the performance of the other corps commanders and unable to identify satisfactory replacements.

Satisfied that he had reached a stalemate at Spotsylvania, Grant, aware that his other offensives in Virginia in the Shenandoah Valley and along the James River had bogged down, decided to move by Lee's right flank once more, with Hancock's men leading the way. In sending the II Corps out ahead of the main body, Grant hoped to lure Lee into attacking that force out in the open, thus presenting the Federals with an ideal opportunity to engage an unfortified enemy. It was a daring plan, and implicit in it was Grant's trust that if Lee came after Hancock, the hero of Gettysburg could handle the situation until reinforcements arrived.[24]

Lee did not take the bait. He preferred to shift once more to block the Union advance by taking position along the North Anna River. On May 23 Hancock ordered his men forward, smashing past Confederate defenders, crossing the river, and establishing a bridgehead on the south bank. The resulting deployment of Union forces along the river offered Lee an opportunity to strike at either flank, with the Yankees having to cross the river twice to reinforce the threatened position, but the Confederates were unable to take advantage of this (in part because Lee was experiencing poor health, just like Hancock). On the twenty-fourth the II Corps engaged the Confederates without result; two days later Grant commenced another move by his left to Totopotomoy Creek. He ordered Hancock to spearhead yet another assault on May 31, but the corps commander soon reported that the enemy was strongly entrenched and that an attack would most likely fail at significant cost. Determined to avoid another setback, Grant shifted to his left once more. On June 1 lead elements of the Army of the Potomac reached a crossroads called Old Cold Harbor, near the site of the 1862 battle of Gaines's Mill. There, they clashed with Lee's men; Grant intended to resume the offensive the next day, using the II and VI Corps along with Maj. Gen. William F. "Baldy" Smith's recently arrived XVIII Corps (detached from Maj. Gen. Benjamin Butler's Army of the James at Bermuda Hundred along the James River).[25]

The planned assault did not come off on June 2. Hancock's corps spent much of the day marching and countermarching, a victim of poor maps and a guide's mistake. Grant postponed the morning attack. Then, with the II Corps still struggling to get into position, he postponed it yet again until the early dawn hours of June 3. The delay proved costly, buying enough time for the Confederates to erect a strongly fortified defensive line from which they could cut down nearly any attack. In this they were aided inadvertently by Hancock, Smith, and Wright. None of the corps commanders took much time to reconnoiter the ground in front of them or in making plans to coordinate their efforts. Grant had left Meade in charge of this assault, and the hero of Gettysburg fell short of preparing for the next day's events.

In the early morning hours of June 3, the three Union corps surged forward in a massive frontal assault against a well-prepared line of defenders. Although Hancock's men actually breached the enemy position at two points, it proved impossible to hold on to those gains. Meade's failure to coordinate the attacks meant that all three corps fanned out on their own, leaving their flanks vulnerable to enemy fire. Grant urged the Army of the Potomac's commander to press forward where there might be a prospect of success but added that "the moment it becomes certain that an assault cannot succeed suspend the offensive."[26]

Meade asked his corps commanders if they believed it would be worthwhile to strike once more. Hancock did not, and he declined to order his men to renew the attack. By midday Grant, after visiting the corps commanders and then Meade, halted the offensive. It was a bloody repulse that would grow even more horrible and futile in the retelling over the years. Yet the failure of Meade, Hancock, and the other corps commanders to reconnoiter the ground in front of them and their inability to plan a coordinated attack eliminated whatever chance there was of success and contributed to the terrible toll in casualties.[27]

In the wake of Cold Harbor, Grant decided that it was time to try to approach Richmond by swinging south across the James River to take Petersburg, south of the capital. With that city in Union hands, Richmond was sure to fall. Once more Hancock led the advance of the Army of the Potomac. Yet as his men approached the James, the general's Gettysburg wound continued to act up on him, and on the morning of June 13, Meade's aide Lyman came across Hancock sitting on the grass, nursing his wound by pouring water over it.[28]

The II Corps reached the James on the afternoon of the thirteenth and commenced crossing the next day. Meade ordered Hancock to await the issuing of rations before he advanced on Petersburg in support of Smith's attack. The delivery of these rations (which Hancock had claimed were unnecessary) was delayed, and the corps waited for several hours before deciding to resume marching to the front on June 15. A bad map complicated the task and added to the confusion and frustration as the men tramped through the heat and dust; an order from Grant urging Hancock to hurry forward to assist Smith in an evening assault placed more pressure on the officers and men. As Hancock later noted, only now did he understand his mission: he had no idea why he was doing what he was doing until receiving this dispatch (followed by one from Smith).[29]

Much would be made later of confusing orders and the lack of coordination, with many fingers pointed at Grant's inability to handle all that was before him. There is much merit to this criticism, but one might also wonder why Meade seemed rather passive about what was going on. The wrangling about rations simply delayed the advance at a moment when time was precious and every lost minute gave the Confederates new opportunity to respond; that Hancock did not know his objective (and seemed unwilling to inquire) strains credulity.

Once Hancock knew what he was supposed to do, he undertook to move his command to the front, with two divisions arriving at the rear of Smith's corps within hours (Barlow's division struggled to find the correct way forward). Conferring with Smith, Hancock learned that he had already attacked once that evening with some success, although the Confederates were still in front. Waiving seniority (and thus command on the field), Hancock placed his men at Smith's disposal, and Smith used them to relieve his men at the front. That decision marked the end of fighting for the day, a choice that played into Confederate hands as they received reinforcements and strengthened their position. What Hancock could not have known at the time was that Smith had been in position for most of the day to launch an attack with overwhelming force but had delayed and procrastinated for hours. Whereas Hancock often neglected the importance of reconnaissance in preparation for an attack, Smith (perhaps with memories of Cold Harbor in his mind) had spent far too much time personally assessing the enemy's position. It did not help that he was feeling under the weather.[30]

Yet one must wonder what had happened to the Hancock of Gettysburg in front of Petersburg. Did he trust Smith in ways that he did not trust Maj. Gen. Oliver O. Howard on July 1 at Cemetery Hill? Might not he have been laboring under impaired health and exhaustion? Had he grown so frustrated during the preceding six weeks that he was no longer as assertive as he once was, and that perhaps he was not nearly as eager to exercise initiative? Was he simply worn out physically, mentally, and emotionally? So suggested Gibbon when he noted that Hancock seemed "irritable" and "out of temper" when he returned from meeting with Smith.[31]

Even Theodore Lyman, who marveled at Hancock's appearance (particularly the general's compulsion to have a clean white shirt always at hand, except when it came to send a flag of truce at Cold Harbor), shook his head sadly. Certainly, Hancock's men were tired after a day of marching, "but, oh! That they had attacked at once. Petersburg would have gone like a rotten branch." That nothing was done struck Lyman as remarkable. "In war there is a critical instant—a night—perhaps only a half hour, when everything culminates," he observed. "He is the military genius who recognizes this instant and acts upon it, neither precipitating nor postponing the critical moment. There is thus good reason why great soldiers should be so rare that generations pass without producing a single one." However able he was, Hancock fell short of that admittedly high standard that day.[32]

Over the next several hours, the II Corps high command did not always acquit itself well. Hancock found fault with Gibbon and Birney for failing to respond with alacrity to his orders looking to an attack on June 16. That afternoon Meade arrived at the front and took charge; in later afternoon Hancock's three reunited divisions launched an attack on Confederate entrenchments, only to discover that the enemy was now reinforced and prepared to repulse a frontal assault. It may well be that in any case the attackers no longer were in any shape to advance with enthusiasm: Hancock and other observers saw that they were exhausted and lacked inspiration. "I do not think the men attack with persistence," the corps commander noted; "they appear to be wearied."[33]

The six weeks of campaigning had also taken its toll on Winfield Scott Hancock. His Gettysburg wound continued to cause him trouble. He found it hard to move, whether on foot or mounted on a horse. On June 17 the pain became so overwhelming that he turned over command of the corps to Birney and removed himself to his tent to recuperate. It proved a restless respite. By June 18, when Meade attempted one final time to take Petersburg, the bickering among the corps commanders suggested that all had taken enough. "Everyone was near the breaking point," noted Lyman. Nor did the men fight well, understandably so. "It was just as I expected—forty-five days of constant marching, assaulting and trenching are a poor preparation for a rush," the staffer observed, concluding: "You cannot strike a blow with a wounded hand."[34]

That was certainly part of the story. But the II Corps of 1864 was so unlike its predecessor from the previous year that the fact that it broke down was, in retrospect, no surprise. The reorganization of 1864 left units with new and unfamiliar comrades, while the approaching departure of those three-year men who had not reenlisted meant that many soldiers were aware that they needed to survive but a short time before they returned home safe and sound. The continuous combat wore away at the physical and mental well-being of the men—and their commanders too, including an already-ailing Hancock. Raw replacements and conscripts of dubious value did not make up for these losses.[35]

Just how wounded the II Corps was became evident several days later, even as its commander continued to recuperate. On June 22 it performed badly when a Confederate attack stopped them well short of the Weldon Railroad, a critical lifeline between the Southern heartland and Petersburg. Some two thousand Yankees surrendered: most observers believed that Birney was not equal to the task of corps command and cited Hancock's absence as contributing to the disaster. Hancock also grew restless when he read newspaper criticisms of his performance before Petersburg on June 15, reports that bore signs of Smith's malignant gossip and faultfinding with others. Defending his command, the general showed a vigor that would have been better applied to the management of his command, and in this case he proved more successful. Neither Grant nor Meade blamed Hancock for what had happened (and not happened) on June 15. Before long Grant, tired of Smith's carping at everyone, relieved him of command. As for Hancock, his reputation remained intact, and he would continue to be known as the Army of the Potomac's best corps commander until his departure in the fall of 1864.[36]

FOR SOME FORTY-SIX DAYS, Winfield Scott Hancock had directed the operations of the II Corps, from its breaking winter quarters north of the Rapidan and Rappahannock to his reluctant relinquishment of command outside Petersburg. During that time, he emerged as the most reliable infantry corps commander available to Generals Grant and Meade. As the latter observed, Hancock "is the only one of my corps commanders who will go right in when I order him."[37] Doubtless this was true, in that Hancock proved more responsive and reliable than his peers. Burnside stumbled throughout the campaign, confirming the negative assessments circulated by his many critics within the Army of the Potomac. Sedgwick's death overshadowed his subpar performance in the Wilderness, and Wright took time to rise to his new responsibilities. By the end of the campaign, Warren was so unhappy and embittered that Meade came close to relieving him: that fate was reserved for Smith, whose criticisms about everyone else proved unbearable. Nevertheless, Grant believed that if Meade was transferred elsewhere, Hancock should inherit command of the Army of the Potomac.[38]

Part of the mixed performance of the II Corps was due to the featured role it came to play in some seven weeks of continuous combat operations. Time and again Grant and Meade came to rely upon Hancock's troops to deliver decisive blows as their faith in other corps commanders waned. Both men spoke highly of his generalship, with Meade going so far as to assert: "No commanding general ever had a better lieutenant than Hancock. He was always faithful and reliable."[39] In relying upon him to strike critical blows, however, both Grant and Meade came to rely upon the II Corps too much. Over weeks of relentless fighting, this could not help but take its toll, and by the third week of June, the corps was simply worn out. Nor did it help that the divisions it inherited from the III Corps in the reorganization of the Army of the Potomac proved to be inferior in composition, with a significant number of regiments looking forward to their discharge that spring. At times the primary responsibility for the shortcomings in the corps's performance lay elsewhere, particularly with the actions of army headquarters, where Grant often proved impulsive and stubborn and Meade seemed overwhelmed with the responsibilities before him in conducting sustained offensive operations.

Yet Hancock must bear responsibility for some of his command's shortcomings. He feuded with his division commanders. He proved lax when it came to reconnoitering enemy positions prior to attacks and mismanaged assaults on May 6, May 12, and June 3. Perhaps his best day was in rescuing Barlow's division on May 10 along the Po River. He was also cautious at times, and his behavior before Petersburg betrayed a man who might have been all too prone to hesitation in light of previous setbacks. At times it became clear that coordinating the movements of several divisions as they approached the enemy taxed his abilities.

There were other reasons why the II Corps did not fare well during the Overland Campaign that were not due to Hancock's performance. Several times poor staff work (especially in guiding Hancock's men to the front) rendered offensive operations problematic, especially at Cold Harbor and the advance on Petersburg. While the nearly constant campaigning took its toll on the officers and men of the II Corps, it also wore heavily upon Hancock as well. The general had not recovered from his Gettysburg wound, nor had he quite mastered the art of overseeing the operations of a corps.

Reflecting on the campaign in later years, Francis Walker argued that the nature of the fighting that spring "offered few opportunities for brilliant actions" and tended "to destroy reputations, and not to make them." He added that Hancock proved particularly hampered by the change in fighting "since those qualities in which he pre-eminently excelled, namely, tactical skill and personal influence over his soldiers in critical moments, were, on most of the battlefields of 1864, largely neutralized by the nature of the country."[40] In short, the Wilderness was not Williamsburg, Spotsylvania was not Gettysburg, and the marching and assaulting from Cold Harbor to Petersburg was unlike anything anyone had experienced. There would be no paintings of generals on horseback or fine equestrian monuments to mark the spot where a commander performed great deeds.

Walker may have had a valid point, but his argument obscures a much larger truth. Winfield Scott Hancock had never exercised command of a corps in conducting offensive operations. His experiences at Gettysburg were unusual and had little to do with the responsibilities of corps command. Yes, at critical moments the personal presence of a corps commander might well prove crucial, but these generals had far less control of battlefield tactics than did brigade and division commanders, while preparation for battle and controlling and directing one's subordinates proved more appropriate tasks than those listed by Walker as Hancock's strengths. Compared to his peers, Hancock performed well, and his superiors recognized that fact. In turn, that led to an overreliance upon a general who, much like his men, wore down during the campaign as he struggled to deal with the aftereffects of a still-painful wound. That he endured as well as he did might speak to a different sort of heroism, but it should also help explain why his performance did not reach its previous heights. Hancock the Superb ended the Overland Campaign as a general who had done well enough just to endure.

NOTES

1. For example, Stephen R. Taaffe's *Commanding the Army of the Potomac* (Lawrence: University Press of Kansas, 2006) describes the rise and fall of that army's numerous corps commanders, but at best it describes their performances without addressing the responsibilities of corps command and how well those who served in that capacity fulfilled those obligations.

2. The best biographies of Hancock remain Glenn Tucker, *Hancock the Superb* (Indianapolis and New York: Bobbs-Merrill, 1960); and David M. Jordan, *Winfield Scott Hancock: A Soldier's Life* (Bloomington and Indianapolis: Indiana University Press, 1988). Also valuable are Francis A. Walker, *General Hancock* (New York: D. Appleton, 1894); and Perry D. Jamieson, *Winfield Scott Hancock: Gettysburg Hero* (Abilene, Tex.: McWhiney Foundation Press, 2003).

3. Jordan, *Winfield Scott Hancock*, 74.

4. Tucker, *Hancock the Superb*, 13; Jordan, *Winfield Scott Hancock*, 100. A. M. Gambone, *Hancock at Gettysburg . . . and Beyond* (Baltimore: Butternut and Blue, 2002) contains much useful information about Hancock's performance at Gettysburg.

5. Tucker, *Hancock the Superb*, 165–67.

6. Walker, *General Hancock*, 148–49.

7. Jordan, *Winfield Scott Hancock*, 104–7.

8. Taaffe, *Commanding the Army of the Potomac*, 126–27.

9. Francis A. Walker, *History of the Second Army Corps in the Army of the Potomac* (New York: Charles Scribner's Sons, 1887), 404–5.

10. Richard F. Welch, *The Boy General: The Life and Careers of Francis Channing Barlow* (Kent, Ohio: Kent State University Press, 2005), 90; Theodore Lyman, *Meade's Army: The Private Notebooks of Lt. Col. Theodore Lyman*, ed. David W. Lowe (Kent, Ohio: Kent State University Press, 2007), 118.

11. Lyman, *Meade's Army*, 121–22.

12. On the Wilderness, see Gordon C. Rhea, *The Battle of the Wilderness, May 5–6, 1864* (Baton Rouge: Louisiana State University Press, 1994).

13. Theodore Lyman, *Meade's Headquarters, 1863–1865: Letters of Colonel Theodore Lyman from the Wilderness to Appomattox*, ed. George R. Agassiz (Boston: Atlantic Monthly, 1922), 91–92.

14. Lyman, *Meade's Headquarters*, 96; Tucker, *Hancock the Superb*, 192–93.

15. Lyman, *Meade's Headquarters*, 94, 96; Rhea, *Wilderness*, 340–43; Alexander S. Webb, "Through the Wilderness," in *Battles and Leaders of the Civil War*, ed. Robert U. Johnson and Clarence C. Buel, 4 vols. (New York: Century, 1887–88), 4:163.

16. Webb, "Through the Wilderness," 163.

17. On Spotsylvania, see Gordon C. Rhea, *The Battles for Spotsylvania Court House and the Road to Yellow Tavern, May 7–12, 1864* (Baton Rouge: Louisiana State University Press, 1997); Lyman, *Meade's Army*, 151.

18. Rhea, *Spotsylvania*, 121–32.

19. Ibid., 135–42, 161–77.

20. Ibid., 221–25.

21. Ibid., 230–38, 316.

22. Jordan, *Winfield Scott Hancock*, 131–33.

23. Lawrence A. Kreiser Jr., *Defeating Lee: A History of the Second Corps, Army of the Potomac* (Bloomington: Indiana University Press, 2011), 154–55. Also of interest is Walker, *History of the Second Army Corps*.

24. Gordon C. Rhea, *To the North Anna River: Grant and Lee, May 13–24, 1864* (Baton Rouge: Louisiana State University Press, 2000), 155–59, 191–93, 212–16, 222–25, 236–40.

25. These operations are discussed in ibid., 280–358.

26. Grant to Meade, June 3, 1864, in *The Papers of Ulysses S. Grant*, ed. John Y. Simon et al., 32 vols. (Carbondale: Southern Illinois University Press, 1967–2012), 11:14n. On Cold Harbor, see Gordon C. Rhea, *Cold Harbor: Grant and Lee, May 26–June 3, 1864* (Baton Rouge: Louisiana State University Press, 2002).

27. Tucker, *Hancock the Superb*, 226–27.

28. Lyman, *Meade's Army*, 201; Theodore Lyman, "Operations of the Army of the Potomac, June 5–15, 1864," *Papers of the Military Historical Society of Massachusetts*, vol. 5, *Petersburg, Chancellorsville, Gettysburg*, ed. Theodore F. Dwight (Boston: Houghton Mifflin, 1906), 19.

29. Jordan, *Winfield Scott Hancock*, 141–43.

30. A good summary of these operations can be found in Edwin C. Bearss, with Bryce A. Suderow, *The Petersburg Campaign: Volume One: The Eastern Front Battles, June–August 1864* (El Dorado, Calif.: Savas Beatie, 2012), chap. 2.

31. Jordan, *Winfield Scott Hancock*, 146.

32. Lyman, *Meade's Headquarters*, 162–63.

33. Jordan, *Winfield Scott Hancock*, 147.

34. Ibid., 147–48; Lyman, *Meade's Headquarters*, 168–70.

35. For a recent discussion of these factors, see Carol Reardon, *With a Sword in One Hand and Jomini in the Other: The Problem of Military Thought in the Civil War North* (Chapel Hill: University of North Carolina Press, 2012), 92–123.

36. Jordan, *Winfield Scott Hancock*, 145–46, 148; Brooks D. Simpson, *Ulysses S. Grant: Triumph over Adversity, 1822–1865* (Boston: Houghton Mifflin, 2000), 338–49, 357–58.

37. Rhea, *Spotsylvania*, 5.

38. Tucker, *Hancock the Superb*, 233.

39. John W. Forney, *Life and Military Career of Winfield Scott Hancock* (Philadelphia: Hubbard Brothers, 1880), 326.

40. Francis A. Walker, "General Hancock," in *Papers of the Military Historical Society of Massachusetts*, vol. 10, *Critical Sketches of Some of the Federal and Confederate Commanders*, ed. Theodore F. Dwight (Boston: Houghton Mifflin, 1895), 61–62.

CONTRIBUTORS

THOMAS G. CLEMENS received his B.A. and M.A. degrees in history from Salisbury State University and his doctorate at George Mason University. He is professor of history emeritus at Hagerstown Community College and has contributed numerous essays and reviews to a wide variety of academic and popular history publications, including *Maryland Historical Magazine*, *America's Civil War*, and *Civil War Regiments*. A popular tour guide and president of Save Historic Antietam Foundation, he is one of the nation's leading authorities on the Battle of Antietam and the editor of an acclaimed two-volume edition of Ezra Carman's *The Maryland Campaign of 1862*.

JOHN J. HENNESSY is the chief historian at Fredericksburg and Spotsylvania National Military Park. He has worked for the New York State Historic Preservation Office and, in the dawn of his career, at Manassas National Battlefield. He is a graduate of the University at Albany (New York) and is the author of *The First Battle of Manassas: An End to Innocence, July 18–21, 1861*, and *Return to Bull Run: The Battle and Campaign of Second Manassas* as well as dozens of articles, essays, and reviews on history and preservation.

KENNETH W. NOE is Draughon Professor of Southern History at Auburn University. He received his graduate degrees from Virginia Tech and the University of Illinois and has contributed dozens of essays, articles, and reviews to academic and popular-history publications. He is also the author of the award-winning *Perryville: This Grand Havoc of Battle*, *Reluctant Rebels: The Confederates Who Joined the Army after 1861*, and *Southwest Virginia's Railroad: Modernization and the Sectional Crisis* and coeditor of *Politics and Culture of the Civil War Era* and *The Civil War in Appalachia*.

ETHAN S. RAFUSE received his B.A. and M.A. degrees in history at George Mason University and his Ph.D. in history and political science at the University of Missouri–Kansas City. He has taught Civil War and military history at the U.S. Military Academy at West Point and is a professor of history at the U.S. Army Command and General Staff College. His publications include *McClellan's War: The Failure of Moderation in the Struggle for the Union*, *The Ongoing Civil War: New Versions of Old Stories*, *Robert E. Lee and the Fall of the Confederacy*, and numerous essays, articles, and book reviews.

BROOKS D. SIMPSON is an ASU Foundation Professor and member of the Honors College faculty at Arizona State University. His many publications include *The Reconstruction Presidents*, *Ulysses S. Grant: Triumph over Adversity, 1822–1865*, *Union and Emancipation: Essays on Race and Politics in the Civil War Era*, and *The Civil War in the East: Struggle, Stalemate, and Victory*. In 1995 he was a Fulbright Scholar at Leiden University.

MARK A. SNELL received his B.A. from York College of Pennsylvania, an M.A. in U.S. history from Rutgers University, and his Ph.D. in history and public administration from the University of Missouri–Kansas City. He is a retired army officer who taught history at the U.S. Military Academy at West Point and Shepherd University, where he also served as founding director of the university's George Tyler Moore Center for the Study of the Civil War. Since 1993 he has been director of the George Tyler Moore Center for the Study of the Civil War at Shepherd University, where he is also an associate professor of history. He is the author, editor, or coeditor of four books, including *From First to Last: The Life of Major General William B. Franklin*, *Dancing along the Deadline: The Andersonville Memoir of a Prisoner of the Confederacy*, and *Bugle Resounding: Music and Musicians of the Civil War Era* and has published numerous essays and reviews. Snell served as the visiting senior lecturer at the Royal Military Academy, Sandhurst, in the fall of 2008.

CHRISTOPHER S. STOWE received his Ph.D. in history from the University of Toledo and is associate professor of military history with the U.S. Marine Corps Command and Staff College, Quantico, Virginia. His publications include articles in *Northwest Ohio History*, *Columbiad*, and ABC-CLIO's *Encyclopedia of the American Civil War* plus several reviews for periodicals. His first full-length book, a biography of George Gordon Meade, is under contract with the Kent State University Press.

STEVEN E. WOODWORTH received his Ph.D. from Rice University, is professor of history at Texas Christian University, and is author, coauthor, or editor of thirty-three books. He is a two-time winner of the Fletcher Pratt Award of the New York Civil War Round Table (for *Jefferson Davis and His Generals* and *Davis and Lee at War*), a two-time finalist for the Peter Seaborg Award of the George Tyler Moore Center for the Study of the Civil War (for *While God Is Marching On* and *Nothing but Victory*), and a winner of the Grady McWhiney Award of the Dallas Civil War Round Table for lifetime contribution to the study of Civil War history.

INDEX

Abbott, Henry L., 264
Acworth, Ga., 237
Adairsville, Ga., 232, 233
Adjutant General's Office, 17
Alabama, 96, 248
Alabama units: 23rd Alabama Infantry, 171
Alexandria, La., 192, 201, 202, 207, 208, 212, 213, 214, 215, 216
Alexandria, Va., 23, 71, 73
Allatoona, Ga., 234
Allatoona Creek, 237
Anderson, George B., 69
Anderson, Thomas M., 58
Anderson, Richard H., 134
Antietam, Battle of (1862), 41–42, 43, 44, 58, 61, 62, 69, 80, 81, 82, 84–89, 95, 114, 116, 119, 126, 152, 262, 268
Antietam Creek, 83, 84
Antietam National Battlefield, 80
Appalachian Mountains, 221
Appomattox Campaign (1865), 6, 152
Appomattox River, 67
Aquia Landing, Va., 38
Arizona, 68
Arkansas, 161, 198, 205
Arlington, 70, 71, 73
Army Corps, Union:
—I (Army of the Potomac) 75, 84, 86, 88, 95, 119, 124, 137, 150, 152, 182, 264; (Army of the Ohio) 98, 104, 105, 106, 107
—II (Army of the Potomac) 11, 78, 83, 84, 88, 129, 137, 261, 262, 263, 264–65, 267, 268, 270, 271, 272, 273, 275, 276–77; (Army of Virginia) 80; (Army of the Ohio) 98, 104, 105
—III (Army of the Potomac) 29, 30, 124, 133, 264, 265, 277; (Army of the Ohio) 98, 99, 100, 101, 102, 103, 104
—IV, 227, 232, 239, 243, 246
—V (Army of the Potomac) 30, 32, 34, 35, 41, 42, 45, 79, 84, 94, 112, 119, 120, 121, 122, 124, 127, 130, 136, 137, 138, 142, 143, 145, 150, 264, 268
—VI (Army of the Potomac) 30, 124, 138, 151, 181, 184, 264, 267, 268, 272
—VII, 77, 194
— IX, 84, 267
—XI, 130, 136, 137, 265; XII, 61, 62, 78, 79–81, 82, 83, 84, 85, 86, 88–89, 94, 95, 130, 131
—XIII, 160, 163, 170, 174, 184, 191, 192, 193, 194, 198, 200, 204, 205, 206, 207, 212
—XIV, 227, 232, 243, 246, 247
—XV, 160, 163, 164
—XVI, 198
—XVII, 9, 156, 157, 159, 160, 163, 164, 165, 170, 198
—XVIII, 272
—XIX, 10, 184, 186, 187, 191, 196, 197, 198, 200, 202, 203, 204, 207, 211, 212, 213, 216, 218
—XX, 10, 225, 230, 232, 234, 237, 238, 239, 240, 242, 243, 247, 249, 250, 251–52
Army of Kentucky, 96
Army of Northern Virginia, 10, 11, 12, 61, 83, 118, 124, 129, 182, 183, 216, 263, 265, 268
Army of Observation, 65
Army of Tennessee, 245

Index

Army of the Cumberland (as Army of the Ohio) 96, 109; 221, 223; and Atlanta Campaign, 225–26, 227, 228, 234, 235, 238, 239, 240, 243, 244, 245, 246, 247, 250
Army of the Gulf, 216
Army of the James, 272
Army of the Mississippi, 97
Army of the Ohio, 225, 227, 229, 234, 239, 240, 242, 243, 246
Army of the Potomac, 3–4, 6, 7, 8, 9, 10, 14, 15, 18, 20, 21, 23, 27, 36, 37, 44, 74, 75, 77, 78, 112, 113, 117, 118, 119, 122, 126, 140, 144, 145, 148, 152, 177, 182, 183, 199, 216, 221, 222, 223, 224, 230, 245, 250, 253, 261, 262; and Chancellorsville, Campaign/Battle of, 129, 135, 136, 139; and Fredericksburg, Campaign/Battle of, 181–82; and Gettysburg, Campaign/Battle of, 143, 144; and Maryland Campaign/Battle of Antietam, 41, 62, 79, 81–82, 89; and Mud March, 123–25, 130, 150; and Overland Campaign, 265–66, 267, 271, 272, 273, 276, 277; and Peninsula Campaign/Seven Days' Battles, 29, 30, 31, 33, 34
Army of the Tennessee, 157, 198, 199, 201, 221; and Atlanta Campaign, 227, 228, 234, 250, 251; and Vicksburg Campaign, 175, 177
Army of Virginia, 35, 38, 40, 78, 80
Atchafalaya River, 195
Atlanta, Campaign/Battle of (1864), 10, 221, 225–52, 253, 254
Atlanta, Ga., 97, 199, 244, 245, 246, 250, 253
Atlantic Coast, 64, 66
Auchmuty, Richard, 136
Auger, Christopher C., 80
Austerlitz, Battle of (1805), 2
Austin, Tex., 69
Austria, 98
Averell, William Woods, 18
Aztec Club, 91

Babcock, Samuel, 64
Backus, Electus, 65

Bailey, Joseph, 209, 214, 215, 216
Baker's Creek, 170, 172, 173
Ball's Bluff, Battle of (1861), 24, 184
Banks, Mary, 184
Banks, Nathaniel P., 10, 73, 78, 79–80, 94, 154, 181, 183–84, 185, 190, 192, 194, 197, 219; and Red River Campaign, 198, 199, 200, 201, 202, 204, 205, 206, 207, 208, 209, 210, 212, 213, 214, 215
Banks's Ford, 123, 124, 129, 131, 132, 133, 134
Bardstown, Ky., 98
Barlow, Francis C., 265, 267, 268, 269, 271, 274, 277
Barlow, Samuel L. M., 26
Barnard, John G., 71
Barnes, James, 132
Barnett, Correlli, 109
Baton Rouge, La., 184, 192
Bayou Baxter, 161
Bayou Boeuf, 201
Bayou Dupont, 202
Bayou Macon, 161, 162
Bayou Pierre, 210
Bayou Teche, 191, 192, 194
Beaumont, Tex., 185, 187
Beauregard, Pierre G. T., 3, 12, 66, 73
Beaver Dam Creek, 32
Bell, Henry H., 185, 190
Bellagio Plantation, 160
Benedict, Lewis, 208, 209
Benjamin, Charles F., 151–52
Bermuda Hundred, 272
Berwick, La., 190
Berwick Bay, 186, 190, 195
Biddle, James C., 134, 136, 138, 141, 152
Biddle, William, 34
Big Black Bridge, Battle of (1863), 174
Big Black River, 164, 174
Birney, David, 265, 267, 269, 270, 275
Black Hawk, 201
Bladensburg, Md., 70
Blair's Landing, 210

Index

Bleeding Kansas, 262
Board of Engineers, 63–64, 66
Bolton, Miss., 170
Boomer, George B., 172
Boonsboro, Md., 82, 83, 84
Boston Harbor, Mass., 67
Bottom Hill, 104
Bourcet, Pierre de, 2
Bowen, John, 157, 172
Boyle, Jeremiah, 99, 100
Bragg, Braxton, 97, 98, 100, 101, 104, 105, 107, 109, 221
Brazos Santiago, Tex., 194
Brewster, Charles, 53
Bristoe Station, Battle of (1863), 264
Brock Road, 266, 267
Broglie, Victor-Francois de, 2
Brooks, William T. H., 151
Buchanan, James, 98
Buckhead, Ga., 246
Buckingham, William A., 87
Buell, Don Carlos, 8, 96, 97, 98, 99, 100, 108, 109; and Perryville, Campaign/Battle of; 101, 103, 104, 105, 106, 107
Buena Vista, Battle of, 66, 67
Bullock House, 137
Bull Run, 39
Bull Run, First Campaign/Battle of. *See* Manassas, First Campaign/Battle of
Bull Run, Second Campaign/Battle of. *See* Manassas, Second Campaign/Battle of
Burbridge, Stephen B. , 193
Bureau of Military Information, 127
Burlington, Vt., 15
Burns, William W., 17
Burnside, Ambrose E., 5–6, 38, 39, 40, 44, 57, 83, 84, 114, 119, 120, 121, 122, 125–26, 127, 129, 130, 133, 151, 154, 181, 182, 223, 224, 253; and Fredericksburg, Campaign/Battle of, 113; and Mud March, 123–25; and Overland Campaign, 267, 268, 269, 271
Burnt Hickory, Ga., 235

Burnt Hickory Road, 237
Butler, Benjamin, 272
Butterfield, Daniel, 19, 34, 119, 120, 121, 127, 138, 143, 152, 257; and Atlanta Campaign, 225, 228, 229, 230, 231, 232–33, 236, 237, 238, 239, 240, 243, 249–50
Buzzard's Roost, 227

Cadiz, Spain, 114
Calcasieu River, 187
Calhoun, John C., 2, 62
California, 157, 222, 224, 262
Cameron, Robert A., 205, 206, 207
Camp Breckinridge, 107
Camp Butler, 75
Camp Hamilton, 75, 92
Canada, 62
Candy, Charles, 247
Cane River, 213
Cape Hatteras, 74–75
Carman, Ezra, 80, 95
Carrion Crow Bayou, 192, 193
Carter, Eugene, 114
Carter, Hill, 56
Casey, Silas, 151
Cassville, Ga., 231, 232, 233, 234
Castel, Albert, 241, 253, 254, 258
Cedar Mountain, Battle of (1862), 80, 183
Cemetery Hill, 274
Cemetery Ridge, 263
Champion Hill, 170, 171, 172, 173
Champion Hill, Battle of (1863), 170–73, 174, 177
Chancellor, Francis, 132
Chancellor House, 132, 137
Chancellorsville, Campaign/Battle of (1863), 6, 10, 113, 129–40, 141, 145, 177, 245, 251, 262
Chancellorsville, Va., 131, 132–33, 135, 136, 137, 265, 266
Chandler, Zachariah, 24, 93, 121
Charleston Harbor, 64
Chase, Salmon P., 28, 72, 74, 78, 224

287

Index

Chattahoochee River, 234, 238, 243, 244, 245, 246, 249
Chattanooga, Siege/Battle of (1863), 10, 217, 221, 223, 224, 255
Chattanooga, Tenn., 96, 97
Chesapeake Bay, 26, 117
Chicago, Ill., 42
Chickahominy River, 31, 32, 33
Chickamauga, Campaign/Battle of (1863), 10, 221
Chillicothe, Ohio, 15
Choiseul, Étienne-François duc de, 2
Churchill, Thomas J., 207, 209
Cincinnati, Ohio, 17, 97, 108
Clemens, Thomas G., 7, 8
Clinton, Miss., 169
Clinton Road, 169
Clyde, Ohio, 157
Coburn, John, 230, 244
Cochrane, John, 121, 182
Cockspur Island, 64
Cold Harbor, Battle of (1864), 272–73, 274, 277
Collier Road, 247
Colorado, 68
Colt's Firearms, 216
Columbian Register, 46
Columbus, Ohio, 70
Comstock, Cyrus B., 269, 270
Conasauga River, 231
Connecticut, 183
Connecticut units: 16th Connecticut Infantry, 81
Coosawattee River, 231, 232
Copperheads, 254
Corinth, Battle of (1862), 158, 218
Corinth, Miss., 96, 99, 106, 158
Corps of Engineers, 62, 62, 64, 67, 79, 157
Corps of Topographical Engineers, 114, 181
Couch, Darius N., 129, 135, 138, 140, 143, 262
Covode, John, 122
Cox, Jacob, 81

Crawford, Samuel, 81, 86, 88, 89
Crittenden, John J., 98
Crittenden, Thomas L., 98, 106
Crocker, Frederick, 186, 187, 188, 189, 190
Crocker, Marcellus, 166, 168, 172, 173
Cruft, Charles, 99, 109
CSS *Virginia,* 75
Cumberland, Md., 64
Cumberland Gap, 107
Cumberland River, 158
Curtin, Andrew G., 141–42, 155

Dallas, Ga., 234, 235, 237
Dalton, Ga., 256
Davis, Jefferson, 67, 68, 91, 245
Davis, Jefferson C., 96, 97, 109
Decker Farm, 134
Delafield, Richard, 64
Democratic Party, 17, 26, 97, 262
Dennis, Elias S., 165–66, 167
Department of Arkansas, 194, 198
Department of California, 68, 69
Department of New Mexico, 68, 69, 73
Department of Northeastern Virginia, 72, 74, 91
Department of Oregon, 69
Department of Texas, 69
Department of the Gulf, 10, 182, 184, 197, 198
Department of the Ohio, 97
Department of the Pacific, 92
Department of Virginia, 75, 77, 93
Department of Washington, 71, 74, 91
Detroit, Mich., 150
District of Columbia, 70
District of West Tennessee, 158
Division of the Mississippi, 224
Dix, John, 73, 77, 154
Dixville Crossroads, 107
Dogwood Valley, 227
Doubleday, Abner, 150
Dowling, Dick, 186
Duerson's Mill, 134

Dug Gap, 227
Dunham, Cyrus, 100
Dutton, George, 63
Dwight, William, 207, 208, 210
Dyer, Clarence, 79, 83, 87

Early's Creek, 247
East Woods, 61, 85, 87, 88
Edward's Station, 168, 170
Ellsworth, Elmer, 71, 73
El Paso, Tex., 69
Ely's Ford, 131, 265
Ely's Ford Road, 136, 137, 138
Emancipation Proclamation, 35, 37, 41
Emerson, Frank, 204
Emory, William H., 204, 205, 206, 207, 208, 209, 213
Etowah River, 232, 234
Euharlee Creek, 234

Falmouth, Va., 112, 113, 124, 129, 131, 140
Farragut, David G., 16
Fite's Ferry, 231
Flood, Patrick H., 87
Florida, 64, 73
Field's Ferry, 231
Fisher, Horace N., 106, 107
Forsyth, James W., 83
Fort DeRussy, 201
Fort Griffin, 185, 186, 187, 188, 189
Fort Hamilton, 64
Fort Monroe, 29, 75, 77, 92
Fort Pulaski, 64
Fort Quitman, 69
Forts Henry and Donelson, Campaign/Battles of (1862), 158, 163
Fort Smith, 199
Fort Steilacoom, 68
Fort Sumter, 122, 150
Fort Texas (Brown), 65, 69
Fort Washington, 70
Fort Winthrop, 64

Fort Yuma, 68
Foster, John, 154
Fourteen Mile Creek, 166, 167
France, 183
Frankfort, Ky., 101
Franklin, Anna, 184, 189, 190, 191, 192, 193, 194, 195, 198, 202, 207, 212, 213, 214
Franklin, La., 201, 219
Franklin, William B., 5–6, 9–10, 12, 24, 30, 57, 58, 59, 76, 77, 78, 81, 121, 123, 124, 125, 130, 149, 151, 181–220; described, 181; and Fredericksburg, Campaign/Battle of, 181–82; and Mansfield, Battle of, 204–7; and Pleasant Hill, Battle of, 209–10, 214–15; and Red River Campaign, 198–216; and Sabine Pass Expedition, 185–89; wounded, 206
Fredericksburg, Campaign/Battle of (1862), 5–6, 9, 10, 113, 114, 119, 120, 122, 140, 151, 181–82, 262, 268
Frederick, Md., 78
Fredericksburg, Va., 31, 32, 36, 38, 123, 129, 130, 133, 134, 138
Frémont, John C., 73
French, William B., 78
French Revolution, Wars of, 1
Fry, Speed S., 99, 101, 102, 103, 104

Gaines's Mill, Battle of (1862), 33, 272
Gallup, George, 240
Galveston, Tex., 69
Garland, John, 65
Geary, John W., 225; and Atlanta Campaign, 227, 228, 229, 230, 231, 233, 234, 235, 236, 237, 238, 239, 240, 242, 243, 244, 246, 247, 248, 257
General Orders No. 8, 125
General Orders No. 25, 200
General Orders No. 45, 196
General Orders No. 47, 133
Georgetown, D.C., 70
Georgia, 64, 170, 232, 252, 254
Georgia Railroad, 246

Index

Germanna Ford, 131, 265
Getty, George W., 267
Gettysburg, Campaign/Battle of (1863), 6, 8, 9, 10, 143–44, 146, 177, 183, 261, 262–63, 264, 265, 271, 273, 274, 275, 277, 278
Gibbon, John, 43, 47, 53, 58, 263, 265, 267, 269, 271, 274, 275
Gilbert, Charles C., 8, 96–111; assessed, 108–9; described, 99–101; and Perryville, Campaign/Battle of, 100–7
Gilgal Church, 238
Gillem's Bridge, 234
Gilmor, Harry, 216
Glendale, Battle of (1862), 33, 34, 119
Gooding, Michael, 106–7
Goodrich, William, 89
Gordon, George, 81, 89
Gould, John M., 61, 84, 95
Grand Encore, La., 201, 202, 207, 210, 211, 212, 213, 214, 215
Grand Gulf, Miss., 160, 163, 164, 165
Grant, Julia, 185
Grant, Ulysses S., 9, 73, 98, 146, 148, 152, 154, 156, 157, 181, 183, 200, 215, 216, 217, 221, 222–23, 224, 225, 238, 254, 255; and Overland Campaign, 261, 265, 267, 268, 269, 270, 271, 272, 273, 276, 277l; and Vicksburg Campaign, 158, 159–60, 162, 163, 164, 165, 168, 169, 170, 171, 172, 173, 174, 175, 176, 177
Gravelly Plateau, 232
Graveyard Road, 156
Great Redoubt, 174, 175
Greeley, Horace, 47, 114
Green, Thomas, 193, 194, 195
Greene, George S., 80, 81, 88, 89
Green Springs, Ohio, 157
Gregg, John, 166–67, 168
Griffin, Charles, 58, 120, 132, 133, 134, 136
Grover, Cuvier, 191, 201, 212
Guadalupe Hidalgo, Treaty of, 68
Gulf of Mexico, 185, 195
Gunpowder River, 216

Hadley, Mass., 222
Hagerstown Pike, 86
Halleck, Henry W., 37, 38, 41, 73, 77, 78, 96, 97, 108, 114, 118, 119, 129, 140, 143, 144, 157, 158, 182, 194–95, 197, 198–99, 200, 224, 252
Hampton Roads, Battle of (1862), 75
Hampton Roads, Va., 64, 75
Hancock, Winfield Scott, 10–11, 135, 261–79; assessed, 276–78; described, 262; and Cold Harbor, Battle of, 272–73; and Gettysburg, Campaign/Battle of, 262–63; and Overland Campaign, 265–73; and Petersburg, First Offensive, 273–76; and Spotsylvania Court House, Battle of, 269–71; and Wilderness, Battle of the, 265–68; wounded, 263, 271, 273, 275
Hankinson's Ferry, 164
Hanover Court House, Battle of (1862), 31, 56
Hanover Junction, Va., 31
Hardee, William J., 104
Hard Times Landing, 163
Harney, William S., 92
Harper's Weekly, 237
Harrison, Benjamin, 257
Harrison's Landing, Va., 34
Harrison's Landing Letter, 53, 56
Hartford, Conn., 108, 216
Hartwood Church, 130
Hattaway, Herman, 11
Hawley, Michael J., 87
Hay, John, 19, 48
Hayes, Rutherford B., 47
Haynes Bluff, 160
Hays, William, 264
Hebert, Walter H., 254
Heintzelman, Samuel P., 4, 12, 27, 29, 30, 31, 76
Hennessy, John J., 7, 152
Hickenlooper, Andrew, 175, 176
Hill, Ambrose P., 266, 267, 268
Holmes, Samuel E., 172
Holt, Joseph, 46, 98, 99

Index

Hood, John Bell, 88, 229, 230, 231, 232, 233–34, 236, 237, 240, 242, 245, 246, 247, 248, 250
Hooker, Joseph, 6, 10, 30, 43, 58, 81, 83, 84, 85, 86, 88, 89, 95, 113–14, 119, 120–21, 124, 125, 126–27, 128, 143–44, 145, 150, 151, 152, 155, 182, 183, 221–60; assessed, 253–54; and Atlanta Campaign, 225–53; and Chancellorsville, Campaign/Battle of, 129, 130, 131, 132–35, 136, 137, 138, 139, 140, 141, 142, 223; and Chattanooga, Siege/Battle of, 221, 223, 224; described, 222–23; and Kolb's Farm, Battle of, 239–42; and New Hope Church, Battle of, 235–37; and Peachtree Creek, Battle of, 246–49; and Resaca, Battle of, 228–31; wounded, 89
Houston, Tex., 185
Hovey, Alvin P., 170, 171, 172, 173
Howard, Oliver O., 143, 177, 221, 274; and Atlanta Campaign, 227, 229, 230, 234, 239, 240, 243, 246, 251; and Chancellorsville, Campaign/Battle of, 130, 131, 136, 138, 251
Howell Mill Road, 248
Humphreys, Andrew, 94, 120, 131, 133, 134, 137
Hungarian Revolution, 98
Hunter, David, 215

Illinois, 161, 254
Illinois units: 8th Illinois Infantry, 168; 36th Illinois Infantry, 102; 20th Illinois Infantry, 167; 75th Illinois Infantry, 103
Indiana, 96, 101, 254
Indiana units: 10th Indiana Infantry, 101, 102; 23rd Indiana Infantry, 167
Inspector General's Office, 67
Iowa, 165
Iowa units: 27th Iowa Infantry, 212
Irwin, Richard B., 199

Jackson, Andrew, 115
Jackson, Battle of (1863), 169, 173, 177
Jackson, James S., 99, 109
Jackson, Miss., 164, 165, 166, 168, 169

Jackson Road, 156, 170, 171, 172, 173, 174, 175
Jackson, Thomas J. "Stonewall," 31, 32, 38, 39, 40, 79–80, 134, 135, 136, 137, 182, 183
James River, 33, 34, 56, 67, 117, 118, 123, 129, 271, 272, 273
J. A. Rawlins, 161, 162
Jena-Auerstadt, Battle of (1806), 2
Johnson, Ludwell, 209
Johnston, Albert Sidney, 73
Johnston, Joseph E., 3, 12, 73, 169, 227, 228, 229, 231, 232, 233, 234, 235, 239, 240, 241, 242, 243, 244, 245
Joint Committee on the Conduct of the War, 4, 24, 35, 56, 93, 121–22, 129–30, 182, 210
Jomini, Antoine-Henri, 32
Jones, Patrick, 247
Jordan, David, 262

Kearny, Philip, 30, 53, 87
Keedysville, Md., 84
Keil, F. W., 100–101
Kelly's Ford, 129, 130
Kennedy, Joseph C. G., 37, 38, 39, 40
Kennesaw Mountain, 238, 242, 243
Kentucky, 8, 96, 97, 98, 99, 101, 104, 107
Kentucky units (Union): 10th Kentucky Infantry, 101; 14th Kentucky Infantry, 240
Kernstown, Battle of (1862), 79
Kerrigan, James, 51
Key, John J., 58–59
Keyes, Erasmus D., 4, 27, 29, 31, 76
Kilpatrick, Hugh Judson, 227, 228
Kingston, Ga., 232, 233
Kolb's Farm, 239, 240
Kolb's Farm, Battle of (1864), 239–42, 245

Lake Providence, 160, 161, 162, 163
Landram, William J., 204, 205
Laurel Hill, 269
Lebanon Road, 104
Lee, Albert, 191, 192, 200–201, 202, 203, 204, 205, 207, 210

291

Index

Lee, Robert E., 11, 32, 34, 38, 61, 64, 66, 73, 118, 119, 121, 123, 129, 130, 133, 136, 138, 143, 145, 152, 155, 183, 265, 268–69, 270, 271, 272
Lee, Stephen D., 11
Lee and Gordon's Mill, 227
Lexington, Ky., 100
Library of Congress, 47
Liddell, St. John R., 104
Lincoln, Abraham, 4, 7, 8, 18, 23, 25, 27, 28, 29, 30, 31, 32, 35, 36, 37, 38, 40, 41, 42, 43, 44, 45, 46, 50, 58, 59, 70, 71, 77, 96, 97, 100, 113, 114, 118, 121, 125, 127, 128–29, 140, 142, 143, 144, 151, 182, 183, 190, 192, 194, 197, 216, 223, 232, 253, 254
Line, George, 84, 87
Logan, John A., 164, 165, 166, 170–71, 172–73, 175, 176, 250
Lookout Mountain, Battle of, 221, 224
Long Bridge, 70
Long Island, 254
Longstreet, James, 39, 47, 267, 268
Loring, William W., 157
Lost Mountain, 238
Louisiana, 160, 162, 163, 192, 197, 200, 248
Louisiana State University, 11
Louisville, Ky., 96, 98, 99, 100, 101, 102
Louisville and Nashville Railroad, 97, 100
Lowe, Thaddeus, 23, 29, 52
Lyman, Theodore, 20, 265, 267, 268, 269, 273, 274, 275
Lyon, Nathaniel, 73, 87

Mackville Road, 104
Macland Road, 239
Maine units: 2nd Maine Infantry, 19, 20, 34; 10th Maine Infantry, 61, 87, 88, 95; 30th Maine Veteran Volunteers, 202
Malvern Hill, Battle of (1862), 33–34, 44, 48, 49, 136
Manassas, First Campaign/Battle of (1861), 3, 17, 18, 19, 22, 24, 74, 181
Manassas, Second Campaign/Battle of (1862), 5, 7, 14, 34, 38–40, 41, 42, 45, 46, 47, 58, 77, 80, 81, 119, 120, 181
Mansfield, Battle of (1864), 10, 204–7, 212
Mansfield, Edward, 91
Mansfield, Henry, 62
Mansfield, Jared, 62, 63
Mansfield, John, 62
Mansfield, Joseph K. F., 6, 7–8, 61–95; assessed, 88–90; and defense of Washington, 70–73; and Maryland Campaign/Antietam, Battle of, 78–79, 80–88; mortally wounded, 61, 87; and Peninsula Campaign, 75–77; prewar life and military career, 62–69
Mansfield, Joseph T., 65
Mansfield, La., 201, 205
Mansfield, Louisa (Mather), 64
Mansfield, Mary (Fenno), 62
Mansfield, Samuel M., 64, 79, 83
Mansfield Road, 207, 208, 209
Marble, Manton, 26, 27–28, 30, 32, 42–43, 45, 55, 57, 58
Marcy, Randolph, 17, 29, 30
Marengo, Battle of (1800), 2
Marietta, Ga., 234, 235, 238, 239, 240, 243
Marietta Road, 237
Marshall, Elisha G., 55
Marshall, Tex., 199
Martindale, John H., 19–20, 21, 22, 31, 34–35, 44, 51, 57, 55, 56, 58
Marye's Heights, 113, 182
Maryland, 21, 51, 61, 70, 78, 80, 89, 94, 143
Maryland Campaign (1862), 9, 10, 62, 82–89, 94, 119, 121, 181
Massachusetts, 126, 183, 197, 198, 202, 252
Massachusetts units: 10th Massachusetts Infantry, 53; 18th Massachusetts Infantry, 20; 20th Massachusetts Infantry, 264; 22nd Massachusetts Infantry, 22
McCall, George, 32
McClellan, George B., 7, 9, 14, 17–18, 19, 20, 21, 22, 23, 24, 25–26, 36–37, 38, 39, 40–42, 43,

292

Index

44–45, 46, 47, 48, 50, 51, 52, 54, 56, 57, 58, 59, 61, 66, 70, 71, 72, 73, 74, 91, 113, 114, 117, 118, 120, 121, 125, 127, 145, 150, 216, 222, 262; and Maryland Campaign/Antietam, Battle of, 41–42, 78, 79, 80, 81, 83–84, 89; and organization of corps, 4, 5, 27, 30, 76; and Peninsula Campaign/Seven Days' Battles, 28, 29, 30, 31–33, 34, 35, 75–76, 77,
McClernand, John A., 160, 163, 164, 168, 169, 170, 173, 177
McClure's Ford, 231
McCook, Alexander M., 97, 98, 105, 106, 107, 108
McCook, Daniel, 104
McCook, Edward, 235
McDowell, Irvin, 3, 4, 24, 27, 28, 31, 32, 36, 39, 72, 73, 74, 75, 76, 151
McLaws, Lafayette, 134
McMillan, James, 207
McMurry, Richard, 260
McPherson, James B., 9, 156–80; assessed, 176–77; and Atlanta Campaign, 227, 228, 229, 231, 234, 238, 245, 246, 250, 251, 252, 256; and Champion Hill, Battle of, 170–73; described, 156–58; mortally wounded, 250; and Raymond, Battle of, 165–68; and Vicksburg Campaign, 156, 158–77
McPherson, James M., 61
McQuade, James, 138
Meade, George G., 6, 8–9, 66, 112–55, 182, 183, 261, 263; assessed, 144–46; and Chancellorsville, Campaign/Battle of, 129–40; described, 112–13, 114–20; and Fredericksburg, Campaign/Battle of, 114, 119; and Mud March, 123–25; and Overland Campaign, 266, 267, 268, 269, 270, 271, 272–73, 275, 276; wounded, 119
Meade, John Sergeant, 126
Meade, Margaretta, 112, 117, 119, 123, 124, 125, 126, 127, 128, 130, 133, 137, 140, 142, 144, 146
Mechanicsville, Battle of (1862), 32

Mexican-American War (1846–1848), 2–3, 17, 65–66, 99, 115–16, 181, 222, 262
Mexico, 65, 67, 68, 73, 91, 101, 117, 183
Mexico City, 17, 183, 262
Michigan, 24, 116, 121, 150, 254
Michigan units: 8th Michigan Battery, 166, 168
Middle Road, 170, 172
Middletown, Conn., 62, 64, 87
Middletown, Md., 79, 82
Military Department of Washington, 70
Miller Cornfield, 88
Milliken's Bend, 160
Mine (Mineral Spring) Creek, 135
Mine Run, 265
Mine Run, Campaign/Battle of (1863), 264, 269
Mineral Springs Road, 135
Mississippi, 158, 160, 161, 163, 164, 165, 168, 169
Mississippi Central Railroad, 158, 159, 163
Mississippi River, 2, 9, 10, 67, 157, 158, 159, 162, 183, 184, 185, 189, 192, 198
Mississippi Squadron, 216
Missouri River, 162
Mitchell, Robert B., 99, 105, 106, 107, 109
Mobile, Ala., 97, 183, 215
Monett's Ferry, 213
Monroe, James, 62
Monroe Doctrine, 183
Monterrey, Battle of, 65
Montgomery Square, Pa., 262
Morell, George, 19, 30, 31, 34–35
Mormon War (1857), 17
Morton, Oliver, 96, 97
Mott, Gershom, 265, 267, 268, 269, 270
Mott's Run, 132
Mud March (1863), 123–25, 130, 150
Mule Shoe, 270
Munfordville, Ky., 100

Nancy's Creek, 246
Napoleon (field gun), 1

Index

Napoleonic Wars, 1–2
Nashville, Tenn., 96, 97, 99, 107
Natchitoches, La., 201, 202, 203, 204, 212
National Home for Disabled Volunteer Soldiers, 216
National Road, 64, 82
Nelson, William C., 96, 97, 98, 99, 100, 109
New England, 62, 183, 191
New Haven, Conn., 46, 62
New Hope Church, 235, 236, 237
New Hope Church, Battle of (1864), 236–37, 239, 245
New Iberia, La., 190, 191, 192, 193
New Jersey, 45, 247
New Jersey units: 13th New Jersey Infantry, 81
New Mexico, 68
New Orleans, La., 182, 184, 185, 186, 189, 190, 191, 200, 208, 216
New Orleans Era, 206
Newton, John, 121, 182, 246, 247, 248
Newton Ferry, 231
New York, 20, 26, 51, 64, 191, 211, 240
New York, N.Y., 47, 64, 157
New York Herald, 142
New York Loyal National League, 122–23
New York Times, 46, 139
New York Tribune, 47, 141
New York units: 9th New York Cavalry, 37, 57; 13th New York Infantry, 19, 20, 21; 25th New York Infantry, 51; 107th New York Infantry, 81, 83, 87; 114th New York Infantry, 196
New York World, 26, 30, 42
Nickajack Creek, 244
Nicodemus Mill, 83, 84
Noe, Kenneth W., 8
Norfolk, Va., 76–77
Norristown, Pa., 262, 263
North Anna River, 272
North Carolina, 64, 74
North Woods, 85
Norwalk Academy, 157

Ohio, 17, 24, 70, 72, 97, 99, 122, 254
Ohio River, 8, 97, 162
Ohio units: 1st Ohio Light Artillery, 101; 20th Ohio Infantry, 167; 35th Ohio Infantry, 100
Old Baldy, 130
Old Cold Harbor, 272
Old Mine Road, 134
Oostanaula River, 229, 231
Opelousas, La., 192, 193, 199, 201
Orange and Alexandria Railroad, 119
Orange Plank Road, 131, 132, 133, 135, 265, 266, 267
Orange Turnpike, 131, 132, 133, 135, 136, 138
Ord, Edward O. C., 184, 193, 218
Osterhaus, Peter J., 164
Otto Cornfield, 82
Ottoman Empire, 98
Overland Campaign (1864), 11, 261, 265–73, 277, 278
Owen, Samuel W., 51
Owen's Mill, 235

Pace's Ferry, 246
Pacific Coast, 67
Palmer, John, 227, 240, 243, 246, 247
Partridge, Alden, 63
Pasquotank River, 64
Patterson, Robert, 17, 73
Peach Orchard, 263
Peachtree Creek, 246, 247
Peachtree Creek, Battle of (1864), 246–49, 250
Peachtree Road, 246
Pea Ridge, Battle of (1862), 98
Pemberton, John C., 157, 158, 168, 169, 170, 172, 173, 174, 176
Peninsula Campaign (1862), 7, 10, 28–35, 37, 75, 118, 181, 208
Pennsylvania, 32, 122, 141, 143, 144, 145, 155
Pennsylvania Avenue, 112
Pennsylvania Reserves, 114, 120, 149
Pennsylvania units: 3rd Pennsylvania Cavalry, 51; 46th Pennsylvania Infantry, 87; 124th

294

Pennsylvania Infantry, 81, 86; 125th Pennsylvania Infantry, 81, 86, 95; 128th Pennsylvania Infantry, 81, 86; 132nd Pennsylvania Infantry, 82
Perryville, Campaign/Battle of (1862), 8, 101–7, 108–9
Perryville, Ky., 103, 105, 109
Petersburg, First Offensive, 273–75, 277
Petersburg, Va., 11, 216, 262, 273, 274, 275, 276, 277
Peters Hill, 104, 105
Phelps, John W., 75
Philadelphia, Pa., 112, 114, 144, 157, 208, 262
Pickell, John, 21, 22, 51
Pickett's Mill, 237
Pine Mountain, 238
Pleasant Grove, 206, 207
Pleasant Hill, Battle of (1864), 209–10, 214–15
Pleasant Hill, La., 201, 203, 204, 206, 207, 208, 210, 211
Poland, 98
Polk, Leonidas, 104
Pope, John, 5, 14, 35, 36–37, 38–39, 40, 41, 44, 45, 46, 47, 56, 57, 59, 77, 80
Po River, 269, 277
Porter, David, 16
Porter, David Dixon, 16, 163, 199, 201, 202, 209, 212, 214, 215
Porter, Fitz John, 5, 7, 12, 14–60, 76, 77, 78, 81, 84, 120; assessed, 45–48; described, 16–19; and Manassas, Second Campaign/Battle of, 38–40; and Maryland Campaign/Antietam, Battle of, 41–42; and Peninsula Campaign/Seven Days' Battles, 28–35
Porter, John, 16
Port Gibson, Battle of (1863), 164, 173, 177
Port Hudson, La., 183, 184, 218
Portsmouth, N.H., 14, 16
Potomac Creek, 127
Potomac River, 70, 78, 80, 143, 223
Powder Springs Road, 243
Powder Springs-Marietta Road, 239, 240, 241

Powell, Samuel, 105
Preliminary Emancipation Proclamation, 42, 43, 44, 58, 116
Prokopowicz, Gerald, 109
Prospect Hill, 113
Providence, Miss., 160, 161
Puget Sound, 68
Pumpkinvine Creek, 235

Ransom, Thomas E., 200, 204, 207
Rapidan River, 11, 80, 129, 131, 265, 276
Rappahannock River, 67, 113, 120, 122, 123, 124, 129, 130, 131–32, 134, 135, 136, 139, 143, 144, 152, 181, 182, 276
Raymond, Battle of (1863), 165–68, 173, 177
Raymond, Miss., 165, 166, 167, 168
Raymond Road, 170
Red River, 160, 162, 194, 195, 197, 198, 199, 201, 206, 209, 210, 211, 214
Red River Campaign (1864), 10, 181, 200–216
Reno, Jesse, 6, 87
Republican Party, 6, 7, 9, 20, 21, 24, 27, 37, 41, 44, 93, 97, 113–14, 118, 120, 121, 126, 197, 222, 254
Resaca, Battle of (1864), 229–31
Resaca, Ga., 228, 229, 230, 231, 232, 236, 245, 256
Reynolds, John F., 6, 47, 137, 138, 139, 140, 141, 142, 143, 151, 182
Rhode Island, 269
Richardson, Israel B., 69, 83, 84, 262
Richmond, Fredericksburg, and Potomac Railroad, 127–28
Richmond, Ky., 96, 99, 100, 109
Richmond, Va., 26, 30, 31, 32, 72, 76, 77, 117, 118, 119, 123, 129, 133, 268, 273
Ringgold Gap, 221
Rio Grande, 65
River Road, 133, 134
Roach Farm, 165
Roberts, Benjamin S., 59
Roberts, Charles, 34, 35
Rochester, N.Y., 51
Rocky Face Ridge, 226, 227, 228

Index

Ropes, John, 28–29, 47
Rosecrans, William Starke, 107, 154, 158
Russell, William Howard, 23

Sabine City, Tex., 185
Sabine Crossroads, 205
Sabine Crossroads, Battle of. *See* Mansfield, Battle of
Sabine Pass, 186, 187
Sabine Pass Expedition (1863), 181, 185–89, 190, 194, 217
Sabine River, 185, 187, 190, 206, 208
Saint Augustine, Fl., 64
Saint Croix, V. I., 62
Saint Johns River, 64
Saint Marys River, 64
Salem Church, 138
San Antonio, Tex., 69
Sanborn, John G., 168, 172
Sandtown Road, 237, 239
San Francisco, Ca., 157
Santa Anna, 66
Savage Station, Battle of (1862), 33
Savannah River, 64
Saxe, Maurice de, 253
Schoepf, Albin F., 98–99, 103, 106, 107, 108, 109
Schofield, John M., 225, 227, 229, 230, 231–32, 234–35, 238, 239, 240, 241, 242, 244, 245, 246, 255
Schurz, Carl, 151
Scott, Winfield, 3, 17, 18, 66, 67, 68, 70, 71–72, 73, 74, 75, 91
Sears, Stephen W., 61, 140
Second Seminole War, 64
Sedgwick, John, 6, 47, 50, 78–79, 129, 133, 138, 141, 268, 269, 276
Senate Committee on Military Affairs, 21
Seven Days' Battles (1862), 6, 7, 32–34, 36, 77, 119, 120, 181, 213
Seward, William H., 37, 38, 114
Sharpsburg, Md., 83, 84, 88
Shaw, Robert Gould, 42
Shaw, William T., 208, 209
Shenandoah Valley, 17, 31, 32, 79, 271
Shenandoah Valley Campaign (1862), 32, 79, 183
Sheridan, Philip, 99, 100, 102, 104, 105, 106, 107
Sherman, William T., 18, 198, 199, 201, 204, 213, 220, 221, 223, 224, 225; and Atlanta Campaign, 227, 228, 229, 230, 231, 232, 233, 234, 235, 236, 237–38, 238–39, 241–42, 243, 244, 245, 246, 249, 250, 251–52, 253–54, 256–57, 259, 260; and Chattanooga, Siege/Battle of, 224; and Vicksburg Campaign, 160, 163, 164, 168, 169,
Shiloh, Battle of (1862), 96, 97, 99, 158, 163
Shirley Plantation, Va., 56n51
Shreveport, La., 196, 197, 198, 199, 201, 204, 206, 210, 211
Shreveport Road, 202, 205, 206
Sickles, Daniel E., 6, 127, 133, 135, 138–39, 142, 143, 152, 232
Sigel, Franz, 124
Simonson, Peter, 230
Simpson, Brooks D., 10
Slocum, Henry W., 131, 132, 134, 135, 140–41, 252
Smalley, George W., 58, 141
Smith, Andrew J., 198, 201, 204, 207, 208, 209, 210–11, 212, 213
Smith, Edmund Kirby, 104, 203
Smith, John E., 167, 171
Smith, William F., 121, 125, 184, 185, 194, 217, 223, 255, 272, 273, 274, 276
Smoketown Road, 84, 85, 87, 88
Snake Creek Gap, 227, 228
Snell, Mark A., 9
South Carolina, 64
Southern Railroad of Mississippi, 168
South Mountain, 82
South Mountain, Battle of (1862), 82, 83, 128
Sparrow, Edward, 160
Spotsylvania Court House, Battle of (1864), 269–71, 277
Spotsylvania Court House, Va., 268
Springfield, Ill., 254

Index

Springfield Pike, 103, 104
Stanley, David S., 229, 230
Stanton, Edwin M., 25, 27, 28, 30, 31, 34, 35, 36, 40, 44, 56, 75, 97, 108, 120, 128, 182
Stedman, Edmund C., 26–27
Steedman, James, 103, 107
Steele, Frederick, 194, 199
Stevenson, Carter L., 172
Stevenson, John D., 167, 168, 171, 172, 173, 175
Stone, Charles P., 184, 192, 193, 195, 208, 209
Stoneman, George, 129, 151
Stoneman's Switch, Va., 127
Stones River, Battle of (1862–1863), 227
Stowe, Christopher S., 8, 9
Stuart, James E. B., 137
Suffolk, Va., 71, 77, 78, 93
Sullivan's Island, 64
Sumner Edwin V., 4, 27, 76, 81, 83, 84, 88, 89, 91, 94, 124, 151
Sunflower Creek, 160
Sunken Road, 262
Sykes, George, 30, 58, 120, 132, 133, 134, 135, 136

Tabernacle Church, 133, 135
Tallahala Creek, 165
Taylor, Jeremiah, 87, 88
Taylor, Richard, 192–93, 195, 196, 202, 203, 204, 205, 206, 207, 209, 210, 213, 214
Taylor, Zachary, 65, 66, 91
Taylor's Ridge, 227
Tennessee, 8, 100, 107
Tennessee River, 96, 97, 158
Tennessee units: 3rd Tennessee Infantry, 167
Tensas River, 161, 162
Texas, 65, 69, 73, 183, 185, 192, 194, 197, 199, 206
Texas units: 6th Texas Cavalry, 195; 7th Texas Infantry, 167
Thayer, Sylvanus, 63, 79
Third Louisiana Redan, 174, 175, 177
Thomas, Francis, 51
Thomas, George H., 97, 98, 99, 101, 106, 107, 225; and Atlanta Campaign, 227, 228, 229, 230, 231, 232, 235, 236, 238, 239, 240, 241–42, 243, 244, 246, 247, 249, 251, 252, 255, 256
Tibbets, Howard, 217
Tilghman, Lloyd, 157
Todd's Tavern, 265
Totopotomoy Creek, 272
Totten, Joseph, 62, 67
Townsend, George, 36
Trans-Mississippi, 10, 181
Trans-Mississippi Department, 203
Trickum's Post Office, 227
Tucker, Glenn, 262
Tupelo, Miss., 97
Turner's Ferry Road, 243
Turner's Gap, 82, 83
Twiggs, David, 69
Tyler, Erastus B., 137
Tyler, Tex., 196
Tyndale, Hector, 89

United States Capitol, 70, 181
United States Census Bureau, 37
United States Congress, 6, 7, 8, 16, 20, 21, 24, 25, 43, 44, 47, 51
United States Ford, 129, 131, 136, 138, 139
United States Military Academy. *See* West Point
United States Senate, 22, 24, 108
United States Treasury Department, 181, 198
United States units: 12th U.S. Infantry, 58
United States War Department, 21, 65, 144, 150, 159
University of Missouri-Kansas City, 11
Upton, Emory, 269–70
USS *Arizona*, 186, 188, 189
USS *Clifton*, 186, 188, 189
USS *Congress*, 75
USS *Fanny*, 74
USS *Granite City*, 186, 187, 188, 189
USS *Monitor*, 75
USS *Sachem*, 186, 188
Utah, 68, 69

Van Dorn, Earl, 158
Vermont, 46
Verrazano Narrows, 64
Vicksburg, Miss., 156, 158, 159, 160, 163, 165, 168, 169, 173, 174, 175, 176, 183, 185, 197, 199
Vicksburg, Siege and Assaults at (1863), 174–76
Vicksburg Campaign (1863), 6, 9, 158–76, 177, 218, 224
Villanow, Ga., 227
Virginia, 3, 15, 16, 17, 30, 36, 38, 39, 40, 41, 45, 64, 70, 71, 117, 118, 119, 144, 145, 199

Wade, Benjamin F., 24, 25, 122
Wadsworth, James, 27, 29, 151
Wainwright, Charles S., 145
Walker, Francis A., 263, 265, 277, 278
Walker, John G., 206
Walker, William H. T., 233
War of 1812, 2, 66
Ward, William T., 230, 231, 238, 243, 244, 246, 247–48, 259
Warren, Gouverneur K., 6, 47, 135, 136, 143, 264, 268, 269, 271, 276
Warren, Joseph, 87
Washburn, Cadwallader C., 192, 218
Washington, D.C., 4, 8, 9, 17, 18, 19, 20, 21, 23, 27, 28, 35, 36, 37, 38, 39, 40, 45, 46, 47, 51, 57, 64, 68, 70, 71, 74, 75, 76, 78, 79, 92, 97, 98, 99, 107, 112, 113, 114, 118, 119, 122, 123, 126, 138, 139, 142, 143, 144, 145, 146, 158, 181, 182, 185, 223, 232, 252, 253, 254, 270
Washington, George, 238
Washington Aqueduct, 70, 71
Webb, Alexander S., 137, 141, 268
Weber, Max, 78, 93
Weitzel, Godfrey, 186, 187, 188, 191
Weldon Railroad, 275
Welles, Gideon, 94, 190, 215
West Chickamauga Creek, 227
Western and Atlantic Railroad, 228, 231, 237
West Gulf Blockading Squadron, 185
West Indies, 62

West Point, 7, 9, 11, 17, 20, 21, 36, 62, 63, 64–65, 66, 72, 73, 79, 99, 113, 114–15, 116, 117, 120, 157, 181, 185, 194, 209, 222, 262
West Woods, 88
Wheatfield, 263
Whig Party, 37
White House, 70, 112
White Oak Swamp, Battle of (1862), 33
Whitney, Otis, 212
Wilder, John T., 100
Wilderness, Battle of the (1864), 265–68, 276, 277
Wilderness, The, 131, 132, 134, 135, 136, 138, 145, 265, 268
Willard Hotel, 112, 113
Williams, Alpheus S., 79–80, 225; and Atlanta Campaign, 228, 229, 230, 231, 233, 236, 237, 240, 241, 243, 244, 245, 246, 247, 248–49, 253; and Maryland Campaign/Antietam, Battle of, 78, 81, 83, 84, 85–87, 88, 89, 94
Williams, George F., 139
Williams, James, 87
Williams, Seth, 17
Williams, T. Harry, 11
Williamsburg, Battle of (1862), 30, 262, 277
Wilson, Henry, 21–22, 24, 35, 41, 47, 52, 55
Wilson's Creek, Battle of (1861), 99
Wolfe, James, 87
Wood, James, 233
Woodworth, Steven E., 9
Wool, John, 73, 75, 76, 77, 91
World War I, 109
Worth, William, 65
Wright, Horatio G., 97, 100, 109, 269, 272, 276
Wright, J. M., 107

Yazoo River, 160
York, Pa., 181, 182
York River, 117
Yorktown, Va., 28, 29, 77
Young's Point, 160

Zoan Church, 133, 134, 135

www.ingramcontent.com/pod-product-compliance
Lightning Source LLC
Chambersburg PA
CBHW030609230426
43661CB00053B/1902